ARTHURIAN LITERATURE

XX

ARTHURIAN LITERATURE

Incorporating *Arthurian Yearbook*

ISSN 0261–9946

Editor: Keith Busby, *University of Wisconsin, Madison*

Assistant Editor: Roger Dalrymple, *St Hugh's College, Oxford*

Editorial Board
James Carley, *York University*
Julia Crick, *University of Exeter*
Tony Hunt, *University of Oxford*
Marianne Kalinke, *Illinois University*
Norris Lacy, *Pennsylvania State University*
Ceridwen Lloyd-Morgan, *National Library of Wales*
Felicity Riddy, *University of York*
Alison Stones, *University of Pittsburgh*
Toshiyuki Takamiya, *University of Keio*
Raymond H. Thompson, *Acadia University*

Arthurian Literature is an interdisciplinary publication devoted to the scholarly and critical study of all aspects of the Arthurian legend in Europe in the medieval and early modern periods. Articles on writings from later periods are included if they relate very directly to medieval and early modern sources, although the editors welcome bibliographical studies of all periods. Articles may be up to 20,000 words in length; short items, of under 5,000 words, are published as Notes. Updates on earlier articles are also welcomed.

Material for consideration can be sent to the addresses below, or directly to Boydell & Brewer: contributors should follow the style sheet printed at the end of volume XII of the series.

Professor Keith Busby
Department of French and Italian
University of Wisconsin-Madison
618 Van Hise Hall
Madison
WI 53706
USA

Dr Roger Dalrymple
St Hugh's College
Oxford
OX2 6LE

The contents of previous volumes are listed at the back of this book.

Arthurian Literature XX

General Editor
KEITH BUSBY

Associate Editor
ROGER DALRYMPLE

D. S. BREWER

First published 2003
D. S. Brewer, Cambridge

ISBN 0 85991 798 3

D. S. Brewer is an imprint of Boydell & Brewer Ltd
PO Box 9, Woodbridge, Suffolk IP12 3DF, UK
and of Boydell & Brewer Inc.
PO Box 41026, Rochester, NY 14604–4126, USA
website: www.boydell.co.uk

A catalogue record for this book is available
from the British Library

Library of Congress Catalog Card Number: 83–640196

This publication is printed on acid-free paper

Printed in Great Britain by
The Cromwell Press Ltd, Trowbridge, Wilts

CONTENTS

GENERAL EDITOR'S FOREWORD

Vol. XX of *Arthurian Literature* continues the policy of alternating theme issues and miscellanies. This varied collection includes studies of major Arthurian works and authors in Old French, Middle High German, Middle English, and, moving closer to the present day, of one important novel by C. S. Lewis. Gerald Seaman revisits a controversial textual crux in Chrétien's *Yvain*, which scholars debated vigorously in the late 1980s. The question of Chrétien's elusive 'vanz' also raises wider issues concerning the very nature of medieval textuality, with which scholars have not fully come to grips. In studying the narrative function of clothing in Chrétien's romances, Monica Wright's article reminds us of the close structural and linguistic relationship between text and textile, a notion that has been the object of a number of recent studies. The legacy of Wolfram von Eschenbach is one of the most fascinating aspects of medieval German literary history, and Richard Barber and Cyril Edwards translate and discuss an enigmatic and linguistically difficult passage from *Der jüngere Titurel*. Jane Dewhurst's article on *Der arme Heinrich* studies this pious tale in the context of its generic affiliations; while not strictly speaking an Arthurian romance, it deserves consideration here as a work of one of medieval Germany's most distinguished practitioners of the genre. According to Dinah Hazell, Thomas Chestre's Middle English adaptation of Marie de France's *Lanval* uses the *lai* as a vehicle for social criticism; her study demonstrates that *Sir Launfal* is in many ways paradigmatic of the uses to which French romance is put in later medieval England. The evolution of Arthurian romance in Middle English is also the primary concern in Krista Sue-Lo-Twu's study of *The Awntyrs off Arthure*, where the text is seen not only as a commentary on the potential and limitations of Arthur's reign, but also on the strengths and weakness of the romance genre itself. The figure of Arthur is central to Tamar Drukker's examination of the Middle English Prose *Brut*, whose author appears to depict a rather eclectically ambiguous sovereign. Edward Donald Kennedy looks at the delicate political implications of the *Morte Darthur* and its ramifications for the imprisoned Malory, possibly hoping from a pardon from Edward IV. In the final essay, Janina Traxler considers the way in which C. S. Lewis transforms and employs the figures of Uther Pendragon and Merlin in *That Hideous Strength*.

I should like to express special thanks to my Associate Editor, Roger Dalrymple, for his help with this issue.

Keith Busby
The University of Wisconsin-Madison

I

REASSESSING CHRETIEN'S ELUSIVE *VANZ*

Gerald Seaman

When Chrétien de Troyes received his commission for the *Chevalier de la Charrette* from Marie de Champagne (sometime after her 1159 marriage, and probably late in the decade between 1170 and 1180), the stakes for him were undoubtedly high. Although the poet had already successfully established a reputation for himself with works like *Erec et Enide* and *Cligés*, the *Chevalier de la Charrette* presented Chrétien with his first occasion for literary patronage and it also thrust him into a new and more prestigious literary arena, one where he would encounter competitive relationships with other authors writing under patronage. Gautier d'Arras himself had cultivated literary patronage ahead of Chrétien, and he had secured commissions from the likes of Beatrix of Bourgogne (wife of Frederick Barbarossa) for his *Ille et Galeron* (*c.* 1167–70), and also from the Countess Marie for *Eracle* (*c.* 1164–71), a work that Gautier eventually completed for Baudoin de Hainaut.[1] To judge from the prologue to the *Charrette*, this new literary dynamic may have caused Chrétien to adopt a rhetorical stance that departed significantly from his previous efforts, and as a consequence his attempt to obtain 'the conditions of *benevolentia*, *docilitas*, and *attentio* in his audience' necessarily resorted to the alternative uses of the *ab adversariorum* and the *ad iudicum persona* approaches as they were recommended by Cicero and Quintillian.[2]

---

[1] P. Nykrog attests that 'Gautier d'Arras lived, and continues to live, in the shadow of Chrétien de Troyes. In modern times, his reputation has ascended, discreetly, in the wake of his great contemporary's.' There is no reason to disagree with this point, especially for the period following the composition of the *Chevalier de la Charrette*. When Gautier was commissioned for *Eracle* and for *Ille et Galeron*, however, one suspects that it was he, and not Chrétien, who occupied a position of literary stature and eminence, and it appears that he did so before the ascent of Chrétien de Troyes. See P. Nykrog, 'Two Creators of Narrative Form in Twelfth Century France: Gautier d'Arras, Chrétien de Troyes', *Speculum* 48 (April 1973), 258–76 (p. 259). For more on the relationship between Chrétien and Gautier, also see C. Pierreville, *Gautier d'Arras: L'Autre Chrétien* (Paris, 2001). According to Pierreville, 'on le voit, non seulement le poète [Gautier] est le contemporain de Chrétien de Troyes, mais il a aussi évolué dans les mêmes cours, en particulier celle de Champagne, puisque la comtesse Marie est également l'instigatrice du *Chevalier de la Charrette*. Cette proximité spatiale et temporelle avec un romancier si illustre que le Champenois a desservi notre auteur' (p. 15).

[2] T. Hunt, 'The Rhetorical Background to the Arthurian Prologue: Tradition and the Old French Vernacular Prologues', *Forum for Modern Language Studies* 6 (1970), 1–23 (p. 3). Also see T. Hunt,

Mentioned in the very first verse of the text, Marie de Champagne is indeed a commanding presence in the *Charrette*, and Chrétien's humble deference before his patron is transparent throughout the prologue. There are no self-aggrandizing references to the author's craft and legacy, as there were with *Erec et Enide* and its now famous reference to the '*mout bele conjointure*' (very elegant composition, v. 14) and the boastful assertion that the tale will survive as long as 'Christianity' (or the 'era of Chrétien') endures ('*tant con durra crestiantez*', v. 25).[3] There is, furthermore, no bio-bibliographical catalog of prior acts and works, in the manner of the *Cligés* prologue; no references to books, or to ancient and modern models of chivalry and learning arise in the opening verses of Chrétien's tale of Lancelot and Guenevere. On the contrary, Chrétien avers in the *Charrette* that he is working in the exclusive service of the Countess, achieving by the application of his own particular talent and effort a tale whose subject matter, meaning, and guiding principles were provided to him by his patron.[4]

In style heretofore atypical of Chrétien, the *Charrette* prologue's *ad iudicum persona* praise is couched in preterition and understatement and it is self-consciously cautious about crossing the line between propriety and impropriety. In this connection, fourteen of the prologue's short twenty-nine verses are dedicated to a rhetorical confrontation with an unnamed third party whose past encomium of a patron has purportedly crossed that line, and whose work Chrétien has therefore set out to critique, better, and effectively silence by an ingenious use of two mock citations. Scholars, including those who edited Chrétien's complete works for the Pléiade, generally accept that, in these citations, the *Charrette* prologue contains a parodic commentary on Gautier d'Arras and there is considerable evidence to support this claim. Specifically, there can be no doubt that the opening verses of the *Charrette* express a critique of the rhetorical attitude of Gautier toward Beatrix of Bourgogne in *Ille et Galeron*, where the poet promised to espouse temperance in his address to his patron and yet immediately followed this claim with a lengthy prologue (134 verses) filled with elaborate and intemperate imagery praising the honor and the glory of the 'greatest empress who ever lived':

Aïe, Dieus, sainz esperiz!	Help me God, holy spirit
Qu'a le milleur empereriz	That I may, to the greatest empress
Qui onques fust, si com je pens,	Who I believe has ever lived,
Otroi men servise et men sens:	Grant my service and my knowledge
Tel me couvient; atempreüre	As I should; temperance
Vueil metre en ceste trouveüre	I would like to instill in this composition
Et trouver atempreement,	And to compose temperately

'Tradition and Originality in the Prologues of Chrestien de Troyes', *Forum for Modern Language Studies* 8 (1972), 320–44.

3   See Chrétien de Troyes, *Oeuvres Complètes*, ed. D. Poirion (Paris, 1994), hereafter referred to as Pléiade; and Chrétien de Troyes, *Erec et Enide*, ed. M. Roques, CFMA 80 (Paris, 1981).

4   See verses 21–29 of the Pléiade edition and of *Le Chevalier de la Charrette*, ed. M. Roques, CFMA 86 (Paris, 1983). Hereafter referred to as CFMA.

Mais que de loer seulement	Except when praising
Celi qui a honeur enclose[5]	The person who embodies honor.

With consummate poetic skill, Chrétien de Troyes artfully telescoped and condensed the lyrical flourishes and poetic exaggerations of *Ille et Galeron* into a concise and elegant eulogy of Marie de Champagne, and he did so by suggestively deploying precise passages and terminology from Gautier's prologue. Chrétien's most obvious reference to Gautier begins with a biting rhetorical question:

dirai je: 'Tant come une jame	Shall I say that a precious gem
vaut de pailes et de sardines	Is worth as many pearls and sards
vaut la contesse de reïnes?'	As the countess is worth queens?
(vv. 16–18)	

Chrétien's reply to Gautier, and his criticism of the praise of Beatrix, can be noted here in two instances. First, in terms of the image, Gautier referred to Beatrix in remarkably similar language, comparing her to a gem as well:

Quant nestre fist si bele geme	Upon the birth of such a beautiful gem
Se pour çou non que lour vaillance	It came to pass that other ladies
Pert mains et mains a d'aparance	Though still worthy,
Par l'oneur qu'en cesti s'aüne	Became more and more diminished
(vv. 80–83)	By the honor vested in her

Further, Chrétien's repetition of the verb '*vaut*' at the beginning of verses 17 and 18 is a clever sonorous recall of verses and rhyming words that occur at almost exactly the same spot in Gautier's prologue:

Pour Dieu, que monte ne que *vaut*?	My God, how does one praise what
Ne sai pour quoi nus se tra*vaut*	is not worthy?
Pour chose qui fausse en le fin	I do not know why one would work
(vv. 15–17; emphasis mine)	For something that was fake in the end.

The literary and historical brilliance of this effort is remarkable, as it demonstrates a rare poetic achievement that ultimately elevated Chrétien and the Countess while using Gautier's own words against him.[6]

The prologue to the *Chevalier de la Charrette* thus clearly gains its greatest rhetorical force from the author's ability to combine appropriate and meaningful praise for Marie de Champagne with a forceful reproach to Gautier.

---

5   Verses 1–7 of E. Löseth's edition (Paris, 1890). Unless otherwise indicated, all translations from Old French to English in this essay are my own.

6   It is interesting to note that, regarding the gem imagery, Pierreville suspects that Gautier may have been aware of Chrétien's parody and that the author may have revised subsequent versions of his prologue as a result: 'Les piques que Chrétien de Troyes lui destine dans *Le Chevalier de la Charrette* sont peut-être venues jusqu'à lui, puisque les vers 79–88 n'apparaissent pas dans le manuscrit de Wollaton, comme si Gautier d'Arras avait voulu corriger son incipit en le ramenant à 74 vers, ce qui réduit considérablement l'éloge de Béatrix' (pp. 55–56).

Chrétien's expressed intent to present his work in the service of the Countess without flattery was in the mind of this reader unquestionably sincere, and his self-effacing, though sometimes playful, attitude toward his patron is woven so intricately into his prologue that no amount of scholarly teasing could unravel it. With a deft touch, Chrétien successfully maintained this deferential stance toward Marie while at the same time engaging in a round of rhetorical sparring with Gautier that exhibits a manifestly contrary impulse. Toward Gautier, Chrétien displayed no self-deprecation or humility because he had a different rhetorical purpose: to demonstrate the superiority of his own narrative art and therefore to burnish his literary reputation in immediate and lasting fashion.[7]

The historical record of Chrétien's eclipse of Gautier remains unintentionally blemished, however, by the fact that one of the *Charrette* prologue's central images, a crucial expression of praise of Marie, and the first mock citation of Gautier, has defied satisfactory interpretation, largely because the manuscript tradition presents us with a significant and multifaceted textual difficulty in verses 12–13. Four manuscripts are extant containing the *Charrette* prologue: Paris, Bibliothèque Nationale, f. fr. 794 (C; known as the Guiot copy); Paris, Bibliothèque Nationale, f. fr. 12560 (T); Escorial, Bibl. Monast., M.III.21 (E) and Princeton University Library, MS Garrett 125 (G). The conflicting renderings of the prologue in these manuscripts have troubled scholars for over a century, and Karl Uitti has described verses 12–13 as a *locus desperatus*.[8] These verses, in particular, are nearly inscrutable, indeed. But scholars have nonetheless made extensive studies of the *Charrette* prologue, relying on what are ultimately unsatisfactory interpretations of these crucial verses in praise of Marie de Champagne. And we have done so despite reasonably favorable physical evidence (the extant prologues to Chrétien's romance are not incomplete, damaged, or difficult to read).[9] The Pléiade and the CFMA editions together reproduce the same versions of the verses, in defiance of excellent manuscript counter evidence. And, as we shall

---

[7] The stylistic, structural, and rhetorical features of the *Charrette* prologue indicate that Chrétien was walking a fine line, trying to accomplish with concision and subtlety what Gautier himself could not accomplish. There is moreover an historical importance to this prologue, as there is to Chrétien's other prologues, and this is true not only because it cites the relationship between Chrétien and Marie de Champagne but also because it gives definition to an authorial impulse and purpose (also seen in the prologues to *Erec*, *Cligés*, and *Perceval*) to endure and to prevail. For more on this and similar matters, see especially M. Zink, *De la Subjectivité littéraire* (Paris, 1985); D. Kelly, *The Art of Medieval French Romance* (Madison, 1992) and G. Seaman, 'Signs of a New Literary Paradigm: The "Christian" Figures of Chrétien de Troyes', in *Nominalism and Literary Discourse: New Perspectives*, ed. H. Keiper, C. Bode and R. J. Utz, Critical Studies 10 (Amsterdam and Atlanta, 1997), pp. 87–109.

[8] See K. D. Uitti, 'Autant en emporte *Li Funs*: Remarques sur le prologue du *Chevalier de la Charrette* de Chrétien de Troyes', *Romania* 105, no. 2 (1984), 270–91.

[9] Today's leading editions, from CFMA and the Pléiade, indicate some textual variants, as one would expect, but they do so in a way that is not entirely complete for the verses in question. W. Foerster's late nineteenth-century edition was more thorough in this regard. See *Der Karrenritter (Lancelot) und das Wilhelmsleben (Guillaume d'Angleterre) von Christian von Troyes* (Halle, 1899).

4

see below, even readings advocated as alternatives to standard editions present their own unfortunate shortcomings.[10]

For Chrétien's prologue, the physical evidence, then, although favorable, and compelling in many instances, cannot be considered wholly reliable. Reputable scholars read the same evidence completely differently. Looking hard enough, and in the right light, hoping for a breakthrough like Henry Dexter Learned's with *Eulalia*,[11] we will probably not ever discover the word beneath the word and thus clarify the elusive meaning of verses 12–13 of the *Chevalier de la Charrette*. For accuracy, to be sure, we must continue to cleave to the manuscripts; but for understanding the physical evidence, we will have to seek clarity beyond a purely comparative, linguistic, or etymological study of the words on the page. If reports on the physical evidence are contradictory, and unsatisfactory, it is clearly not enough to choose the best reading based on the manuscripts alone. Something more eclectic is required, involving other, external, evidence, scholarly judgment and a sound argument as to how and why Chrétien's verses are related to, and clarified by, his other writings, the writings of a peer such as Gautier, and by contemporary historical and cultural evidence.[12] As I will contend here, compelling evidence does indeed exist in support of a satisfactory reading of these verses. In its corroboration of the manuscript readings, furthermore, this evidence conclusively answers many of the hitherto unanswered questions about Chrétien's eulogy of the Countess. Most importantly, this evidence allows us to reformulate the verses in a way that is at once coherent, convincing, and consistent with Chrétien's narrative art and with the imagery of the *Charrette* prologue.

---

[10] As published in the CFMA and Pléiade editions, the verses in the left column below are from the mid thirteenth-century champenois manuscript BN f. fr. 794. On the right are verses from the late thirteenth-century picardian manuscript Princeton University Library, MS Garrett 125:

9	si deïst et jel tesmoignasse		9	Si deist et jel temoignasse
10	que ce est la dame qui passe		10	Que ce est la dame ki passe
11	totes celes qui sont vivanz		11	Toutes celes ki sunt vivans
12	*si con li funs passe les vanz*		12	*Tant com le fu passe li vens*
13	*qui vante en mai ou en avril*		13	*Qui en mai vente u en avril*

In translation, these manuscripts yield remarkably dissimilar images:

9	one could say, and I would attest		9	one could say, and I would attest
10	that this is the lady who surpasses		10	that this is the lady who surpasses
11	all those who are now living		11	all those who are now living
12	*as the zephyr surpasses the winds*		12	*as vapors are dispersed by the wind*
13	*when it blows in May or April*		13	*when it blows in May or April*

[11] In 1941, Learned read *aduret*, rather than *adunet*, in the *Eulalia* manuscript, using daylight and a magnifying glass, and in a single stroke corrected a serious misreading and granted lasting meaning and coherence to a previously nonsensical verse. This event was illustrated most recently in *The Future of the Middle Ages: Medieval Literature in the 1990s*, ed. W. D. Paden (Gainesville, FL, 1994).

[12] This is certainly the lesson we have learned from statements on text editing such as the following: A. Foulet and M. B. Speer, *On Editing Old French Texts* (Lawrence, KS, 1979); P. Dembowski, 'Intertextualité et critique des texts', *Littérature* 41 (1981), 17–29 and (among other works) K. D. Uitti, 'Poetico-Literary Dimensions and the Critical Editing of Medieval Texts: The Example of Old French', in *What is Literature? France 1100–1600*, ed. F. Cornilliat, U. Langer and D. Kelly (Lexington, KY, 1993).

A Review of the Problem and Some of its Solutions

```
 9   si deïst et jel tesmoignasse
10   que ce est la dame qui passe
11   totes celes qui sont vivanz
12   si con li funs passe les vanz
13   qui vante en mai ou en avril
```

Let us begin with a shared conclusion: by casting '*li vens*' in the nominative singular case, the Garrett manuscript at Princeton furnishes us with a reading that is superior to the Guiot copy (and, by extension, to the Pléiade and CFMA editions) whose text (quoted above) reads '*les vanz*', in the plural oblique case.[13] Moreover, BN f. fr. 12560 also renders '*li venz*' in the nominative singular such that, for both manuscripts, these verses could be read:

<table>
<tr><td>. . . li venz</td><td>the wind</td></tr>
<tr><td>Qui vente en mai ou en avril</td><td>That blows in May or April</td></tr>
</table>

There is obviously a particular merit in accepting this variant and therefore in correcting '*les vanz*' to '*li vanz*': it allows the wind to blow. Indeed, the merit is such that we ought to adopt the nominative singular as the preferred reading, and not as a variant at all, for the following reasons. It is not an exception (two of the four extant prologues render the word this way) and it is not an anachronism, the manuscripts attest to that. The structure is also grammatically possible, and the rhyme and meter of the verse are unaffected by the change. Finally, to put things even more simply, it just makes sense for wind to blow. With all other things being equal, one might ask, why would the wind do anything else?

Relying exclusively on Garrett, however, also raises some questions. Although we can be satisfied that '*li vens*' in the nominative singular is correct, '*le fu*' in the oblique case, as Garrett renders it, provides us with a reading that is both intriguing and exceptional. The three other *Charrette* manuscripts with prologues, BN f. fr. 794 (Guiot), BN f. fr. 12560, and Escorial, Bibl. Monast., M.III.21 (E) do not, in fact, agree with Garrett. The Guiot copy and BN f. fr. 12560 each give '*li funs*' in the nominative singular; Escorial gives its own unique reading, '*li feuz*', in the nominative singular as well, and none of these shows evidence of missed annotation, or of hesitant or confused transcription. Translators such as Frappier have given the modern French equivalent '*zéphyr*' for '*li funs*', and the Pléiade edition, following an argument that reaches all the way back to Foerster and the first edition of the *Charrette*, casts the word as '*le foehn*' in its translation. In each case, relying on the nominative singular '*li funs*', while simultaneously trusting that the plural oblique '*les vanz*' of the Guiot copy was correct, has led the scholars in question to a particularly vexing conundrum: finding a way for the subject '*li*

---

13 K. D. Uitti, 'Autant en emporte'.

funs' to go with the verb '*vante*'. As the Old French editions (exclusive of Uitti-Foulet), and almost all the modern French translations indicate,[14] the conundrum was (not so neatly) resolved by what might best be described as reasoning in reverse. If '*li funs*' actually 'blows' (as the manuscripts say it does) then it must be some kind of wind. From there, tenuous etymology was deployed to link '*li funs*' with the peculiarly German wind '*le foehn*', and the whole questionable enterprise was bolstered by the confident editorial assertion that, because Marie de Champagne's father-in-law was German, such a reading was 'not impossible'.[15]

One must concur with Uitti here that the etymological argument presented above is seriously flawed. Moreover, its attempt to force a meaning into and from an unchangeable context reveals the potential confusion that may result from remaining overly faithful to modes of text editing in the 'best manuscript' tradition.[16] Furthermore, let me add for my part that additional evidence may be invoked to question the claim that '*li funs*' is a wind that blows. Indeed Chrétien's second romance, *Cligés*, provides convincing validation for this critique as it is here that we discover the only other occurrence of '*funs*' in all of Chrétien's works:

Si se cuevre et çoile chascuns	Thus each covers and conceals himself
Si que n'an pert flame ne funs	So that neither flame nor smoke arises
Del charbon qui est soz la cendre	From the coal that is under the cinder
(vv. 601–603, Pléiade;	
vv. 595–597, CFMA)[17]	

In this, the unique attested instance outside of the *Charrette* prologue, '*funs*' is clearly associated with smoke and fire; it is not any kind of special wind at all.[18]

It is unfortunate, then, that the Pléiade and CFMA editions of the *Chevalier de la Charrette* publish an irreparably nonsensical prologue. Accepting the clearly convincing evidence that '*funs*' is not '*le foehn*', however, could be a first step toward establishing coherent meaning. Garrett and BN f. fr. 12560

---

[14] One exception is *Le Chevalier de la Charrette*, ed. C. Méla (Paris, 1992). For verses 10–14, Méla provides a reasonably elegant misreading:

Que ce est la dame qui passe	que c'est la dame qui surpasse
Totes celes qui sont vivanz	toutes celles qui sont en vie
Si con les funs passe li vanz	comme surpasse tout parfum la brise
Qui vante en mai ou en avril	qui vente en mai ou en avril.

[15] On this point, see the editor's footnote on this verse in the Pléiade edition: 'Enfin si le mot (föhn) est bien germanique, il est ancien: était-il impossible pour une cour française de le connaître? Remarquons que le père d'Henri de Champagne était allemand, et qu'il s'agit ici de parodier le prologue d'*Ille et Galeron* écrit par Gautier d'Arras pour Béatrix, l'impératrice du Saint Empire romain germanique' (p. 1256).

[16] See Uitti, 'Autant en emporte', pp. 274–75.

[17] *Oeuvres Complètes* and *Cligés*, ed. A. Micha, CFMA 84 (Paris, 1982).

[18] Douglas C. Walker's *Lexique d'Ancien Français* (Calgary, 1998; available at http://www.acs.ucalgary.ca/%7Edcwalker/Dictionary/dict.html), an electronic database of prominent words found in Tobler-Lommatzsch's *Altfranzösisches Wörterbuch* (Berlin, 1925), lists *fun* and *fum* as synonyms. Uitti's reading of Garrett casts *fu* as the etymological forebear to the modern French *fumée*.

compel us to acknowledge the flaw of the Guiot copy and they also require us to accept that, by logic, by grammar and by physical evidence '*li vanz*' is the only possible subject of the verb '*vanter*'. One might, of course, attempt to argue that '*funs*' (smoke/fire) could 'blow' (*vante*), but why would it do so specifically in May or April?[19] And how would it surpass or disperse the winds, '*les vanz*'? Clearly, then, even a change in the definition of '*funs*' would not suffice to make the verses in the Guiot copy any less incoherent. BN f. fr. 794 might indeed be our best Chrétien manuscript, but its rendition of verses 12–13 of the *Charrette* is obviously imprecise and, in my view, it is an evident betrayal of whatever image Chrétien might have originally attempted to convey of his patron, Marie de Champagne.

This, of course, is the key point: Beyond all the philological questions, it is ultimately and indisputably Chrétien's image of Marie that is at issue in this prologue. Given what we know of the Countess of Champagne, and of her role as a literary patron, Chrétien undoubtedly crafted this image of Marie with great care, drawing at once on his complete set of rhetorical skills and on the diverse and sophisticated body of knowledge he had acquired as a student of the seven liberal arts. While there are many gaps in the historical record, we do know for certain that the Countess was a significant figure in the landscape of the late twelfth century,[20] and it is useful to recall here some of the pertinent details of her life. Born in 1145 to King Louis VII of France and his first wife Eleanor of Aquitaine, Marie was a patron to authors such as Chrétien and Gautier d'Arras, and a nominally central figure in Andreas Capellanus' *Art of Courtly Love* (*De arte honeste amandi*). Together with Chrétien and Gautier, authors including Gace Brulé, Pierre de Celle, and Conon de Béthune all shared associations with the Countess of Champagne and there is further evidence that Marie commissioned a vernacular translation of Genesis in 1190.[21]

In overview, Marie's life might be best described as a series of curious dramas interspersed in an already unusual existence.[22] Because she was the daughter, and firstborn, of a mother presumed to be barren, Marie was from birth hailed as a miracle child, the glorious fulfillment of Bernard of Clairvaux's prayers for divine intercession on behalf of the royal couple, and a girl whose life portended great things.[23] While still very young, indeed just a

---

[19] As Uitti points out, Foerster attempted to maintain the etymological (and the logical) link between *funs* and wind by viewing it as a possible derivative of the Latin *favonius*, the west wind, associated with Spring. Unfortunately, such an etymology is incorrect. See Uitti, 'Autant en emporte', p. 274.

[20] See, among other works, A. Kelly, *Eleanor of Aquitaine and the Four Kings* (New York, 1958); J. F. Benton, 'The Court of Champagne as Literary Center', *Speculum* 36 (1961), 551–91; J. H. Martin McCash, 'Marie de Champagne and Eleanor of Aquitaine: A Relationship Reexamined', *Speculum* 54 (1979), 698–711; E.-R. Labande, 'Les Filles d'Aliénor d'Aquitaine: étude comparative', *Cahiers de Civilisation Médiévale* 29 (1986), 101–12 and P. Bourgain, 'Aliénor d'Aquitaine et Marie de Champagne mises en cause par André le Chapelain', *Cahiers de Civilisation Médiévale* 29 (1986), 30–36.

[21] Labande, 'Les Filles d'Aliénor', p. 103; Benton, 'The Court of Champagne'.

[22] This two-paragraph overview draws in large part on Labande, 'Les Filles d'Aliénor d'Aquitaine', pp. 101–104.

[23] According to W. Williams, on the occasion of an 1144 conference at St Denis, 'St Bernard so rebuked

child, Marie nearly became the next Queen of England, but Henry II Plantagenet's request for her hand, opposed by Bernard on the grounds of consanguinity, was never granted. In 1152, still at a tender age, Marie witnessed the incautious removal of her own mother from the French throne ostensibly for failing to give Louis a male heir. Later, in one of history's ironies, Eleanor herself ascended to the English throne in her daughter's place, and eventually became the mother of Henry II Plantagenet's five sons.

There is no evidence that Marie had anything other than a quiet marriage herself to Henry the Liberal of Champagne. She gave him two boys and two girls, and served as regent after the Count went away on crusade in 1179. Though Henry returned from the East, he died shortly thereafter, in March 1181, and Marie took up her role as regent again until 1187, when she turned authority over to her eldest son, also named Henry. Along with Richard the Lionheart and Philippe Augustus, the younger Henry set off on his own crusade in 1190; he died while away at Acre, falling from a window in September 1198. In total, then, Marie was regent of Champagne almost without interruption from 1179–1187 and from 1190 until her death, probably in Meaux, in 1198. This is a fact of considerable significance, for it not only establishes the Countess, for a period of nearly a decade and a half, as the undisputed and sole head of an influential and powerful medieval aristocratic family and the governing authority of an important county. It also underlines her status as a person of sufficient intelligence, strength of character and means to negotiate the complexities of the competing interests of the kings of England and France, and to maintain successfully the enterprise of her husband and sons in their absences and after their deaths.

In the case of Marie's place in the prologue to the *Chevalier de la Charrette*, scholarly attention has been paid almost exclusively to describing Chrétien's compositional practices via the signal terms '*san*' and '*matière*' given in verse 26 and, according to the poet, provided by his patron.[24] Given this scholarly consensus that Marie played some kind of quasi-authorial role in the creation of the *Charrette*, and in the light of what we know of her leadership status within twelfth-century feudal hierarchies, it is somewhat irregular that scholars continue to accept a canonical prologue depiction of the Countess that is flawed, distorted and ultimately incorrect.

[Eleanor] for abusing her influence that she was subsequently moved to confide in him the fact of her sterility, and to beg him to pray that she might have a child. The chronicler records that the Abbot of Clairvaux required as the condition of his prayers that she should amend her ways as the king's evil genius, that Louis himself pressed him to grant her request, and that at about the same time in the following year a child was born. This would have been their eldest daughter, Mary': *Saint Bernard of Clairvaux* (Manchester, 1935), p. 215. Also noted in Labande, 'Les Filles d'Aliénor d'Aquitaine', n. 1, p. 102.

[24] See for example, W. A. Nitze, '*Sans et Matière* dans les oeuvres de Chrétien de Troyes', *Romania* 44 (1915), 14–36; D. Kelly, *Sens and Conjointure in the Chevalier de la Charrette* (The Hague and Paris, 1966); J. Rychner, 'Le prologue du *Chevalier de la Charrette*', *Vox Romanica* 26 (1967), 1–23; J. Frappier, 'Le Prologue du *Chevalier de la Charrette* et son interprétation', *Romania* 93 (1972), 337–77 and M.-L. Ollier, 'The Author in the Text: The Prologues of Chrétien de Troyes', *Yale French Studies* 51 (1974), 26–41.

As we have seen, if we use Guiot, verses 12–13 only make sense if we perpetually misread them and thereby subject the text to a fate that its author and Marie surely would have regretted. In this connection, the version produced in Garrett provides limited consolation. By accepting Garrett's reversal of subject and object cases, and relying on Chrétien's predilection for chiasmus, Uitti proposes to read verses 12–13 in the following way: 'Tant com le fu passe li vens/ Qui en mai vente u en avril' ('Tout comme sur les effluves du sol l'emporte la brise/ Qui souffle en mai ou en avril'). Although faithful to Garrett and to Old French grammar this reading of Chrétien's image is nonetheless inelegant. We should recall that Chrétien is indeed talking about other noble ladies, and for that reason it is somewhat inconceivable that, in praise of Marie, he would have elided these others to 'les effluves du sol'. We can, furthermore, be reasonably sure that Chrétien, even in his parody of Gautier d'Arras, would not have constructed such an unfortunate couplet, one whose base message evinced derogatory mockery of his patron's superior class and ken. It may be reasonably assumed, moreover, that Marie was pleased by the way in which Chrétien depicted her above other ladies. But it also safe to say that, for her own pleasure, she would never have stooped so low as to permit her poet, in a romance imbued with Marie's own 'matière', 'san' and 'comandemanz' to deride her peers.

It is clear that the reading in Garrett is unsatisfactory. We cannot be content with it because the imagery explicitly contradicts Chrétien's intention and practice. By undermining the essential elements of *praeteritio* and *meiosis* that permeate Chrétien's prologue, and by weakening the poet's critique of Gautier, the comparison of '*la brise*' to '*les effluves du sol*' not only impoverishes Chrétien's poetics but it also, and more significantly, turns Marie from an exalted lady of praiseworthy modesty into a vain and derisory figure.

We return, then, to our recurring dilemma: how do we establish a 'best' reading from the manuscripts when none of them makes perfect sense? As I have said, we obviously need other evidence, from Chrétien himself, and from what we know of his experience and intellectual background. To begin, I propose that we reexamine our terms (specifically '*vanz*') and that we ask ourselves the following question: Why would Chrétien compare Marie de Champagne to the wind in the first place?

Wind, Weather and Medieval Cosmology

Unlike '*funs*', the term '*vanz*' frequently recurs in Chrétien's romances. When part of a nautical reference, '*vanz*' is exclusively related to seafaring conditions that have a positive effect on the story's protagonists. In *Cligés*, for example, as Alexandre prepares to depart for Arthur's court, we read:

Au port truevent lez la faloise	In port, near the cliff they find
Les mariniers dedanz les nes.	The sailors in their ships
La mer fu peisible et soes,	The sea was peaceful and smooth

Li vanz dolz et li airs serains.	The wind was gentle and the air calm
(vv. 242–45, Pléiade;	
vv. 238–41, CFMA)[25]	

The same favorable conditions obtained for Alexandre's return journey to Athens with Soredamour and Cligés himself:

A Sorlan monterent sor mer	At Shoreham they embarked over sea
Au congié de tote la cort.	And took leave of the entire court
Boen vant orent, la nes s'an cort	They had good wind, and the ship sailed
Assez plus tost que cers qui fuit.	More swiftly than a fleeing stag
(vv. 2424–27, Pléiade;	
vv. 2402–405, CFMA)	

In *Perceval*, finally, the wind plays a kind of miraculous ex-machina role and can be said to account in large part for the survival of the victims of Clamadeu's siege at Beaurepaire:

Ce jor meïsmes uns granz vanz	That very day a large wind
Ot par mer chaciee une barge	Drove a barge from the sea
Qui de fromant portoit grant charge	With a great payload of wheat
Et d'altre vitaille estoit plainne.	And full of other foods
Si com Deu plot, antiere et sainne	As God wished, safe and sound
Est devant le chastel venue	It arrived right in front of the castle
(vv. 2526–31, Pléiade;	
vv. 2524–29, Roach)[26]	

Each in their own way, then, these examples associate gentleness and opulence with the wind. If, as Uitti contends, Chrétien was deploying a chiasmus in verses 12–13 of his prologue, our association of Marie de Champagne with the wind ('*li vens*') should therefore be permeated by an extended isotopia of courtliness, one that goes beyond the season of May and April to incorporate the sweet qualities of good fortune and generosity.

This is not, however, the only kind of wind to be found in Chrétien's texts. In fact, one could forcefully argue that such a courtly wind is exceptional, rather than prototypical, for his work. Elsewhere in the romances, it is indeed more frequent that we find wind associated with foul weather that threatens Arthur's knights. A crucial nexus for analyzing this phenomenon is presented by the intertextually linked *Chevalier de la Charrette* and the *Chevalier au Lion* (hereafter referred to as *Yvain*). In contrast to *Cligés* and *Perceval*, neither of these romances deploys the wind as part of a nautical image, nor do they place wind within the isotopia of courtliness mentioned above. Rather wind in these two texts is almost without exception detected in the context of pernicious, and more extensively detailed, meteorological conditions.

In *Yvain*, '*vanz*' and its verb '*vanter*' occur more frequently than in any of

---

25 CFMA gives 'l'orez' for 'la mer' in verse 240.
26 Chrétien de Troyes, *Le Roman de Perceval*, ed. W. Roach (Geneva and Paris, 1959). The Roach edition contains slight variations due to a difference in base manuscript.

Chrétien's other works. It should be no surprise to learn that, with only one exception, this wind blows at the Barenton Fountain. By virtue of the fountain's central status in the story, we can conclude, therefore, that weather itself occupies a critical discursive role in this romance. As Danièle James-Raoul points out in her meteorological study of the *Conte du Graal* and Wolfram von Eschenbach's *Parzival*, Chrétien has very precise, but limited, knowledge of medieval meteorology, and he deploys this knowledge intentionally for narrative and symbolic purposes.[27] In this connection, it is clear in *Yvain* that the weather of the fountain episode presents itself to Calogrenant and Yvain as an enemy as formidable as any living knight. Recalling the words of the wild woodsman, should one pour the water on the stone at the fountain:

La verras une tel tanpeste	There you will see such a tempest
Qu'an cest bois ne ramanra beste,	That no beast will remain in the wood
Chevriax ne cers, ne dains ne pors,	Neither roe nor stag, nor buck nor boar
Nes li oisel s'an istront fors;	Not even the birds will remain
Car tu verras si foudroier	For you will witness lightning
Vanter, et arbres peçoier	Wind and split trees
Plovoir, toner, et espartir,	Rain, thunder, and bolts
Que, se tu t'an puez departir	Such that, if you are able to escape
Sanz grant enui et sanz pesance,	Without great harm and great pain
Tu seras de meillor cheance	You will have had better luck
Que chevaliers qui i fust onques	Than any knight before you
(vv. 395–405, Pléiade;	
vv. 397–407, CFMA)[28]	

For purposes of the *Yvain* narrative, the storm at the fountain serves a dual function: As part of a clever prolepsis, it forecasts success for Yvain where Calogrenant has failed. Similarly, when, at the end of the story, a return to the fountain is again necessary, the actual return of the knight is coupled with a kind of narrative flashback that emphasizes Yvain's imminent rehabilitation into the world of Arthurian chivalry and courtly love after his bout of madness in the woods. Though the narrative, as it brings us back to the fountain, does not explicitly take the reader back in time (as a flashback would), it accomplishes this symbolic temporal displacement via the device of *interpretatio/ expolitio*, prescribed by Mathew of Vendôme for 'elaboration by repetitive or incremental statement'.[29] Indeed, verses 6519–28 (Pléiade; vv. 6507–16, CFMA) serve to repeat and recall the earlier fountain episodes by employing a shared syntagmatic reference to the weather conditions of Yvain's initial, solo, departure for the fountain challenge:

---

[27] D. James-Raoul, 'D'une météorologie l'autre: le temps qu'il fait du *Conte du Graal* de Chrétien de Troyes au *Parzival* de Wolfram von Eschenbach', in *Le temps qu'il fait au Moyen Age: Phénomènes atmosphériques dans la littérature, la pensée scientifique et religieuse*, ed. C. Thomasset and J. Ducos (Paris, 1998), pp. 209–230.

[28] Chrétien de Troyes, *Le Chevalier au Lion (Yvain)*, ed. M. Roques, CFMA 89 (Paris, 1982).

[29] D. Kelly, *The Art of Medieval French Romance* (Madison, 1992), 56.

Et panse qu'il se partiroit	So he thinks that he will depart
Toz seus de cort, et si iroit	All alone from court, and so will go
A sa fontainne guerroier;	To do battle at the fountain
Et s'i feroit tant foudroier,	And he will make it thunder greatly
Et tant vanter, et tant plovoir,	Blow great wind and rain mightily
Que par force et par estovoir	Such that by strength and by necessity
Li covanroit feire a lui pes,	He will succeed in subduing it
Ou il ne fineroit ja mes	Or never see the end
De la fontainne tormanter,	Of the fountain's tempest
Et de plovoir, et de vanter	Rain and wind.

As James-Raoul informs us, 'le temps qu'il fait est symbole d'une réalité transcendentale, il signifie aussi une présence et une volonté divines'.[30] Meteorological forces, therefore, as part of a greater cosmological scheme, can be seen as reflections either of God or of nature. In *Yvain*, Calogrenant's story underscores the relationship of weather to the sacred:

Mes Dex tost me rasegura	But soon afterward God reassured me
Que li tans gaires ne dura,	That the weather would not last
Et tuit li vant se reposerent;	And all the winds died down
Des que Deu plot, vanter n'oserent	As God wished it, the winds no longer dared to blow
Et quant je vis l'air cler et pur,	And when I saw the air clear and pure
De joie fui toz asseür;	I was comforted by joy
Que joie, s'onques la conui,	For joy, if one has ever known it
Fet tost oblïer grant enui	Makes one completely forget great worries
(vv. 449–56, Pléiade;	
vv. 451–58, CFMA)	

Surviving the weather at the fountain, then, is clearly meant as a sign of election, a fact that is equally true for Calogrenant as it is for Yvain and perhaps for all Arthurian knights. This survival has further significance for our understanding of Chrétien's text because it indicates the author's conscious incorporation into his narrative of a current of medieval beliefs and superstitions about meteorology and weather that dates back to the ancient world and that was also present in the mythologies of Gaul prior to the arrival of the Romans.[31] Before Chrétien's day and even well after it, weather as an enemy, Chantal Connochie-Bourgne explains, unleashed its forces against humans in forms that were perceived to be personifications of evil spirits.[32] Calogrenant's belief that God has interceded on his behalf, to calm the weather and return 'joie' to the knight's world, can therefore be said to foreground a specific cultural attitude toward the weather, one that was bound up with medieval perceptions of the cosmos.

---

[30] See James-Raoul, 'D'une météorologie l'autre', 219.
[31] On this last point, see especially P. Walter, *Canicule: Essai de mythologie sur 'Yvain' de Chrétien de Troyes* (Paris, 1988).
[32] C. Connochie-Bourgne, 'Le temps qu'il fait . . . expliqué par les premières encylopédies en langue française (XIIIe siècle)', in *Le temps qu'il fait au Moyen Age: Phénomènes atmosphériques dans la littérature, la pensée scientifique et religieuse*, ed. C. Thomasset and J. Ducos (Paris, 1998), 31.

A hint of this cosmological perception is provided to us in a revealing passage from the *Charrette*. Immediately following the episode where Lancelot has lifted the lid from the tomb we discover his damsel companion (who does not know Lancelot's name) praising his qualities to the hermit in terms of the weather:

Et son non, s'ele le savoit,	And his name, if she knew it
Li pria qu'ele li deïst	He asked her to tell him
Tant que cele li regeïst	And she replied to him
Qu'ele nel set, mes une chose	That she did not know, but one thing
Seürement dire li ose,	She dared certainly to tell him
Qu'il n'a tel chevalier vivant	That there was no such knight living
Tant con vantent les quatre vant	As far as the four winds blow.
(vv. 1954–60, Pléiade;	
vv. 1948–54, CFMA)[33]	

Depicting the wind as the instrument of fame, rumor, or reputation (whether positive or negative), is a commonplace topos in western literature from the classical age up to today. In his praise for Lancelot, Chrétien clearly portrays the wind as such an instrument, and this is not the first such instance in his romances; Chrétien also presented wind in this manner in *Cligés* and in *Yvain*.[34] One recalls that, before Fénice confessed her 'illness' to Thessala (i.e. her love for Cligés), she swore her nurse to silence. In that exchange, Chrétien, significantly, also deployed the '*vivant: vant*' rhyme:

– Mestre, por neant en parlez	– Mistress, you will cease such talk
Quant serai certainne et seüre	When I am definitively reassured
Que vos ja par nule avanture	That there is no chance that you
N'en parleroiz a rien vivant	Will repeat what I say to any living thing
– Dameisele, certes li vant	– Certainly young lady the winds
An parleront einçois que gié	Will speak of this before I do
Se vos ne m'an donez congié	If you do not grant me leave to do so
(vv. 3108–14, Pléiade;	
vv. 3086–92, CFMA)	

---

33 One quickly notes the *vivant: vant* rhyme for its repetition of the rhyming words of the prologue, *vivanz: vanz*. (The phonology of the rhyme, of course, would not be the same, presuming there was no failure to pronounce final consonants.) With specific reference to this comparison, Uitti asks the following question: 'Avons-nous affaire ici à une phrase toute faite qui relèverait du style courtois en général?' Considering the evidence he presents from the *Chèvrefeuille*, we might certainly agree that this is indeed the case. The clear rhetorical purpose of Uitti's question, however, is to help him demonstrate that courtly literary style in general supports Chrétien's *usus scribendi* in particular, an association that would further buttress the Garrett manuscript's pairing of the noun 'vanz' (in the subject case) with its eponymous verb, 'vanter'. We have already concurred with Uitti on this point, if for different reasons. However, although there is no reason to disagree that this is hyperbolic praise, we shall discover below that such praise of Lancelot is fundamentally different from Chrétien's praise of Marie in his prologue. Uitti, 'Autant en emporte', 286.

34 Though the connection can only be suggested, one might suspect that Chrétien was punning on 'wind' to advance his own fame and reputation in the final verses of the prologue to *Erec et Enide* where he boasts (*vante*): 'Des or comancerai l'estoire/ qui toz jorz mes iert an mimoire/ tant con durra crestïantez/ de ce s'est Crestïens *vantez*' (vv. 23–26).

In *Yvain*, Chrétien depicts the wind in a similar fashion:

As oroilles vient la parole	The word came to his ears
Ausi come li vanz qui vole	Like the wind in flight
(vv. 157–58, Pléiade;	
vv. 157–58, CFMA)	

The image of the four winds in the *Charrette*, however, extends the topos from *Cligés* and *Yvain* and grants the wind a significance that is greater than our understanding of it as a kind of voice. Rather, the wind that expresses Lancelot's fame represents nature in all its expansiveness, an image that predates Chrétien and again has its origins in Greco-Roman traditions. In this connection, Barbara Obrist's 'Wind Diagrams and Medieval Cosmology' provides a definitive perspective on the role played by the wind in medieval conceptions of the natural world and the greater cosmos.[35] '*Quator a quadris uenti flant partibus orbis*' and '*Quatuor a quadro consurgunt limite venti,*' the opening verses of these medieval wind poems attributed to Suetonius,[36] obviously underlie Chrétien's citation concerning '*les quatre vant*'. Together with Isidore of Seville's '*De nominibus ventorum*', these texts all clearly relate the four cardinal winds to the four cardinal directions[37] and thus place the winds in a metonymical relationship to the cosmos. The implications of this for Chrétien are that, beyond any sort of courtly stylistic *usus scribendi*, we discover a kind of scientific and historical grounding for the author's basic point: that his knight Lancelot has no match in all the natural world.

Elements in Praise

The same grounding for the damsel's praise of Lancelot may be invoked to assist us in our understanding of the prologue's praise for Marie de Champagne. As Obrist makes clear, medieval wind diagrams incorporated texts concerning winds into their composition and structure, and thus they provided a graphical representation of meteorological and cosmological knowledge in the Middle Ages. We can safely assume that Chrétien was acquainted with this kind of knowledge, although there is perhaps no way for us to be absolutely certain of it. It should be noted, however, that, with respect to Chrétien's knowledge of medieval arts of poetry and rhetoric, we have made a similar assumption. Indeed, taken as a whole, the prologue to the *Chevalier de la Charrette* has been treated as one of Chrétien de Troyes' most significant literary statements. From William Nitze to Douglas Kelly, scholars have traced Chrétien's compositional practice to the influences of his own schooling in the liberal arts.[38] Others, like Rychner, and Ollier, have focused

---

[35] B. Obrist, 'Wind Diagrams and Medieval Cosmology', *Speculum* 72 (1997), 33–84.
[36] Obrist, 'Wind Diagrams', 38–39.
[37] Obrist, 'Wind Diagrams', 38–40.
[38] See for example, Nitze, '*Sans et Matière*' and Kelly, *Sens and Conjointure*.

more narrowly on interpreting the meaning of the *Charrette* prologue itself
and on analyzing '*sans*' as it describes the status of the author, his story, and
the relationship of both to Marie de Champagne.[39] In broad terms, then, the
history of scholarship on the *Charrette* prologue informs us that the eulogy of
the Countess is not just a fine example of Chrétien's art. It is also an excellent
indicator of the poet's literary range and intellectual preparation.[40] If there is a
key to Chrétien's compositional method, then, and to the stock of knowledge
that informed his romances, Chrétien scholars of every stripe and from every
period agree that we may find it somewhere in the author's Latin training/
influences and in the medieval curriculum.[41]

Failing incontrovertible physical evidence, therefore, it is to be hoped that
such a key may prove useful as we try to understand verses 12–13. As indicated by the work of the eminent scholars mentioned above, there are many
points of connection between Chrétien's education, his experience, and his
literary work. It is reasonable for us to believe that his knowledge of the winds
came from the sources given above, and perhaps from a variety of others, but
it is also very likely that such scientific and historical knowledge was transmitted to Chrétien via literary traditions. In fact, Ovid's story of the creation in
the *Metamorphoses* appears to have had a direct influence, if not on the
author, at least on the perspectives of his times:

> The air hung over all, which is as much heavier than fire as the weight of water
> is lighter than the weight of earth. There did the creator bid the mists and clouds
> to take their place, and thunder, that should shake the hearts of men, and winds
> which produce lightning and thunderbolts. To these also the world's creator did
> not allot the air that they might hold it everywhere. Even as it is, they can scarce
> be prevented, though they control their blasts, each in his separate tract, from
> tearing the world to pieces. So fiercely do these brothers strive together. But
> Eurus drew off to the land of the dawn and the realms of Araby, and where the
> Persian hills flush beneath the morning light. The western shores which glow
> with the setting sun are the place of Zephyrus: while bristling Boreas betook
> himself to Scythia and the farthest north. The land far opposite is wet with

---

[39] See Rychner, 'Le prologue du *Chevalier de la Charrette*', and Ollier, 'The Author in the Text'.
[40] The well-known opening verses from the prologue to *Cligés* indicate that, at the very least, Chrétien
was well acquainted with Ovid. Consider verses 1–8.

Cil qui fist d'Erec et d'Enide	The author of Erec et Enide
Et les comandemanz d'Ovide	Who translated Ovid's Commandments
Et l'Art d'amors an romans mist,	And his Art of Love
Et le Mors de l'espaule fist,	And who wrote the Shoulder Bite
Del roi Marc et d'Ysalt la blonde,	And of King Mark and fair Isolde
Et de la hupe et de l'aronde	And who composed the metamorphosis
Et del rossignol la muance,	Of the hoopoe, the swallow and the nightingale
Un novel conte rancomance	Begins a new tale.

[41] An example of this is Uitti's analysis of the relationship between Chrétien's *Erec et Enide* and
Martianus Capella's *De nuptiis Philologiae et Mercurii*: 'A propos de philologie', *Littérature* 41
(1981), 30–46. Also see his 'Vernacularization and Old French Romance Mythopoesis with Emphasis
on Chrétien's *Erec et Enide*', in *The Sower and his Seed: Essays on Chrétien de Troyes*, ed. R. T.
Pickens (Lexington, KY, 1983), 81–115.

constant fog and rain, the home of Auster, the South-wind. Above these all he placed the liquid, weightless ether, which has naught of earthy dregs.[42]

The medieval wind diagrams described by Obrist follow closely on this Ovidian division of the four cardinal winds according to their names, qualities, and geographic origins. Similarly, such diagrams also attest to the enduring, ancient, conception of the natural universe as it is divided into the four elements. In this connection, Ovid's creation story provides another concise example of the kind of knowledge we can assume for Chrétien:

God – or kindlier Nature – composed this strife; for he rent asunder land from sky, and sea from land, and separated the ethereal heavens from the dense atmosphere. When thus he had released these elements and freed them from the blind heap of things, he set them each in its own place and bound them fast in harmony. The fiery weightless element that forms heaven's vault leaped up and made place for itself upon the topmost height. Next came the air in lightness and in place. The earth was heavier than these, and, drawing with it the grosser elements, sank to the bottom by its own weight. The streaming water took the last place of all, and held the solid land confined in its embrace.[43]

Taken together, these two citations from Ovid reflect the basic Aristotelian scheme of the natural universe. As Obrist explains

In the all-pervasive Aristotelian scheme, 'natural' places were allotted to these elementary constituents, the earth making up the lower and central part, fire the upper and peripheral one; these places were determined by the opposites heavy and light. The cohesion of the whole structure was guaranteed by the cyclical transformation of the elements one into another, which was explained by way of a further set of opposites, namely, hot and cold, dry and humid. Respectively, two of these qualities were assigned to each element, and these were thought to be the product of the cyclical association and dissociation of qualities (for example, fire resulted from the combination of hot and dry). Depending upon the ecliptic course of the sun, the whole process became manifest through seasonal change.[44]

---

[42] F. J. Miller, trans., *Metamorphoses* I (Cambridge, MA, and London, 1984 (reprint)). The Latin text of verses 52–68 reads as follows: 'Inminet his aer, qui, quanto est pondere terrae/ Pondus aquae levius, tanto est onerosior igni./ Illis et nebulas, illis consistere nubes/ Iussit et humanas motura tonitrua mentes/ Et cum fulminibus facientes fulgura ventos./ His quoque non passim mundi fabricator habendum/ Aera permisit; vix nunc obsistitur illis,/ Cum sua quisque regat diverso flamina tractu,/ Quin lanient mundum; tanta est discordia fratrum./ Eurus ad Auroram Nabataeaque regna recessit/ Persidaque et radiis iuga subdita matutinis;/ Vesper et occiduo quae litora sole tepescunt,/ Proxima sunt Zephyro; Scythiam septemque triones/ Horrifer invasit Boreas; contraria tellus/ Nubibus adsiduis pluviaque madescit ab Austro./ Haec super inposuit liquidum et gravitate carentem/ Aethera nec quicquam terrenae faecis habentem.'

[43] In Miller's edition, the Latin text of verses 21–31 reads as follows: 'Hanc deus et melior litem natura diremit./ Nam caelo terras et terris abscidit undas/ Et liquidum spisso secrevit ab aere caelum./ Quae postquam evolvit caecoque exemit acervo,/ Dissociata locis concordi pace ligavit:/ Ignea convexi vis et sine pondere caeli/ Emicuit summaque locum sibi fecit in arce;/ Proximus est aer illi levitate locoque;/ Densior his tellus elementaque grandia traxit/ Et pressa est gravitate sua; circumfluus umor/ Ultima possedit solidumque coercuit orbem.'

[44] Obrist, 'Wind Diagrams', 35.

For the Middle Ages we know that 'in most handbook summaries four (major) winds, four parts of the world, four elements ('bodies'), four seasons, four humors, etc. are correlated'.[45] Isidore of Seville's *De Natura Rerum* assumed such a correlation, and was a significant medieval source of cosmological and medical knowledge.[46] This is an important fact and it denotes a critical corpus of shared knowledge that connects medieval medical theory with the cosmological models described by medieval wind diagrams and Ovid's *Metamorphoses*. As we also know, the teaching of medical theory in France began with Bishop Fulbert and the School of Chartres in the late tenth and early eleventh centuries, and theoretical knowledge of medicine was a standard component of the liberal arts curriculum by Chrétien's day.[47] That Chrétien studied medical theory himself is therefore highly likely, if not a virtual certainty.[48]

Isidore of Seville's medical writings remind us that medical theory, as Chrétien would have known it, was predicated on Latin models that associated the four elements (Earth, Water, Air, and Fire) the four seasons (Autumn, Winter, Spring, and Summer), the four humors (Black Bile, Phlegm, Blood, and Yellow Bile), and the four temperaments (Melancholic, Phlegmatic, Sanguine, and Choleric). In these models, good health was considered to be the result of proper balance and of cyclical patterns; one's temperament was directly related to the balance of one's humors, and these in turn were related to the seasons and their associated elements. Returning to our earlier question, then, we can begin to understand why Chrétien compared Marie de Champagne to the wind in the prologue to the *Charrette*. To all appearances, Chrétien deployed wind in his comparison of Marie to other noble ladies for reasons that go beyond courtliness and literary style. On a much more profound level, he chose to praise Marie in terms of the wind because such wind was a commonplace feature of an obvious, medieval, cosmological hierarchy extending from Greco-Roman traditions and known to the author through literary, scientific, medical and historical sources, and also through medieval wind diagrams. What place Chrétien intended Marie to occupy in

---

45 Obrist, 'Wind Diagrams', 72.
46 See W. D. Sharpe, MD, trans., *Isidore of Seville: The Medical Writings. An English Translation with Introduction and Commentary* (Philadelphia, 1964).
47 L. C. McKinney, *Bishop Fulbert and Education at the School of Chartres* (Notre Dame, 1957) and *Early Medieval Medicine, with Special Reference to France and Chartres* (Baltimore, 1937).
48 By experience, Chrétien probably also knew about the practice of medicine, the use of ointments and herbs for healing, for example, but medical practice itself was not necessarily a part of the curriculum. Medicine of this type was often practiced by women with special skills, as in the case of Erec's nurses, the damsel that healed Yvain, and of Thessala who concocted the sleeping potion for Fenice. The connection between Chrétien's world and Salerno and Montpellier, significant centers of medieval medical learning, may also extend beyond the references in *Cligés*. The physician to Philip Augustus (Aegidius Corboliensis) was trained in Salerno and the well known *Regimen Sanitatis Salernitanum* was written on the cusp of the twelfth century for Robert, Duke of Normandy, eldest son of William the Conqueror (John Harington, trans., *The School of Salernum: Regimen Sanitatis Salernitanum* [New York, 1970], 24–26). Richard the Lionheart also went to Salerno, in 1199 on his way to Palestine (*The School of Salernum*, 29). More could be said, but there are already enough points of contact here for a safe assumption that Chrétien had good knowledge of Salerno and of medicine, perhaps even more knowledge that he ever conveyed in his romances.

this hierarchy, however, is not perfectly clear. Further investigation into this question is therefore required before we can attempt to decipher accurately verses 12–13 of the prologue.[49]

To better illustrate the kinds of hierarchical systems alluded to in the opening verses of the *Charrette*, two diagrams published with Obrist's article merit our attention. One particular depiction of Isidore's cosmological scheme and medical theory, from Munich, Bayrische Staatsbibliothek, deserves special emphasis for the hierarchies it establishes among the elements, the seasons, and the temperaments:

Fire	Air	Water	Earth
Summer	Spring	Winter	Autumn
Choleric	Sanguine	Phlegmatic	Melancholic

Of similar importance for our understanding of the intersection of Isidore's theories and medieval wind diagrams is the eleventh-century computistical miscellany Obrist publishes from Dijon, Bibliothèque municipale, MS 448 which gives the following hierarchies:

Air	Fire	Earth	Water
Spring	Summer	Autumn	Winter
Sanguine	Yellow Bile	Black Bile	Phlegm
Infancy	Adolescence	Maturity	Old Age

The significant difference between these two diagrams is that Isidore's model is ordered according to a counterclockwise cyclical evolution of the seasons. (Summer, at the top, is surrounded by its two adjacent seasons, Autumn on the left and Spring on the right, and is directly opposite its contrary season, Winter). The Dijon manuscript, by contrast, distributes the elements, the seasons, and the humors, according to a clockwise progression of the four stages of life (infancy, adolescence, maturity, old age). This minor difference in distribution is not significant to our discussion. The greater point is that wind diagrams, Ovid's creation story, and Isidore's medical theory each in their turn relied on the same hierarchical arrangements and on the same principle of a 'cyclical transformation of the elements one into another'[50] to express an understanding of the natural universe.

---

49 The full complexity of Chrétien's image would not likely have been apparent to his audience or to his patron, but there is no clear artistic necessity for such transparency. Moreover (as we shall see below), the simple relation of inferior to superior in the image would not have been difficult to comprehend, given other factors. Admittedly, Chrétien did write for his contemporaries, but he just as certainly wrote for posterity. His prologues make it altogether clear that Chrétien, though respectful of his patrons, wanted to be appreciated not exclusively for his relationship to them, but rather for his superior literary merits whence he would earn a place in the historical record. As every negative statement directed toward Gautier in the *Charrette* prologue suggests, the pantheon of literary history (as Chrétien would have envisaged it) despises loquacious, obsequious flatterers, themselves the most transparent poets of all.

50 Obrist, 'Wind Diagrams', 35.

According to Obrist, in the Dijon diagram, 'the winds appear to dominate over the elemental and humoral transformations as they manifest themselves in the seasonal cycle and the corresponding ages of man'.[51] In this way, wind would seem to occupy a superior position with respect to the aforementioned components of the medieval cosmological scheme. Generally speaking, indeed, 'the diagrams correlate categories in such a way that the reader is immediately able to detect a certain hierarchy, for example, that winds dominate elements and seasons, and not vice versa'.[52] Such a conception, however, seems to diverge from Ovid's cosmological vision in the *Metamorphoses* where winds are clearly confined to the sphere of air. One recalls that 'the air hung over all, which is as much heavier than fire as the weight of water is lighter than the weight of earth. There did the creator bid the mists and clouds to take their place, and thunder, that should shake the hearts of men, and winds which produce lightning and thunderbolts'.[53]

Thirteenth-century meteorological theorists such as Guillaume de Conches shared Ovid's (and by extension Aristotle's) conception of the four cardinal winds. As Isabelle Vedrenne informs us, 'Guillaume de Conches rappelle l'existence de quatre vents principaux: le Zéphyr à l'Occident, l'Eurus à l'Orient, le Borée au Septentrion et l'Auster au Midi.'[54] Also in the thirteenth century, Gossuin de Metz depicted the winds as 'l'air agité' by the confluence of ocean waters.[55] Chrétien de Troyes himself also seems to have shared the conceptual connection that depicted the winds as residing within the sphere of air, as the frequent recurrence of winds and storms in *Yvain* suggests. In *Cligés*, furthermore, the connection of wind and air is twice made explicit. The first instance has already been mentioned, in the nautical reference concerning Alexander's journey to Arthur's court. Let us emphasize here, however, that, in this image of the peaceful sea, Chrétien expressly pairs the favorable wind with 'calm air':

Au port truevent lez la faloise	In port, near the cliff they find
Les mariniers dedanz les nes.	The sailors in their ships
La mer fu peisible et soes,	The sea was peaceful and smooth
Li vanz dolz et li airs serains.	The wind was gentle and the air calm
(vv. 242–45, Pléiade; vv. 238–41,	
CFMA; emphasis mine)	

In our earlier wind citation from *Yvain*, finally, we can see another intimate cosmological relationship between wind and air

---

[51] Obrist, 'Wind Diagrams', 71.

[52] Obrist, 'Wind Diagrams', 73.

[53] *Metamorphoses* I, 52–56.

[54] I. Vedrenne, 'Temps et climat', in *Le temps qu'il fait au Moyen Age: Phénomènes atmosphériques dans la littérature, la pensée scientifique et religieuse*, ed. C. Thomasset and J. Ducos (Paris, 1998), pp. 80–81.

[55] Connochie-Bourgne, 'Le temps qu'il fait', p. 41.

Et tuit li vant se reposerent;	And all the winds died down
Des que Deu plot, vanter n'oserent	As God wished it, the winds no longer dared to blow
Et quant je vis l'air cler et pur,	And when I saw the air clear and pure
De joie fui toz asseür;	I was comforted by joy
(vv. 451–54, Pléiade; vv. 453–56, CFMA; emphasis mine)	

According to Gossuin de Metz, 'l'air est constitué de couches successives' and can be described according to the following divisions: (i) 'l'air souterrain'; (ii) 'l'air mis en mouvement par les courants aquatiques souter-rains, et désigné ensuite comme *vent*'; and (iii) 'l'air *esperitels, purs, naiz*'.[56] In the storms at the Barenton fountain, and in the examples taken from *Cligés*, it is clear that Chrétien is alluding to this second kind of air 'désigné comme *vent*'; we might even go so far as to say that the first *Cligés* citation indicates that the author had knowledge of the conceptual relationship between ocean conditions and the winds.

According to Connochie-Bourgne, Gossuin's 'air *esperitels, purs, naiz*' is distinct from air as an element and therefore we should understand it as belonging to a different cosmological sphere, and thus as occupying a different place within the hierarchy of the elements. Indeed, air, in this latter sense, connotes 'la région des corps incorruptibles' and is used at times to designate ether or fire.[57] Ovid's creation story speaks in similar terms about ether, placing it, with fire, above the winds. (Let us recall that 'above these all (i.e. the four cardinal winds) he (the creator) placed the liquid, weightless ether, which has naught of earthy dregs').[58] For Connochie-Bourgne, Gossuin's distinction of an 'air *esperitels*' was intended to avoid any confu-sion between 'le feu élémentaire' and 'le feu terrestre', and it therefore fulfilled an important pedagogical imperative. Indeed, 'c'est bien dans une région aérienne, ordinairement appelée ciel ou air que nous voyons étoiles filantes et comètes, même si les théoriciens, les philosophes, la désignent comme région ignée . . . Dernière des sphères élémentaires, elle s'étend jusqu'à celle de la lune. C'est en quelque sorte un air supérieur, sec, chaud, subtil et lumineux.'[59]

The *Yvain* reference to the '*air cler et pur*' is suggestive of the sort of polyvalence that inhered in medieval perceptions of air: when Calogrenant speaks of the '*air pur*', we imagine (following Gossuin) that he is talking about the heavens (and the reference to God would underscore that point); when he refers to the '*air cler*', however, it appears that he means something more down to earth, something akin to a sky cleared of winds, clouds, and rain. This distinction is especially important for understanding the prologue to the *Chevalier de la Charrette*: Wind, as it is associated with weather, is clearly

---

56 Connochie-Bourgne, 'Le temps qu'il fait', p. 37.
57 Connochie-Bourgne, 'Le temps qu'il fait', p. 37.
58 *Metamorphoses* I, 67–68.
59 Connochie-Bourgne, 'Le temps qu'il fait', pp. 37–38.

confined to the sphere of air, third in the hierarchy of the four elements. By association with this element, wind further connotes specific associations to seasons, humors, and temperaments. Such a wind cannot, therefore, dominate the element of fire, because this latter is associated with the incorruptible heavens, a sphere that was, as Gossuin tells us, frequently regarded in the Middle Ages as a kind of superior air. In such a medieval view of the cosmos, then, fire in its celestial space would have been superior to, and unaffected by, such earthbound meteorological phenomena as winds, storms, and rains.

In Connochie-Bourgne's words, 'le feu élémentaire ne se voit pas comme se perçoit le feu terrestre'.[60] Chrétien often evokes the 'feu terrestre' in his romances, sometimes in a positive light, but more frequently as a dangerous and destructive force. The fire of the hearth is associated with lodging and the court, and by extension with culture, opulence and safety, especially in the case of Chrétien's *Perceval*.[61] Fire represents the flame of love in the heart in the *Charrette*.[62] Elsewhere in Chrétien's romances, however, fire is the instrument of capital punishment (in *Cligés*, *Yvain*, the *Charrette*, and *Perceval*); it is used to burn villages (*Yvain*), and it is the breath of the serpent (*Yvain*).

The 'feu terrestre' and the 'feu élémentaire' are nonetheless frequently related in Chrétien's romances via synecdoche. In fact, cosmological comparisons predicated on the inferiority of the light of earthly fire to the light of celestial bodies can be found so consistently in Chrétien's writings that we might consider such imagery to be an essential component of his poetics. In *Cligés*, for example, after the Oxford tournament, the story's eponymous hero is praised in the following terms:

Vostre acointance chiere avons,	We hold your acquaintance dear
Et molt vos devrïens amer,	And should favor you very much
Et prisier et seignor clamer,	And honor you and call you lord
Qu'a vos n'est nus de nos parauz.	For none of us is your equal
Tot autresi con li solauz	Just as the sun
Estaint les etoiles menues,	Outshines the lesser stars
Que la clartez n'an pert es nues,	Whose light disappears from the clouds
La ou li rai del soleil nessent:	When the rays of the sun emerge
Ausi estaignent et abessent	Thus are our deeds
Noz proesces contre les voz,	Eclipsed and outshined by yours
Si soloient estre les noz	Though ours should be
Molt renomees par le monde	Renowned throughout the world
(vv. 4988–99, Pléiade; vv. 4948–59, CFMA; emphasis mine)	

When discussing Gauvain and Lunette in *Yvain*, furthermore, Chrétien deploys strikingly similar terminology:

Savez de cui je vos voel dire?	Do you know who this is?
Cil qui des chevaliers fu sire	The man who is lord of all knights

---

60 Connochie-Bourgne, 'Le temps qu'il fait', p. 37.
61 See vv. 3092–3101, Pléiade. The Roach edition of these same verses contains slight variations.
62 See vv. 3753–63, Pléiade; vv. 3745–3755, CFMA.

Et qui sor toz fu reclamez	And who is acclaimed above all
Doit bien estre solauz clamez.	Should be called the sun
Por monseignor Gauvain le di,	I am speaking of my lord Gawain
Que de lui est tot autresi	By whom
Chevalerie anluminee,	All chivalry is illuminated
Come solauz la matinee	As morning is lit by the sun
Oevre ses rais, et clarté rant	Spreading its rays and giving light
Par toz les leus ou il s'espant.	In all the places it touches
Et de celi refaz la lune	And this other one is the moon
Dom il ne puet estre que une,	And there can only be one
De grant foi et de grant aïe.	Of such great faith and assistance
Et neporoec, je nel di mie	I don't only say this, however,
Seulemant por son grant renon	Because she is well renowned
Mes por ce que Lunete ot non	But because Lunete is her name

(vv. 2401–16, Pléiade; vv. 2401–16, CFMA; emphasis mine)

Further on in this same romance, Chrétien bestows praise on Yvain in terms of the synecdoche of the 'feu terrestre' and the 'feu élémentaire':

Et dïent que buer seroit nee	They say she would be fortunate
Cui il avroit s'amor donee,	To whom he would give his love
Qui si est as armes puissanz	He who is so strong in battle
Et desor toz reconoissanz,	And obliging above all others
Si con cierges antre chandoiles	Like a torch among candles
Et la lune antre les estoiles	And the moon among the stars
Et li solauz de sor la lune	And the sun above the moon

(vv. 3245–51, Pléiade; vv. 3239–45, CFMA; emphasis mine)

In *Perceval*, finally, the brilliant light of the grail itself is described using the same kind of cosmological hierarchy and imagery discovered in *Yvain* and *Cligés*:

Quant ele fu leanz antree	When she entered the room
A tot le graal qu'ele tint,	Bearing the grail
Une si granz clartez an vint,	A light so bright came off it
Ausi perdirent les chandoiles	That the candles lost their luster
Lor clarté come les estoiles	Just as the stars lose their brightness
Qant li solauz lieve, et la lune	When moon and sun rise

(vv. 3224–29, Pléiade; vv. 3224–29, Roach; emphasis mine)[63]

Such shared figurative language in Chrétien's romances is surely more than a coincidence; it indicates a clear poetic practice and intent. Further, the frequency and context of this shared language is convincing evidence that Chrétien relied on his vision of the cosmos and its hierarchical system of elements to construct his most powerful comparisons. As the preceding examples make abundantly clear, to bestow praise on his superior characters

---

[63] The Roach edition of these same lines contains slight variations.

(Gawain, Yvain, and Cligés) and to depict the superlative nature of what will later be interpreted as a Christian relic, Chrétien associated Arthurian knights and the grail with the qualities of fire and the celestial spheres, and thus elevated them all to a status unequaled by anything on earth.

It is highly likely that Chrétien's praise of Marie de Champagne partakes of this same figurative language and that it thus relies on these same hierarchical visions of the cosmos. In fact, if we recall our earlier claim that verses 10–13 constitute a mock citation of Gautier d'Arras, then this contention becomes a virtual certainty, as Gautier employed exactly the same cosmological comparisons, and the same synecdoche of celestial light and earthly light, to praise Beatrix of Bourgogne in the prologue to *Ille et Galeron*:

Car del soleil palist le lune,	For the moon pales before the sun
De le lune palist l'estoile,	And the stars before the moon
Del cler jour palist le chandoile,	And a candle before the light of day
Et li argenz de l'or recuit	And silver yields to gold
(vv. 84–87)	

Knowing that, in this precise instance, Chrétien's preferred figurative language for depicting exemplarity throughout his romances finds a point of intersection with his literary challenge to Gautier in the prologue to the *Chevalier de la Charrette* is invaluable. It helps us to clarify the poet's comparison of Marie to other ladies in verses 12–13 of the *Charrette* and it allows us to avoid some of the pitfalls of previous interpretations.

Proposing a New Reading of Verses 12–13

As noted earlier, the Pléiade and CFMA editions, comparing '*funs*' and '*vanz*', relied on a suspect interpretation of '*funs*' as a kind of wind. However, the logic of the analogy presented in this reading was flawless and, as it followed the kind of medieval principles of *similitudo* found in Averroes and St Thomas (among others), it was very likely reflective of Chrétien's original intention: If Marie was superior to other ladies, then this particular wind ('*li funs*') must be superior to other kinds of winds ('*les vanz*'). In Thomistic language, such an analogy describes 'resemblance according to priority and posteriority' an operation that links 'the possession of an analogous perfection more properly or perfectly by one analogate than by the other(s) with either causal participation or the analogy of eminence'.[64] In simpler terms A is above A' as B is above B'. The reading in the Garrett manuscript, however, does not follow the principles of resemblance and eminence and therefore it relies on a much less fortunate analogy: Marie is superior to other ladies as wind ('*li vens*') is superior to earthly exhalations ('*le fu*'). A is to A as B is to

---

[64] G. P. Klubertanz, SJ, *St Thomas Aquinas on Analogy: A Textual Analysis and Systematic Synthesis* (Chicago, 1960), pp. 107–108.

C. Asymmetrical and logically faulty, the already inelegant metaphor of Garrett is also infelicitous, and its accuracy as a reflection of Chrétien's original text should be discounted.

Addressing the question of textual symmetry, and keeping in mind the principles of resemblance and eminence, should further assist us as we attempt to reply to the question of what place Chrétien intended Marie to occupy in the hierarchies evoked above. In this connection, let us look closely again at verses 10–13 of the prologue to the *Chevalier de la Charrette*:

> que ce est la dame qui passe
> totes celes qui sont vivanz
> si con li funs passe les vanz
> qui vante en mai ou en avril   (Pléiade and CFMA editions)

Leaving aside the question of the case of '*vanz*' (which, as we have argued above should be nominative rather than oblique), it is immediately apparent that Chrétien deployed here a pattern of analogies that relied structurally on the repetition of two phrases using the verb '*passer*', each of which were articulated around the comparative adverbial expression '*si con*', such that:

> La dame . . . passe/ totes celes

is symmetrically balanced by its comparison to

> Li funs passe les vanz.[65]

As given above (and as one would read in the Pléiade and CFMA editions) these two phrases depict a perfectly parallel structure of subject ('*la dame*', '*li funs*'), verb ('*passe*') and object ('*totes celes*', '*les vanz*'). By its word order, and the adverbial 'si con', this structure privileges and gives emphasis to the superior term of the comparison ('*la dame*', '*li funs*'), and thereby places wind ('*les vanz*') and the other noble ladies ('*totes celes*') in the inferior position. The rendering from the Garrett manuscript, however, disrupts this parallel, and, via its chiasmus, reverses the superior and inferior terms of the comparison:

> La dame . . . passe/ totes celes

> Le fu passe li vens

By all accounts, the elegant symmetry of the Guiot copy would be compelling were it not for the fact that the etymological argument deriving '*li funs*' from the Latin *favonius* (the west wind, and the wind of Spring) is easily falsified; and were it not for the evidence that shows '*funs*' to be associated with fire and

---

65 *Si con*, an adverb of comparison, derives from the Latin *quomodo* and, in my view, is a crux in our understanding of these verses as a parallel construction, with Marie surpassing others '*quomodo*' (in the same fashion that) *funs* surpasses *vanz*. For more on *Si con*, see Kr. Nyrop, *Grammaire Historique de la langue française*, VI (Copenhagen, 1930), p. 18.

25

smoke. Between the Guiot copy and Garrett, it may be argued that the latter represents the best possible *grammatical* structure, and yet, despite Chrétien's predilection for chiasmus, the verses are awkward, and the imagery impoverished. Moreover, as we should already suspect, the superior term of Chrétien's comparison is not the wind of April or May, but something different entirely.

Based on BN f. fr. 12560, a third reading of Chrétien's image is also possible. This reading, however, relies on a double nominative in verse 13:

> La dame . . . passe/ totes celes

is analogous to

> Li funs passe li venz

One might hasten to concur with Uitti that this version of verse 13 makes no grammatical sense. And yet, there is something curious here that deserves our attention. Let us begin by looking back at verses 10–11 and analyzing them more closely, phrase by phrase, paying special attention to parts of speech and word order:

La dame . . . passe/ totes celes	Subject – Verb – Object
Totes celes qui sont vivanz	Subject – Verb

By looking at the verses in this schematic way, it becomes apparent that Chrétien employed '*totes celes*' both as the object of the verb '*passer*' and (via the relative pronoun '*qui*') as the subject of '*sont vivanz*'. We can conclude from this that the poet constructed his verse using a clever double nominative. The relative pronoun '*qui*' did not alone allow him to do this; the coincidence of nominative and oblique forms in the feminine plural declension also granted the poet the necessary linguistic flexibility to accomplish this image.

Similarly, when viewed schematically, verses 12–13 of BN f. fr. 12560 yield a strikingly exact parallel to verses 10–11:

Li funs passe li venz	Subject – Verb – (Subject/Object?)
Li venz/ Qui vente en mai u en avril	Subject – Verb

If we can assume that Chrétien was deploying a parallel construction here, then we can conclude that, like '*totes celes*' in the previous phrase, '*li venz*' in this latter phrase serves at once as the object of the verb '*passe*' and as the subject (again, via '*qui*') of '*vente en mai u en avril*'. Several questions, however, remain to be resolved. To begin with, how is the reader supposed to decide whether '*li funs*' or '*li venz*' is the subject of '*passe*' in verse 12? This question willfully deploys an anachronistic attitude toward the medieval text in anticipation of its response. The *listening* public of Chrétien's day surely would not have stumbled over '*li venz qui vente*', a locution that Uitti has called a 'phrase toute faite', and for that reason, it is very unlikely that this double nominative structure would have produced any confusion. Further, because the parallel between verses 10–11 and 12–13 is so strong, it seems even more doubtful that a member of the medieval public would have hesitated for even a moment over these verses that have caused us, the contemporary critics, so much confusion.

Another, more difficult, question also imposes itself here. Could it not be the case that this double masculine nominative structure in verses 12–13, because it runs counter to what we assume to be good Old French grammar, is simply a mistake? The response, of course, is that it may indeed represent a mistake at some unknown (and ultimately unknowable) level of manuscript production and reproduction. Alternatively, such a construction may have been of a kind with the sorts of grammatical variations one inevitably discovers in a language that is in the process of evolving away from synthetic forms and toward analytic syntax.[66] From what we have discovered in verses 10–11, the suggestion that these verses represent a purely grammatical mistake appears less convincing than evidence that the manuscript legacy of the *Charrette* contains more than one error in the transcription of the two crucial terms of Chrétien's comparison, i.e. '*funs*' and '*vanz*'. Furthermore, if Chrétien never deployed a similar construction in his works, we might very easily dismiss such an occurrence as an unfortunate scribal error. The facts, however, do not support this argument. Indeed, especially in phrases implying a comparison, and the use of a relative pronoun, it appears that the double nominative is not absolutely exceptional. The following example from *Erec et Enide* is indicative:

Mes plus luisanz estoit li crins	But the hair was more splendid
Que li filz d'or qui mout est fins	Than a very fine golden thread
(vv. 1645–46, Pléiade; vv. 1637–38, CFMA)	

An even more convincing instance of a masculine noun serving as object of one verb and subject of another (via the relative pronoun 'qui') occurs in *Yvain*:

Je sui, ce voiz, uns chevaliers	I am, you see, a knight
Qui quier ce que trover ne puis	Who seeks what he cannot find
(vv. 356–57, Pléiade; vv. 358–59, CFMA)	

---

[66] As Glanville Price has noted in *The French Language: Present and Past* (London, 1971): 'In OFr there are numerous instances of the use of the inappropriate case, and especially of the use of the oblique where the nominative might have been expected' (p. 96). Price considers this to be an indication that the two-case system was breaking down even in its earliest stages of existence. He further comments, in this connection, that the case system was weakened by 'a growing tendency to adopt certain fixed word orders, with the result that the function of a noun in a sentence was well enough indicated by its position' (p. 98).

To all appearances, then, the double nominative masculine structure from BN f. fr. 12560 cannot be dismissed out of hand on the grounds that it is 'ungrammatical'. Chrétien deployed similar constructions elsewhere, and it is plausible that the poet used such a structure as he constructed his praise of Marie in verses 12–13.

Because such a reading has the merit of completing the symmetry of the structure begun in verses 10–11, and because BN f. fr. 12560 also allows the wind to blow, we have discovered in this manuscript significant evidence for our investigation into Chrétien's original image. We also, and unfortunately, can discover here one important impediment: BN f. fr. 12560, like Guiot, also employs '*li funs*' in its comparison, a term that continues to present us with difficulties. From what we know of '*li funs*', and from what we have learned in general about wind, it is certain that Chrétien was not comparing '*li vanz*' to any other kind of wind, nor was he comparing it to the '*les effluves du sol*'. This being the case, we are challenged to maintain our symmetrical analogy for the prologue, adhering to resemblance and eminence, and thus to produce a satisfactory metaphor and an elegant image of Marie. The cosmological models discussed above can help us meet this challenge, but as we do so we must also look to lessons from other manuscripts for guidance.

By all corresponding textual accounts, the '*vanz qui vante en mai ou en avril*' is evocative not just of a courtly season (Spring) but also of the wind's corresponding element (air). Thence the wind connotes a specific place in the cosmological hierarchy, above the sphere of water, but below the sphere of fire. Based on the hierarchy of the elements alone, therefore, it would be a plausible and coherent comparison to place Marie above other noble ladies, just as fire rises above wind. Indeed, such a comparison would be based on perfectly analogous terms – the '*air agité désigné comme vent*' and the '*air supérieur*' associated with the sphere of fire – and so would complete, with perfect symmetry, and in adherence to the principles of resemblance and eminence, the parallel construction with verses 10–11. The uncertainty remains, however, of whether the manuscripts can support this type of comparison.

As one might expect, the *Charrette* manuscripts are equivocal on this point, though they do furnish us with some guidance. The Escorial manuscript indeed gives '*li feuz*' in the nominative singular, as the subject of the verb '*passe*', and thus as the correlative comparative term to Marie in its version of verse 12. Unfortunately, Escorial repeats the same troubling variant as the Guiot copy, rendering '*les vanz*' in the plural oblique. Based on the preponderance of evidence presented above, however, it is incumbent upon us to argue that '*les vanz*' (plural oblique) is a shared error across the manuscripts, one that must be corrected to '*li vanz*' so that the wind, as it should, may be allowed to blow. Further, given what we now know of Chrétien's knowledge of wind diagrams, medical theory, and cosmological schemes, we should also accept that '*li feuz*' is a better reading than '*funs*' or '*fu*' whose various interpretations as '*foehn*' and '*effluves*' have produced unsatisfactory results (though the relationship, discovered in *Cligés*, between '*funs*' and smoke and fire suggests that modern readings have strayed farther from the connotation of 'fire' than might have the actual medieval ones). Moreover, because there is evidence that the masculine double nominative was indeed possible within comparisons in Old French, I would propose that the manuscripts allow, that Chrétien's *usus scribendi* supports, and that medieval cosmological models prescribe the following rendition of Chrétien's verses:

Si deïst et jel tesmoignasse	One might have said, and I can attest to the fact,
Que ce est la dame qui passe	That this is the lady who surpasses
Totes celes qui sont vivanz	All those who are now living
Si con li feuz passe li vanz	Just as fire rises above the wind
Qui vante en mai ou en avril	That blows in May or in April
(vv. 9–13)	

Adopting this reading of the *Charrette* prologue implies that we have made thorough enough investigation into the text, its manuscripts, Chrétien's art, and medieval intellectual traditions to accommodate the inevitable, and lingering, uncertainty that attends Chrétien's praise of Marie de Champagne. Such accommodation, however, is not detrimental to our understanding of verses 12–13; knowing that fire rises above wind, as Marie rises above other noble ladies, enriches our appreciation of Chrétien's art and work and allows for an image that is beautiful and coherent on multiple levels. With a comparison predicated on the hierarchical place of wind within models of the natural universe, Chrétien constructed verses 12–13 not just for the purpose of elevating Marie above her peers. Chrétien's praise of his patron also served, by extension, to laud her health and temperament by means of an image that relied on models associating elements, seasons, humors and temperaments. By *distancing* Marie from the wind ('*li vanz qui vante en mai ou en avril*'), the poet placed her above the element (air, known to be turbulent, to carry disease, and suspected of harboring evil spirits), the humor (blood, characteristic of childhood) and the temperament (sanguine, implying naiveté) connected to Spring and its wind. We should take care to remind ourselves, however, that these models denoted balance and motion, as in a turning of the spheres, and so we should emphasize that Chrétien's praise of Marie did not indicate a binary type of opposition between the Countess and other noble ladies. Instead, the author clearly viewed his patron as representative of the healthy balance that arises in that authentically medieval moment of perfect synchronicity when the elements (air and fire) seasons (Spring and Summer), humors (blood and yellow bile) and temperaments (sanguine and choleric) harmoniously coalesce.

II

THEIR CLOTHING BECOMES THEM: THE NARRATIVE FUNCTION OF CLOTHING IN CHRETIEN DE TROYES

Monica L. Wright

If medieval verse romance could be compared to a tapestry, Chrétien de Troyes would be one of the genre's finest weavers.[1] One might ask, then, how he came to spin such beautiful tales. One answer to this question lies in the romancer's aptitude in using well-chosen structuring devices in his works, ones that tie together different parts of the narrative, allowing them to reflect and complement each other. In fact, all of the elements of Chrétien's texts are intricately intertwined to form a cohesive whole; that is, each serves a specific narrative function crucial to the text. Among these elements is clothing, which provides Chrétien with a remarkably efficient tool with which to weave.

Because clothing (defined liberally to include all types of vestimentary objects, armor and adornments) is so easily associated metonymically with the character who wears it, articles of clothing offer a second textual representation of a given character – the first being the character himself as he is represented in the text. This second representation works within a signifying system that allows the reader to understand more fully the character and his relationships with others.[2]

Lacy has noted that it is precisely from their narrative context that objects have meaning within a medieval text.[3] Chrétien uses clothing in varying degrees and for different interpretive purposes. I will attempt to analyze many

---

[1] Eugène Vinaver uses the term 'tapestry' to describe medieval romance in *Form and Meaning in Medieval Romance* (New York, 1966), p. 10.

[2] By signifying system, I mean a socially based representational system that ascribes meaning to the articles of clothing a person wears. This meaning involves class distinctions, rank and role within a class, sexuality and information about interpersonal relationships. My argument is that the clothing signifying system apparent in the romances of the twelfth century is distinct from the pre-existing real-world vestimentary code (on which it is nonetheless based) in that it has a greater degree of flexibility, thus a greater capacity for expression of ambivalence and ambiguity.

[3] N. J. Lacy, *The Craft of Chrétien de Troyes: An Essay on Narrative Art* (Leiden, 1980), p. 16. In his 'Thematic Structure in the *Charrete*', *L'Esprit Créateur* 12 (1972), 13–18, Lacy discusses the structural principle of 'thematic analogy' which 'consists of the reflection of the central theme or intrigue of the work in numerous other episodes' (p. 13). I would argue that Chrétien's use of clothing is a device of this nature.

of these functions in order to understand better Chrétien's genius and what he calls in his prologue to *Erec et Enide*[4] his *conjointure*.[5]

In a related study, Sturm-Maddox and Maddox have analyzed the function of clothing in Chrétien's *Erec et Enide*.[6] They conclude that the main reason for the couple's wanderings is their need to evolve socially from their initial status as youths to husband and wife and finally, to king and queen. Both their social evolution and their relationship with each other are fully represented by the descriptions of their clothing and their acts of dressing and undressing. They must, as the saying goes, grow into their clothes. At every level, clothing provides the reader with a means to interpret Erec and Enide's moral, social and interpersonal reality. The technique is remarkably efficient inasmuch as it requires very little elaboration while still conveying the information that the reader needs to understand the text. Chrétien chooses to show, to represent, rather than to tell, and what results from the mimetic device is a text that is richer in detail without losing its subtlety. Chrétien will use this type of narrative description to the same end throughout his other four romances.

To begin my treatment of the textual function of clothing, I will first explore the romance *Cligés*.[7] When the Greeks arrive in the Arthurian court, they immediately remove their mantles as they go before Arthur (315–17) in order to show the king their respect. Several lines later, the poet once again emphasizes this deference when he describes Alexandre as 'Desfublez fu devant le roi' (334). Chrétien's insistence here underlines the immense respect that Alexandre bears for this king, and he does so by representing an act of undressing oneself as an honoring gesture. Later, the king will reciprocate this respect when he gives Alexandre his armor (1123–35). The vestimentary gift is an equally honoring gesture in which the donor symbolically dresses the recipient. In the same way that Alexandre disrobes to demonstrate deference to the king, Arthur will have Alexandre dressed in armor that is twelve times more valuable than the armor he gives to the other Greeks. The cycle of mutual honoring is completed by the queen's gift of the *chemise* into which Soredamors's hair is sewn.[8] This gesture not only represents the honor that the Arthurian court wishes to bestow upon Alexandre, but also ultimately precipitates the expression and realization of love between Alexandre and Soredamors, thus becoming a plot motivator. It is significant both that the

---

4   *Erec et Enide*, ed. M. Roques (Paris, 1952), vs. 14.
5   For an extensive discussion of Chrétien's notion of *conjointure*, see D. Kelly, *The Conspiracy of Allusion: Description, Rewriting and Authorship from Macrobius to Medieval Romance* (Leiden, 1999), and *The Art of Medieval Romance* (Madison, 1992).
6   S. Sturm-Maddox and D. Maddox, 'Description in Medieval Narrative: Vestimentary Coherence in Chrétien's *Erec et Enide*', *Medioevo Romanzo* 9 (1984), 51–64. J. Le Goff, 'Vestimentary and Alimentary Codes in *Erec et Enide*', in *The Medieval Imagination*, trans. A. Goldhammer (Chicago, 1992), pp. 132–50, contends that Erec's masculine superiority over Enide is encoded in the couple's clothes. Like Strum-Maddox and Maddox, Le Goff examines Chrétien's use of clothes to represent rites of passage but does not develop it as systematically as they do.
7   *Cligés*, ed. A. Micha (Paris, 1957).
8   Le Goff claims that 'the queen's gift of clothing is a female equivalent of dubbing' (p. 136). His assertion creates a strong parallel between Arthur's gift of armor and Guenevere's gift of clothing.

queen's gift comes in the form of a vestimentary object, additionally so because Soredamors made the *chemise* herself, and that Alexandre's beloved is physically present in the gift through the hair sewn in its seam. The text requires a closing of the honoring-through-clothing cycle: the two vestimentary gifts given to Alexandre by the king and queen answer the double mention of Alexandre's removing his mantle before Arthur. Soredamors's hair functions here as a synecdochical substitution for her. Hair is not simply an adorning element (hair being the part of the body that we most readily may alter for aesthetic purposes): it is a tiny physical piece of Soredamors herself. The poet describes the hair as being more beautiful, and thus more valuable, than the gold strand that is sewn into the other seam of the *chemise* (1558). Yet the burgeoning love between Alexandre and Soredamors shows most clearly the hair's true worth. The queen uses the *chemise* with its hair as a means to coax the two would-be lovers into a confession of their mutual love, despite their best attempts to hide it from the world as well as each other.[9]

If Alexandre arrives at Arthur's court in a position of deference, Cligés, his son, arrives with the intention of proving from the beginning his vast prowess, but wishes to remain anonymous. To this end he disguises himself in choosing to wear suits of armor of four different colors on the four days of combat in the tournament (4536–916). From this difference alone we may see the chasm that divides the son from the father.[10] Cligés will repeat to a large extent the actions of his father, but he will invert them at many turns. Here, the image of the father kneeling before King Arthur after having removed his mantle contrasts dramatically with the image of the son intentionally confusing the court by neither revealing his identity nor allowing the court to recognize immediately that he is the same knight from day to day. Arthur bestowed the gift of armor upon Cligés's father; now Cligés uses his several suits of armor to confuse Arthur and his knights as to his identity.

An even greater contrast is apparent in the relationships that the father and the son have with their respective lovers. Alexandre meekly hides his feelings toward Soredamors despite the complete legitimacy of their mutual feelings.[11] Nonetheless, the two are discovered by the queen, who initiates a symbolic

---

[9] Lacy has asserted that the her hair 'serves not only as a symbol and reminder of Alexandre's and Soredamors's love but as the actual instrument by which it was discovered and encouraged by the queen' (*Craft*, p. 83).

[10] Peter Haidu discusses at length the parallel between the father and son in *Cligés* in his *Aesthetic Distance in Chrétien de Troyes: Irony and Comedy in 'Cligés' and 'Perceval'* (Geneva, 1968), pp. 63–70. He explains Alexandre's actions in terms of his belonging to a proto-courtly generation whereas Cligés's generation may be viewed as fully courtly. Haidu argues that in many ways the son surpasses the father, particularly with regard to self-confidence within the courtly milieu. I do not disagree with Haidu's analysis; rather, I find his positing of a generational gap that divides the chivalric realm an extremely satisfactory explanation of the reasons for differences between father and son. However, I would characterize the resulting contrast in temperament in another way: whereas I think Alexandre embodies meekness and deference (with the exception of his very early behavior at his father's court), Cligés is, in my estimation, almost brazen in his deeds.

[11] Lacy, *Craft*, p. 82.

intimacy between them in the abstract physical contact provided by the hair in the *chemise*. Cligés and Fénice, on the other hand, are forced into secrecy by the illicit nature of their adulterous love. They proceed to a truly physical intimacy, at which point they are discovered 'nu a nu' (6362–68). The legitimate love of Alexandre and Soredamors is evoked by an object of clothing, whereas the illicit love between Cligés and Fénice is most clearly represented by the discovery of the two lovers lying nude together, or in complete absence of clothing. This nudity is an instance of undressing oneself, but unlike Alexandre's deferential undressing act which opens this discussion, Cligés et Fenice in no way show deference to the emperor by their act; indeed, their nudity represents their betrayal of the emperor. Not only has their undressing gone too far and into nudity, adultery and shame, but it also specifically insults the emperor, forcing Cligés to flee rather than come into the emperor's presence. The romance opens with one undressing act: Alexandre's coming before the king in a position of deference with his mantle removed. It closes with the inverted reflection of the first undressing act: Cligés fleeing the emperor after being discovered nude with the empress.

Chrétien elaborates on nudity, or the lack of proper clothing, in *Le Chevalier au lion*,[12] by assigning it a place of predominance both as a direct reflection of the major theme of the romance – Yvain's moral and social devolution and evolution – and as a major plot motivator. Yet, even before Yvain's madness and nudity, there are some important mentions of clothing which are thematically analogous to later episodes in the narrative. When we see Laudine for the first time, she is grieving the death of her husband and is ripping and tearing her clothes (1159). A brief time later, when King Arthur comes to her land and finds Yvain married to this maiden, the poet gives us a description of her clothing, stating that she is 'plus bele que nule contesse' (2359–70). These two passages punctuate the period of time during which Laudine progresses from a loss of social status with no one to defend her fountain to an elevated state in which she has the most valiant knight of the Arthurian court at her side. This passage is an inverted foreshadowing of the progression that Yvain will make from sanity and social status to madness and outcast status. Yvain's plight is also represented with vestimentary imagery. Even as the maiden messenger arrives to deliver her message to Yvain, the clothing image is operative. When she approaches the encampment of Arthur's knights, she removes her mantle. Her undressing action can be seen not only as an honoring gesture toward the king, whom she cordially and respectfully greets, but also as a dishonoring gesture toward Yvain, whom she shames publicly with the admonitions that her lady has sent (2704–72). Immediately upon hearing the news that his lady has reclaimed the ring, the symbol of her love for him, Yvain destroys his clothes, slipping into madness (2806), his nudity becoming a sign of his madness and his retreat from society. Without his sanity, Yvain has lost his ability to function in society,

---

[12] *Le Chevalier au lion*, ed. M. Roques (Paris, 1960).

and without his clothes, Yvain has lost his social identity. The hermit with whom he has his first social contact during his madness recognizes him as mad from the fact that he is nude (2832), while the ladies who once knew him have a difficult time recognizing him undressed (2892–912). Furthermore, Yvain himself, once he comes back to his senses and recognizes his nudity, is ashamed and quickly dresses himself in the clothing that the damsels have left for him (3020–22).

Yvain is not the only character in the romance for whom shame is linked to the absence of clothing. The giant who menaces Gauvain's relatives threatens that he will take the gentleman's daughter and will reduce her to state of lice-ridden nudity (4116). The giant himself is described primarily with regard to his poor accoutrements, emphasizing the shameful state of his life (4086–95). Lunete's fall from grace is characterized by her reduction to near-nudity. She is taken to be burned at the stake 'trestote nue en sa chemise' (4316). However, as the other ladies realize that Lunete has been too harshly judged, they lament the fact that Lunete can no longer provide them with beautiful clothes to wear (4360–61). In the end, they decide to send a mantle to her to cover herself, thus reducing her shame (4368–73). Finally, the situation of the three hundred *tisseuses* represents a notable irony within the text: these wretched women are forced to toil to make clothing but are themselves dressed completely in rags (5294–96). Their near-nudity represents their powerlessness, vulnerability and lack of social status, while their work provides to others what they are denied. In all of these cases, Yvain provides deliverance from shame and nudity. Yvain has thus come full circle: he first saves Laudine from her grief, then he himself endures madness and nudity but manages with some help to return to sanity and society, and finally he must save others from their shame and nudity, which ultimately wins back the love of Laudine. Yvain's clothing and nudity provide a direct parallel to his changing social identity, but in *Le Chevalier de la charrette*, Chrétien will use clothing in a much more nuanced way to create the identity of perhaps his most mysterious knight.

Like in *Cligés*, Chrétien continues to use dressing and undressing to structure his narrative in *Le Chevalier de la charrette*.[13] However, at the beginning of this romance, there is a predominance of dressing scenes, in particular those in which the hero of the romance, Lancelot, is honored by the various people he encounters during his adventures. Lancelot's hosts give him, at almost every home that lodges him, a fur mantle; occasionally he receives the mantle directly from the shoulders of another person, a sign of extreme deference and honoring. At the castle of the lady whose lodging is dependent upon his sleeping with her, the lady dresses him, as is customary, in a fur mantle; however, during the pretend rape scene one of the lady's assailants tears the mantle (1144). We may initially consider this act of specialized undressing to be one of aggression and dishonoring, yet since the assailant does not destroy

---

[13] *Le Chevalier de la charrete*, ed. M. Roques (Paris, 1958).

the mantle, only tear it a bit, we come to understand that Chrétien is showing us that this act of tearing is quite carefully controlled and that ultimately the dishonoring is only temporary and slight. Indeed, it is a false dishonoring which mirrors perfectly the acts of the assailant toward the lady. When Lancelot first enters into the false rape scene, the poet explains that the lady is nude to the navel (1080). Again, the fact that her nudity is partial signals that the rape is not a real one: all is for show. What is real, however, is Lancelot's prowess and chivalric merit, as he comes to the aid of the maiden. The defense that he mounts on her behalf as well as the courtly way in which he behaves toward her as she offers her body to him later that evening lead her to the realization that this knight is indeed a worthy one.

> Si est an sa chambre venue
> et si se couche tote nue,
> et lors a dit a li meïsmes:
> 'Des lores que je conui primes
> chevalier, un seul n'an conui
> que je prisasse, fors cestui,
> la tierce part d'un angevin;
> car si son ge pans et devin,
> il vialt a si grant chose antendre
> qu'ainz chevaliers n'osa enprendre
> si perilleuse ne si grief;
> et Dex doint qu'il an veigne a chief.'   (1267–78)

(And she went into her room and went to bed completely nude and then said to herself: 'Since the time that I first made the aquaintance of a knight, there is not one but this knight whom I would esteem a third of an angevin; for as I think and surmise, he has set himself upon a quest more perilous and painful than any other knight has ever dared to undertake. May God grant him success in it!')

The scene between Lancelot and the maiden is particularly interesting with regard to the use of vestimentary imagery. The bed to which the maiden leads Lancelot for their night together is covered in perfectly white sheets (1195–99), evoking an impression of purity. This image both defies the lady's amorous attempts and reinforces their ultimate failure, for Lancelot rejects her advances. Lancelot, however, reveals his lack of interest in sleeping with her only after the two have gotten into bed together. What is remarkable in this passage is the care with which Chrétien points out that neither Lancelot nor the maiden has removed his or her *chemise*.

> Un covertor de .II. dïaspres
> ot estandu desor la couche;
> et la dameisele s'i couche,
> mes n'oste mie sa chemise.
> . . .
> Et il se couche tot a tret,

mes sa chemise pas ne tret
ne plus qu'ele ot la soe feite.   (1200–03; 1213–15)

(A covering of two embroidered silk panels was spread over the bed; and
the young lady lay upon it but did not remove her *chemise*. . . . And he lay
down at once; like her, he did not remove his *chemise*.)

Just as the earlier dishonoring was a false one, so this intimacy is equally false.
Upon making this discovery, the lady excuses herself, undresses herself in her
own chamber, and remarks that Lancelot is a truly worthy knight. The lady's
undressing herself, like the white bedsheets, contrasts and answers both the
rape scene, in which the wrong person attempts to undress her, and Lancelot's
rejection, in which the right person refuses to undress her. Lancelot implicitly
honors her by leaving her clothed, while the rapist, albeit a false one,
dishonors her: Lancelot's honoring answers the prior dishonoring. The lady's
undressing herself signals her deference toward Lancelot and her esteem for
him, even though he is absent from this honoring act. The very next view that
both the lady and we, as readers, have of Lancelot is as a fully armed knight,
ready to continue his quest of the queen.

Isnelemant et tost se lieve.
Et li chevaliers se resvoille,
si s'atorne et si s'aparoille
et s'arme, que nelui n'atant.
La dameisele vient a tant,
si voit qu'il est ja atornez   (1282–87)

(Quickly and early she rose from bed. The knight awoke and dressed;
with no help from anyone, he prepared himself and armed himself. At this
moment the young lady arrived and saw him already attired.)

This image of Lancelot is certainly the only aspect of this episode that
unequivocally rings true: the lady has honored him only to provoke his assistance during the staged rape in which both she then he are falsely dishonored,
and she has attempted to force him into a false intimacy by insisting that the
only way that she will allow him to be lodged in her castle is if he sleeps with
her. This attempt at intimacy is foiled, however, by the worthiness of the
knight, and the image of Lancelot armed and ready to face the only *aventure*
that matters to him is, in fact, the only aspect of the episode in which appearance corresponds to reality.

Lancelot's single-mindedness with regard to finding the queen is an inte-
gral part of his identity. His dedication to his task is never more apparent than
when he climbs into the cart to reach her more quickly. However, the text is
replete with references to his special aptitude for a different task, namely, the
liberation of the people of Logres from Meleagant. Several episodes accen-
tuate the fact that he fits the requirements of his task so precisely, including
the one in which Lancelot borrows armor from one of his hosts to fight the
proud knight. The text emphasizes that these arms fit Lancelot extremely

well, so well in fact that one would believe he had been born wearing them: 'qu'il fu ensi nez et creüz/ de ce voldroie estre creüz' (2675–76). Chrétien insists that his readers believe him, and the author's emphasis serves to identify Lancelot both with the armor and as the obvious savior of the captives. Lancelot fits his armor and his destiny perfectly, unlike Gauvain, who has failed at his mission and is finally found at the Pont soz Eve, bobbing up and down in the water with his armor spread about on the shore (5104–28). Obviously, Lancelot has the appropriate tools for the job while Gauvain is decidedly lacking. Yet, herein lies an artful subtlety in Chrétien's text: although all of the romance's characters conclude that the earlier episodes are signs of Lancelot's particular aptitude for the task, they do not understand that Lancelot, while well suited for the liberation of the people of Logres, is undertaking the task for very different reasons. Since the people of Logres will be freed from Meleagant along with the queen, Lancelot is only incidentally their liberator. He is the knight worthy of the task of liberation, yet he pursues this task only to fulfill his own desires.[14] Therefore, his identity as the worthy liberator is only superficial, in the same way that the cart was only superficially shameful and that the rape scene was staged. First and foremost he wishes to save his lady, the queen, and his ability to remain focused on her never waivers.

Lancelot demonstrates a remarkable fixation upon the queen, slipping almost into idolatry when he finds the comb that Guenevere has lost in the woods (1348–499). When he finds the comb, he allows the maiden with him to keep it, provided she give him the hairs entangled in its teeth. Lancelot's fascination with the hair is very obvious to the maiden, but the reader who has been allowed to read into Lancelot's thoughts knows that the queen has consistently occupied his mind, sometimes to the point that he does not notice when he is addressed. We must wonder, then, why Lancelot needs the hair to remind him of the queen. The answer lies both in the ease with which he abandons the comb in favor of the hair, and in what transpires later in the text. On the night of the lovers' tryst, Guenevere awaits Lancelot in a *chemise* that the poet takes care to describe as 'molt blanche' (4579). Although Guenevere will shortly commit adultery, the image that Chrétien gives us of her at this point in the romance is one of purity. This very subtle clue is perhaps the only one that the reader receives that the tryst later might be the first sexual contact between Lancelot and the queen. If this is the case, Lancelot's touching the hair represents their first physical contact. There is a clear progression within the text: at first, Lancelot has a completely abstract image of the queen; then through the hair he is able to feel her physically; and, finally, the two are united in the tryst. Significantly, Guenevere is the only person capable both of naming him and of recognizing Lancelot when he is disguised for the tournament (5636–37), indicating that the queen knows him so intimately that she recog-

---

[14] D. Kelly calls Lancelot 'a figure rich in contrast, indeed in contradictions', *Sens and Conjointure in the Charette* (The Hague, 1966), p. 206.

nizes him in any situation, thus in any clothes. For Guenevere, Lancelot's identity, like his attention for the queen, remains constant, regardless of his clothing. Chrétien creates an identity for Lancelot that only one other character is capable of perceiving. For everyone else, Lancelot remains an enigma.

Whereas in Chrétien's *Charrette* characters other than the queen are incapable of deciphering the hero's identity, in *Le Conte du Graal*,[15] the hero is initially incapable of deciphering anything. As Lacy notes, Perceval's main problem is that he fails to interpret properly the appearance of objects in order to arrive at an understanding of them and their place in the world.[16] This situation is never more obvious than when he confuses the knights he sees in his mother's forest first for devils, then for angels (127–45). When he sets out to find King Arthur so that he, too, can be a knight, he is attracted simply to their appearance rather than to their social function. Significantly, he begins his quest dressed inappropriately for his new calling: he wears the Welsh clothes that his mother has made for him (584–91), repeatedly refusing to abandon them in favor of a more courtly costume. With Ivonet, he gives reasons for his refusal, citing the inferiority of the clothing that Ivonet proposes. Perceval not only refuses these clothes, he insults them, insisting that the ones that his mother made for him are far superior (1132–52). However, we know that the clothes he describes as inferior are of the finest materials, and we understand that the notion of dressing the part of a knight is completely lost upon Perceval. Yet, despite his refusal to wear the clothes of a knight, he does manage to acquire a suit of armor, although he has no idea how to use his arms.[17]

At the next stop on Perceval's journey, he encounters Gornemant, who, we learn, is not only a valiant knight but also a perfectly courtly gentleman. It is finally Gornemant who, if unable convince to Perceval of the superiority of the courtly clothes, at least can persuade him to wear them to please his new mentor. Gornemant also takes it upon himself to teach Perceval how to use his armor. When he asks Perceval if he knows how to use his armor, the youth replies that he only knows how to put it on and take it off (1370–77). This is significant in light of the fact that the function of arming and disarming a knight held such prominence in the textual world of Chrétien. Not only is his knowledge extremely superficial on a practical level, but also his understanding that there could be social or relational implications to the acts of

---

15 *The Story of the Grail (Li Contes del Graal), or Perceval*, ed. R. T. Pickens, trans. W. W. Kibler (New York, 1990).

16 *Craft*, pp. 16–20.

17 In fact, Perceval's very procurement of the set of armor evokes and reinforces his complete misunderstanding of its use and purpose, for once he has killed the Red Knight in order to take his armor, Perceval believes he must resort to chopping the knight to bits in order to remove his armor: 'Mes einz avrai par charbonees/ Trestot esbraoné le mort/ Que nule des armes an port,/ Qu'eles se tienent si au cors/ Que ce dedanz et ce defors/ Est trestot un, si con moi sanble,/ Qu'eles se teinent si ansamble' (vss. 1116–20). It is only with the arrival of Yonez that Perceval is instructed in the appropriate removal of armor, although he remains unaware of its use.

arming and disarming is completely absent. Perceval thus fails both to know and to understand.

By the time Perceval reaches the castle where Blanchefleur lives,[18] he has almost entirely overcome his shortcomings for the chivalric world. Upon his arrival in the castle, Blanchefleur's servants disarm him (1756), that is, he is perceived for the first time as a true knight. They further honor him by bringing a fur mantle for him to wear (1760). Perceval is now fully educated in his use of arms and fully courtly, and others take him to be a knight and treat him with the appropriate respect. The two notable exceptions to this general attitude toward the new knight are the lack of attention accorded him as he exits the Grail Castle, and the admonition he receives from the pilgrims on Good Friday. These rejections are represented by vestimentary symbols as well. Although the inhabitants of the Grail Castle receive Perceval with much honoring, bringing him mantles and allowing him to sleep in the bed of the Fisher King, they completely ignore him the following morning; no one arms him, no one answers his calls, and no one bids him farewell (3325–87). This cold treatment is the direct result of Perceval's failure to ask the question that would have healed the Fisher King and his lands. The inhabitants of the Grail castle extended great hospitality to Perceval, only to find that his chivalric training had undermined the very reason he had been sent into their midst. Their overwhelming disappointment in him is demonstrated textually by their refusal to answer him, arm him or dress him.

This episode contrasts greatly with Perceval's sojourn in Blanchefleur's castle. Although he is received in the same fashion – with great hospitality – his subsequent treatment by Blanchefleur and her people is vastly different. We may understand this difference in light of Perceval's great success at Blanchefleur's castle, whereas he fails at the Grail Castle. Blanchefleur, unlike the Fisher King, has found in Perceval her savior, and she no longer feels that she needs the assistance of others while he is at hand. In fact, after the night of love between Blanchefleur and Perceval, she returns to her chamber in the morning and does not call her servants to come dress her. She willfully dresses herself to demonstrate her newfound ability to defend herself against her foe, whereas Perceval at the Grail Castle is forced to fend for himself as the inhabitants abandon him. In one case dressing oneself is a positive act of self-sufficiency; in the other it is a condition imposed upon an individual by those he has disappointed.

The second rejection that Perceval receives is from the pilgrims on Good Friday who admonish him for wearing armor on this sacred occasion (6212–66). Thus it is specifically for becoming too involved in the chivalric world that Perceval endures this affront, and his armor becomes a sign of shame. At this point in the text, Perceval has forgotten the church, his courtly clothing, and the clothing that his mother made for him. He is presented to us

---

[18] For a discussion of the historical plausibility of the description of Blanchefleur's dress, see R. Abbott, 'What Becomes a Legend Most?: Fur in the Medieval Romance', *Dress* 21 (1994), 4–16.

as a chivalric shell. Yet it is precisely at this moment that Perceval remembers these objects and regrets having forgotten them, and when he arrives at the home of the hermit, he 'Se descent et si desarme' (6305), an undressing act that removes the shame of forgetting who he is and from whence he came. Since this instance is the last reference to the clothing of Perceval and in light of the fact that so much of the early part of the romance was devoted to describing his accoutrements in detail, we may assume that he has lain his arms aside forever, rejecting the Arthurian chivalric world for the religious one that he now seeks with his uncle the hermit. Perceval has undergone a series of great changes: from a youth dressed in the Welsh fashion who confuses the appearance of knights with that of angels, to a brave and chival-rous knight who sports courtly clothing when not in battle, then to a tired and disillusioned knight who wears nothing but his armor. Finally, he abandons his armor for what we can probably assume to be the clothes of a religious hermit.[19] In the end he is not far from where he started. Through the description of his clothing, Chrétien demonstrates clearly every step Perceval takes on his journey.

A final clothing reference of interest in *Le Conte du Graal* occurs in the episode in which Gauvain approaches Perceval to coax him to return with him to Arthur's court (4315–511). After Sagremor and Keu are each defeated by Perceval, Gauvain decides that he should like to approach this young knight (who is contemplating the drops of blood in the snow) in a non-threatening manner, by going to speak with him and ask him to come to court rather than going to fight with him. Keu quickly insults Gauvain, by subtly accusing him of cowardice: 'Certes, en un bliaut de soie/ Porroiz ceste besoigne faire/ Ja ne vos i covenra traire/ Espee ne lance brissier' (4356–26). Gauvain explains that he is simply trying to approach this man in a human fashion, but Arthur urges him to wear his armor: 'Or m'i alez donc, fait li rois,/ Que molt avez dit que cortois./ S'estre puet, si l'en amenez,/ Mais totes vos armes prenez/ Que desarmez n'iroiz vos pas' (4345–49). Here, Arthur is saying to his nephew, 'Go, and be as courteous as you wish, but be a knight first. Wear your arms.' Gauvain does as his uncle wishes and wears his armor, but he addresses him 'Sanz fere nul felon sanblant' (4400). Unlike his negative reaction to Sagremor's and Keu's threats, Perceval's reaction to Gauvain's genteel tone and patient understanding is positive. Gauvain alone has risen to the occasion that Perceval has offered to Arthur's knights, understanding that there exists a means other than through the knightly order, represented by armor, to have a civilization. However, his strict and almost blind allegiance to the king stunts his attempt to participate in it fully, as his wearing his armor despite his incli-nations to the contrary indicates. This moment most clearly indicates that

---

[19] Of course, it may have been that Chrétien's plan was instead to create a synthesis of Arthurian and reli-gious knighthood. In the absence of an ending for the romance, however, such an assertion remains speculative. My interpretation here is based on what *does* appear in the text, rather than on what might have appeared, had he finished the romance. This clothing act is, in fact, Perceval's last and, moreover, his last action in the romance.

Perceval will surpass the order of the Arthurian realm. Gauvain does succeed in bringing Perceval to the court, but the two remove their armor before they enter, signifying that they have made human rather than knightly contact.

Chrétien's use of clothing is thus pervasive and fulfills a variety of different narrative functions. The very common motif of clothing as an indicator of status presents itself throughout the works. As Sturm-Maddox and Maddox have noted, Erec and Enide's wanderings are a direct result of their need to evolve into the new social beings that they must become in their new roles first as spouses, then as king and queen, dressing the part. Chrétien employs the theme of undressing oneself as a sign of respect and deference. He also utilizes the theme of dressing another as an act of honoring. In *Cligés* the tales of the father and son inversely mirror each other: the father openly paying respect to the king and secretly longing for his love, the son covertly entering the Arthurian world and ultimately exposing his illicit love, caught in a shameful display of nudity. Chrétien explores the notion that nudity is shameful in *Le Chevalier au lion*. Yvain's state of dress mirrors his passage from husband and knight to madness, nudity and outcast status, and back again to husband and knight. Similar passages of other characters mirror Yvain's passage. In *Le Chevalier de la charrette*, Chrétien explores clothing as an identity both constant and shifting, calling appearances and motivations into question throughout the romance. Finally, in *Le Conte du Graal*, Perceval's evolution as a knight is marked by his clothing, as is his final atonement, with regard both to the Lady of the Tent and to his family. Gauvain attempts to gain entrance into the celestial realm that Perceval inhabits, as he attempts to leave behind his knightly trappings but fails because of his close ties with Arthur.

Clothing, described in detail or merely mentioned, serves as a structuring device in the romances of Chrétien. The clothing of the characters who populate his romances reflects the major themes of each romance, and the description of their clothing efficiently and eloquently conveys much information concerning the characters' social or moral status, their motivations and attitudes, and their relationships with others. Furthermore, each mention or description of clothing serves the text in its own way, deriving its meaning from its unique context, and lending to Chrétien's work a vitality as the reader must interpret for herself at every moment. Finally, Chrétien de Troyes' use of clothing as a narrative tool that is touched, as are all of his tools, by the hand of a master artist, plays a greatly important role in his romances: it is a part of his *molt bele conjointure*.

III

GENERIC HYBRIDITY IN HARTMANN VON AUE'S
DER ARME HEINRICH

Jane Dewhurst

Introduction

In his introduction to *Alterität und Modernität*, Hans-Robert Jauss illustrates the intensity of the debate surrounding the relationship between medieval literature and modern genre theory with an anecdote. In 1965, the editors of the GRLMA were so determined to assert the validity of genre categories in the face of the 'individualistic' aesthetics of critics such as Benedetto Croce, that they called on no lesser authority than Pope Pius XII, an enthusiast of Protestant 'literary' studies of the Bible, to support their cause.[1] This supplementation of generic conventions with religious authority provides some indication of the extent to which generic classification is bound up with the fate of the literary institution itself. Sacralised by constant use, genre categories acquire the status of universal, suprahistorical norms or 'archetypes', and are often applied indiscriminately to all historical periods. On the basis of these purportedly fixed and delimited categories, canons have been formed, and the literary products of previous centuries organised into a succession of peaks and troughs, geniuses and epigones, or a gradual progression towards a *telos*.[2] Given the investment of both literary criticism and literary history in generic conventions, it is hardly surprising that they should be regarded as sacrosanct in some quarters, and that the highest authority should be brought to bear on the heretic who challenges their validity.

Yet research into medieval criteria for classifying literary works, as well as into the circumstances of medieval textual production and transmission, has

---

[1] H.-R. Jauss, *Alterität und Modernität der mittelalterlichen Literatur* (Munich, 1977), p. 35. I would like to thank Dr Mark Chinca and Dr Sebastian Coxon for their comments on an earlier version of this article.

[2] For examples of different strategies of literary history and taxonomies, see D. Perkins, *Is Literary History Possible?* (Baltimore and London, 1992). Literary histories of the Middle Ages traditionally privilege the *Blütezeit* as the apogee. See, for example, H. de Boor, *Die höfische Literatur: Vorbereitung, Blüte, Ausklang 1170–1250*, Geschichte der deutschen Literatur von den Anfängen bis zur Gegenwart 2 (Munich, 1969); W. Haug, *Literaturtheorie im deutschen Mittelalter von den Anfängen bis zum Ende des 13. Jahrhunderts* (Darmstadt, 1985).

demonstrated that such isolating and normative conceptions of genre cannot be applied to the texts of the Middle Ages without jarring anachronism. Medieval rhetorical treatises show a remarkable lack of concern with generic classification, concentrating instead on the poetic styles and repertoires that stood at the disposal of all authors.[3] Few generic terms circulate, and those that do can be employed with bewildering looseness, cutting across the boundaries laid by modern criticism.[4] Thomasin von Zirklaere, for example, groups together literary figures from the *matières de Rome*, *Bretagne* and *France* under the collective term *aventiure* to illustrate his commentary on the moral status of vernacular narratives. Thomasin's evaluation of contemporary literature proceeds according to the criteria of *wârheit* and *lüge*: the ideological question whether the *aventiure* carry any moral or spiritual significance (lines 1118–26).[5] Such indications that generic expectations were primarily rooted in dichotomies such as religious/secular, Latin/vernacular, written/oral, cast further doubt on the heuristic value of our modern arsenal of generic terms.[6]

Another feature of medieval narrative that militates against normative systems of classification is its high level of intertextuality. The webs of intertextual reference that can be discerned in the prologues, excursuses and narrative scenarios of much Middle High German literature indicate that authors are familiar with the preceding Latin and vernacular traditions, and are eager to situate themselves within these traditions by associating themselves with or disassociating themselves from their predecessors.[7] The literary practice of *imitatio* creates complex filiations between texts; however, *imitatio* can also be practised subversively, in order to establish a negative dialectic between texts and their related ideological positions. Authors can suggest generic affiliation in order to mislead their audience and inhibit interpretation, allegorical repertoires playing host to obscene humour, courtly texts distancing themselves more or less explicitly from the ideology they appear to promote.[8]

These intricacies of textual production present scholars of medieval literature with something of a two-horned problem. On the one hand, normative genre conceptions fail to do justice to such intertextual transitions and to the

---

3 See H. Dubrow, *Genre*, The Critical Idiom 42 (London and New York, 1982), pp. 52–5; A. Fowler, *Kinds of Literature: An Introduction to the Theory of Genre and Modes* (Oxford, 1982), pp. 142–7; Jauss, *Alterität*, p. 108; A. Butterfield, 'Medieval Genres and Modern Genre Theory', *Paragraph* 13 (1990), 184–210.

4 See Dubrow, *Genre*, p. 54.

5 *Der Wälsche Gast*, ed. H. Rückert, Bibliothek der deutschen Literatur 30 (Quedlinburg, 1852); cf. Haug, *Literaturtheorie*, pp. 228–40.

6 On the complex dynamics between the classical and the emerging vernacular tradition, see Haug, *Literaturtheorie*; on the confrontation of vernacular literature with the oral culture, see U. Liebertz-Grün, *Aus der Mündlichkeit in die Schriftlichkeit 750–1320*, Deutsche Literatur: Eine Sozialgeschichte, 3 vols. (Reinbek bei Hamburg, 1988), I.

7 See Haug, *Literaturtheorie*; on intertextuality in the Arthurian romance, see F. Wolfzettel, *Artusroman und Intertextualität*, Beiträge zur deutschen Philologie 67 (Gießen, 1990).

8 See Butterfield, 'Medieval Genres'. On irony in the courtly romance, see P. Haidu, *Aesthetic Distance in Chrétien de Troyes: Irony and Comedy in 'Cligès' and 'Perceval'* (Geneva, 1968); D. H. Green, *Irony in the Medieval Romance* (Cambridge, 1979).

combinatory practices of medieval authors. On the other, if we abandon such categories and foreground the redeployment and recycling of motifs and discourses we effectively reduce the entire corpus of literature to an undifferentiated mass of such motifs and discourses. What is more, we forego the possibility of discerning dominant patterns of repetition and interaction within the literary corpus, and of reconstructing medieval frameworks of association for texts on the basis of the intertexts to which they allude, the codicological groupings in which they are found in manuscript compilations, and so on.[9] A middle ground has been found by Jauss, whose dynamic conception of genre allows us to view such categories as always and necessarily provisional, without denying them all heuristic and constitutive value. Jauss sees genre as an element of the *Erwartungshorizont* that the reader or audience brings to the text, subject to continual modification through the interaction of public expectation with literary creativity.

Jauss's suggestions for a revision of the critical tool of genre in order to take reader response into account seem all the more pertinent given the present climate of interest in such issues as scribal innovation and manuscript compilation, and in their implications for our understanding of medieval textuality.[10] The historicisation of the medieval text as unstable, subject to the vicissitudes of manuscript transmission, has established beyond doubt that, when dealing with medieval literature, the stable text, like the stable genre, is a critical fallacy.[11] The medieval text is not an isolated and self-sufficient unit; rather it is implicated in an on-going process of reinterpretation. Thus scribal revisions and the activities of manuscript compilers provide us with vantage points for examining the potentialities of the text itself. The scribal variant can crystallise alternative readings of a text or alert us to its loci of controversy or instability. The transposition of the text into different codicological contexts can shed light on the elements that were perceived as dominant by different medieval audiences, and in some cases can effectively expand or modify a text's meaning. These material records of what Jauss refers to as the 'Prozeß fortgesetzter Horizontstiftung und Horizontveränderung' allow us to bring

---

9   On precisely this problem, with reference to the *Mären*, see the exchange between J. Heinzle, 'Märenbegriff und Novellentheorie: Überlegungen zur Gattungsbestimmung der mittelhochdeutschen Kleinepik', *Zeitschrift für deutsches Altertum* 107 (1978), 121–38, 'Altes und neues zum Märenbegriff', *Zeitschrift für deutsches Altertum* 117 (1988), 277–96 and H.-J. Ziegeler, *Erzählen im Spätmittelalter: Mären im Kontext von Minnereden, Bispeln und Roman* (Munich and Zurich, 1985), pp. 5–28.

10 See, for example, J. Bumke, 'Der unfeste Text: Überlegungen zur Überlieferungsgeschichte und Textkritik der höfischen Epik im 13. Jahrhundert', in *Aufführung und Schrift in Mittelalter und früher Neuzeit*, ed. J.-D. Müller (Stuttgart and Weimar, 1996), pp. 118–29, also 'Autor und Werk: Beobachtungen und Überlegungen zur höfischen Epik', in *Philologie als Textwissenschaft: Alte und neue Horizonte, Zeitschrift für deutsche Philologie (Sonderheft)* 116 (1997), 105–35; work in the burgeoning field of manuscript studies includes H. Kuhn, 'Versuch einer Literaturtypologie des deutsche 14. Jahrhunderts', in *Typologie Litteratum: Festschrift für Max Wehrli zum 60. Geburtstag*, ed. S. Sonderegger, A. Haas and H. Burger (Zurich and Freiberg, 1969), pp. 261–80; A. Mihm, *Überlieferung und Verbreitung der Märendichtung im Spätmittelalter* (Heidelberg, 1967); S. Westphal, *Textual Poetics of German Manuscripts, 1300–1500* (Columbia, 1993).

11 See Bumke, 'Der unfeste Text', 'Autor und Werk'.

our conception of text and genre and the interaction between the two more closely in line with medieval poetics.[12] Their witness becomes invaluable when the generic affiliations of a text are plural or difficult to gauge in 'positivist' terms.[13]

My focus in this essay will be Hartmann von Aue's *Der arme Heinrich*, a text that has consistently proved resistant to generic classification. Hartmann is known primarily for his reworkings of Chrétien de Troyes' *Erec et Enide* and *Yvain*, which adapt the narratives to the ideological requirements of German knighthood; his *Erec* is generally considered to have inaugurated the literary fashion in Germany for reworking French narratives based on the *matière de Bretagne*.[14] As I will demonstrate, *Der arme Heinrich* clearly shows affiliations with this genre: the work remains close to the narrative scheme of romance throughout, the echoes of *Erec* and *Iwein* are unmistakable, and, in all but one version, its final narrative and ideological posture is emphatically that of a romance.[15] However, the text also appropriates and mobilises heterogeneous discourses from works of different generic and ideological affiliations. I will attempt to locate some of these intertextual strands by examining the text in diachronic series, as a transformation of preceding discourses, which is itself subject to transformation in the course of its transmission. I will therefore use generic *termini* provisionally and with a view to submitting them to critical scrutiny. In addition to Jauss's conception of genre as subject to diachronic change, my investigation is also informed by feminist literary criticism. In examining the text's affinities with different generic discourses, I will focus on its representation of gender roles and relations on the grounds that gender systems and ideologies are important constituents of the horizons that frame the production and reception of literary texts, and are also necessarily mediated by these texts.[16]

As I will demonstrate, the heterogeneous generic and ideological discourses mobilised by the text converge on the figure of the unnamed girl. These discourses beleaguer her character and her body from the outset, and anticipate her dramatic displacement from the centre of the narrative in the sacrifice scene. Thus the character of the *maget* represents a source of narrative plurality, a challenge to the text's univocality and a witness to its hybridity. The scribal adjustments to which the text is subject in the course of its transmission, and the codicological contexts in which it is placed by manuscript compilers, indicate that the heterogeneity that underlies her character

---

12 Jauss, *Alterität*, p. 119.
13 See Butterfield, 'Medieval Genres', pp. 184–7.
14 See, most recently, Sylvia Ranawake, 'The Emergence of German Arthurian Romance: Hartmann von Aue and Ulrich von Zatzikhoven', in *The Arthur of the Germans*, ed. W. H. Jackson and S. Ranawake, Arthurian Literature in the Middle Ages 3 (Cardiff, 2000), 38–53 (p. 38). On Hartmann as spokesman and ideological codifier of knighthood in Germany, see W. H. Jackson, *Chivalry in Twelfth-Century Germany: the Works of Hartmann von Aue*, Arthurian Studies 34 (Cambridge, 1994).
15 See below, p. 33.
16 See F. Jameson, *The Political Unconscious: Narrative as a Socially Symbolic Act* (Ithaca and New York, 1981), p. 79; S. Gaunt, *Gender and Genre in Medieval French Literature* (Cambridge, 1995), pp. 3–21.

was not lost on later medieval audiences. My examination of the text in diachronic series is thus simultaneously a study of the dynamic continuum of a particular complex of gender constructs, which, like genre categories, are intrinsically unstable and open, continually subject to transformation and reinterpretation.

Der arme Heinrich: A Genre Experiment

In the famous opening lines to *Der arme Heinrich*, Hartmann signals his anomalous status as *ein ritter sô gelêret*, a knight who enjoys the benefits of a clerical education, and who thus occupies an intermediate position between the knighthood and the clergy (lines 1–2).[17] An almost exact repetition of this formulation occurs in *Iwein*, where it serves to establish the author's credentials as a literate representative of courtly culture (lines 21–2).[18] In *Der arme Heinrich*, the sense of a shared social *habitus* is enhanced by the local character of the material. The narrator informs his audience that the narrative will feature *ein herre* [. . .] / *ze Swâben gesezzen* ('a lord living in Swabia'[19]), and draws on the conventional catalogue of courtly values in order to describe his protagonist (lines 30–46). However, in contrast to the *Iwein* prologue, Hartmann here paratactically links his desire to please his audience to an additional religious intention: he wishes to write of *sô gewanten sachen, / daz gotes êren toehte / und da mite er sich möhte / gelieben den liuten* (lines 12–15) ('things of such a nature which would do honor to God and with which he could endear himself to his fellow men'). The religious tenor is enhanced by his appeal to the audience to intercede with prayer on his behalf (lines 21–5). The Christian formulations, many of which are redolent of the epilogue to the hagiographic text *Gregorius*, suggest that any *lêre* the poet transmits in this work will be far removed from the ideological remit of King Arthur.[20]

The indeterminate nature of *Der arme Heinrich*, with its combination of courtly and religious signals, poses a problem of generic classification which has consistently vexed modern critical discussion, leading critics through almost the entire gamut of generic possibilities. Early studies of the work

---

[17] Unless otherwise stated, all references are to *Der arme Heinrich*, ed. U. Rautenberg (Stuttgart, 1993). On the chronology of Hartmann's works, see P. Wapnewski, *Hartmann von Aue* (Stuttgart, 1979), pp. 19–23; F. Neumann, ' "Der arme Heinrich" in Hartmanns Werk', in *Kleinere Schriften zur deutschen Philologie des Mittelalters* (Berlin, 1969), pp. 225–55; C. Cormeau and W. Störmer, *Hartmann von Aue: Epoche – Werk – Wirkung* (Munich, 1993), pp. 25–32.

[18] References are to *Iwein*, ed. G. F. Benecke, K. Lachmann and L. Wolff, 7th edn (Berlin, 1968).

[19] All translations of *Der arme Heinrich* are taken from F. Tobin's 'The Unfortunate Lord Henry' in *German Medieval Tales*, ed. F. G. Gentry, The German Library 4 (New York, 1983), pp. 1–21. Translations from all other works are my own.

[20] Wapnewski suggests that *Der arme Heinrich* and *Gregorius* signpost a 'gegenhöfische Wendung' in Hartmann's career, *Hartmann von Aue*, p. 118. However, given Hartmann's chivalric self-stylisation, his concern for the public reception of his work, and the courtly setting of his narrative, this seems a rather extreme formulation.

drew on largely formal criteria to argue a genetic relationship with the *Novelle*, a view that has since been discredited on the grounds that it attributes rather a high degree of prescience to the late twelfth-century author.[21] The text's religious content has prompted comparisons with hagiographic or homiletic texts;[22] however, the closing sequence, with its affirmation of *süeze[n] lanclîp* ('a long and happy life'), has generally caused critics to resort to compound definitions.[23] The fact that *Der arme Heinrich* follows the basic tripartite scheme of the romance, with the knight's initial fall from grace followed by a departure on *aventiure* which eventually culminates in his restoration to chivalric exemplarity, sealed with a feudal marriage, has also not gone unnoticed.[24] Recently, critics have suggested a proximity to the *Märe*, on the grounds of the text's formal properties and the nature of its transmission.[25] These difficulties of generic attribution are indices of broader problems concerning the relation between the religious and secular elements of the work. Cormeau considers the text to be pervaded by an irreconcilable dualism: 'Die sinnlich-reale Ebene und die symbolisch-religiöse decken sich nicht ohne Widersprüche und vor allem nicht mit letzter Sicherheit der Zuordnung.'[26] Seiffert also considers the text thematically plural, arguing that the terms 'religious' and 'courtly' or 'worldly' 'do not always yield a precise critical framework for an assessment of the poem'. His observation of 'a certain ambivalence in the theme, balanced as it is between the religious and the erotic', leads him to classify the text as 'a genre experiment'.[27]

The terms used by Hartmann himself to describe the work further underline this problem. In the prologue he refers to a source which he has adapted: *nu beginnet er iu diuten / ein rede, die er geschriben vant* (lines 16–17) ('Now he will begin to interpret for you a tale which he found written'), and qualifies

---

[21] On *Der arme Heinrich* as a *Novelle*, see J. Klein, *Geschichte der deutschen Novelle* (Wiesbaden, 1954), p. 27; H. Kuhn, *Annalen der deutschen Literatur* (Stuttgart, 1962), p. 132; H. Eggers, 'Rezension zu B. Nagel', *Euphorion* 48 (1954), 102–4 (p. 102). On the invalidity of the term *Novelle* for the analysis of medieval literature, see H. Fischer, *Studien zur deutschen Märendichtung des 15. Jahrhunderts* (Tübingen, 1968), pp. 30–1; Heinzle, 'Märenbegriff'.

[22] H. Sparnaay states that the text is 'wesentlich legendarischer Natur', *Verschmelzung legendarischer und weltlicher Motive in der Poesie des Mittelalters* (Halle, 1922), p. 126; A. Schirokauer describes it both as a 'Ritterlegende' and a 'Büßergeschichte', 'Zur Interpretation des "Armen Heinrich" ', *Zeitschrift für deutsches Altertum* 83 (1951), 59–78 (p. 67); H. Moser suggests an affiliation to the 'Mirakelerzählung', 'Hartmanns "Armer Heinrich" – eine Mirakelerzählung', in *Festschrift für J. Trier*, ed. H. Beckers and H. Schwarz (Cologne and Vienna, 1975), pp. 321–9.

[23] G. Ehrismann classifies the text as a 'Legendennovelle', *Geschichte der deutschen Literatur bis zum Ausgang des Mittelalters*, 3 vols. (Munich, 1922–35), II, 200; P. Anderson describes it as a 'courtly epic which blends the secular and the religious', 'Court and Anti-Court in Hartmann von Aue's "Der arme Heinrich" ', *New German Studies* 7 (1979), 167–87 (p. 185). On the affirmation of the secular in Hartmann's Arthurian romances, see R. Endres, 'Die Bedeutung von *güete* und die Diesseitigkeit der Artusromane Hartmanns', *Deutsche Vierteljahrsschrift für Literaturwissenschaft und Geistesgeschichte* 44 (1970), 595–612.

[24] See, for example, Wapnewski, *Hartmann von Aue*, pp. 115–16.

[25] See Cormeau and Störmer, *Hartmann von Aue*, p. 145; Westphal, *Textual Poetics*, p. 113.

[26] C. Cormeau, *Hartmanns von Aue 'Armer Heinrich' und 'Gregorius': Studien zur Interpretation mit dem Blick auf die Theologie zur Zeit Hartmanns* (Munich, 1966), pp. 12–13.

[27] L. Seiffert, 'The Maiden's Heart: Legend and Fairy-Tale in Hartmann's *Der arme Heinrich*', *Deutsche Vierteljahrsschrift für Literaturwissenschaft und Geistesgeschichte* 37 (1963), 384–405 (p. 397).

this statement several lines later: *Er las daz selbe maere, | wie ein herre waere | ze Swâben gesezzen* (lines 29–31) ('The story which he read tells of a lord living in Swabia').[28] The term *maere* does not necessarily suggest any relation to the genre category designated by this term in modern criticism, as the texts placed in this category are generally dated to the thirteenth century and later, and there is little evidence that they were considered a single genre formation by medieval authors. For Düwel the terms used by Hartmann are primarily references to his source. He interprets the term *rede* as signalling an affiliation to the tradition of spiritual/exemplary literature, but points out that the syntax is ambiguous and the term could refer to the source text, to Hartmann's adaptation, or to both.[29] The ambiguity is of course increased by the fact that no such source has been found. It is thus unclear whether Hartmann is claiming an exemplary status for his own *diutunge* or merely presenting it as an adaptation of an exemplary *rede*.

The experimental and thematically heterogeneous character of *Der arme Heinrich* links it to *Gregorius*, to which it is also chronologically close.[30] Both works adapt material that is religious in character.[31] However, neither of the two narratives confines itself to the merely exemplary, showing a narrative breadth and concern for psychological verisimilitude that is beyond the scope of the schematic *exemplum*.[32] In addition, both adapt certain structural and thematic constellations from the courtly romance, in order to place them in experimental dialectic with the didactic content. The institution of chivalry, as well as its broader social milieu, become a theatre for dramatising the relationship between God and man, the logical impasse of original sin and the possibility of salvation through the condescension of the divine *arzât*. Hartmann also weaves the courtly theme of *minne* into the theological subject matter, by grafting a marriage plot onto both narratives.

The most common approach to *Der arme Heinrich* engages primarily with the theological subject matter. The exemplary courtly protagonist, abruptly divorced from God's favour and from society like his biblical counterpart Job, is taken to exemplify the existential dilemma of post-lapsarian man.[33] The

---

[28] The B version, which can be found in the Heidelberg (Universitätsbibliothek, cpg 341, fols. 249r–258v) and so-called Kalocsa (Cologny, Biblioteca Bodmeriana, cod. Bodmer 72, fols. 256r–265r) manuscripts, has *ditz buoch*, lending the work a more authoritative, historiographical aspect. See K. Düwel, *Werkbezeichnungen der mittelhochdeutschen Erzählliteratur* (Göttingen, 1987), p. 255.

[29] Düwel, *Werkbezeichnungen*, p. 84. See also Ehrismann, *Geschichte*, II, 199.

[30] For an analysis of *Gregorius* prologue as a programmatic experimentation with the conventions of the legend, see Haug, *Literaturtheorie*, pp. 134–54; on the heterogeneity of *Gregorius* and *Der arme Heinrich*, see Jackson, *Chivalry*, pp. 147–8.

[31] *Gregorius* is an adaptation of an Old French *vita*. No direct source for *Der arme Heinrich* has been found; however, the motif of leprosy as a manifestation of sinfulness, and the soteriology of the cure, are redolent of the *Sylvesterlegende* as well as the *Amis et Amiloun* tradition. See S. N. Brody, *The Disease of the Soul: Leprosy in Medieval Literature* (Ithaca and London, 1974), pp. 147–73; K. Ruh, 'Hartmanns "Armer Heinrich": Erzählmodell und theologische Implikation', in *Medievalia Litteraria: Festschrift für H. de Boor*, ed. U. Henning and H. Kolb (Munich, 1971), pp. 315–29.

[32] See Haug, *Literaturtheorie*, pp. 146–54.

[33] On the Job and Absalom typology, see G. Datz, *Die Gestalt Hiobs in der kirchlichen Exegese und 'Der arme Heinrich' Hartmanns von Aue* (Göppingen, 1973); P. Wapnewski, 'Poor Henry – Poor Job: A

---

peasant girl is seen as the opposite pole in the dialectic: an embodiment of pre-lapsarian innocence. By emphatically espousing the *contemptus mundi* ideology, she relativises the values of the chivalric order, and her altruism mediates Heinrich's spiritual awakening.[34] He subsequently submits unquestioningly to God's will: *swaz dir got hât beschert, | daz lâ allez geschehen* (lines 1254–5) ('May God's will in my regard be done'), and ascends to a new height of chivalric exemplarity, this time remaining conscious of his indebtedness to divine grace: *er wart rîcher vil dan ê | des guotes und der êren. | daz begunde er allez kêren | staeteclîchen hin ze gote* (lines 1430–33) ('He was better off than before in material wealth and honor. All this he referred to God with great constancy'). The period of *versuochunge* thus culminates in an affirmation of human and chivalric existence lived *sub gratia*. Whereas for Gregorius earthly *minne* is a road to sin, for Heinrich it takes on a redemptive character. His claim: *daz ich von dirre guoten maget | mînen gesunt wider hân* (lines 1494–5) ('that I have this wonderful girl [. . .] to thank for having my health again') suggests that the girl's dedication to him has a spiritual value, that it too is a vehicle for God's grace. The stereotypical romance conclusion here marks the triumph of this spiritually exalted form of love, purged through the will to self-sacrifice, which has the power to level social differences and to bind together all social orders in an idyllic *communitas*.[35]

Critics have displayed unflagging energy in mining *Der arme Heinrich* for such religious symbolism, and using it as the basis for global interpretations. A great deal of ink has been spilt on local theological points such as the precise nature of Heinrich's sin, or the taxonomy of his penitence.[36] Due to the experimental heterogeneity of the text, such an obsessive focus on the religious axis can produce at best only a partial reading, and the resulting interpretations frequently abstract from actual configurations of plot and character to such a degree that they fail to say anything illuminating.[37]

Most importantly, the homogenising thrust of such interpretations cuts swathes through much of the text's internal ambivalence, and remains obliv-

Contribution to the Discussion of Hartmann von Aue's so-called "Conversion to an Anti-Courtly Attitude" ', in *The Epic in Medieval Society: Aesthetic and Moral Values*, ed. H. Scholler (Tübingen, 1977), pp. 214–25.

34 On the tradition of theorising virginity as man's best image of perfection, and consequently as a counter to man's post-lapsarian alienation, see R. H. Bloch, *Medieval Misogyny and the Invention of Western Romantic Love* (Chicago and London, 1991), pp. 93–112; J. Wogan-Browne, 'The Virgin's Tale', in *Feminist Readings in Middle English Literature: The Wife of Bath and all her Sect*, ed. R. Evans and L. Johnson (New York, 1994), pp. 166–7.

35 Cf. F. Beyerle, '*Der arme Heinrich* Hartmanns von Aue als Zeugnis mittelalterlichen Standesrechts', in *Kunst und Recht: Festgabe für H. Fehr* (Karlsruhe, 1948), pp. 42–5; K. H. Borck, '*Nû ist si vrî als ich dâ bin*: Bemerkungen zu Hartmanns Armen Heinrich, v. 1497', in *Medium aevum deutsch: Festschrift für K. Ruh*, ed. D. Huschenbett (Tübingen, 1979), pp. 37–50; P. Boon, 'Die Ehe des "Armen Heinrich" ', *Neophilologus* 66 (1982), 92–101; H. Freytag, 'Ständisches, Theologisches, Poetologisches: Zu Hartmanns Konzeption des *Armen Heinrich*', *Euphorion* 81 (1987), 240–61.

36 See, for example, Schirokauer, 'Zur Interpretation', pp. 66–70; Neumann, 'Der arme Heinrich'; Seiffert, 'The Maiden's Heart', p. 386.

37 For example, Seiffert's unhelpful classification of the sacrifice scene as a 'mystery', 'The Maiden's Heart', p. 398.

ious to the subtleties of Hartmann's experimental poetics. The notorious 'Mehrschichtigkeit' of Hartmann's narratorial commentary, which can make pronouncements or suggest criteria for interpretation only to qualify and apparently to contradict them at a later stage, has the effect of holding meaning in suspense.[38] In addition, the narrative structure of the work is extremely conflictual, incorporating two character perspectives and concomitant narrative programmes that cannot easily be made to converge, and can only be synthesised by cranking up the machinery of divine intervention. The result is that the text's theological *sensus* sits rather uneasily on a dissonant amalgamation of generic discourses and ideological stances.

A Conflict of Narratives

That these problems of generic classification are symptomatic of a more fundamental disjunction in the narrative has been noted by various commentators. Seiffert argues that the text is composed of two interdependent narratives of the main characters' development which together form a 'chiasmus'.[39] Cormeau and Störmer tread carefully: 'Zwei Figuren bestimmen den Erzählablauf [. . .]; ihre Zuordnung zueinander ist nicht auf einen einfachen Nenner zu bringen'.[40] One of the most valuable insights into the narrative structure has been provided by Ruh, whose research into the possible sources and analogues of the leprosy legend leads him to identify a further intertextual layer grafted onto the composite combination of romance and exemplary narrative. He states that Hartmann's narrative represents a 'Mischtypus' consisting of '[der] Heilsgeschichte Heinrichs und, darin eingeschlossen, [der] Erzählung von dem opferwilligen Pächtermädchen'.[41] Narrative tension arises from the competition between these two models which 'beide zusammen verschiedenen Zielen entgegengehen'.[42] The two models are necessarily divergent, as the girl's 'Hohes Lied der Opferbereitschaft' is geared towards the completion of the sacrifice, whereas Heinrich's 'Heilsgeschichte' depends on his prevention of the sacrifice and his renunciation of her voluntary death. Thus the sacrifice scene forms the pivot of both narratives. Ruh considers the text's interpretative difficulties to be located at this point of suture: 'präzis an der Nahtstelle des Modells'.[43]

Ruh's insight that the *maget*'s self-sacrifice is embedded in the overarching narrative of Heinrich's spiritual and physical restoration highlights the asym-

---

[38] Cf. S. Ranawake, 'Mehrschichtigkeit des Erzählkommentars bei Hartmann von Aue', in *Akten des V. Internationalen Germanisten-Kongresses*, ed. L. Forster and H.-G. Roloff, Jahrbuch für internationale Germanistik A (Cambridge, 1976), II, 414–24.

[39] Seiffert, 'The Maiden's Heart', p. 389.

[40] Cormeau and Störmer, *Hartmann von Aue*, p. 144.

[41] Ruh, 'Hartmanns "Armer Heinrich" ', p. 322. Cf. J. Fourquet's formal analysis of the plot structure in 'Zum Aufbau des "Armen Heinrich" ', *Wirkendes Wort, Sonderheft* 3 (1961), 12–24.

[42] Ruh, 'Hartmanns "Armer Heinrich" ', p. 328.

[43] Ruh, 'Hartmanns "Armer Heinrich" ', p. 322.

metrical relationship between the two characters and their respective narratives. It thus represents an important qualification of theological readings which stress the symbolic symmetry of the leper – maiden opposition, or of structural analyses which relate their positions to thematic polarities such as worldliness and contempt of the world.[44] In fact, although there is virtual critical consensus concerning her symbolic function, attempts to read the *maget*'s character for psychological consistency have been beset by difficulties. Whereas earlier scholarship celebrated her as 'une jeune illuminée' or an 'engelgleiche Legendengestalt',[45] there has since been a trend of explaining irregularities in her representation by classifying her as psychologically anomalous.[46] Assessments of her motivation range from accrediting her with the purest form of altruism and Christian *caritas* to hypothesising sublimated love for Heinrich and charging her with selfishness.[47] This plurality of interpretations is indicative of the problems surrounding the integration of the girl's narrative.

As I will demonstrate, the inconsistencies in her representation can be explained by the fact that the girl is a confection of incompatible generic stereotypes, a literary fantasy whose shape is dictated by the demands of the narrative. As her narrative function is plural, her actions are supplied with different and often contradictory motivations.[48] It is for this reason that attempts to reach global understanding of her character, insensitive to the specific transitions within the narrative, reach such paradoxically polarised conclusions.

Diu reine maget

At the beginning of the scene in Salerno, the doctor gives a graphic description of the operation he is about to perform. He paints a lurid picture of physical mutilation, which is offered to the girl and the audience as a mental spectacle: *ich binde dir bein unde arme. / ob dich dîn lîp erbarme, / so bedenke disen smerzen: / ich snîde dich zem herzen / und brichez lebende ûz dir. [. . .] ezn geschach nie kinde alsô wê* (lines 1089–96) ('I bind your arms and legs. If

---

[44] See, for example, Seiffert, 'The Maiden's Heart', pp. 388–9; D. Duckworth, *The Leper and the Maiden: Hartmann's 'Der arme Heinrich'* (Göppingen, 1996).

[45] F. Piquet, *Étude sur Hartmann d'Aue* (Paris, 1898), p. 286; Schirokauer, 'Zur Interpretation', p. 75. Cf. Ehrismann, *Geschichte*, II, 202; Sparnaay, *Hartmann von Aue: Studien zu einer Biographie*, 2 vols. (Halle, 1933–8) II, 10.

[46] See E. Rose, 'Problems of Medieval Psychology as Presented in the "Klein Gemahel" of Heinrich the Unfortunate', *Germanic Review* 22 (1947), 182–7; Wapnewski, *Hartmann von Aue*, p. 117.

[47] For an interpretation of her actions as a manifestation of *caritas*, see H. B. Willson, 'Symbol and Reality in "Der arme Heinrich" ', *Modern Language Review* 53 (1958), 526–36. W. Wackernagel and W. Toischer, eds., *Der arme Heinrich Herren Hartmanns von Aue, mit Anmerkungen und Abhandlungen von Wilhelm Wackernagel* (Basel, 1885), pp. 214–15, Piquet, *Étude*, pp. 287–8 and Rose, 'Problems', p. 186, all attribute her behaviour to a frustrated attraction to Heinrich. She is charged with selfishness by J. K. Bostock, ed., *Der arme Heinrich: A Poem by Hartmann von Ouwe* (Oxford, 1969), p. 24, and Wapnewski, *Hartmann von Aue*, p. 96.

[48] See T. Buck, 'Hartmann's "Reine Maget" ', *German Life and Letters* 18 (1965), 169–76.

you have any regard for your physical well-being, then consider the suffering yet to come. I cut into you all the way to your heart and tear it still beating from you. [. . .] Never has a child suffered as you are going to'). She responds provocatively, in cutting, sardonic terms, confident in her anticipation of spiritual triumph: *geturret ir mich snîden, / ich tar ez wol erlîden.* [. . .] *wan dehein nôt sô grôz ist, / die sich in eines taces vrist / an mînem lîbe genden mac, / mich endunke, daz der eine tac / genuoc tiure sî gegeben / umbe daz êwige leben* (lines 1128–48) ('If you are not afraid to cut me open, I certainly have the courage to suffer it. [. . .] For no bodily suffering that is over with in one day is so great that I should think that this one day was too high a price to pay for eternal life'). The ghoulish description of mutilation, and the denigration of ephemeral suffering by opposition to the eternal rewards of the afterlife, are all standard ingredients of a genre which enjoyed huge popularity during the high and later Middle Ages: the virgin martyr legend. In the legend of St Agatha, Quincianus, the heathen aggressor, describes the torture to which Agatha will be subjected if she fails to submit to his desires in terms similar to those used by the doctor: *ich wil dich lan / peinigen noch anderswie, / daz dir gescach so we nie* (lines 29–31[49]) ('I wish to have you tortured in such a way, that you never before felt such pain'). In the legend of St Margaret, Olybrius is similarly forceful in his threats: *ich wil vil herte not / an dich legen unz uffen tot* (lines 23–4) ('I wish to cause you very great suffering, until you die'). The women's responses ring with self-assurance and faith that their actions receive divine sanction. St Agatha is so secure in her faith: *daz ich geduldigen mut / in allen not enpfa / und dine pine gar versma, / darinne ich denke wesen vro* (lines 38–41) ('that I will bear all suffering patiently, and completely despise your punishments, in which I believe I will rejoice'). Margaret invokes an economy in which physical suffering is proportional to heavenly reward: *ie grozer not der lib hat, / ie grozer lon die sele entphat* (lines 73–4) ('The greater suffering the body bears, the greater reward the soul receives').

At the time when Hartmann was writing, female hagiography would have circulated largely in Latin passionaries. There is some evidence for an onset of a vernacular tradition in the twelfth century, however, and the narratives enjoyed wider dissemination as homiletic *exempla* in sermons.[50] The virgin martyr *passiones* feature a female protagonist who transcends the social order and attains sanctity, largely through her adamant defence of her chastity in the face of threatened sexual assault and actual physical torture. Along with a general contempt for the ephemeral boons of worldly existence, the legends incorporate a powerful anti-matrimonial thrust, opposing the virgin's aspiration to become a *sponsa Christi* to the social role of wife and dynastic

---

[49] Unless otherwise stated, citations from the legends are from *Das Passional: eine Legenden-Sammlung des dreizehnten Jahrhunderts*, ed. F. K. Köpke, 3 vols. (Quedlinburg, 1852), I.

[50] See H. Rosenfeld, *Legende* (Stuttgart, 1961), pp. 35–56; T. Heffernan, 'An Analysis of Narrative Motifs in the Legend of St Eustace', in *Medievalia et Humanistica: Studies in Medieval and Renaissance Culture*, ed. P. M. Clogan (Cambridge, 1975), pp. 66–8. Of course as a *literatus*, Hartmann may well have been familiar with the Latin versions.

continuator that is laid down for her by society. To a large extent, then, the texts stage a gender war, pitting the lone female against the coercive demands and sadistic violence of a malign pagan patriarchy. Subtending these heroics of virginity is a somatised economy of representation, in which the martyr's body becomes a site of contestation between her own desire for transcendence and the very different agendas of the dynastic order and lascivious onlookers. Thanks to the increasing permeability of the borders between hagiography and romance, the model of femininity constructed in the virgin martyr legends also enjoyed a wider circulation, inspiring narratives of a more secular bias whose female protagonists suffer repeated torments and assaults on their *integritas*.[51]

The heroines of the *passiones* exemplify a sensational and monomaniacal subjectivity, grounded entirely in their chastity and their religious faith. The typical protagonist is aged in her early teens, and much of the conflictual drama of the narrative arises from the fact that she has reached marriageable age and is vulnerable to the unwelcome advances of suitors.[52] In her attempts to fend off these advances, the will to *integritas* emerges as her most essential moral impulse. Many of the heroines of Middle High German legends make recurrent use of the terms *muot* and *wille* when expressing their determination to dispose over their own sexuality. Juliane, married against her will and wishing to preserve *den iren lip reinen*, responds to paternal pressure to consummate the marriage decisively: *ja han ich, vater <min>, / einen vesten muot pegriffen, / du mag mir niht gescaden / dehein wereltlichen dro* (lines 83–6) ('I have formed a firm resolve, my father, you cannot harm me with any wordly threat').[53] Agnes assures her suitor: *wand sich nimmer me ergit / min wille in dinem willen* (lines 76–7) ('for my will shall never become your will'). Martyrdom is presented as the apotheosis of this extreme formulation of subjectivity, and is often welcomed. Juliane states: *von diu vertige mich enzit / mit der marter du niht enpit. / daz du mir wellest heizen tuon, / mir ist vil lieb dar zuo* (lines 158–61) ('Let me be ready in time and you not wait to carry out the martyrdom. What you would have me do pleases me very much'). Agatha rejoices: *wie rechte wol mir ist / in dirre heiligen vrist, / die ich nu habe uf erde, / die ich gemartert werde, / wand ich mit willen bin daran* (lines 17–21) ('How glad I am of this holy space of time I have on earth in which I will be martyred, for it is my wish'). By mapping volition entirely onto virginity, these narratives construct a rarefied form of female moral and physical purity.

The tender age and atypical *güete* of the *maget* in *Der arme Heinrich* place her in the ambit of the hagiographic narrative, where youth is often contrasted

---

[51] For example, the Griselda and Crescentia traditions.

[52] On the youth of female saints, see D. Weinstein and R. M. Bell, *Saints and Society: The Two Worlds of Western Christendom, 1000–1700* (Chicago, 1982), pp. 228–32.

[53] I am citing Priest Arnold's *Juliane*, which is thought to date from the twelfth-century. In *Die religiösen Dichtungen des 11. und 12. Jahrhunderts*, ed. F. Maurer, 3 vols. (Tübingen, 1964–70), I, 7–51.

with divinely bestowed moral precociousness.[54] The oration scene, in which the previously docile and silent child suddenly takes centre stage to wield the topics of theological doctrine and the structures of rhetorical disputation, seems less incongruous when read as a divinely inspired manifesto of virginal heroics.[55] As she only rises to the status of a speaking character when she learns of her possible role as an instrument of Heinrich's recovery, virginity forms the keystone of the girl's emergent identity and of her volition: *ich bin ein maget und hân den muot* (line 562) ('I am a virgin and have the right disposition'). Her participation in the narrative is almost entirely geared towards proving that she meets the additional requirement of being *des willen, daz sî den tôt durch* [Heinrich] *lite* (lines 448–9) ('would be willing to suffer death for [Heinrich's] sake'); towards establishing her credentials as a mature volitional agent, as opposed to an impulsive *kint*. She expresses her aspiration to sexual abstinence and martyrdom in formulations remarkably close to those that recur in hagiographic texts: *ich wil mich alsus reine | antwürten in gottes gewalt* (lines 698–9) ('I wish to deliver myself into God's dominion as pure as I am now'); *ez ist mir komen ûf daz zil, | des ich got iemer loben wil, | daz ich den jungen lîp mac geben | umbe daz êwige leben* (lines 607–10) ('I have the opportunity, and because of it I shall always praise God, of being able to give my young body in return for eternal life'). In the sacrifice scene, her volition and her virginity are effectively equated when they are subsumed under the unspecific moral terms *genuoc unwandelbaere* and *vollen guot* (lines 1172; 1175).

In the wider compass of prescriptive writings on virginity, marriage is frequently denigrated as a form of socio-economic and sexual slavery, in contrast to the personal autonomy of union with Christ.[56] There are resonances of these topics in the *maget*'s speech. She independently challenges her parents' view of marriage as the most attractive social destiny for their child, representing it as a bleak gamble between *nôt* and *tôt* (lines 765–6). It entails a brand of worldly toil that is specific to women:[57] *ich* [. . .] *bin mit*

---

54 She is eight at the neginning of the narrative in one manuscript, which would make her eleven or twelve at the time of the sacrifice, twelve in another.
55 On the rhetorical proficiency – the *simplicitas* – of the virgin martyrs, see Wogan-Browne, 'The Virgin's Tale', p. 179.
56 On the *Speculum virginum* tradition, see M. Bernards, *Speculum Virginum: Geistigkeit und Seelenleben der Frau im Hochmittelalter* (Cologne, 1955).
57 Cf. K. Smits, 'Bemerkungen zu den Motiven der Diesseitsflucht und Ehe-Flucht im *Armen Heinrich* Hartmanns von Aue', in *Festschrift für Siegfried Grosse zum 60. Geburtstag*, ed. W. Besch (Göppingen, 1984), pp. 433–49 (p. 440). On the denigration of marriage in virginity treatises, see Wogan-Browne, 'The Virgin's Tale', p. 169. Similar sentiments are expressed in the thirteenth-century Middle English virginity treatise *Hali Meiðhad*, where the *seli freodam* of marriage to Christ is compared to *a mannes þeowdom*, ed. B. Millett, EETS o.s. 284 (London, 1982), p. 5. In the German-speaking sphere, Elisabeth of Schoenau and Hildegard of Bingen both laud the spiritual and physical emancipation of virginity over encasement in the institution of marriage: see E. Gössmann, 'Das Menschenbild der Hildegard von Bingen und Elisabeth von Schönau vor dem Hintergrund der frühscholastischen Anthropologie', in *Frauenmystik im Mittelalter*, ed. P. Dinzelbacher and D. R. Bauer (Ostfildern, 1985), pp. 24–47 (pp. 32–3 and 42–3). With specific reference to *Der arme Heinrich*, see also M. H. Jones, 'Changing Perspectives on the Maiden in *Der arme Heinrich*', in *Hartmann*

ganzer arbeit | geschieden von gemache | mit maneger hande sache, | diu den wîben wirret | und si an vreuden irret (lines 767–72) ('my lot is [. . .] a life filled with hardship and far from comfort with all sorts of things that cause women trouble and lead them astray from joy'). Marriage to Christ, conversely, is described as a condition opposed to earthly marriage, characterised by *vreude âne arbeit*, stability and material comfort (lines 779–96). St Agnes similarly exalts the boons of union with her heavenly spouse, contrasting his riches with the paltry bribes that her suitor offers her: *sine groze richeit | verre uber dich ich schowe* [. . .] *die engele sin im undertan; | sunne und mane besundern | sich siner schone sundern; | sin richtum ewiclichen stat* (lines 22–31) ('I value his great riches far above yours [. . .] the angels serve him; sun and moon obey his grace; his empire endures for ever'). The peasant girl's speech reads like a rustic contrafacture to this. The impeccable courtly spouse celebrated by Agnes becomes *ein vrîer bûman*. His superior attributes are similarly described in terms of the girl's earthly experience: *im gât sîn phluoc harte wol, | sîn hof ist alles râtes vol, | da enstirbet ros noch daz rint, | da enmüent diu weinenden kint* (lines 779–82) ('His plow works very well for him, his farm is filled with all provisions. There neither horse nor cattle die. There one is not vexed by crying children.'). Her words have a figurative reach, allegorising the farm as a metaphor for the state of mankind after the Fall. However, they are also compelling on a literal level in their evocation of the physical *duresse* and claustrophobia of a peasant wife's existence.

Yet the dramatic constellations in *Der arme Heinrich* also deviate significantly from the clearly partisan framework of the *passio*.[58] The latter is predicated on an irreducible opposition between the protagonist and her immediate social context, in which even the girl's family is aligned with patriarchal brutality. The virgin is described as *diu gotes maget, diu gotes getriuwe* (line 23; lines 26, 40; line 69, etc.); the pagan tormentor is denounced as *der bose man, ein tuvels sun* (line 65; line 10; line 58). By contrast, Hartmann places his *maget* in the bosom of her loving family, and as a result her desire for death is presented altogether more equivocally.[59] Her parents deplore her decision, her mother suggesting that she would be transgressing the fourth commandment (lines 638–43). Alongside her desire for martyrdom, various other motivating factors are invoked as proofs, only some of which could be considered contingent on her spiritual aspirations. In addition to the rewards that she expects to reap in heaven, the narrator grounds her decision in her altruistic devotion to Heinrich: *daz sî benamen ir leben | umbe ir herren wolde geben* (lines 527–8) ('she would in fact give her life for her lord'). Yet the girl also

---

von Aue: Changing Perspectives. London Hartmann Symposium 1985, ed. T. McFarland and S. Ranawake (Göppingen, 1988), 211–31 (pp. 219–22).

58 On the binary structure of the *passio*, see C. F. Altman, 'Two Types of Opposition and the Structure of Latin Saints' Lives', in *Medievalia et Humanistica*, ed. Clogan, pp. 1–11.

59 On the discrepencies between the girl's portrait of family life on a farm, and the peasants' *reinez leben* as it is portrayed in the narrative, see Smits, 'Bemerkungen', pp. 442–6.

refers to concerns of a very material nature regarding her own and her family's future: if Heinrich, their protector and benefactor, were to die: *so müeze wir verderben* (line 624) ('we shall [. . .] go to ruin'). Her anti-matrimonial statements are over-determined by her suggestion that she would in any case be of little value within a marital economy, and by her reference to the misery of spinsterdom (lines 747–55). The contradictions in the girl's speech are typical of the architectonics of medieval disputation, which was more concerned with pursuing one subject from different angles than with unifying all topics within a controlled argument. Such 'multifacetedness' may even elicit approval from the modern reader as a 'deeper' or more 'realistic' mode of characterisation. However, it represents a clear departure from the black-and-white characterisation of many of the virgin martyrs.

Hartmann's failure to organise his narrative and character configurations according to a diametrical opposition between good and evil is at the root of a troubling ambivalence which colours the girl's characterisation and actions. Although she is presented as a vehicle of divine *güete*, and the narrator explicitly states that her actions are inspired by God (lines 1037–40), it remains unclear to what extent her absolute will to death is endorsed by the narrative. In the absence of a direct compulsion, such as the threat of sexual violation which frames the virgin martyr's death as less than entirely voluntary, the girl's will to die is presented as disquietingly self-motivated.[60] The problem of evaluating her character is compounded by the transitions and dislocations in her motivation, and particularly by the suggestions of narcissism which sporadically emerge in her self-justificatory monologues (lines 820–1; 828–30).

The interpretative stakes are at their highest in the sacrifice scene. In the virgin martyr legends, the accounts of the torture scenes are interspersed liberally with epithets affirming the iniquity of the torturers and the virtue of the virgin. Narratorial comment and divine intervention also conduce certainty about the semiotics of the violence inflicted on the virgin's body, underwriting the perspective of the virgin and negating the objectifying gaze of the tormentors who believe that the torture signifies their own power. Hartmann's *maget* seems to contend as powerfully as the martyrs for semantic control, anticipating the *süeze not* of the knife wounds as signification of her martyrdom. Cross-examined by the doctor in an exchange not unlike the interrogations to which the virgin martyrs are subjected, she responds by taunting him, casting aspersions on his professional capacities and even on his masculinity. In contrast, she asserts he own superior will-power and moral endowments as a woman: *ich bin ein wîp und hân die kraft* (line 1128) ('I am a woman and have the nerve'). Yet her statements of autonomous will are undercut by reminders of the instrumental nature of her sacrifice, a disjuncture that is highlighted when the doctor concludes the interview by reporting

---

[60] An element of compulsion is generally present in the *passiones*, as an entirely voluntary death was considered a violation of the sixth commandment in post-Augustinian thought.

back to Heinrich: *iuwer maget ensî vollen guot* (line 1177) ('Your girl is completely suitable [good].').[61] Although she is the triumphant subject of her own narrative of martyrdom, in the narrative of Heinrich's restoration her role is that of a sacrificial object. This doubling of the girl's role introduces an ironic tension into her anticipation of spiritual apotheosis.

Hartmann's adaptation of the virgin martyr legend is thus more of an annexation: the generic allusion serves to legitimate the sacrifice plot, and to render the girl's desire for death to some degree plausible and intelligible to his audience. Yet he also insinuates more equivocal elements in preparation for the change in narrative direction in the sacrifice scene. Heinrich's intervention to prevent the sacrifice is followed by a reversal on the moral axis that links him to the *maget*. Her grandiose spiritual aspirations dashed, the girl vilifies Heinrich as a *werltzage*, but her words are placed in a framework which presents them as a breach of prevailing codes of behaviour: *sî brach ir zuht und ir site* (line 1284) ('She acted not as she usually did nor in accordance with her upbringing.). Heinrich, by contrast, is rehabilitated by the same gesture as: *ein vrumer ritter* / [. . .] *dem schoener zühte niht gebrast* (lines 1340–1) ('an able knight [. . .] who never was lacking in refinement and good breeding'). The narrator continues to describe her as *guot*, and even expresses sympathy with her predicament, but his moral *parti pris* for Heinrich is clear. The girl's declamations are described as *schelte*; they appear as the petulant reaction of a character denied narcissistic fulfilment. As the girl subsequently recedes from the centre of the action, the narratorial gloss in this scene appears to give the last word on her conduct. It has certainly formed one of the main reference points for negative evaluations of her character.[62]

This moral equivocation in Hartmann's presentation of the girl is necessary because the ideology she represents is to be overridden by another set of concerns. The text's generic affiliations extend beyond the religious/ exemplary, and the narrative assigns a further function to the girl: that of the *gemahel*. This generic role is predicated on a view of feminity and female sexuality that is entirely at odds with the ideology of *virginitas* that underpins the virgin martyr legend. As the girl is forced to act out the incompatibilities between these roles, the romance ingredient further problematises a unified reading of her character and actions.

---

[61] G. Eis notes the discrepancy between this scene and the hagiographic torture scene: 'In den für die seelsorgerische Praxis brauchbaren Legenden [. . .] werden die Richter oder Folterknechte, die Hand an die Heiligen legen [. . .] stets mit Abscheu überhäuft und meistens auch streng bestraft. [. . .] Der 'Arzt' hätte mindestens geblendet werden müssen', in 'Salernitanisches und Unsalernitanisches im "Armen Heinrich" des Hartmann von Aue', in *Hartmann von Aue: Wege der Forschung*, ed. H. Kuhn and C. Cormeau (Darmstadt, 1957), pp. 135–50 (p. 149). On the ambiguity of *guot*, see below, pp. 000–0.

[62] See Seiffert, 'The Maiden's Heart', p. 389; H. B. Willson, '*Ordo* and the Portrayal of the Maid in *Der arme Heinrich*', *Germanic Review* 44 (1969), 83–93 (pp. 90–1).

Dâz er sî sîn gemahel hiez

Announcing her intended self-sacrifice to Heinrich, the *maget* justifies her decision by invoking the superior value of Heinrich's life over her own: *ir hât uns doch gesaget, / ob ir hetet eine maget, / diu gerne den tôt durch iuch lite, / dâ soldet ir genesen mite. / diu wil ich weizgot selbe sîn: / iuwer leben ist nützer dannez mîn* (lines 921–26) ('you told us that if you had a virgin who would willingly suffer death on your account, you would thereby be healed. I myself want to be that girl, so help me God. Your life is more useful than mine.'). Enite, forbidden *an den lîp* from communicating with Erec, decides on similar grounds to warn him of the impending attack by bandits: *bezzer ist verlorn mîn lîp, / ein als unklagebaere wîp, / dan ein alsô vorder man, / wan dâ verlür maniger an. / erst edel unde rîche / wir wegen ungelîche. / vür in wil ich sterben / ê ich in sihe verderben* (lines 3168–75) ('Better I am lost, a woman over whom no-one will sorrow, than such an excellent man, for that would be a loss for many. He is noble and rich; we are of unequal worth. I would rather die for him than see him perish.').[63] The final two lines are said in inverted order by the *maget* herself (lines 563–4). The parallel with the romance lady invites a different generic perspective on the girl's self-sacrificial stance, associating it with the selfless and redemptive love of the lady for her ethically or physically debilitated knight, which mediates his restoration to chivalric exemplarity.[64] Tobler, who bases her reading of *Der arme Heinrich* entirely on such a conception of love, says of the resonances between the two female characters: 'Hier wie dort is es die frauliche Liebe, die zu diesem Opfer bereit macht.' She continues, in panegyric mode: 'Liebe, deren Wert es ist, daß sie nur als Hingabe leben kann, ist sie doch das einzige Gut, das sich allein im Verschenken bildet und vermehrt.'[65]

The romance plot of *Der arme Heinrich* is adumbrated from an early stage. While the girl is still being referred to as a *kint*, and has not yet said a word, Heinrich showers her with gifts that belong to the semiotics of courtly love – *spiegel unde hârbant* [. . .] *gürtel unde vingerlîn* (lines 336–8). Implicit references to the ritual framework of marriage are sustained alongside the elaboration of the sacrifice plot. Heinrich prepares for the departure for Salerno by endowing the girl with the apparel of a courtly lady: *swaz ouch der maget tohte, / daz wart vil schiere bereit: / schoeniu phärt und rîchiu kleit, / diu sî getruoc nie vor der zît, / hermîn unde samît, / den besten zobel, dem man vant, / daz was der mägede gewant* (lines 1020–26) ('What was suitable for the girl was quickly ready. Beautiful horses and expensive clothes which she had never worn before: ermine, velvet, and the best sable one could find.

---

63 All references are to *Hartmann von Aue, Erec*, ed. T. Cramer (Frankfurt am Main, 1972).

64 On the parallels between Enite and the *maget*, see W. C. McDonald, 'The Maiden in Hartmann's *Armer Heinrich*: Enite redux?', *Deutsche Vierteljahrsschrift für Literaturwissenschaft und Geistesgeschichte* 53 (1979), 35–48; also Smits, 'Bemerkungen'.

65 E. Tobler, '*daz er si sin gemahel hiez*: Zum *Armen Heinrich* Hartmanns von Aue', *Euphorion* 81 (1987), 315–29 (pp. 322–3).

Those were the girl's clothes.'). We might compare here *Erec*, in which the ceremonial dressing of Enite in courtly garb functions as a kind of rite of passage, initiating her into courtly culture and signalling her new identity as wife. Following the aborted sacrifice we are told that Heinrich *sîne maget wider kleite*, and the radical change in her social status at the end of the work is anticipated by Heinrich's endowment of her: *sîner gemaheln er dô phlac | mit guote und mit gemache | und mit aller slahte sache | als einer vrouwen ode baz* (lines 1446–9) ('His bride he treated as a courtly lady or even better, giving her all sorts of things and seeing to her pleasure.'). This recurrent use of romance semiosis renders the amorous plot difficult to disentangle from the sacrifice plot.

The romance construction of femininity and its mediation of gender relations through the discourse of courtly love have been submitted to gender-oriented analysis in the recent past, mostly in the ambit of French medieval studies.[66] The theory of 'the traffic in women' formulated by Lévi-Strauss and subsequently subjected to feminist criticism, has provided a particularly rich vein for the analysis of romance poetics.[67] Roberta Krueger's study of the rhetorical and narrative strategies of romance reveals a double standard, which accords value to female initiative and volition only insofar as they support the feudal marriage economy. Romance heroines are praised most highly when they demonstrate unswerving commitment to the values of sexual fidelity and self-sacrifice, and subordinate their desires entirely to the patriarchal system.[68] As this economic and ethical system relies on the absolute complicity of women with their instrumentation, it is also necessarily characterised by ambiguity, dogged by the persistent danger that, to use Lévi-Strauss' original formulations, the individual woman may cease to function merely as a 'sign' and instead become a 'generator of signs'.[69] Active female volition, the arrogation by a female character of the right to dispose over her own sexuality, or to impose meaning independently on her person and actions, are all necessarily anathema within this system.

Many of these tensions are focused in *Der arme Heinrich*, with its amalgamation of both romance and virgin martyr perspectives on the nuptial passage of the *maget* from paternal custody to marital union. In a society structured around atavistic lines of descent, this moment of liminality focused

---

66 For a gender-oriented analysis of Hartmann's *Erec*, see G. Steiner, *Das Abenteuer der Regression: Eine Untersuchung zur phantasmagorischen Wiederkehr der 'verlorenen Zeit' im 'Erec' Hartmanns von Aue* (Göppingen, 1983).

67 C. Lévi-Strauss, *The Elementary Structures of Kinship*, trans. J. H. Bell, J. R. von Sturmer and R. Needham (Boston, 1969); for a feminist response to this 'grand theory' see G. Rubin, 'The Traffic in Women: Notes on the "Political Economy of Sex" ', in *Toward an Anthropology of Women*, ed. R. Reiter (New York, 1975), pp. 157–210. For applications of Rubin's interpretation to romance, see R. Krueger, *Women Readers and the Ideology of Gender in Old French Verse Romance* (Cambridge, 1993), pp. 143–53; S. Kay, *The Chansons de geste in the Age of Romance: Political Fictions* (Oxford, 1995), pp. 204–7.

68 Krueger, *Women Readers*.

69 Lévi-Strauss, *Elementary Structures*, p. 496.

many feudal concerns relating to lineage and female sexuality.[70] The presentation of virginity within female hagiography and theological treatises as a state to be preserved at all costs in order to befit the martyr for union with Christ, stands in stark contrast to the feudal encoding of sexual continence as a guarantor of legitimacy in primogeniture. From a romance perspective, virginity literature represents a rival semiotic system which accords the woman mastery over her own sexuality and raises the spectre of independent female volition. The doubling of the *maget*'s narrative role as both sign and generator of signs therefore brings considerable ideological stakes into play concerning the roles and subject positions offered to the historical woman by the opposing discourses of feudal marriage and sexual abstinence.

In both *Erec* and *Der arme Heinrich*, the marriage transaction is carried out without consultation of the woman. Heinrich consults only the barons and knights of his *familia* whereas Erec negotiates Enite's marriage with her father. Furthermore, in both cases, the two parties in the exchange are separated by a gulf in social and economic status. The origins of both Enite and the *maget* are inferior to those of the knightly protagonist. Enite's family is *edelarm*, her father having been impoverished by a feud (lines 406–10). The girl's father, by contrast, is a *vrîer bûman* who has benefited from his lord's generosity for some time (lines 267–87). Enite is presented as being of negligible value within the marital economy, a factor which apparently constitutes a direct impediment to marriage (lines 534–49). The *maget*'s marital value is dependent on the patronage of her lord; his death will therefore deprive her of the means to a social identity (lines 747–53). The narrow confines of the unmarried girls' existence stand in sharp contrast to the wealth and the broad sphere of social agency enjoyed by the male protagonist.

Yet both works embellish this discrepency in social circumstances by transposing dependency onto the knight. In *Erec*, the temporary presentation of the knight as *habelôs* acts as a frame for the marriage proposal. Heinrich is also transposed into a situation of dependency, having suffered a diminution of his social and material *werde*. In contradiction to this, however, his relations with the peasant and his family are set within the framework of the family's indebtedness to him. As the narrator indicates, Heinrich does not so much throw himself on the mercy of the peasant family during his sojourn on the *geriute* as collect the revenue for his previous acts of generosity: *swaz er im hete ê gespart, | wie wol daz nû gedienet wart | und wie schône er sîn genôz!* (lines 285–7) ('Whatever Heinrich had spared him earlier, how that was now repaid!'). The *maget* and her parents frequently invoke their reliance on Heinrich's protection and material support as the foundation of their own *guot unde êre*, with the result that he still appears as their benefactor (line 495; cf. also lines 424, 617–24). It is also worthy of note that Heinrich does not seem to be short of disposable income throughout his illness. He supplies

---

[70] See Wogan-Browne, 'The Virgin's Tale', pp. 196–7; Gaunt, *Gender and Genre*, pp. 185–98. In 'Bemerkungen', Smits sees marriage as a unifying motif of *Der arme Heinrich*, overlooking the tension with *virginitas*.

the *maget* with a courtly wardrobe, and pays the doctor in silver following the aborted sacrifice (lines 1020–26; 1279). Insofar as material endowments and social status translate into agency or narrative advantage, then, the knight and the *maget*'s family undoubtedly *wegen ungelîche*. The presentation of Heinrich as a *dürftige* therefore appears as an exaggerated and somewhat disingenuous fiction.

The *maget*'s self-sacrifice is bound into this relationship of ethical and economic indebtedness. The negotiations that take place around her turn her into an economic and semiotic object, defined in terms of her use value for Heinrich's recovery. Her father implicitly commodifies her, presenting her as recompense for Heinrich's previous generosity: *ir hât uns vil verre | geliebet und gêret: | daz enwaere niht wol gekêret, | wir engultenz iu mit guote* (lines 974–7) ('you have been very good to us and shown us great respect. The only fitting response for us is to repay you in kind.'). Handing over his daughter, he makes the instrumental nature of the gift explicit: *nû lâze iuch got mit ir genesen* (line 985) ('May God let you be healed through her.'). However, the term *guot* also echoes the descriptions of the girl as an embodiment of *güete* throughout the early stages of the narrative. It is this essential moral quality which draws her to the leper and which, according to the narrator, is also at the root of her will to self-sacrifice (lines 520–23).[71] The term *guot* recurs when Heinrich thanks the family for the gift of their daughter: *Heinrich [. . .] begunde sagen in | grôze gnâde allen drin | der triuwen und des guotes* (lines 1013–15) ('Heinrich thanked all three of them for their loyalty and generous care'). This time, the immediate context is ethical; however, as the reported speech appears as a direct response to the father's offer, it carries the same commodifying resonances. The semantic ambivalence of the word *guot* aptly illustrates the collusion of ethical and the economic frameworks in transforming the *maget* into an object of exchange. She is put into circulation as a *guot*, just as she is troped as an embodiment of *güete*. The latter, as the moral disposition that equips her to fulfil the role of sacrificial object, determines her value as the former, as an instrument of Heinrich's restoration. Moreover, viewed through the generic lens of romance, the exchange of the *maget* takes place under the auspices of marriage to Heinrich. This undercurrent of sexual exchange is enhanced by his subsequent clothing of her as a courtly *vrouwe* in preparation for their departure.

A similar operation of metaphorisation and instrumentation can be perceived in the embellishment of the *maget*'s self-sacrifice as a manifestation of *triuwe*. The glorification of female fidelity and devotion, maintained against all odds and throughout all physical trials, is an intrinsic element of romance semiosis. In *Erec*, the knight's military trials are intercalated with tests of Enite's *triuwe*, in which she withstands abduction and threatened sexual assault, not to mention Erec's threats of brutal punishment. In her anal-

---

71 An analysis of the moral/spiritual significance of the term *güete* in Hartmann's romances can be found in Endres, 'Die Bedeutung von *güete*'.

ysis of the *cycles de la gageure* Roberta Krueger interprets this positive valuation of fidelity as a strategy which recuperates female autonomy for the overarching androcentric ideology. By linking female volition and agency with such values as obedience and the adamant defence of chastity, these texts deploy female characters as signs to shore up the feudal marriage system.[72] This strategy is made quite explicit in *Erec*. Following the long period of his estrangement of Enite, the narrator tells us that Erec realises his brutal treatment: *was durch versuochen getân / ob si im waere ein rehtez wîp* ('had been in order to test whether she was a good wife for him'). He is now assured: *daz er an ir haete / triuwe unde staete / unde daz si waere / ein wîp unwandelbaere* (lines 6781–91) ('that he had found a loyal and constant woman in her').[73] The narratorial glosses on the girl's conduct bring similar ethical values into play, lauding *des kindes triuwe* and subordinating her moral steadfastness to the purpose of Heinrich's recovery by describing her as *genuoc unwandelbaere* (line 1001, line 1172). This ethic of female self-denial and subservience is reaffirmed in the conclusion, where the *maget*'s role in bringing about Heinrich's *gesunt* is presented as an argument for her suitability as a wife (lines 1493–5).

Yet the ambiguity of the *maget*'s position as both sign and generator of signs is reflected in her elaboration of a rival semiotics. In dialogue with her parents, the girl anticipates her own spiritual enrichment when she consigns economic gain to the afterlife. Speaking to the doctor, she presents her own life as an economic stake with which she hopes to win *sus gewisse[n] lôn(e)*. Her admonitions to her parents to remember *wes ich mir selber schuldic bin* ('what I owe to myself') and *mine triuwe an mir selber* ('I must be true to myself') sit uneasily with her assimilation to the romance discourses of exchange and passive subservience (lines 835, 820–21). Thus the representation of her trajectory towards martyrdom as a manifestation of feminine devotion and self-denial creates a rather incongruous double vision, the romance gloss thinly overlaying the *maget*'s emphatic statements of self-affirmation.

The incongruity of this amalgamation of romance and virgin martyr discourses around the *maget* is concentrated in certain emblems and tableaux. The courtly transformation of the *maget* prior to the couple's departure for Salerno results in a somewhat dislocative representation of her as prospective bride of both Christ and Heinrich. Signifying the social identity that is to be conferred on her by feudal marriage, the courtly apparel grotesquely envelops the *lip* that she wishes to offer up *alsus rein* to God. In the sacrifice scene, a similar potential for dissonance arises when Heinrich perceives her naked body, glossed with implicit reference to Genesis as an image of pre-lapsarian purity (line 1196), as *minneclich*.[74] The eroticisation of the female body is not

---

72 Krueger, *Women Readers*, pp. 128–37.
73 On the centrality of *triuwe* and *güete* to Enite's characterisation, see K. Pratt, 'Adapting Enide: Chrétien, Hartmann and the Female Reader', in *Chrétien de Troyes and the German Middle Ages*, ed. M. Jones and R. Wisbey (Cambridge, 1993), p. 81.
74 *Si enschamte sich niht eins hâres grôz.* Cf. II Genesis 2:25. The erotic nature of the scene has been noted by only a minority of scholars, notably Seiffert, 'The Maiden's Heart', H. Sacker, *An Introductory*

unusual in the torture scenes of virgin martyr hagiography, where the outwardly spiritual nature of the narrative serves to officialise the voyeurism to some degree.[75] The juxtaposition of the erotic and the spiritually exalting is also a staple of secular genres such as romance and lyric; here *minne* frequently appears as a didactic theme, a secular modulation of the tropes and language of spiritual instruction. However, this conflation of the spiritual and the erotic is notoriously unstable. In narratives with both religious and secular subject matter, it can be slanted away from the spiritual/didactic and towards the scabrous and grossly embodied, frequently tipping into self-criticism or parody. The doubt as to whether *Der arme Heinrich*'s affiliations are sacred or secular increases the ambivalence of this pivotal scene, with its sensual focus on the female body. Among the interpretative possibilities that it offers is the crass sexual objectification of the martyr who believes she is about to assume spiritual purity through chaste death. I will be discussing the parodic potential of this scene more fully in next section.

Heinrich's intervention to prevent the sacrifice inaugurates the assimilation of the *maget* to the stereotypical romance ending. His proprietorial gesture of clothing *sîne maget* is followed by an abrupt and somewhat crude divine intervention which *schiet sî dô beide / von allem ir leide* ('freed them both from all their miseries'), curing Heinrich and throwing a veil over the *maget*'s character which is not lifted for the remainder of the narrative (lines 1367–8). The expediency of this narrative artifice as a means of accommodating the girl to the altered narrative frame is self-evident. The author is liberated to wind up his romance plot without having to concern himself with the question of how his eloquent advocate of virginity will react to being transformed into a wife.

As God's privileged minion, Heinrich is 'miraculously' endowed with the means of expressing his gratitude to the *maget* and her family. The concatenation of gifts, including the endowment of the farmer with ownership of his farm and the provision for the girl as for a *vrouwe*, serves as a prelude to Heinrich's marriage suit. The expedient nature of these gifts comes to light when Heinrich expresses his preference for the *maget* and assures his barons: *nû ist si vrî als ich dâ bin* (line 1497) ('she is just as freeborn as I am'). The assertion is fraught with contradictions. By endowing the *maget*'s father with ownership of his farm, and the *maget* herself with the economic resources of a courtly *vrouwe*, Heinrich enhances her social status and thus effectively places her on the marriage market. The paradoxical nature of the girl's 'freedom' thus reflects the contradictory nature of the woman's position within a gift economy, as both subject with personal preferences and sign whose volition must remain subordinate to the patriarchal economy. Given her silence in

---

Middle High German Text: Hartmann von Aue's 'Der arme Heinrich' (London, 1964), p. 84, and J. Margetts, 'Observations on the Representation of Female Attractiveness in the Works of Hartmann von Aue with Special Reference to *Der arme Heinrich*', in *Hartmann von Aue: Changing Perspectives*, ed. T. McFarland and S. Ranawake, pp. 199–210.

[75] See Wogan-Browne, 'The Virgin's Tale', p. 175.

the final scene, juxtaposed with the eloquence of the reinstated, opulent feudal lord, given also the unilateral nature of the marriage declaration, we may find Heinrich's insistence on their equal status rather incongruous.

From Saint to Shrew?

Having examined the affinities between *Der arme Heinrich* and texts from both religious and courtly traditions, I will now turn my attention to a genre that is generally considered to be parasitic on both: the *Märe*. Scholarship has been consistently vexed by questions relating to the limits, the coherence, and the internal systematisation of this genre. Critics have attempted to identify generic markers by isolating common themes, motifs or narrative techniques, but have found themselves spectacularly unable to agree on even such apparently basic questions as whether individual texts are predominantly humorous or predominantly didactic.[76] Fischer's codification of the genre by means of opposition with other traditions has been attacked on various grounds; however, the heuristic advantages offered by his loose classificatory grid, which allows for border zones and experimental mixtures, have ensured its lasting currency.[77] Perhaps this flexible and very Jaussian framework provides the only viable terminological and conceptual apparatus for analysing texts that cast their referential nets so wide, frequently drawing on narrative themes and repertoires, social structures and articles of faith in order to subvert them or to supplant their original meaning.

The narratives that are now considered to constitute the *Märe* corpus have generally been dated to the thirteenth century and later. However, many of them derive from twelfth-century French or even Latin sources, and scholars generally postulate a preceding oral circulation.[78] The traditional specification of the early thirteenth century as the *terminus post quem* may well be connected to the (now discredited) prejudice that the *Mären* constitute a 'bourgeois' genre, performed to a different kind of audience from that which commissioned and enjoyed courtly texts. In fact, few of the texts can be dated

---

[76] H. Fischer's delimitation of a 'Denkmälerliste' in his *Studien* has proved most influential. Further attempts at delimitation and internal subdivision include K.-H. Schirmer's *Stil- und Motivuntersuchung zur mittelhochdeutschen Versnovelle* (Tübingen, 1969), and Ziegeler's narratological study in *Erzählen im Spätmittelalter*. See J. Suchomski, *'Delectatio' und 'Utilitas': Ein Beitrag zum Verständnis mittelalterlicher komischer Literatur* (Bern, 1975), pp. 173–202, E. Stutz, 'Der Codex Palatinus Germanicus 341 als literarisches Dokument', *Bibliothek und Wissenschaft* 17 (1983), 8–26 (pp. 20–3) on the inseparability of the humorous and the edifying in the *Märe*.

[77] Fischer defines the *Märe* as: 'eine in paarweise gereimten Viertaktern versifizierte, selbständige und eigenzweckliche Erzählung mittleren [. . .] Umfangs, deren Gegenstand fiktive, diesseitig-profane und unter weltlichem Aspekt betrachtete, mit ausschließlich (oder vorwiegend) menschlichem Personal vorgestellte Vorgänge sind', *Studien*, pp. 62–3. For a critique of this definition, see Heinzle, 'Märenbegriff'.

[78] See J. Bumke, *Geschichte der deutschen Literatur im hohen Mittelalter* (Munich, 1990), p. 289. As Hartmann could read French, he may well have come into contact with the Old French versions.

definitively, as they rarely carry authorial signatures or references to their socio-historical context.

The brevity and unity of the action in *Der arme Heinrich*, its convergence on one dramatic visual scene, the pastoral setting with its 'realistic' detail and the relative sparsity of narratorial reflection and intervention all align it with the *Märe*.[79] The focus on the body as a spectacle and a site of contestation between conflicting social codes is also analogous to many of the narratives in this corpus. The text's religious and courtly bias may at first sight seem to be at odds with Fischer's list of the generic characteristics of *Märe* narratives; however, many of the narratives included by Fischer in his 'Denkmälerliste' are couched in courtly discourse, whilst others incorporate religious content either directly or allegorically as part of the compulsory officialising thread of *utilitas*.[80] Religious content can even be subordinated to humour: texts belonging to the sub-category of *Schwankmäre* frequently mimic allegorical repertoires, patterns of expiation or typological structures in their narrative organisation in order to exploit them for casuistic purposes, or to debunk them by redirecting them towards the corporeal or the scatological.[81] This corrosive humour can similarly be turned against the pseudo-religion of courtly love, parodying courtly euphemism by making quite explicit reference to sexual matters in apparently abstract and euphemistic language. Hagiographic narratives, and particularly *passiones*, proved highly adaptable to comic ends thanks to their focus on the corporeal.

The *maget*'s bid for narrative supremacy in the sacrifice scene is explicitly formulated as a challenge to a matrix of gender norms. Vaunting her own feminine perfection, she accuses the doctor of emasculate behaviour: *iuwer rede gezaeme einem wîbe*, [. . .] / *iuwer angest ist ze grôz*, / *dar umbe daz ich ersterben sol* (lines 1122–5) ('You talk like a woman [. . .] Your qualms about my dying are excessive.'). Yet the subsequent presentation of her diatribe against Heinrich as a breach of *zuht* reverses the character configuration to cast her as a foil to Heinrich's exemplary self-control and adherence to the dictates of *schoene*[*n*] *zühte*. The gender configurations at this point bring to mind those *Schwankmären* which dramatise conflicts between the sexes. In such narratives, the machinations and insubordination of the female protagonist can sometimes set the hierarchical organisation of the entire social edifice in play. However, elsewhere, the conflict is subtended by the narrator's

---

[79] Cf. Cormeau and Störmer: 'Nahe verwandt ist das Märe: wenige auserwählte Szenen, zudem mit genrehaft realistischen Zügen', *Hartmann von Aue*, p. 145; the text is classified as a *Märe* on the basis of its form and its transmission by Mihm, *Überlieferung*, p. 48, and Westphal, *Textual Poetics*, p. 113.

[80] See Suchomski, *'Delectatio'*, pp. 166–7.

[81] See, for example, *Der Herrgottschnitzer* in *Neues Gesamtabenteuer: Das ist Fr. H. von der Hagen Gesamtabenteuer in neuer Auswahl. Die Sammlung der mittelhochdeutschen Mären und Schwänke des 13. und 14. Jahrhunderts*, ed. H. Niewöhner and W. Simon, 2nd edn (Zurich, 1967), pp. 229–33, which derives its humour from the convergence of literal and allegorical registers on the body of the priest; also *Das Almosen*, in *Neues Gesamtabenteuer*, ed. Niewöhner and Simon, pp. 53–7, where humour arises from the substitution of corporeal *amor* for Christian *caritas*. On the *Schwank* as a subcategory of the *Märe*, see Fischer, *Studien*, pp. 101–9; on the difficulty of making a hard and fast distinction between the *Schwank* and other kinds of *Märe*, see Suchomski, *'Delectatio'*, pp. 173–202.

endorsement of the normative model of the man's ethical superiority and the woman's necessary subordination. In such texts, anxieties concerning female agency, speech and bodily conduct are articulated within moralistic or humorous plots that violently overturn or wittily debunk female control.

The insubordinate female is a character type particularly prevalent in those *Schwankmären* that deal with the theme of *Frauenzuht*, where she frequently acts as a testing-ground for male supremacy. The husband who subjugates his wife through the calculated deployment of force is presented as a paragon of virtuous masculinity. The chivalric protagonist of *Die Zähmung der Widerspenstigen* who succeeds in 'taming' both his wife and his mother-in-law (the latter with a knife!) is described as being *menliches muotes*; the husband in *Die eingemauerte Frau* is characterised similarly positively as *ein riter tugend rîche*. Failure to subordinate one's wife is represented as detrimental to masculinity: the husband in *Von dem übelen wîbe*, who allows the marital hierarchy to be destabilised, is compared negatively with chivalric heroes of romance and epic.[82] In such narratives of *Frauenzuht*, the taming of the tongue, a symbol of the subversive incontinence and wilfulness of the female protagonist, is a particular desideratum. The woman's speech is sometimes successfully harnessed in the service of the dominant hierarchy, as in the case of the proselyte in *Die eingemauerte Frau*. Elsewhere she merely acquiesces to male control, or her complaints are defused through humour. With a shift in generic perspective, the *maget* in *Der arme Heinrich* could similarly be viewed as an insubordinate female who is 'tamed', divested of all moral authority to the advantage of her male companion, and subsequently reduced to silence.

As I argued above, the incongruous combination of semiotic codes in the sacrifice scene endows it with a parodic potential analogous to the brand of humour that occurs frequently in the *Schwankmären*. The 'realistische Kraßheit' of the sacrifice scene in *Der arme Heinrich* has not gone unnoticed by critics. However, they have generally sought to assign an allegorical function to it or to sentimentalise it as an element of the romance plot.[83] In an article on this scene, John Margetts broke new ground when he noted that the tools which are to be the instruments of the girl's martyrdom – the *mezzer* and the *wezzestein* – are attested in the Swabian dialect dictionary and in songs by (Pseudo-) Neidhart and Oswald von Wolkenstein as euphemisms for the male and female genitals. *Wetzen* is frequently used as a metaphor for copulation.[84] Margetts also points out that Heinrich's 'spiritual awakening', his conversion

---

82 *Die Zähmung der Widerspenstigen*, in *Neues Gesamtabenteuer*, ed. Niewöhner and Simon, pp. 1–35; *Die eingemauerte Frau*, in *Der Stricker, Verserzählungen 1–11 mit einem Anhang: Der Weinschwelg*, ed. H. Fischer, ATB 53 and 68 (Tübingen, 1967), pp. 55–65; *Von dem übeln Wîbe*, ed. K. Helm, ATB 46 (Tübingen, 1955).

83 See B. D. Haage, 'Der Harmoniegedanke in mittelalterlicher Dichtung und Diätetik als Therapeutikum: Das mystische Leben in der Welt ohne die Welt im *Armen Heinrich* Hartmanns von Aue', in *Psychologie in der Mediävistik* (Göppingen, 1985), pp. 171–96; Sieffert, 'A Maiden's Heart', pp. 391–2.

84 Margetts, 'Observations', p. 202.

to a *niuwen muot*, is described sufficiently ambiguously for it to carry the additional meaning of sexual arousal. For Margett, this 'spiritual-sexual double-entendre' infuses the sacrifice scene with 'the atmospheric smell of sado-masochism'. His article is eloquent on the tendency of the bulk of scholarship to embellish the allegorical level of signification, thereby suppressing this troubling confection of violence, voyeurism and sexual attraction, which he describes as 'an important element of almost taboo proportions'.[85]

Margetts' analysis focuses solely on such potentially disquieting elements of the double-entendre. As a consequence, he does not consider that the linguistic duplicity that he identifies may have been a source of humour for a medieval audience. The plurality of linguistic codes underlies much of the humour in the *Schwankmären*, where language frequently functions as an alibi, a means of circumventing the codes of conduct enforced by social institutions. By inventing alternative narratives for their behaviour, adulterers can conceal their misconduct; sexual propositions can be obscured beneath a veil of innuendo.[86] An implicit presentation of the apotheosis of *virginitas* as intercourse would produce an analogous brand of scabrous humour. The *maget*'s confident assertions of her own femininity and her provocative challenge to the doctor: *lat sehen, welh meister ihr sit* (line 1156) ('Show what kind of doctor [master of your trade] you are.') would acquire sexual connotations, implying that the aspiring martyr is compliant with her own defloration. Such a reading of the sacrifice scene finds the well-worn antifeminist topos of female concupiscence pitted subversively against a model of female perfection with considerable ideological and doctrinal cachet.[87]

Margetts' assertions should be treated with a certain amount of caution. Thanks to the semantic fluidity of much Middle High German vocabulary, it is often difficult to ascertain when irony is intentional and when it is merely accidental.[88] In the absence of an explicit textual signal, the question whether Hartmann knew the scabrous narratives of the *Maren* corpus and was intentionally including such elements in his work must ultimately remain a tantalising speculation. There can be no doubt, however, that the *Schwankmäre* constituted a part of *Der arme Heinrich*'s horizon of reception, and that later medieval audiences whose responses were informed by the heuristic codes of this genre would have been sensitive to such burlesque undercurrents. When placed within this generic framework, the narrative may have provoked an

---

85 Ibid., p. 205.

86 See M. Chinca, 'Taming and Maiming: The Body in Some Middle High German *Maeren*', in *Framing Medieval Bodies*, ed. S. Kay and M. Rubin (Manchester, 1994), pp. 187–210.

87 Cf. for example, *Mären* such as *Das Häslein* and *Der Sperber*, in which an *ingénue* is tricked into having intercourse by a male protagonist, but finds it very much to her taste. They can be found respectively in *Gesammtabenteuer: Hundert altdeutsche Erzählungen: Ritter- und Pfaffen-Mären, Stadt- und Dorf-Geschichten, Schwänke, Wundersagen und Legenden . . .*, ed. F. H. von der Hagen, 3 vols. (Stuttgart and Tübingen, 1850), II, 1–18, and *Der Sperber und verwandte mhd. Novellen*, ed. H. Niewöhner, Palaestra: Untersuchungen aus der deutschen und englischen Philologie 119 (Berlin, 1913), pp. 15–51.

88 See Green, *Irony*, pp. 5–6.

entirely different order of ethical response from the audience. The *maget*'s ambitions may have appeared as gender insubordination rather than as the virgin martyr's laudable pursuit of spiritual perfection. Furthermore, the double-entendre in the sacrifice scene may have provided an effective means of disclaiming her narrative, and retroactively casting her ambitions in a parodic light.

My purpose in drawing out these parallels with scurrilous *Schwankmären*, and with texts that are generally classified as misogynist, has been to demonstrate the potential of *Der arme Heinrich* to admit readings that are far removed from the courtly, or theological and apotheosising interpretations that form the staple of modern secondary literature. Moreover, the comparison suggests that *Der arme Heinrich* primarily opens itself to such readings in its deeply problematic inscription of female agency and the female body, elements of the text that have received little critical recognition. The parallels with the *Schwankmäre* thus further illustrate the location of the *maget* at the nexus of the text's generic potentialities. Moreover, as I will demonstrate in my analysis of the text's transmission and of the codocological contexts in which it was placed, this element formed a point of engagement for fourteenth-century scribes and manuscript compilers. The latter in particular appear to have found resonances of the *Schwankmäre* in Hartmann's text.

A Philological Fracas

The transmission of *Der arme Heinrich* is characterised by a high degree of textual instability.[89] The text has reached us in three complete versions: A, Ba and Bb.[90] The latter two versions are almost identical and presumably originated in the same *scriptorium*. Three fragments are also in existence: C, D and E. Priority has traditionally been given to A over the other manuscripts; however, the fact that the fragmentary versions often concur with B against A casts doubt on this hierarchisation. Various methods have been employed in the attempt to construct an edition from this fluid textual tradition, ranging from the conservative approach of Hermann Paul, who based his edition entirely on the A redaction, to the more interventionist attempts to construct a text, 'wie ihn Hartmann gedichtet haben könnte', undertaken by a succession of editors.[91] This tendency towards intervention has been accompanied by a

[89] Bonath, citing Leitzmann, asserts: 'daß bei einer Edition des Armen Heinrich nur eines sicher ist: das "quälende Gefühl der Unsicherheit" ', *Hartmann von Aue: Der arme Heinrich*, ed. H. Paul and G. Bonath, ATB 3, 15th edn (Tübingen, 1984), p. 17.

[90] The following *sigla* will be used to refer to the different versions: Strasbourg, Johanniterbibliothek, A 94, fols. 24v–36v = A; Heidelberg, Universitätsbibliothek, cpg 341, fols. 249r–258r = Ba; Kalocsa, Erzbischöfliche Bibliothek, MS 1, now Geneva-Cologny, Cod. Bodmer 72, fols. 256r–265r = Bb; Berlin, Staatsbibliothek, MS Germ., fol. 923, no. 7a = C; Munich, Bayerische Staatsbibliothek, cgm 5249, nos. 29a and 30a = D; Munich, Bayerische Staatsbibliothek, cgm 5249, no. 29b (Benediktbeuern) = E. See *Der arme Heinrich*, ed. Bonath, pp. 6–7.

[91] For example, *Der arme Heinrich von Hartmann von Aue. Überlieferung und Herstellung*, ed. E. Gierach (Heidelberg, 1913); *Hartmann von Aue: Der arme Heinrich*, ed. H. Paul and A. Leitzmann,

widening of the angle of vision to include the variant readings offered by the fragments, in particular the newly discovered Benediktbeuern fragment (E).

When dealing with the medieval text it is important to be aware that the modern edition is an artifice with no claim to authenticity as a medieval literary creation, and, furthermore, that it represents a drastic reduction of the scribal tradition. Textual criticism has accorded increasing importance to the variant in the recent past, shedding its obsession with reconstructing the 'original' and treating each scribal redaction as a text with its own integrity and claim to critical attention. This new approach to the phenomenon of variance has considerable implications for genre analysis. The variant readings and narrative perspectives that are offered and renounced in the course of the text's transmission can effectively reorganise the text into dominant and subordinate elements, perhaps to the extent of fundamentally altering its generic character. Variant redactions can alert us to the latent generic potentialities of the text, and to the loci of instability where generic discourses intersect.

One of the most striking instances of variance in the *Armer Heinrich* transmission is the alternative conclusion offered in the B version (lines 1491–512). Following the marriage between Heinrich and the girl, the narrator informs us: *nach wertlicher wone | wolden sie beide niht | zweier engel zu versicht | schien an in beiden | do sie sich musten scheiden* (lines 1492–6) ('Neither of them was inclined towards worldly customs. The destiny of two angels appeared to them; then they had to part.').[92] The conversion and rejection of the worldly shifts the text away from the romance, and closer to the ambit of hagiography, a shift that is complemented by the rejection of the *werltlicher wone* of marriage. The final lines describe Heinrich's embarkation on a spiritual career: *er hette sie wohl beslafen | nach wertlichem schafen | vor gote er sichez getroste | er tet sich in ein kloster* (lines 1497–1500) ('He had slept with her according to worldly customs. He renounced this before God and entered a monastry.')

The variant ending in B thus substitutes sexual abstinence and world renunciation for marital bliss and world affirmation. As such, it may betoken an unease on the part of the scribe concerning the transition from the spiritual to the worldly in the A version. However, although the variant ending affirms the ideology of abstinence expounded by the *maget* in her oration, it significantly also affirms the displacement of the *maget* as narrative agent. Instead, it is Heinrich who heroically renounces the pleasures of the flesh; the *maget* is relegated to the position of a passive instrument of these pleasures (*er hete sie wohl beslafen* (line 1497)).

The most controversial loci of variance, however, are the two occasions where first the doctor and then Heinrich recount the conditions for the cure. The variant versions read as follows:

ATB 3, 7th edn (Halle, 1930) and all subsequent ATB editions of the text; also the edition by F. Neumann (Stuttgart, 1959), and, most recently, Rautenberg's edition of 1993.

93 My citations of the variants are all taken from Gierach's edition (Heidelberg, 1913), which publishes the different redactions (except for E) in parallel.

ir muozent haben eine maget	*ir soldet haben eine mait*
die vollen erbere	*vollen vriebere*
unde ouch des willen were	*die in dem willen were*
daz siu den tot durch iuch litte	*daz si den tot gerne lide*
(A lines 224–8)	*daz man si zwischen iren brusten snite*
	(B lines 206–10)

('You will have to find a virgin who [is completely pure?/fully able to marry? and] would be willing to suffer death [for your sake/by being cut between her breasts.]')

mir wart niht anders do gesaget	*mir wart anders niht gesait*
wan daz ich muoste han eine maget	*ich solde haben eine mait*
die volle manbere	*die in dem willen were*
und ouch des willen were	*daz si niht verbere*
daz siu den tot durch mich litte	*daz si den tot gerne lite*
unde man si zuo dem herzen snitte	*daz man si zwischen iren brusten snite*
(A lines 445–50)	(B lines 413–18)

('I was told nothing else but that I would have to find a virgin who was [fully able to marry?/willing?] and would be willing to suffer death for my sake, that the doctor would cut her [open to the heart/between her breasts].')

The slippage between the three adjectives *êrbere*, *manbere* and *vriebere* is revealing. *Erbere* has been glossed by commentators as 'in jeder Hinsicht vollkommen makellos', with the possible added connotation of 'geschlechtlich unberührt';[93] *manbere* evidently refers to the girl's marriageability. The meaning of *vriebere* is contested: Jacob Grimm suggested that it means 'mannbar, freibar'; however, Ranke shifts the vowel to give *vrîbaere*, which he glosses as 'in seinem Entschluß völlig frei'.[94] The link made in A between moral purity and marriageability, and the presentation of both as pre-conditions for the girl's participation in the narrative, are suggestive of the glorification of female sexual purity in order to shore up feudal marriage that I described previously as a characteristic strategy of romance. *Vriebere* may have been sufficiently semantically loose to elide marriageability with the quality of being able to make independent decisions, and thus provides a neat way of side-stepping the issue of female choice and of obscuring the coercion implicit in the marriage plot. However, this direction of autonomy towards marital alliance sits uneasily with the stress on the autonomous *wille* to death as the accompanying credential demanded of the maiden.

The amount of critical attention that has been bestowed on this *crux philologorum*, and the conspicuous failure of scholars to agree on its meaning,

---

[93] This reading and interpretation is favoured by F. Saran, *Das Übersetzen aus dem Mittelhochdeutsch* (Halle, 1930), pp. 45 and 51; also by T. van Stockum, 'Eine crux philologorum: Die prognostisch-therapeutische Formel im "Armen Heinrich" des Hartmann von Aue', *Neophilologus* 48 (1964), 146–50.

[94] J. and W. Grimm, eds., *Der arme Heinrich von Hartmann von Aue: Aus der Straßburgischen und Vatikanischen Handschrift* (Berlin, 1815), pp. 5 and 9; F. Ranke, 'Mhd. *Vrîbaere* "frei im Entschluß, freiwillig" ', *Zeitschrift für deutsches Altertum* 79 (1942), 178; see also Wackernagel's edition of 1885, pp. 64–6.

seem to indicate an awareness of its underlying paradoxes. One of the most remarkable features of the philological debate is the disfavour with which *manbere* has generally met; this despite the fact that the term occurs in the A redaction, whose witness is usually given priority. Critics have generally been guided in their recommendations by their generic and interpretative prejudices. Having classified the text as a legend, Ranke considers the term to be at odds with the religious content: 'schon der bloße Gedanke an die völlige weibliche Ausgereiftheit des Mädchens [trägt] eine durch *vollen* noch besonders unangenehm betonte körperliche Vorstellung in die reine seelisch-sittliche Welt der höfischen Legende'.[95] Czinczoll concurs: 'Meines Erachtens ist bis jetzt der Ton viel zu stark auf die "Ehefähigkeit" der *maget* gelegt worden', and editors have similarly tended to avoid the term.[96] Some commentators have even resorted to supplying more abstract alternatives that do not occur in any of the variants, for example Ranke's *vrîbaere* and Carl von Kraus' advocacy of *vrambaere* ('herrlich, ausgezeichnet').[97] Throughout the nineteenth century, and for much of the twentieth, *manbere* only found favour with the Grimm brothers. However, the Benediktbeuern fragment (E), which surfaced in the 1960s, brought an additional witness in favour of *manbere*. This find has swayed many subsequent editors towards this reading.[98]

The account of the leprosy cure, with its emphasis on volition, moral or sexual purity and marriageability, concentrates many of the paradoxes of the girl's intermediary position between different generic and ideological discourses. This potent ambiguity may well explain why medieval scribes, as well as modern philologists and textual critics, have felt compelled to gloss and substitute, and thus to continue the semantic battle over her character and her narrative role. The philological debate surrounding the variant descriptions of the cure illustrates how an isolated instance of textual instability can raise larger questions concerning the generic and interpretative frame that is appropriate to a text. It also testifies to the power wielded by philologists and editors to cull sources of dissonance and unease from the medieval text, and thus to bring about significant alterations to its character.

---

[95] Ranke, 'Mhd. *Vrîbaere*', p. 178.

[96] D. Czincoll, 'Eine textkritische Anmerkung zu Hartmanns "Armem Heinrich" ', *Zeitschrift für deutsche Philologie* 85 (1966), 94; for a resumé of the readings favoured by the various editions, see F. Neumann, 'Lebensalter im "Armen Heinrich" Hartmanns von Aue', in *Kleinere Schriften zur deutschen Philologie des Mittelalters* (Berlin, 1969), pp. 95–9; Rautenberg, *Der arme Heinrich*, pp. 98–9.

[97] Ranke, 'Mhd. *Vrîbaere*'; C. von Kraus, '*Vrambaere*; "Armer Heinrich" vs. 225. 447', *Zeitschrift für deutsches Altertum* 82 (1948/50), 73–6.

[98] See ed. L. Wolff (Tübingen, 1972), ed. H. Mettke (Leipzig, 1974), ed. G. Bonath (Tübingen, 1984).

The Manuscripts

The brevity and the short couplet form of *Der arme Heinrich* place it in the category of *Reimpaardichtung*. The codicological practice of collecting texts with this format into specialised manuscripts is attested from the mid-thirteenth century, and these manuscripts have received increasing attention in the recent past as records of the generic consciousness of manuscript compilers.[99] The three extant complete versions of *Der arme Heinrich* are all transmitted in such *Sammelhandschriften*, and it appears that it was only transmitted in isolation in one of the three fragmentary versions to have reached us (C).[100]

Like scribal variation, manuscript layout offers us concrete evidence of how a text was read by a medieval audience. The deliberate ordering of texts within codices is often indicative of the connections between works perceived by medieval audiences. Clues to previous acts of interpretation can be found locally in juxtapositions, as well as in more extensive thematic groupings. When a text is transmitted in multiple manuscripts, each one offers a synchronic still of the reception environment and the place allocated to the text within this environment. From variations in codicological context we can thus infer a great deal about the different faces that a text presented to audiences with differing generic expectations. Given the uncertainty that frequently attends the modern critic's attempts at generic classification, such historical evidence of audience response is invaluable.[101]

The sample contexts in which the fragmentary versions D and E are found attest to a high degree of codicological variance in the *Armer Heinrich* transmission. In fragment D, Freidank's *Von der Bescheidenheit*, a strophic didactic work containing aphorisms and a résumé of salvation history, accompanies our text. In E, however, it is transmitted with a version of the *Märe* of Aristotle and Phyllis.[102] A similar diversity in the codicological frame of our text can be found in the complete versions transmitted in the *Sammelhandschriften*. Here we find, in juxtaposition with *Der arme Heinrich*, a courtly didactic text, a religious narrative, but also several *Mären* dealing with gender relations and containing scurrilous sexual puns. Codicological evidence thus offers much to substantiate the picture I have painted of *Der arme Heinrich* as a protean text with plural generic affiliations.

---

99 The most significant works on codicology in German vernacular manuscripts are Mihm, *Überlieferung*, and Westphal, *Textual Poetics*. Kuhn, 'Versuch einer Literaturtypologie', considers codicology to be a material record of the 'Typen-Bewusstsein der Zeit', p. 122.

100 See Bonath, ed., *Der arme Heinrich*, pp. 5–9.

101 See Butterfield, 'Medieval Genres', pp. 184–7.

102 See Bonath, ed., *Der arme Heinrich*, pp. 10–11. Interestingly, the rubricator of the Benediktbeuern fragment (E) heads the work *diez ist diu aventiure von dem armen Heinrich*, suggesting that he considered the work's affiliations to be primarily courtly. On the use of *aventiure* as a genre designation, see Düwel, *Werkbezeichnungen*, p. 84.

The Strasbourg Manuscript

Manuscript A94, destroyed when the Strasbourg Johanniterbibliothek burned down in 1870, was a *Sammelhandschrift* dated between 1330 and 1350 containing a total of twenty-six didactic and comic texts.[103] The predominance of themes of a courtly and erotic nature has been noted by Sarah Westphal, who analyses the first five texts in the collection as an example of a codicological grouping known as the *minne* constellation. Such constellations juxtapose discursive *Minnereden* with *Mären* of a thematic group classified by Fischer as 'höfisch-gallant', as well as with *Mären* from Fischer's second thematic type, which recount more scurrilous tales of women's erotic exploits and their ability to hood-wink their jealous husbands through *chuendekeit*.[104] Westphal considers this type of constellation, of which the Strasbourg manuscript is the earliest known example, to mark 'a shift in *Mären* reception away from the didactic and exemplary features which they share with the *Bispel* and toward their erotic subject matter and the poetological features that assimilate them to the discourses on love'.[105]

Der arme Heinrich occurs towards the end of this manuscript, in sixteenth place. Westphal notes that the texts placed later in the manuscript show a certain thematic continuity with those occurring at the beginning. Again, morally instructive *reden* are juxtaposed with *Mären* featuring a successful amorous knight in the lead role, and these courtly texts are interspersed with occasional examples of more scurrilous *Mären*. The immediate codicological frame of *Der arme Heinrich* exemplifies this deliberate combination of courtly refinement with scurrilous humour. The work is preceded by a moralistic dialogue, headed in the rubric with the words: *dis ist liebe unde schoene*, and is followed by a *Märe* of Fischer's second thematic type, which the scribe introduces with the words: *dis seit von der wibe list*.[106] The three consecutive tales are linked by their inclusion of colourful and often conflictual dialogue. Yet the controlled rhetoric of the allegorised figures *liebe* and *schoene* differs considerably in tone from the vituperations of the *maget* following the sacrifice scene in *Der arme Heinrich*, as well as from the marital strife of *der wibe list*.

Thematic overlaps can be found between *Der arme Heinrich* and both of the texts that form its frame. The dialogue between *liebe* and *schoene* features a long excursus on love, exalting it in terms reminiscent of the praise of

---

103 For a description and list of the contents of this manuscript, see E. G. Graff, *Diutiska*, 3 vols. (Stuttgart, 1826), I, 314–17; E. Grunewald, 'Zur Handschrift A94 der ehemaligen Strassburger Johanniterbibliothek', *Zeitschrift für deutsches Altertum* 110 (1981), 96–105.

104 Westphal notes that the centrality of such texts in *minne* constellations 'suggests that medieval audiences did not exclude courtly from other expressions of love, but found pleasure and significance in their juxtaposition': *Textual Poetics*, p. 111.

105 Westphal, *Textual Poetics*, p. 115.

106 *Liebe unde schoene* is, as far as I know, only accessible in the *Samlung* [sic] *deutscher Gedichte aus dem XII. XIII. und XIV. Jahrhundert*, ed. C. H. Myller, 3 vols. (Berlin, 1784), I, 24–5. All citations from *Der wibe list* are taken from the *Neues Gesamtabenteuer*, ed. Niewöhner and Simon, in which the *Märe* is published under the alternative title *Das Kerbelkraut*, pp. 96–9.

caritas in St John's gospel. The dialogue is based on the binary opposition between worldly *vanitas*, topically associated with transient beauty, and redemptive, sacralised *liebe*, an opposition that tallies with the didactic content of *Der arme Heinrich*. Indeed, *liebe*'s homiletic excursus includes some of the key terms from the discursive opening of *Der arme Heinrich*. *Schoene* vaunts herself as *weltliche froeiden eine krone* (line 55; cf. *Der arme Heinrich* lines 61–3), and is reproached by *liebe* for her *übermuot* and *hoffart* and for behaving *üppiglich* (lines 68, 166; cf. *Der arme Heinrich* lines 82, 86, 151). It seems reasonable to assume that these thematic and verbal resonances motivated the scribe's decision to juxtapose the two works. The juxtaposition highlights the potential of *Der arme Heinrich* to serve as a narrative illustration of precisely the kind of redemptive love described in the *Minnerede*.[107]

Der wibe list, by contrast, has no pretension to a spiritual *sensus*, remaining anchored in the profane and corporeal. Like many of the narratives commonly assigned to the *Mären* corpus, this narrative accords principal agency to the female protagonist and delights in her subversion of dominant social and linguistic codes. The *Märe* revolves around a scene in which the husband witnesses his wife's adultery, signified by *vier füeze* in the bed, and dramatises the attempt by the wife and her accomplice to supplant his reading of the situation with their own. Through the ruse of the chervil, the wife and the *fügerinne* are able to supply an alternative context for the scene and thereby to discredit the husband's interpretation.[108] Unlike the *maget* of *Der arme Heinrich*, the wife in this *Märe* succeeds in defining her body according to her own signifying agenda and controlling the outcome of the narrative. Yet rather than celebrating their ingenuity, the narrative ends with a resigned address to husbands: *sus kunnen sumelichiu wip / noch wol ir man vertoeren / die ihtes waenent hoeren. / davon nieman enwüete, / daz er sines wibes hüete. / ez ist verloren arebeit* (lines 272–7) ('Thus some women can make fools of husbands when they believe they hear something. Therefore let no-one strive to keep watch on his wife. It is a futile endeavour.'). Within the stated parameters of the *Märe*, then, female autonomy is glossed as morally negative.

The Heidelberg Manuscript

Manuscript cpg 341 contains a total of 213 diverse couplet poems, with secular and sacred themes, and dates from the early fourteenth century.[109] Commentators agree on the monumental importance of this manuscript for

---

107 On the function of the *Mären* in the Strasbourg manuscript as 'Anschauungsbeispiele' of the topics discussed in the *Minnereden*, see Westphal, *Textual Poetics*, p. 109.

108 For an analysis of this *Märe* that engages with this theme, see Chinca, 'Taming and Maiming', pp. 191–2.

109 For a description and discussion of the contents of this manuscript, see G. Rosenhagen, *Kleinere mittelhochdeutsche Erzählungen, Fabeln und Lehrgedichte III. Die Heidelberger Handschrift Cod. Pal. Germ. 341* (Berlin, 1909), pp. 1–41; Mihm, *Überlieferung*, pp. 48–51; E. Stutz, 'Der Codex Palatinus Germanicus 341 als literarisches Dokument', *Bibliothek und Wissenschaft* 17 (1983),

reconstructing the typologies and sub-categories into which scribes and compilers subdivided the massive corpus of *Reimpaardichtung*.[110] Westphal discerns an 'abiding interest in religious writing, especially salvation history' running through the manuscript, but notes at a more local level 'a blending of religious and secular horizons' along with 'a degree of experimentation with the problem of textual likeness'.[111] In contrast to the Strasbourg manuscript, the *Mären* in this manuscript tend to be grouped with *Bispele*, in harmony with the overall didactic emphasis. It is significant given this general religious bias that this manuscript carries the altered version of *Der arme Heinrich*, which substitutes the marriage and *süeze(z) lanclîp* with a career of abstinence for Heinrich.

Occurring in 133rd place, *Der arme Heinrich* is the oldest text in this manuscript. It is situated amidst a group of texts which Rosenhagen identifies as 'größere weltliche Erzählungen', and which he subdivides 'in einen Teil höfisch-idealistischen Stils (128–133) und einen bürgerlich-realistischen Stils (134–39)'.[112] *Der arme Heinrich* would therefore be located on the border between these two groups. The narratives in the earlier group range from the secular/erotic (Dietrich von Glatz's *Der Gürtel*) to tales which incorporate a level of religious meaning (the didactic *Die Mâze*; Konrad von Würzburg's *Heinrich von Kempten*) to the explicitly religiously oriented (Konrad's *Der Welt Lohn*). Those following Hartmann's text are *Mären* dealing with the theme of *Ehekrieg*, and have been attributed to Stricker. The rubricator has preceded Hartmann's narrative with the words *diz ist der arme heinrich / got mach uns im gelich* ('This is [the story of] Poor Heinrich. God make us like him.'), endowing it with an exemplary status which harmonises with the substituted conclusion of Heinrich's withdrawal into a monastery.

One of the most interesting features of the codicological context in which *Der arme Heinrich* is placed in this manuscript is that the original preceding text has been erased, to be replaced by the religious allegorical poem *Von der Barmherzigkeit*.[113] This work narrates the trajectory of salvation history from original sin to Christ's intercession, and thus engages with many of the theological issues that underpin the religious *sensus* of Hartmann's poem.[114]

pp.8–26. A. Bernt, *Altdeutsche Findlinge aus Böhmen* (Brünn, Munich and Vienna, 1943), p. 12, dates the manuscript more precisely to around 1320.

110 See Rosenhagen, *Kleinere mittelhochdeutsche Erzählungen*, p. 1; Kuhn, 'Versuch einer Literaturtypologie', p. 127; Stutz, 'Codex Palatinus Germanicus'. Also I. Glier, 'Zweites Kapitel: Kleine Reimpaargedichte und verwandte Großformen', in *Die deutsche Literatur im späten Mittelalter: Reimpaargedichte, Drama, Prosa 1250–1370* (Munich, 1987), p. 23.

111 Westphal, *Textual Poetics*, pp. 68 and 72. Cf. Rosenhagen, *Kleinere mittelhochdeutsche Erzählungen*, p. 14; Stutz 'Codex Palatinus Germanicus'. Mihm, *Überlieferung*, p. 60, sees a thematic progression from the religious/didactic through miracle narratives to worldly didactic and finally more scabrous texts, but admits that this structure disintegrates less that halfway through the manuscript.

112 Rosenhagen, *Kleinere mittelhochdeutsche Erzählungen*, p. 8; cf. Mihm's largely similar sub-division of the manuscript contents in *Überlieferung*, p. 49.

113 Scientific examinations of the erasures have revealed that many of the erased texts were of a scabrous nature and may therefore have met with the disapproval of the manuscript commissioner. See Mihm, *Überlieferung*, pp. 49–50; Stutz, 'Codex Palatinus Germanicus', p. 23.

114 All citations are from Bartsch's edition of *Von der Barmherzigkeit*, published under the title *Die*

Again, key terms link the texts: mankind's *hochmuot* is condemned, and Christ announces his intention to cure man of his spiritual sickness in words similar to those used by the *maget*: *zum tôde wil ich sin bereit | und für den menschen sterbe, | ê danne er verderbe* (lines 252–4; cf. *Der arme Heinrich* lines 563–4) ('I wish to be ready for death and to die for man, rather than see him perish.'). The descriptions of Christ's curative miracles also complement Hartmann's narrative.

However, as in the case of the Strasbourg manuscript, the codicological frame is heterogeneous. The text following Hartmann's work is a *Märe* whose thematic focus is remarkably similar to that of *Der wibe list. Daz bloch* is again concerned with the social codes that circumscribe the actions of the female subject, and with her ability to circumvent their control.[115] This story of a woman who can only escape the brutal assaults of her husband by feigning death is a bleak commentary on the coercive patriarchal structures of society and the Church. Again, however, *Daz bloch* stands in an antithetical relationship to *Der arme Heinrich*, in that the female protagonist successfully dictates the terms under which she returns to her husband, and thus determines the outcome of the narrative.

The Kalocsa Manuscript

The similarity of the Kalocsa codex (now cod. Bodmer 72) to the Heidelberg manuscript in both content and appearance has led critics to the consensus that the two manuscripts were produced by scribes working in close collaboration, probably in the same *scriptorium*.[116] Indeed, the proximity of the hand used in the Kalocsa codex to that of certain sections of cpg 341 suggests that the same scribe was involved in the production of both.[117] To a large extent, the Kalocsa scribe reproduces the codicological sequence of the Heidelberg manuscript, and he draws on the latter consistently as a source for individual texts. However, he also deviates considerably from this source, making significant changes to the order, and offering corrections and different readings for many of the texts.[118] It is thus clear that the Kalocsa codex is the work of a scribe and

---

Erlösung, ed. K. Bartsch (Quedlinburg, 1858), pp. 9–20. Stutz classifies this work as a *Heilsepik*, 'Codex Palatinus Germanicus', pp. 15–17.

115 References are to Fischer's edition of Stricker's *Verserzählungen*, where *Daz bloch* appears with the title *Der Gevatterin Rat*, pp. 66–91.

116 For a discussion of the contents of this manuscript, and particularly of its relation to cpg 341, see Rosenhagen, *Kleinere mittelhochdeutsche Erzählungen*, pp. 15–20; Mihm, *Überlieferung*, pp. 51–7; Westphal, *Textual Poetics*, pp. 48–9 and 73. See also K. Schneider, 'Cod. Bodmer 72: Sammlung kleinerer mittelhochdeutscher Reimpaardichtungen ("Kalocsa-Codex"; "Gesamtabenteuer")', in *Deutsche Handschriften des Mittelalters in der Bodmeriana* (Cologny–Geneva, 1994), pp. 81–129.

117 See O. R. Meyer, *Der Borte des Dietrich von Glezze: Untersuchungen und Text* (Heidelberg, 1915), p. 22; Mihm, *Überlieferung*, p. 48.

118 See Mihm, *Überlieferung*, pp. 51–4, who notes that the works substituted for erased texts in the Heidelberg manuscript occur in the same location in the Kalocsa codex. This indicates that the Heidelberg codex precedes the Kalocsa.

manuscript compiler of considerable literary discernment, and not merely the product of mechanical copying.

Der arme Heinrich is the 125th text in this codex. The scribe precedes the work with a formulaic introductory couplet, in which he describes it as a *mere rîch*.[119] Significantly, he deviates from the sequence of the Heidelberg manuscript to interpolate five short couplet works between *Von der Barmherzigkeit* and our text.[120] With the exception of *Das Wachtelmäre*, a nonsense rhyme that is absent from cpg 341, the texts are all *Mären* which thematise relations between the sexes, and which occur elsewhere in the Heidelberg codex. They belong towards the jocular/obscene end of the tonal range spanned by the texts of the *Mären* corpus. Alongside *Der Hasenbraten*, a narrative about a wife successfully duping her husband, the scribe includes three scabrous texts dealing explicitly with erotic matters: *Das Almosen*, *Der hohle Baum*, and *Der Sperber*.[121] In these narratives, humour derives from the sexual naivety of one of the protagonists, from motifs of selling or donating love, and from parodic side-sweeps at religious doctrine concerning sexual continence both within and outside the context of marriage. In *Das Almosen*, the fundamental incompatibility between Christian charity and erotic *amor* (often conflated in the amorous rhetoric of romance and *Minnesang*) becomes obvious when a woman commits adultery with a beggar under the pretext that she is merely doing her Christian duty. In *Der hohle Baum*, the Christian ideal of chaste marriage is parodied when a young wife advises her inexperienced husband on how to satisfy her sexually.[122]

Perhaps the most trenchant satire on the religious ideal of sexual continence occurs in the text placed adjacent to *Der arme Heinrich*: *Der Sperber*. This tale of a young novice whose naivety and linguistic incapacity lead her to sell her *minne* to a knight brings into play opposing perspectives on *virginitas* similar to those which, I have suggested, come into conflict in *Der arme Heinrich*. The narrative in *Der Sperber* is based on an opposition between an exemplary representative of the chivalric/feudal society (a *ritter hübesch und gemeit* (line190)) and a vulnerable exemplar of female sanctity. The latter is tempted into prostitution by means of a sparrow hawk, a symbol associated with the aristocracy and with chivalric culture. The audience is invited to admire the linguistic dexterity of the knight, and to maintain an ironic distance from institutionalised chastity. Not only does sexual claustration render the girl vulnerable to the advances of the knight by keeping her in ignorance; its discipline is also entirely contrary to her desires. The girl's development of an

---

[119] See Mihm *Überlieferung*, p. 58. Again, this term should not be taken to be a genre designation.

[120] See Mihm, *Überlieferung*, pp. 52–3; Bonath, ed., p. 9. *Der arme Heinrich* is followed by *Daz bloch*, as in cpg 341.

[121] *Das Wachtelmäre* appears in *Denkmäler deutscher Sprache und Literatur aus Handschriften des 8ten bis 16ten Jahrhunderts zum ersten Male hrsg.*, ed. H. F. Maßmann (Munich, 1827), pp. 105–12. *Der Hasenbraten* and *Das Almosen* appear in the *Neues Gesamtabenteuer*, ed. Niewöhner and Simon, pp. 53–7. *Der hohle Baum* is published under the title *Der wahrsagende Baum* in von der Hagen's *Gesammtabenteuer*, II, 137–44.

[122] See Schirmer, *Stil- und Motivuntersuchung*, pp. 293–4.

insatiable sexual appetite under the tutelage of the knight illustrates a staple of medieval misogyny: the presentation of concupiscence and frailty of the flesh as 'natural' attributes of the feminine.[123]

The characterisation and dialogue of *Der Sperber* resonate to some degree with *Der arme Heinrich*. The young novice is described as *gar unwandelbaere* (line 56; cf. *Der arme Heinrich* line 1172); her life is simple and pious and she has nothing but contempt for worldly pleasures: *ahtete niht umb ein hâr | uf der werelde üppikeit* (lines 70–2) ('did not care one bit for wordly joys'). However, following her transformation from *maget* to *wîp* she provokes the knight indecorously (*mit unsiten*) to restore her *minne*, and praises the knight's sexual prowess to the mother superior: *Er ist rehte ein meister daran* ('He is a true master at it!') (line 217; cf. *Der arme Heinrich* line 1156). The novice's provocative and candid references to her own physical gratification complement the parodic reading of the *maget*'s assertive behaviour in the sacrifice scene that I hypothesised previously. The humour of both texts would be rooted in a scabrous variation on the chastity-testing motif, which subverts rather than upholds the ideal of female sexual continence.[124]

In the fluid context of fourteenth-century codicology, where dichotomies such as religious/worldly and courtly/scurrilous are relativised or dismantled, *Der arme Heinrich* is thus grouped with diverse texts which highlight its interpretative and generic potentialities. In the Strasbourg and Heidelberg manuscripts, the work is preceded by two texts that are earnest in tone and didactic in intention. *Liebe und schoene* borrows the idiom of religious instruction to expound an abstract *Minnelehre*, based on the principle of Christian salvation. Together with *Von der Barmherzigkeit*, it suggests that certain fourteenth-century manuscript compilers concurred with the dominant modern view of *Der arme Heinrich* as a courtly *exemplum*, illustrating the doctrine of Christian redemption. The codicological linkage with the religious text is reinforced in the Heidelberg manuscript by the insertion of an ending of an unequivocally religious cadence. However, traces of a rather less pious predecessor emerge from beneath *Von der Barmherzigkeit*, attesting to a previous act of context-building that implies a rather different view of the text.

Yet the other texts that frame *Der arme Heinrich* confirm that it was not only the religious/exemplary content that motivated the manuscript compilers in their context-building activities. The compilers of all of the manuscripts

---

[123] The satire that this text directs at institutionalised chastity appears all the more deliberate when we compare the Middle High German *Märe* with its French analogue. In *Cele qui fu foutue et desfoutue pour une grue* no opposition is created between chivalric society and female sanctity: the female protagonist is a courtly lady who has been ensconced in a tower by her father: *Fabliaux érotiques: Textes de jongleurs des XIIe et XIIIe siècles*, ed. L. Rossi and R. Straub (Paris, 1992), pp. 185–97.

[124] On the chastity-testing motif, which is common to religious genres such as the virgin martyr legend, to idealistic courtly literature and to the lewd *fabliau*, see Bloch, *Medieval Misogyny*, pp. 93–112; Krueger, *Women Readers*, pp. 128–55.

show a tendency to juxtapose our text with *Mären* which dovetail in their thematic focus on gender as a relationship of control. In two of the texts, the female protagonists, who resist their disenfranchisement in marriage and succeed in circumventing social and marital control, play the most active role. Yet the attitudes that these two narratives inscribe towards the ingenuity of their protagonists differ. In *Der wibe list* the wife's infidelity and linguistic control appear as a problem, reflected in the title and the epilogue. In contrast, the manoeuvres of the wife and godmother in *Daz bloch* are presented as giving the brutal husband his just desserts.

With *Der Sperber*, we are transported from the domain of marriage into the more austere setting of institutionalised female sanctity. Again, the narrative centres on a gender confrontation. However, whereas the female protagonists of *Daz bloch* and *Der wibe list* attain literary empowerment by circumventing the masculine control enshrined in the institution of marriage, here the power relations are reversed. The female protagonist is placed under the aegis of institutionalised chastity, and it is for the chivalric protagonist to test the limits of this institutional control. The humour derives from the ease with which the courtly hero overthrows this bastion of sexual abstention and divests it of its legitimacy. Thus the direct juxtaposition of *Der arme Heinrich* with *Der Sperber* suggests that the compiler either espoused or was inviting a reading of the former text as an ironic commentary on *virginitas* and the resistance to a feudal sexual economy implied by this ideology.

We can therefore infer from the codicological evidence that fourteenth-century manuscript compilers considered *Der arme Heinrich* to be implicated in debates on gender relations, particularly those concerning the legitimacy of female empowerment and sexual agency. The *Mären* concur in presenting female agency as embattled, tightly circumscribed by social and linguistic codes. However, as far as didactic content is concerned, the selection could hardly be more mixed, encompassing both positive and derisively negative responses to the behaviour of the female protagonists. If we are to see these codicological juxtapositions as interpretative reactions to the *maget*'s representation in *Der arme Heinrich*, they aptly reflect the ambivalence and the abrupt shifts in attitude towards the her ambitions in the latter text.

Conclusion

Poised between the sacred and the secular, incorporating a broader social perspective than either of Hartmann's romances, *Der arme Heinrich* evades classification according to canonical paradigms. Yet we would be in error to dismiss the importance of textual and discursive types for reconstructing the literary environment in which the text was produced, for analysing both how it situates itself within this environment and the place that it is allocated by later audiences. In the preceding discussion, I hope to have demonstrated the advantages offered by a more flexible conception of genre; one that pays attention to practices of experimentation, transformation and modulation in the process of textual production, as well as to public expectation and response as they are witnessed by the activities of scribes and codicologists.

The ambiguities and inconsistencies inherent in the *maget*'s characterisation, long noted by critics, become more intelligible if we approach the text with an awareness of the gender roles and relations specific to the genres that constituted the author's literary horizon. The *maget* mediates a dialectic between conflicting generic roles; thus her agency is overdetermined and her representation ambiguous. As heroine of both virgin martyr legend and romance, she is elevated to a position of ideological privilege and narrative control whilst simultaneously being disenfranchised and objectified. The romance narrative rises to prominence, and the martyrdom narrative is definitively suppressed, in the sacrifice scene, a unilateral manoeuvre that is accompanied by a negative moral gloss on the *maget*'s behaviour. In addition, Hartmann potentially builds gratuitous sexual innuendo into the episode at her expense. This would link the text with narratives of *Frauenzucht* and scabrous *Mären* which become prevalent in the fourteenth century, where female agency is frequently encoded as verbal and bodily insubordination, and vengeance is exacted on women who venture outside socially prescribed roles.

However, when it comes to reconstructing generic horizons and discerning relationships of congruence between texts, the scholar of medieval literature is frequently on shaky ground and forced to resort to speculation. It is at this point that the evidence of reception afforded by the text's transmission acquires added importance, as it allows us to situate the work more firmly in the historical context in which it was read, and to compare our own analysis with the responses of medieval audiences. Instability is a key feature of *Der arme Heinrich*'s transmission. The substitute ending offered in the B variant suggests that the scribe viewed the protagonists' narrative aims and respective stances on sexuality as divergent, and that Heinrich's abstinence from *werltliche[r] wone* was intended to alleviate this problem. The scribal alternatives *manbere*, *vriebere*, *êrbere* bear witness to the multiple generic valences of the *maget* by crystallising the various readings that intersect on her body, agency and sexuality. In the context of supposedly 'postivistic' nineteenth-century philology, this instance of variance prompts partisan reactions and a surprising disregard for textual witness.

The disparate manuscript environments in which *Der arme Heinrich* is found can be viewed as codicological reflexes to this indeterminacy. Some of the juxtapositions confirm modern interpretations of *Der arme Heinrich* as a synthesis of amorous courtly narrative and religious parable. However, manuscript compilers, evidently aware of the pliancy of our text, also seem to have enjoyed juxtaposing it with narratives that are far less exemplary in orientation. The compilers of the Strasbourg and Heidelberg manuscripts may well have viewed *Der arme Heinrich* as a fence-sitter located between the spiritual/earnest and the profane/humorous, and have exploited this indeterminacy as a means of bridging between these types. The Kalocsa scribe, in positioning *Der arme Heinrich* next to *Der Sperber*, perhaps aimed to highlight the scabrous potential that I suggested emerges when the exemplary discourse of our text is suspended and it is placed in a different context. Like the philological controversy surrounding the description of the leprosy cure, the codicologists' activities suggest that the girl's agency was regarded as an interpretative crux: *Der arme Heinrich* is juxtaposed in all three manuscripts with texts that focus on female agency, and evince a paradoxical mix of attitudes towards this issue.

A further aspect of the text's diachrony that I have not been able to treat in this essay is the nineteenth- and twentieth-century reception of the text. In addition to the numerous *Volksbücher* and *Volksausgaben* that were published following the text's popularisation by the Brothers Grimm, the work also formed the basis of translations, plays, operettas, ballads, cycles of paintings and engravings, and novellas.[125] The material proved extremely ideologically pliant. The ambiguous act of self-sacrifice, ideologically over-determined and thus vulnerably indeterminate, was repeatedly adapted for nationalist ends, reaching a height of chauvinism with Borchardt's proclamation: 'die Germanin allein darf es wagen, neben die Alkestis der griechischen Sage zu treten'.[126] The *maget* seems have worked a paradoxical power on the imagination of nineteenth-century romanticist philologists, and the shifting incarnations of this figure throughout the nineteenth and twentieth centuries further testify to her amenability to different readings and contextualisations.

The premise that genres are ideological formations that mediate social and historical phenomena begs the question how we are to relate the generic over-determination of the *maget* to the text's socio-historical context. Marianne Wynn recently suggested that her representation should be viewed in the light of the explosion in female piety that took place in the course of the twelfth century. Wynn claims that Hartmann's 'downgrading of the heroine's stature' represents a feudal backlash to the increasing number of women who were choosing to eschew marital destiny and pursue a spiritual career.[127] In subordinating his vocal advocate of virginity to the structures of feudal marriage, Hartmann would therefore be inscribing and attempting to resolve very real social tensions concerning female agency and body politics.

When employed as a means of classification of purportedly universal and enduring validity, genre can only be inhibiting. My aim has been in part to challenge such critical commonplaces. I have also attempted to cast doubt on

---

125 See U. Rautenberg, *Das 'Volksbuch vom armen Heinrich': Studien zur Rezeption Hartmanns von Aue im 19. Jh. und zur Wirkungsgeschichte der Übersetzung Wilhelm Grimms* (Berlin, 1985).

126 Cited by F. Wagner, ' "Heinrich und die Folgen": Zur Rezeption des *Armen Heinrich* bei Hans Pfitzner, Ricarda Huch, Gerhart Hauptmann und Rudolf Borchardt', in *German Narrative Literature of the Twelfth and Thirteenth Centuries: Studies Presented to Roy Wisbey on his 65th Birthday*, ed. V. Honemann (Tübingen, 1994), pp. 261–74 (p. 270).

127 Wynn, 'Heroine without a Name: The Unnamed Girl in Hartmann's Story', in *German Narrative Literature*, ed. Honemann, pp. 245–59. On the burgeoning of institutionalised female sanctity in the late twelfth and early thirteenth centuries, see P. Dinzelbacher and D. R. Bauer, *Religiöse Frauenbewegung und mystische Frömmigkeit im Mittelalter* (Cologne, 1988).

the blanket interpretations and neo-platonising rhetoric of theological readings, and the idealising interpretations based on naïve conceptions of 'femininity' and 'love' as static values implying submission and self-sacrifice. It
has emerged in the course of the discussion that the meanings attached to
textual and gender formations are historically situated, and thus plural, arbi-
trary, and open to constant revision. My exploration of the textual history of
Der arme Heinrich has revealed that both its generic character and its representation of female agency were recognised by medieval audiences as
subjects for debate and material for reinterpretation rather than critical givens.
We should be aware of their approach, and of the new interpretative possibilities that it opens up for us, in our future interpretations of Hartmann's text.

IV

THE GRAIL TEMPLE IN *DER JÜNGERE TITUREL*

Richard Barber and Cyril Edwards

Wolfram von Eschenbach's *Parzival* is familiar territory to Arthurian scholars, long recognised as one of the great versions of the Grail legend; as the source for Wagner's *Parsifal*, it has enjoyed additional currency in modern translations. It is undoubtedly Wolfram's masterpiece; but what is less generally known is that it is not his only work on the Grail. *Parzival* was a relatively popular work in medieval Germany, and a number of manuscripts survive, seventeen of which are complete. In one of these, there are fragments of an unfinished poem, which modern scholars have called *Titurel*, from the name of its hero, who is named in the first line. We quickly learn that Titurel was the first keeper of the Grail, and that in his old age he passed it to his son Frimutel: it is evident that Wolfram is preparing to tell us the history of the Grail from its first appearance, in other words the prehistory of *Parzival*, just as the French writers had created a prehistory of the Grail which found its final form in the *Estoire del Saint Graal*. The first fragment breaks off incomplete, and a second section provides the history of the lovers Sigune and Schionatulander, who figure in the young Parzival's adventures; at their last appearance, Schionatulander has been killed, and Sigune is mourning over his body. It is clear that this was to be the body of the tale, introduced by the Grail episodes, but it is difficult to see how the two were to be balanced: the Grail history is concerned with the high ideals of the company of knights and the kingdom centred on it, while the story of the lovers is the familiar territory of romance. In all, we have about 170 stanzas from Wolfram's hand, of which a handful are of doubtful authenticity.

Just as in the case of Chrétien de Troyes' *Perceval*, the lure of an unfinished masterpiece proved irresistible to later writers, and within half a century of Wolfram's death, the *Titurel* had been completed by an otherwise unknown poet called Albrecht. When this work was rediscovered in the early nineteenth century, it was at first hailed as being a complete poem by Wolfram, but scholars soon realised its uneven quality, and once the original fragments came to light, interest in Albrecht's work declined: the standard edition was only completed in 1995.[1]

---

[1] *Albrechts von Scharfenberg Jüngerer Titurel*, ed. Werner Wolf, completed by Kurt Nyholm, Deutsche Texte des Mittelalters XLV, LV, LXI, LXXIII (Berlin, 1955–95).

The *Jüngere Titurel* or 'Later Titurel', as this work is usually called, sets the romance of Sigune and Schionatulander within an opening and closing framework dealing with the Grail, its early history and its removal to India, where Titurel dies. These passages mirror in a distant way the structure provided by the *Estoire* and *Queste* of the French Lancelot-Grail cycle; the beginning is set in the early days of Christianity, and the conclusion removes the Grail from the eyes of western Christians. Titurel enjoys the same longevity as the biblical patriarchs, abdicating his kingship of the Grail at the age of 450, and dying when he is 500. He is fifty when an angel entrusts the Grail to his keeping, and he at once sets about establishing the Grail kingdom at Muntsalvatsch, in the land called Salvaterre; these are the Munsalvaesche and Terre de Salvaesche of *Parzival*. Albrecht describes Muntsalvatsch as surrounded by impenetrable forest, the Foreist Salvasch, and ringed by thirty miles of mountains; no-one could find their way there, unless the angels so wished, and the castle itself was fortified against all comers.

In Wolfram, by contrast, we learn almost nothing of the physical surroundings of the Grail or of the appearance of the Grail castle. The latter is portrayed only as an impregnable fortress, splendid in its size and power, and luxuriously furnished: this we learn on Parzival's first visit, and at the end of the story we discover that there is also a temple which houses the Grail, either within the castle or in the Grail domains, from which the Grail guardians are called *templeise*. Whether Wolfram intended this name to echo the military order known as the Templars is doubtful; it is perhaps best translated as 'men of the Temple'. All that Wolfram tells us of the Temple is that it contains a font made from a single ruby, mounted on a jasper pedestal.

Albrecht begins his work with a declaration of his religious faith, an extended prayer of some three hundred lines based on the opening of another of Wolfram's works, *Willehalm*. He then incorporates Wolfram's story of Titurel, up to the point where he embarks on the description of the Grail temple. This too draws on Wolfram's manner, with a baroque delight in ornate description and obscure language; but it is a fantasy quite unlike any of Wolfram's flights of imagination. Where Wolfram is always in control of his material, Albrecht, although he is describing an architectural structure, seems to be working without any particular system, delighting in the exuberance of his imagination. It is an extraordinary fantasy, and it is this passage, never previously translated into English, which Cyril Edwards presents below.

Through the thickets of highly coloured language, the underlying intention of the poet is clear: to evoke the image of an incomparable building, far beyond the experience of his audience, of which the focal point is the Grail itself. The Grail moves of its own accord, and at the time of the building of the temple, has never been carried by any mortal being; it hovers in the central sacristy. Later, we learn that the Grail named its bearer, Tschosian (Wolfram's Schoysiane), by writing which appeared on the Grail itself. Around this central miracle rises Albrecht's temple. For Albrecht, the Grail is the centre of an ordered and harmonious state, and its temple not only symbolises that order and harmony, but also the religious function of the Grail, as a mediator of salvation. To the extent that this is a symbolic building, like Chaucer's 'House of Fame' or Lydgate's 'Temple of Glass' – to name but two examples of a longstanding medieval tradition of descriptions of such allegorical buildings – we try to draw its groundplan despite the writer's intentions. Even the texts hinder us: we cannot be sure whether Albrecht intended the temple to have twenty-two or seventy-two choirs or surrounding chapels.[2]

What Albrecht does convey is the image of a shrine decorated in the richest possible manner. He shares Wolfram's enthusiasm for the exotic names of jewels, and also portrays elaborate mechanical devices such as doves and angels controlled by wires, as well as a magnificent array of musical instruments. The effect is purposely overwhelming: this is the greatest and richest of shrines, worthy of that holiest and most miraculous of relics, the self-moving Grail, which even controls the building of its own temple through the writing which appears on it. For Albrecht's concerns, in this section at least, are primarily religious, despite the heaping up of material splendour. In the *Jüngerer Titurel*, the Grail castle scarcely figures in descriptive terms: it is the Grail temple which is the crucial place.[3]

Despite the evidently symbolic intention of Albrecht's work, German scholars have tried hard to propose prototypes for the Grail temple. For example, San Vitale at Ravenna has been suggested on the strength of its octagonal ground plan and the detail of its decoration; but what Albrecht describes is a much more elaborate structure than the elegant simplicity of San Vitale.[4] His vision is not necessarily Gothic, but it is very probable that he is thinking of contemporary architecture rather than the Roman or Byzantine past. Another candidate as model is the Liebfrauenkirche at Trier, a Gothic church in the form of a Greek cross, which its admirers have compared to a *rosa mystica*, a hymn in stone to the glory of the Virgin.

Sulpice Boisserée, one of the first scholars to comment on the text in the early nineteenth century, created a detailed architectural drawing of his reconstruction of Albrecht's imaginary building (fig. 1), giving it seventy-two chapels rather than twenty-two.[5] He argued that a number of features in the description pointed to a Gothic building: the octagonal chapels, the ribbed vaulting with a keystone, the stained glass and the towers with numerous windows and spiral staircases. Other writers have seized on the eventual home of the Grail in the east to argue that its relocation to India at the end of the romance means that some Eastern model lies behind the Grail temple. The most extended of these Oriental theories was set out by Lars-Ivar Ringbom, who identified the temple with the sacred shrine at Siz, birthplace of

---

2   See Wolf, I, 86, stanza 341; he prefers the reading twenty-two to the seventy-two given in the best manuscript. See p. 91 below.
3   Gudula Trendelenburg, *Studien zum Gralraum im "Jüngeren Titurel"*, Göppinger Arbeiten zur Germanistik 78 (Göppingen, 1972), p. 26.
4   Trendelenburg, p. 36; ibid. p. 96 for the Liebfrauenkirche.
5   Sulpice Boisserée, 'Ueber die Beschreibung des Tempels des heiligen Grales in dem Heldengedicht: Titurel Kap. III', *Abhandlungen der philosophisch-philologischen Classe der königlich Bayerischen Akademie der Wissenschaften* 1 (1835), 307–92.

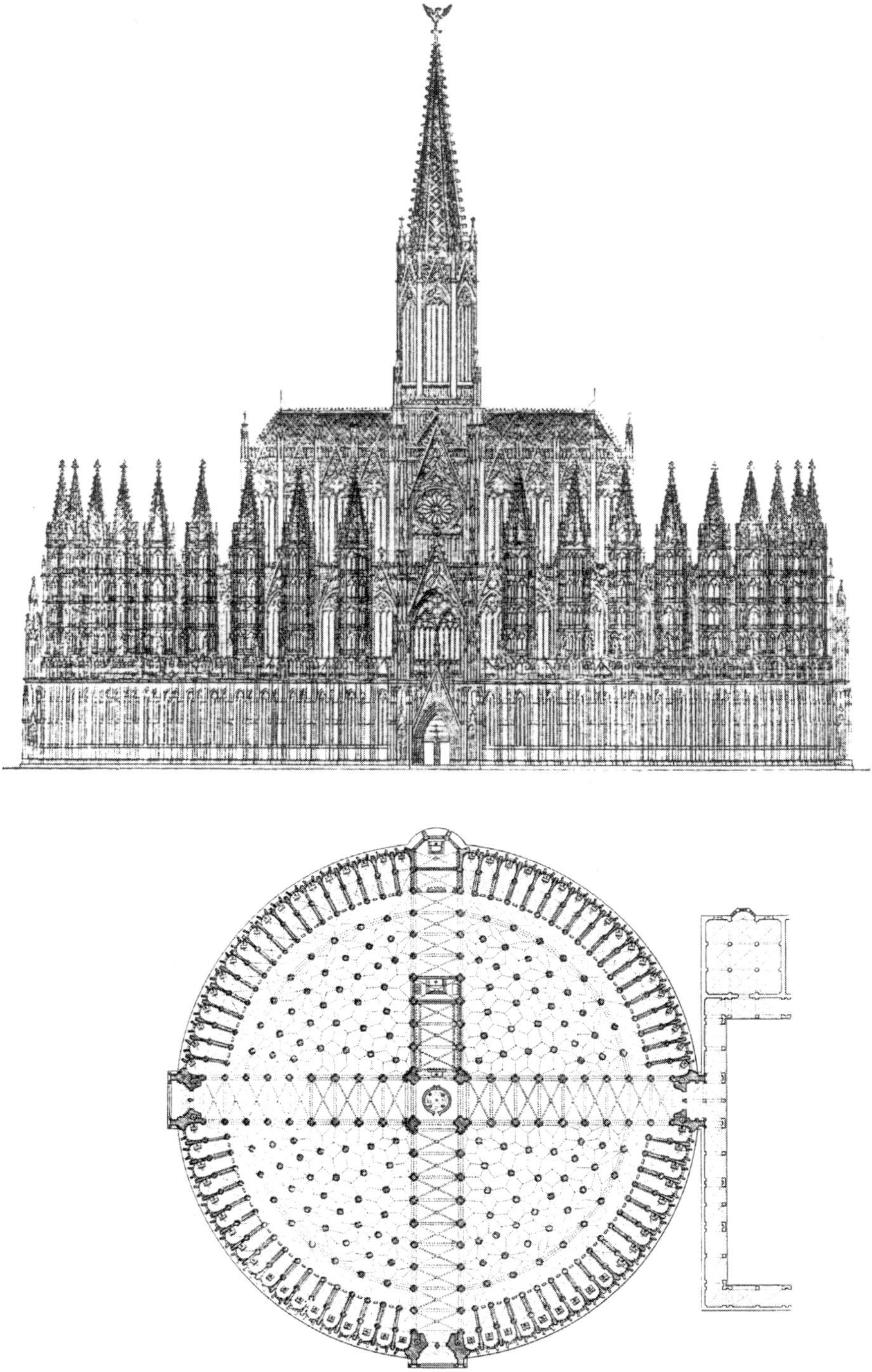

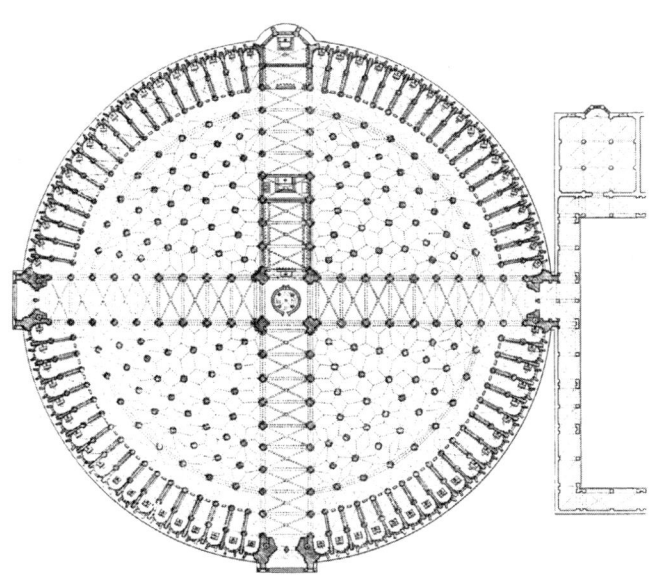

Sketch and plan of the Grail temple after Sulpiz Boisserée.

Zoroaster, and one of the holy places of his fire-worshipping followers.[6] Ringbom suggests that if Wolf is correct in attributing only twenty-two choirs to the temple, we are not looking at a huge building, but at something relatively modest; and he argues that Boisserée's reconstruction is fundamentally flawed in scale. He sees an analogy with the Romanesque octagon of Sankt Gereon in Köln, and traces the unusual groundplan of this building back to Armenia, by way of the ninth-century palace church at Breslau. He identifies a specific type of royal chapel, found at San Lorenzo in Milan, San Vitale in Ravenna, and at Charlemagne's palace at Aachen, all of which are octagonal buildings with a cupola.[7] From Armenia, he moves to Iran, and to the buildings at Siz, claiming that

> the country of Salvatierre and the mountain Monsalvatsche, with its onyx rocks, the imposing walls, with the sanctuary adorned with the cosmos, the secret jewel and the spiritual-chivalric attendants originally had a real existence in Iran.[8]

All this is ingenious, but ultimately far-fetched; as another writer points out, 'if Albrecht's building has a rational plan, it is not based on architectural principles'.[9] Albrecht himself says later in the poem:

> I have built the temple for worthy Christian people so that they may learn the right lessons from it, and want to look faithfully to God through the temple's design.[10]

The Grail temple is replete with symbolism, and its details are more important than such overarching plans as it may possess. Albrecht's unlikely Arthurian temple is here presented to English readers for the first time to judge for themselves, in the hope that they will explore and further illuminate this byway of Grail literature.

---

[6] Lars-Ivar Ringbom, *Graltempel und Paradies: Beziehungen zwischen Iran und Europa im Mittelalter*, Kungl. Vitterhets Historie och Antikvitets Akademiens Handlingar 73 (Stockholm, 1951).
[7] Ibid., p. 167.
[8] Ibid., p. 229: 'das Land Salvatierre und der Berg Monsalvatsche mit seinen Onyxfelsen und den stattlichen Mauern, mit dem kosmisch ausgestatteten Heiligtum, dem geheimnisvollen Kleinod und der geistlichen-ritterlichen Dienerschaft hat ursprünglich in Iran tatsächlich existiert.'
[9] Klaus Zatloukal, *Salvaterre: Studien zur Sinn und Funktion des Gralsbereiches im "Jüngeren Titurel"*, Wiener Arbeiten zur germanischen Altertumskunde und Philologie 12 (Vienna, 1978), p. 195: 'Wenn Albrechts Bauwerk ein Gesamtplan zugrunde lag, so ist er nicht aufgrund von architektonischen Prinzipien erstellt.'
[10] 516.2.

DER JÜNGERE TITUREL strr. 329–439

Here the story commences of how Titurel the pure created in God's honour a temple for the Grail, made of bright precious stones, and otherwise of nothing but red gold – and thirdly of lignum aloe, for such timber as was needed. 329

Their intention was to furnish it in the most luxurious way imaginable. I shall tell you what steps they took to achieve this noble display of wealth. In order that the building should be as lavish as possible it contained no wood except for the seating. The gold and the precious stones brought them frost in winter and coolness with the dew. 330

Questions were therefore put concerning the most favourable precious stones to use. This caused little concern to those who were acquainted through Pythagoras with the ancient art and knew through Hercules of the natural powers of stones. They proffered their expertise here: 331

Stones might readily be found of such a benign nature that they afforded most pure air in summer, and in winter, when fires were lit, yielded heat of such sweet moderation that it suited man's physical needs in the right measure, to his heart's desire. 332

'Asbestos turns to fire,' so the experts proclaimed, 'and as a result all coldness flees from it, and the fire can be perceived to burn constantly; once lit it never dies out.' This was the information that they gave to the king. 333

'An even greater provider of heat in wintertime is heliotrope.[11] If this same stone is dropped into a basin full of gently moving water, then it will indubitably yield coolness in the summer, while in the winter the water will boil vigorously. 334

This beneficial stone has many additional qualities apart from its heating effect: it succours health, good fortune and the intellect. It prolongs life. The stone is most efficacious against lying, deception and poisons. While there is no need of the latter qualities here, the stone is ideally suited for the temple.' 335

Dishonour and poverty were banished from the temple, since the benevolence of the pure Virgin and her Son reign in such sovereign power high over all creation. Titurel the pure and comely was most grateful to them for this. 336

This mountain that towered so high above everything had a rocky base consisting of pure onyx. It was, however, overgrown with plants and grass. The edifice was built upon this, a work of great skill. The stone was hewn in such a way that the like will never be seen again. 337

---

[11] This is the first of many stones which derive from the list in Wolfram von Eschenbach's *Parzival* (ed. Karl Lachmann, Berlin 1926), section 791. Cf. Wolfgang Wegner, *Albrecht, ein poeta doctus rerum naturae? Zu Umfang und Funktionalisierung naturkundlicher Realien im Jüngeren Titurel*, Europäische Hochschulschriften 1562 (Frankfurt am Main, 1996), especially pp. 74–124.

On top of the onyx was a hill, more than six foot high. The king deliberated on the construction of the temple, pondering how he should go about it. The plants, grass and land were then removed from the mountain. He ordered it to be swept bare and ground smooth so that it shone like the moon. 338

Afterwards, as he was pondering on the matter, guidance came to him from the Grail, to enable him to create the temple in the form, dimensions and ornament that he desired. He found these sketched out all around the onyx.[12] 339

He found the foundations sketched out on the stone in elegant proportion, so that he then knew for sure how the work might with skill be carried out. The stone was six foot high, and in width thirty feet all round, from the outer wall to where the steps ascended,[13] 340

Round like a rotunda, so we hear the story tell, broad and high. He could count some twenty-two choirs, all octagonal and projecting forwards.[14] Such luxury would have overwhelmed a poor man. 341

This elegant edifice was borne by pillars of bronze. My heart would rejoice if I were ever to see a temple so rich in all its interior ornament. Each precious stone shone forth in its own colour from the red gold. 342

Where the arches rose to meet the sweep of the flying buttresses many rich designs could be espied, curling above the pillars, beautifully carved, skilfully executed with elaborate ornament. The work was luxuriously embellished with pearls and corals. 343

High above all the pillars, carved and cast, were many angels worthy of high praise, looking as if they had flown there direct from Heaven, joyous in flight, such a sight for sore eyes that even a foolish Waleis[15] might have sworn that he had been caught in the act of smiling. 344

Many images were cast, carved and hewn according to the wishes of the king, crucifixes and images of Our Lady, rendered pure by high art with no thought for the cost – I must needs fall silent in my assessment, I have no grasp of such skills. 345

---

12 The manuscripts diverge radically here, and my translation is a poor compromise. MS H reads: 'the form and dimensions of the temple [were] like the noble palace which Prester John could not forget'. The allusion to Prester John is an echo of Wolfram's *Parzival*, in which Prester John, the Christian priest-king of India, is the son of Feirefiz, Parzival's half-brother, and Repanse de Schoye, the erstwhile Grail maiden.

13 Wolf: 'von der mure unz an der grede uf leite'; MS H: 'Al vmb her von der mure claffter funf biz an der gred vff laite'. The sense is obscure.

14 The architectural detail is obscure. The Heidelberg manuscript refers to seventy-two choirs, which were 'vssen dan. aht egge vnd furgeschozzen/ waz ieglich kor besunder.' Wolf: 'er kunde gepruefen wol zwen und zweinzic koere,/ uzen her dan unde fur geschozzen/ ieglich kor besunder.'

15 *Waleis* hovers in meaning in Arthurian literature between 'Gaul' and 'Welshman', being cognate with both. The adjective *welsch* ofen refers to Italians, such as Thomasin von Zirclaria, author of the MHG work *Der welsche Gast* (*c.* 1225). The only certainty is that a nationality is indicated which is not German. The absence of the English Channel in much Arthurian literature complicates matters; Wales and Gaul are a geographical and racial, Celtic unit. What is unusual here is the suggestion that a *Waleis* are a dour race. MS H has a variant with an anti-Bavarian bias: 'such that a foolish Bavarian might have sworn that it [i.e. the images] were alive.'

Yet my account must proceed: the altars were richly and beautifully adorned, as well befitted God's honour, so masterly, with such a display of wealth that I would be hard put to accord each a separate assessment, even if I had greater powers of discernment. 346

The altars supported all kinds of miraculous decoration: on each stood its own reliquary, tablets, precious images, and on top of all of them stood a rich ciborium, elegantly ornamented with cast metal, with many images of the saints in great glory. 347

Sapphire possesses the noble quality of purging a man's sin from the page, helping him towards God like a watery wave turning a mountainous somersault.[16] This stone's power confers such virtue that a man can lament his sins in true contrition – 348

That is, provided one knows the right kind, for there are three varieties. The kind I have in mind is the best, fully equal to some hundred lands in value. Yet some sapphires can be seen to lose their power, if people are not capable of preserving them properly.[17] 349

God Himself gave in the form of a sapphire that writing to Moses which frees man from all sin – that man who yet abides by the same doctrine, observing all those commandments, five times paired. Thus many of the highest virtues are combined in the sapphire. 350

For this reason the altar stones were entirely of sapphires. Since this stone makes man free of sin, then this was all for the best in the king's view. He cared but little for the expense. 351

Velvet, casting a green glow, cut in circles, hung over each altar, defying dust, and whenever the priest sang, a silken string was pulled. A dove brought an angel, who came flying down from the arch.[18] 352

A wheel took him back again, pierced by string through its middle [?]. The dove moved towards him in flight and met the angel, as if it were flying forth from Paradise, like the Holy Ghost, to the high honour of the mass, the greatest solace of Christendom. 353

The windows were of ornamental glass, rich in strange artistry. I doubt if anyone ever saw or heard the like. The glass filling them was not made of ash, but of bright crystals. There was no question of any expense being spared. 354

Pearls and crystals were placed on the outside of the glass. So much daylight pierced through that the light might easily have caused injury to the eye of a frivolous beholder, if he let his glance linger there. Masterly arts prevented that: 355

Inlay was not spared, designs incorporating pearls, with painting, so that the dazzling shine might be tempered, and to embellish the rich

[16] Wolf: 'mit wazzers unde,/ daz uber sich zu berge da kan fliezen.'
[17] On the obscure sapphire passage see Wegner (as note 11), pp. 100–2.
[18] Or, as MS H would have it: 'an angel brought forth a towel'. The mechanics of this and the following strophe evidently puzzled the scribes.

display to the honour of God and the Grail, for it decorated the temple lavishly. 356

All the designs that the masters cut on the glass and all the different colours that they applied with their brushes were embellished with precious stones, each possessing the same colour, bright, pure and clear. 357

Sapphires were chosen for the azure colour, emeralds for the precious greens. Nothing was neglected there. The same practice applied to the yellow, red, brown and white colours, each according to its kind being embellished with bright stones, no expense being spared in the workmanship. 358

The amethyst is threefold in colour, and in kind. It was not spared here, but employed because of its pure, radiant, very delicate hue and other virtues. One colour it has is purple, another violet, a cure for sickness, 359

And the third colour is bright and clear, like fresh roses. The comely topaz played a valued role. Whoever looks into this stone will find his chin rises whilst his eyes are lowered, strange as it may seem.[19] It has two radiant colours, yellow and golden, unsurpassable. 360

The garnet-hyacinth provided a fiery red hue, the sardonyx supplied a white, enhancing the display. For a contrast penselpix[20] was set. The noble, precious jasper has no less than seventeen colours, and much value is set upon that stone. 361

All the colours would be totally lacking in virtue if the powerful black were not fully in place. This the jasper supplied in abundance. The windows derived radiance from the jasper, and from chrysolite. 362

Chalcophonus,[21] ruby, cornelian[22] and chrysoprase,[23] diparasme[24] bright of hue – sixty colours are attributed to exakorasien[25] –, octalamus,[26] karisian,[27] ardisen.[28] These precious stones are beyond my powers of praise. 363

A wondrous number of pearls and corals were inlaid in the windows. Many a pure, bright ruby shone forth in brilliance like a glowing tinder. The sun adapted its colour to each stone's radiance in turn, as it shone

---

[19] The topaz functions as a distorting mirror. Cf. Wegner, p. 112.

[20] 'penselpix'. Perhaps the basis is MHG *pensel* = brush?

[21] 'alkofone'. Another obscure stone, presumably identical with Wolfram's 'calcofôn' (*Parzival*, section 791, 12).

[22] 'kornvel'. Wegner (p. 94) identifies this tentatively as med. Lat. 'corneolus' = 'cornîol' in Wolfram (*Parzival* 791,13); English 'cornelian' or 'chalcedony'.

[23] 'krisopasien', presumably inspired by Wolfram's 'crisoprassîs' (*Parzival* 741,6; 791,27). Cf. Wegner, p. 96.

[24] 'diparasme'. H: 'Die parsius'. The manuscripts are puzzled by many of these stones, and here even Wegner can provide no solution.

[25] Wegner suggests the multi-coloured stone 'exacontalithus' (p. 87).

[26] H: 'berthalamus'. Perhaps inspired by Wolfram's 'optallîes' (791,5). Wegner suggests that this may mean 'opal' (p. 97) and adduces several parallels.

[27] Another obscure stone. Cf. Wegner, p. 92.

[28] Cf. Wegner, p. 80.

through the windows, creating special optical delights all over the temple. 364

As for the roof, it was of red gold overlaid with niello-work, to prevent the bright reflection of the sun destroying men's eyes. Thus the work was carried out, with masterly skill and cunning. 365

God was ever more giving to pure desire than desirous of it. When king [Titurel] was alive in his glory God gave him guidance which equalled the munificence of Solomon when he built the throne of the Templum Domini in Jerusalem. 366

God gave Solomon the stones, cut to perfection, so that there should be no clamour in Jerusalem. Be they large or small, chisels, hammers and other tools were all to be heard in full measure there. Thus Solomon's labour was graced by God's gift. 367

He retains the same power to afford constant help. It may be read in Holy Writ that He worked much greater miracles than those He accorded to the Grail here, to help those worthy people who would gladly live in His grace. 368

From the providence of Heaven He has amply fed the world. Whoever does His bidding still will find his place in Paradise. If a man preserves his soul pure here against the desire of the flesh he will be amply rewarded by God there. 369

Now the work was so expensive that it could never be completed. Therefore the Grail sent the king guidance in writing. Whatever was needed was found before the Grail, according to the master builder's every desire. 370

Once again the company of the Grail proffered praise and great honour to God for responding so promptly and so very graciously. Small wonder that the building proceeded in praiseworthy fashion. 371

The brilliance of the window-glass was absolutely unnecessary, for many bright stones there gave off an excess of red light. The glare of the stones lit up the bright gold so that it reflected back their brilliance. This great luxury injured many eyes. 372

The choirs within all had dividing walls.[29] For the love of the Highest God they thought nothing of all the expense, as His help gave them such great guidance. Consequently an edifice was built there which has no equal anywhere in the world. 373

Over all the vaulting was the blue of sapphires. To praise the divinity no other stone was intermingled, save the starry light of carbuncles which shone like the sun, whether the night was dim or dark. 374

The vaulting was thus covered with sapphires, of the variety called pure, with carbuncles inserted. Their shine gave off such bright radiance it equalled that of the stars. It was truly a delight for anyone to see who was not troubled by heart's sorrow. 374a

---

[29] Wolf's edition suggests 'walled seating' ('all under sitz mit muore').

The ultimate in joyous expense was not spared there. The golden sun and the silver moon were both taken as models to be imitated in precious stones, their colours both replicated. 375

They manufactured clocks by rich art, with such hidden skill that no eye could ever detect their circling, and yet their signs and circles moved. Golden bells announced to them melodiously the times of the seven days. 376

Not to be omitted were four noble, massive statues of the Evangelists, cast of many kinds of gold, their wings high and stretched out wide. When a man's eye beheld them it was led to God in great joy, 377

Inspired to think in the direction of the Heavenly Throne and to disdain everything which robs mankind of that crown which seats the poor amongst kings. That man who paid no attention to them was thwarted of the heavenly crown. 378

Should I mention paintings? These they wished to dispense with. They held them cheap since they had stones of so many colours, well carved into images and faces. This was executed with such art as matched well the nature of the stone. 379

Wherever the choir turned outwards there was the altar, so that the priest could turn his face correctly to the Orient when he desired to increase the bliss of Christians and God's praise in the Mass. 380

The greatest of the choirs pointed to the Orient. Two entire galleries were given to this direction, for it was dedicated to the Holy Ghost in all elegance of ornamentation, enriched at special expense, since he was the patron of the whole temple. 381

The one next to it was dedicated to the Virgin, who is the mother of that child who has both Heaven and Earth in His power and their population. John was the name of the lord of the third choir. The rest of the twelve disciples were housed close by. 382

The inside of the temple had such rich craftsmanship, built in beauty for the love of God and the Grail, everywhere equally so, save that the choirs lacked such ornament as was bestowed upon the rest of the temple. The whole work was completed in thirty years. 383

There was only one single sanctified altar there, the choirs around it were empty. Such a wonder of wealth was invested in it. In front of the belfry stood rich ciboria with images of the saints. Each carving told its own story there. 384

This same rich temple was devoted to the Grail, so that it could be kept there every day and when it was raised on high a broad and radiant sacristy was visible below. 385

There were three portals; the number is not disputed. One faced towards that corner of the world which is called the Meridian, the other led out to the Occident, and the third to Aquilon, whence blows an ill wind. 386

Their great hall and dormitory faced the Meridian. An elegant cloister lay between; this was indispensable and befitted well the brotherhood. Splendid steps adorned all these portals in princely fashion.　387

The portals were rich in pure red gold, inlaid with such precious stones that I cannot imagine how anyone could afford them. They were, moreover, adorned with locks, richly bolted; nothing on this earth is comparable.　388

Before each of the portals were placed all the different kinds of stones which formed part of that great, rich edifice. There they lay next to one another, each with an inscription giving its name and nature.　389

This, then, was how the portals were decorated, a task carried out with especial luxury. Many wonders were carried out there, much high skill attempted. How many kinds of stones were carved? Five broad circles were formed from them. I believe it lies beyond my powers of description.　390

High above one of the gates, elegantly facing the Occident, was an organ, a construction with a clear, sweet note, a great pleasure to hear; it accompanied the office on feast days, as is still the case all over Christendom:　391

A tree of red gold, equipped with all desirable foliage, twigs and branches, with birds perched everywhere of those kinds whose sweet voices are praised. Wind went in from a bellows, so that every bird sang in its fashion,　392

One high, the other low, depending on the manipulation of the key. Laboriously the sound was conducted back down into the tree. Whichever bird he wished to press into action, the master was well acquainted with the key according to which the birds sang.　393

Four angels were perched on the ends of the branches in immaculate pose, each holding a horn of gold in his hand; these they blew with a great din, whilst with their free hand they beckoned as if to say 'Rise up, all ye dead!'　394

There was the Last Judgment, cast, not painted. The simplicity of the design was intended to reinforce the warning that bitterness ever follows after sweetness, and so when a man is happy he should ever think upon that same sadness.　395

Two most exquisite doors led into each choir there. Between them stood an altar, over which hung chancels, vaulted, supported by two spindle columns, each forming a circle of some six feet, with the area between them filled with special ornament.　396

The doors in front of all the choirs had railings of rich gold, so that people could see and hear better from all directions. The walls by the doors also all had rich railings, closed with clasps, and everything was studded with precious stones.　397

The choirs had a great deal of ornament on their walls, executed in an unusual way; there were massive newels with arches passing over them. Above these were trees of gold in high foliage with birds perched upon them, whose quarrels had all been amicably settled.　398

Whatever invention could imagine was put into practice as far as possible. The arches were intertwined with vines everywhere. Two wound upwards in each case, then bent over each other, hanging over the seats on both sides, some six foot in height. 399

Below that a wood burst forth in wondrous foliage; here roses budded in full bloom, white and red, on bushes and boughs, with green stems and lily-white petals. Flowers of all colours were to be seen there, each image diligently executed. 400

The flowers of all plants, of all the high and noble ones, could be seen all prettily wafting, delightful in their splendour, with their colours and all their forms as they should be, stems, petals and blossoms, the folds and all the leaves made of gold. 401

The vines, though made of robust gold, had a green overlay, as vines should, and also because green emboldens the eye and indeed gave shade against so much dazzling light. That is why in all the choirs the walls were well furnished with emeralds. 402

The leaves hung in thick clusters; when a wind rose they could be heard rustling with a sweet sound, yet without any sudden movement,[30] just as if a thousand falcons were rising into the air in a huge flock, with the golden bells attached to them ringing out. 403

Flying over the vines many bands of angels were to be seen, as if they had been plucked from paradise, and when the stalks of the vine-leaves made the leaves rustle the angels responded with absolutely life-like motions. 404

The highest sacred choir was especially distinguished by its beautiful ornament, greater than that of a hundred other such. Vines and angels were there a-plenty. Wind was conducted there secretly and skilfully by means of bellows. 405

Per music and *per use*[31] and yet softly, in moderation, whenever the wise master gave accompaniment and direction, the organ, together with the clergy, gave forth sweet sounds, like a company of angels – melodies without words, and yet it was beautiful. 406

When this rich ornament gave them so much joy and delight they all alike said: 'God the Father, Lord,' and beat their breasts, 'since you have conferred upon us such glory here, what do you have in store in Heaven, where this is capped a hundred thousand times!' 407

Did they have crypts there? No, God forbid that pure folk should ever associate themselves with false company under the deep earth, as sometimes are assembled in crypts! Christian faith and Christ's office should be proclaimed to us by light. 408

---

30 'sunder schricke'; H: 'ane schrike'. The rare word 'schricke' is in the internal rhyme position; its meaning is uncertain.

31 'Per music und per use'. Latin and German are combined obscurely here.

Small and large crystals like hats,[32] golden and black. Vats of balsam burned as if they were afire. Thrice two hung in each choir, and two more outside in front of the choirs, suspended from rich gold wires.   409

Above angels hovered some twelve feet high, as if they were holding the lights. And above these the wires were invisible, although they had to hold the angels in place high up in the vaulting. Much rich expense was thus employed there.   410

Many angels on the pulpit and on the walls held candles in their hands, some coiled candles, some straight sticks. Altough they were indifferent to high expense and had a great wealth of balsam, they did not wish to dispense with candlelight, conforming to good custom.   411

Many candelabras rich in gold, upon which many candles shone, hung there as perfection required. One angel held two at arm's length, six foot high, so that it seemed he intended to carry the crown towards the skies. No-one could tell that they were suspended from rich gold wires.   412

Whatever kind of voice resounded in the temple, the effect of the preciousness of the gems was that the echo was prolonged far and wide, and on high, too, in a bright, sweet tone, in the same way as a wood echoes the greeting of the birdlets in May.   413

The altars were all decorated in two squares of lights on those occasions when God's honour and our salvation were adorned by pure divine office. The fire of balsam burned there at all times, but the wax candles always had to wait to be lit until the divine office took place.   414

It would be well nigh impossible for me to do justice to so many kinds of adornment by giving each a separate account. Take note that there was nowhere an empty space six foot in length, neither inside or outside the temple, but everywhere there was moulding, engraving and painting of artistic ingenuity.   415

Although it did not cost them a penny [being God's gift], it was nevertheless worthy of high praise. They took solemn counsel in many ways as how to thank God and the Grail. The Grail once again relieved them of lesser cares.   416

The pulpits were provided with ledges and newels all around, with many elegant turrets on top. In all the curves of the pulpits could be seen the apostles, confessors, virgins, patriarchs, martyrs and prophets. Strong matter was inscribed upon their tablets.   417

Also present were those of great sanctity who proffer succour and those who strive towards such sanctity; also those who profited by the charity and mercy of Him who bears the crown in the land of angels. There stood beautiful maidens of whose garlands wonders might be told.   418

Both the small and the great arches, supported by flying buttresses, met at a central point, converging from four directions, and where the

---

[32] 'geliche den hueten'. Sense and syntax are obscure here and in the following half-line: 'gleifer unde rozer' (H: 'ruezzer').

corner points were formed there was no lack of archangels and evangelists in splendour. 419

A cylindrical emerald formed the central joint. They did not omit to have a figure of a lamb cast above it, the cross in its paw, the banner red. This sign has won salvation for us in battle and killed Lucifer in all his power. 420

On the outside there were engravings and sculptures of the dangers incurred by the undaunted Templars in their daily feats of arms, depicting how they fought chivalrously in great peril in the service of the Holy Grail, to protect it against evil people. 421

The corners of the choirs all rose upwards in a curve. The masters spared no pains creating vines, leaves, many kinds of dwarves, finely executed, along with wondrous sea-monsters, which caused many to smile.[33] 422

Between these on the wall were many miraculous carvings. I have a neighbour, and I reckon that if he wanted to look at this wonderful feat of workmanship from one end to the other, he might well be left standing there until he had been eaten out of house and home. 423

Wherever the choirs projected at the corners the king would spare no cost, but had placed on top of each pair high belfries, six such chambers, all identical. Let the incredulous speak of poverty, I'll stick to luxuries. 424

The belfries matched the noble choirs, forming a circular garland to the honour of the Grail, beyond the means of ten kings. Nothing was spared in the cause of splendour. 425

There were eight walls, and just as many corners, equalling the numbers of the choirs. The artistry and expense of the work were carried out to perfection, without any low mouldings. If any one dubs me a liar in this respect, I believe he has seldom been moved by art and expense. 426

Each chamber had three windows in every wall, with spindles of *bradem*[34] carved therein. Eyes looking up to the sun could feast upon this workmanship. The tops of the windows were like that of the temple, with huge ruby-red balls which burned fiercely. 427

On top of these balls were crosses, tall, snow-white, of bright crystal, to ward off the Devil, declaring checkmate to him, and check to all his wiles and temptations. The noble inhabitants of that court were sealed off against all hellish sins. 428

An eagle of red gold, all fire and sparks, was soldered on to each cross. Seeing it from afar, everyone would imagine that the eagle was hovering in the air and would lose sight of the cross from which it took flight. 429

One tower stood in the midst of all this. This rich wonder of work-

---

[33] The manuscripts diverge considerably here, but the ornament and gargoyles are strongly reminiscent of late Romanesque friezes such as those at Königslutter.

[34] 'bradem' remains obscure; presumably it is the name of a precious stone. In the *Martina* of Hugo von Langenstein 'brasime' refers to prase or prasine, a green mineral. Cf. Wegner, p. 82.

manship was crafted of gold from many smithies, together with many thousand radiant, bright, pure stones. Gold and gems combined to decorate this tower, which was the equal in height and breadth of two others.   430

On top of the tower was a sphere, a huge bright carbuncle; its radiance was worthy of praise, serving, when the night was dark, to afford a clear view high and low, so that if the templars found themselves late at night in the woods they might be directed to their rich lodgings by its light.   431

Many another precious stone lent additional guidance, its colour glowing like coals in the fire. All these shone to aid the carbuncle. Let there be no talk of seven stars – there some thousand stars shone brightly.   432

Red here, yellow there, here green, now a dark hue, then a white, a pale, a brown, a blue. Their hearts were emboldened by this joyous radiance, by the power of the gems and by the Grail itself. If any of them were vanquished, it could only be that he had earned it by the mark of sin.   433

The crown of all sounds is the elegant voice of the harp-string with its sweet, light note. Yet this is capped by the *arzibiere*.[35] Two bells had been skilfully cast of this; the clappers were of gold, to perfect the splendour.   434

One served the temple, the other to summon the company to a meeting, when they were called to table or to be rewarded for their battles.[36] They desired no further sound of bells, following the monastic order, for the sake of the law and honour of the Grail.   435

Great splendour of ornament was to be beheld beneath the onyx; fishes and images of all the wonders of the ocean were engraved and cut therein, each in its proper form, behaving just as if they were alive and in the wild,   436

Except that pipes surrounded them from the outside, supplying air.[37] The floor was covered with bright crystals; among them the creatures moved proudly, as if they were living in the waves. Windmills operating from some distance outside employed bellows to effect this *bradem*.[38]   437

Acquaintance with the floor created the optical illusion[39] of a lake rippling with waves, but covered with ice, and yet in such fashion that it was entirely transparent, so one could see the battles and combats of fishes, animals and sea-monsters there.   438

The bishop Penitenze, of the brothers of Parille,[40] wore many garlands accorded him by the French and by the people of many kingdoms; he it was who now willingly consecrated this temple and all the altars.   439

---

35 'arzibiere' remains obscure, perhaps a stone invented by Albrecht. Cf. Wegner, pp. 80–1.
36 'sus an stritliche soldimente'. 'soldimente' means 'reward', but the phrase is obscure.
37 Here too the syntax is obscure.
38 See note 34 above.
39 'Des estriches kunde gap liecht den ougen wise'. Here too the syntax is impenetrable.
40 Parille or Parillus was the grandfather of Titurel the Grail King.

Translator's Note

This section of Albrecht von Scharfenberg's *Der jüngere Titurel* has not to this translator's knowledge previously been rendered into English, although it has been the subject of much scholarly analysis. The strophic numbering is based upon the edition by Werner Wolf: *Albrechts von Scharfenberg Jüngerer Titurel*, Deutsche Texte des Mittelalters XLV, vol. 1 (Berlin, 1955), which is also taken as a base for the translation. The following editions were also consulted: Ernst Droysen, *Der Tempel des Heiligen Gral. Nach Albrecht von Scharfenberg. Juengerer Titurel Str. 319–410* (Bromberg, 1872); Werner Schröder, *Die Heidelberger Handschrift H (cpg 141) des 'Jüngeren Titurel'. Bereinigter Text des ersten Teilstücks (Strophe H 1–661,4) mit den Variationen der Redaktion R*, Akademie der Wissenschaften und der Literatur Mainz, Abhandlungen der geistes- und sozialwissenschaftlichen Klasse, Jg. 1994, Nr. 1 (Stuttgart, 1994); Kurt Nyholm, *Albrechts Jüngerer Titurel. Band IV. Textfassungen von Handschriften der Mittelgruppe*, Deutsche Texte des Mittelalters LXXIX (Berlin, 1995).

It may not be immediately apparent to the reader of this translation that *Der jüngere Titurel* was written at a time in the evolution of German literature, towards the end of the thirteenth century, when style took precedence over content. The poem is a huge essay in the *ornatus difficilis*, in an obfuscatory style sometimes known as 'geblümter Stil'. The difficulties that face the translator of the Grail Temple section are thus considerable and fall into various categories. A number of the technical terms employed by the author, particularly the names for minerals, are not to be found elsewhere in Middle High German, and some have the ring of *ad hoc* coinages; scribal variants show clearly that some were not known to Albrecht's contemporaries. Section 791 of Wolfram von Eschenbach's *Parzival* is the model for Albrecht's lists, but only a small number of the stones in the *Titurel* occur in Wolfram's list. A more recurrent difficulty is the syntax of the MHG, which is frequently obscure, and heavily dependent upon participial and prepositional constructions. At times this clearly puzzled the scribes copying the *Titurel*, who diverge, but frequently without making much sense of the obscurities. Consequently, there is much in this translation that is speculative. The repetitive nature of many of the strophes reflects that of the original. The use of internal rhyme makes considerable demands upon the poet and leads to much rhyme-compulsion, obscurity and repetition. To attempt a verse translation would only exacerbate the difficulties. This prose version is, however, often misleadingly clear.

The work begins with Albrecht's appeal to God for help in the narrative enterprise. The prologue is in part a paean to God the creator. It lays emphasis upon the sacrament of baptism, with water as the holy element. The wording is heavily reliant upon the prologue of Albrecht's model, Wolfram's *Parzival*, as when the theme of despair, *zwîvel*, is introduced. The Trojan and Roman ancestry of Titurel is traced. His grandfather Parillus converts to Christianity.

After Parillus's death, Titurel is born to Parillus's son, Titurison, and his wife, Elizabel. Titurel's upbringing and education are described, his education in letters and in knighthood. His mother seeks to keep him from all knowledge of love, but then a tutor acquaints him with the distinction between secular and divine love. Titurel opts for chastity. He and his father Titurison, in alliance with the Carolingians, wage war successfully on the heathen. There follow some moralising passages, including a dialogue between Wolfram and Lady Adventure. (Only towards the end of the work (strophe 5883, the penultimate strophe in manuscripts C and J) does Albrecht name himself; up to that point he preserves the fiction that the work is the continuation of *Parzival* and *Titurel* by Wolfram himself.) A diatribe against Ovid follows.

An angel announces that the chaste Titurel is called to the Grail. He leaves his tearful parents, and is taken by angels to Foreist Salvaesche, and to the mountain in its midst, Munt Salvasch, the home of the Grail, in the land of Salvaterre. There Titurel decides to build a temple for the Grail. The translated passage follows.

V

THE AWNTYRS OFF ARTHURE AT THE TERNE WATHELYNE: RELIQUARY FOR ROMANCE

Krista Sue-Lo Twu

I

In relation to the central strands of medieval Arthurian tradition, the Middle English *Awntyrs off Arthure at the Terne Wathelyne* appears decidedly peripheral. Next to the foundational historiography of Geoffrey of Monmouth's *History of the Kings of Britain*, the nuanced romances of Chrétien de Troyes, and the tragic, epic *Alliterative Morte Arthure*, the early fifteenth-century *Awntyrs off Arthur* is a late-comer which appears to be derivative in all the worst ways. Also, insofar as the *Awntyrs off Arthure* belongs to the 'Alliterative Revival' of the fourteenth and early fifteenth centuries,[1] it belongs to a set of long-marginalized texts that have received rather less attention than their rhymed, metrical contemporaries with their more patent continuities with later English poetic tradition. The texts of the 'Alliterative Revival' by and large originate in the west midlands and northern outskirts of England, far from the center of power in the metropolitan south.[2] Thorlac Turville-Petre notes that 'its contacts with the poetry of the metropolitan, Chaucerian tradition [whose form and dialect we inherit] seem to have been very slight', as indeed, 'the two schools seem to have ignored one another'.[3]

---

[1] Although evidence points to a certain continuity of alliterative writing in England, stretching from the twelfth through the fifteenth centuries, scholars generally agree that the 'immense and still largely unexplored difference in style and tone between the work of 1200 and that of 1350' (E. Salter, 'The Alliterative Revival I', *Modern Philology* 64 [1966], 164) sufficiently distinguishes later texts as a separate, if perhaps related, concern – whether or not one choses to designate it a 'revival'. Thorlac Turville-Petre emphasizes this point in his observations that 'both the bulk and the high quality of alliterative poetry written in this period of less than a hundred years are remarkable', and that 'there is no suggestion in alliterative poetry that the writers thought of themselves as anything but up to date and following contemporary fashions' (*The Alliterative Revival* [Cambridge, 1977], pp. 26–28).

[2] Thorlac Turville-Petre traces the development of the 'Alliterative Revival' from its establishment in the southwest midlands during the 1340s, through its spread to the northern parts of the west midlands in the 1350s, from whence it spread further north and east, and up into Scotland, in the 1390s, until its decline in the mid-fifteenth century; he notes, however, that in Scotland the form persisted through the sixteenth century (*The Alliterative Revival*, p. 35).

[3] *The Alliterative Revival*, pp. 35–36.

Furthermore, even though scholars mention the *Awntyrs* in their treatment of the 'alliterative school', it has not enjoyed the same attention as such well recognized texts as *Sir Gawain and the Green Knight* or *Piers Plowman*. It comes to us from the margins of the margins.

Scholars have long read the *Awntyrs* as a rather unhappy yoking together of two disparate plot elements, in which first the ghost of Guenevere's mother appears in order to admonish the court for its worldly vices and ambitions, and then in a seemingly unrelated episode, Gawain defends his territorial war prizes against their former lord, Galeron. The general consensus has been that the poem is an overwrought, unwholesome remnant of a greater Arthurian tradition or a pair of pallid imitations of its sources and analogues. *The Awntyrs off Arthure* thus has long suffered from critical neglect due to a scholarly tradition that tends to focus on the poem's formal elements and manuscript history. But this sort of criticism overlooks the sum of its parts. When a case for the poem's unity and coherence is pressed, its literary qualities and generic awareness are brought into relief, revealing a subtle poem which plays on our expectations about Arthur's court and its literary history.

Indeed, the *Awntyrs*' status as a late contribution to the Arthurian legend is not incidental, but crucial, since the poem ultimately functions as a commentary on the limitations of the romance genre. Furthermore, its manipulations of the history, corpus and status of Arthurian literature form its most strident articulation of the topos *sic transit gloria mundi*. Not only do these manipulations question the status of such glory, they question the fiction of such a world. Thus, in reading the *Awntyrs off Arthure* as a meta-Arthurian text, we observe that an intricate unity, terrible and pathetic, does bind together all of its seemingly disparate elements. Furthermore, the variations and repetitions that produce this unity, over and over again reinforce its argument that the aesthetics of chivalry belie its fundamental violence. Finally, the very self-conscious, extravagantly stylized, structure of the poem provides the ironic medium for simultaneously celebrating and mourning the fictions that it contains like a dazzling reliquary for the remains of an ossified discourse of romance.

II

In the late nineteenth century, Hermann Lübke's assertion that the *Awntyrs off Arthure*[4] is actually comprised of two separate poems[5] proved to be so influential in encouraging scholars to consider it a poorly conjoined, bipartite text, that Ralph Hanna's 1974 edition continues to present the poem under the subtitles 'The Awntyrs A' and 'The Awntyrs B', because '*The Awntyrs* may

---

[4] Four manuscripts of the text survive, all dating from the fifteenth century: Bodleian Library, MS Douce 324 (1460–1480); the Ireland-Blackburne MS (1450–1460); Lincoln Cathedral Library, Thornton MS 91 (1430–1440); and Lambeth Palace Library, MS 491 (1400–1425).

[5] H. Lübke, 'The Aunters of Arthur at the Tern-Wathelan, Teil I: Handschriften, Metrik, Verfasser', Inaugural-Dissertation zur Erlangung der Doctorwürde (Berlin, 1883), pp. 20–27.

represent not one poem but two'.[6] Although in 1985, Rosamund Allen[7] declared the debate over its 'organic unity' to be over (5), asserting that such unity 'is now recognised' (5) and that 'few would dispute' A. C. Spearing's arguments[8] regarding the links between the two parts (5, n. 1), the topic refuses to die peacefully, even within Allen's own article. Thus the debate on the structure has so far postponed extensive literary analysis of the text on its own merits and in relationship to the Arthurian canon.

Although Allen tantalizes us with hints of a thesis arguing that the meaning of the poem actually 'concerns the role of women in upper-class society' (6) by means of 'a satire on the chivalric ethos' (5), this thesis receives little development by means of elaboration or textual analysis. Instead, Allen advances her critique of the editing practices that constrain the poem, concluding with the suggestion that Lübke's 'compilation theory' could still be valid, and that it 'may well have been composed in *three* stages' (23, emphasis hers). Finally, to concur with Allen's suggestion that we cannot begin analysis in earnest until we are better able to approximate 'what the author wrote' (25), we risk applying our own anachronistic notion of author-ship to the poem in a manner that neglects the way medieval scribes and readers transmitted and received a possibly composite text. After all, as is the case with most medieval texts, the extant manuscripts of the *Awntyrs* do not preserve the name of the person who composed the poem, because medieval readers did not require the 'author-function' to endorse the literary value of narrative.[9]

Thus, four years after Allen's article, J. O. Fichte still asks if we should even take seriously the last stanza as 'genuine or . . . just added by some kind soul to achieve a semblance of formal closure'.[10] Even more recently, Helen Phillips' 1993 article on the structure and meaning of the poem vigorously expands and recomplicates the debate by considering further possibilities for critical interpretation of the poem based on a possibly *tri*partite structure. The debate regarding structure is alive and well in her assertion that 'none of the manuscripts simply divides the work into two halves to produce the binary

---

6 R. Hanna III, ed., *The Awntyrs off Arthure at the Terne Wathelyn: An Edition Based on Bodleian Library MS Douce 324* (Manchester, 1974), p. 17.

7 R. Allen, 'Some Sceptical Observations on the Editing of *The Awntyrs off Arthure*', in *Manuscripts and Texts: Editorial Problems in Later Middle English Literature. Essays from the 1985 Conference at the University of York*, ed. D. Pearsall (Cambridge, 1997).

8 See A. C. Spearing, 'Central and Displaced Sovereignty in Three Medieval Poems', *Review of English Studies* 33 (1982), and '*The Awntyrs off Arthure*', in *The Alliterative Tradition in the Fourtheenth Century*, ed. B. S. Levy and P. E. Szarmach (Ohio, 1981).

9 In 'What is an Author?', Michel Foucault addresses the changing role of the 'author-function' through-out literary history. He notes that in pre-modern literature, 'scientific' texts required the name of an author for validation and authentication in so far as such a name 'marked a proven discourse', quite the opposite of our current acceptance of scientific information as an internally verified system of truths and methods which does not require an author's name as an 'index of truthfulness' (in *Language, Counter-Memory, Practice*, ed. and trans. D. F. Bouchard [Cornell University Press, 1977], p. 126).

10 J. O. Fichte, '*The Awntyrs off Arthure*: An Unconscious Change of the Paradigm of Adventure', in *The Living Middle Ages*, ed. Böker (Stuttgart, 1989).

structure that has become a standard assumption for modern critics'.[11] To the contrary, Phillips shows how the scribal rubrication of the Ireland manuscript into three fittes presents a strong case against a binary reading, and how the resulting structural complexities carry the themes of territorial sovereignty and the Wheel of Fortune throughout the poem.

Apparently the medieval audience represented by the production of this particular manuscript did not consider it to be a poorly unified bipartite poem. Even if the 'two parts' were composed at different times by different poets, a composer at some point thought that these two parts should go together and combined them, as witnessed by the surviving manuscripts. Moreover, the case for single authorship may be advanced on codicological grounds – no extant manuscripts feature the two parts independently of each other, which we might expect if the parts were ever seen as separable[12] – and on stylistic and thematic grounds, according to Stephen Shepherd's proposition that 'the poem represents an eschatological unity wrought by one poet'.[13] One observes that the *Awntyrs off Arthure* is a tour de force of poetic achievement. It both alliterates and rhymes, employs a metrically regular 'bob and wheel' and concatenates throughout, performing more tricks per stanza than even *Sir Gawain and the Green Knight*.[14] Derek Pearsall lauds it as 'exceptionally advanced and complex',[15] and A. I. Doyle posits that this very complexity in its 'stanzaic and rhyming structure will surely have helped to maintain [the text] in part from corruption'.[16] By means of these structural complexities, the poem offers shifting frames of reference that add up to a unified whole, which, as Spearing asserts, asks 'the reader to participate in the creation of a meaning that is larger than [what each of the parts] possesses in isolation' (249). Furthermore, as Phillips notes, the poem's shifting frames of reference include a variety of allusions to the *Alliterative Morte Arthure* and the Arthur myth at large. Phillips concludes that 'criticism is unlikely to return again to the view that its design is meagre or naive' (88), an observation which invites further consideration of the merits of the *Awntyrs*' design and analysis of the work's place in the medieval English Arthurian tradition.

[11] H. Phillips, 'The *Awntyrs off Arthure*: Structure and Meaning', *Arthurian Literature* XII (1993), p. 65.

[12] One might think, for instance, of the many tales from Chaucer's *Canterbury Tales* that appear independently in fifteenth-century miscellanies.

[13] S. H. A. Shepherd, 'The Awntyrs off Arthure at the Terne Wathelyne', in his *Middle English Romances* (New York, 1995), p. 369.

[14] The poem employs a thirteen-line alliterative and rhyming stanza composed of nine four-stress lines, rhymed ababababc, and a four-line wheel with two to three stresses per line, rhymed dddc (although some scholars might not count it as truly alliterative, because of the homomorphological meter). Iteration generally occurs between the eighth and ninth lines. Concatenation links the stanzas together; the last two short lines of the poem round off the pattern by repeating the first line of the poem. Thorlac Turville-Petre links its nine-line stanzaic pattern with the form adopted by fifteenth- and sixteenth-century Scottish poets (*The Alliterative Revival*, p. 35).

[15] D. Pearsall, 'The Alliterative Revival: Origins and Social Backgrounds', in *Middle English Alliterative Poetry and its Literary Background: Seven Essays*, ed. D. Lawton (Cambridge, 1982), p. 36.

[16] A. I. Doyle, 'The Manuscripts', in *Middle English Alliterative Poetry and its Literary Background: Seven Essays*, ed. D. Lawton (Cambridge, 1982), p. 96.

III

The kingly figure of Arthur unifies the poem. In contrast to many of the Arthurian romances, in which Arthur appears as a figurehead and his court as a point of departure for the adventure, he remains the center of the court and the occasion for action throughout the *Awntyrs off Arthure*. Indeed, the Arthurian court itself, as a social and juridical body, provides the setting for the poem, which meditates on the court's powers and limitations in each of the episodes. Phillips notes that, while modern readers usually do not recognize the passages that describe Arthur's kingly status and power as a distinct narrative element at all, the Ireland manuscript does distinguish this section as a separate fitt (71). This fitt, the second of three, begins with the ghost's prophecy about the doom to befall Arthur's court as a result of his territorial ambitions and ends with Galeron's challenge to reclaim the territories Arthur had taken from him in war. In the middle of the fitt, and thus in the center of the work as a whole, Arthur sits in state at Rondelsette Hall. While Phillips presents this manuscript's divisions as an alternative to the bipartite reading, Arthur's enthronement here at the exact center of the poem, 'soveraynest of al' (358), provides a meridian at which the Arthurian sun has reached its noon.[17] But far from dividing the parts, the centrality of Arthur's kingship here provides a unifying device for the whole poem. Like the sun at noon, Arthur's reign creates its own day from which morning and evening are measured. Arthur's kingly presence illuminates all of the disparate features of the poem: the Ghost's warning to Guenevere regarding the infidelity that eventually will contribute to the dissolution of Arthur's court; its warning to Gawain about the vicissitudes of fortune and the revolutions of power through military conquest; and Galeron's challenge to Arthur's annexation of his lands. Furthermore, the poem's preoccupation with Arthur's kingship and the right relationship between the powers and duties of kingship manifests itself in its constant reference to Arthur by title, 'the King', rather than by name, except in the first and last lines, as if his name were a headnote and footnote to this shining circuit of power.

This centralized image of kingship also makes possible the perfection of the courtly way of life depicted in the poem, and seems to stem from the political context of the mid- to late fourteenth century. Elizabeth Salter finds that 'the facts seem to be clear: the new flowering of alliterative poetry in the west and north midlands coincides almost exactly with a period of remarkable accord between crown and baronage'.[18] And so we see this relationship idealized in Arthur's court. Only at its apex can it create the conditions for the poem's display of peace and leisure, where the court can ride to hunt instead of to war, and a dispute can be settled in tournament rather than in mortal

---

[17] Citations are from S. H. A. Shepherd's edition of the *Awntyrs off Arthure at the Terne Wathelyne* in *Middle English Romances*, based on text of Oxford, Bodleian Library, MS Douce 324 (*D*).

[18] 'The Alliterative Revival I', p. 146.

combat. Hence the poem's continual celebration of this courtly standard provides a logic that unifies the hunt, the occasion for the first *awntyr*, with the duel between Gawain and Galeron, and with the elaborate verse style itself. Each of these elements celebrates the normative aristocratic values of the court, highlighting the aristocracy's aesthetic prerogatives as well as its license to express and contain violence.

In the *Awntyrs*, the hunt takes place strictly at and for the king's pleasure. Other medieval texts also treat the hunt as an exclusively aristocratic pastime. The activity served to identify the military elite, and functioned as a substitution and preparation for war. The game animals legally belong to the king, and the unified participation of the entire court, 'dukes and dussiperes that with the dere dwelles' (4), emphasizes their solidarity. William the Conqueror himself instituted royal hunting preserves in England, restricting hunting in preserves to the king and those whom he personally invited to participate, effecting a royal monopoly on the sport until 1217, when forest hunting rights were extended to the nobility as well.[19] Indeed, the *Awntyrs*' hunt takes place 'in forest frydde' (7). Furthermore, the strict rules and rituals that the govern the hunt offer some constraints upon the violence inherent in the activity. First of all, the hunt limits the killing to animals, allowing an expression of some of the court's bloody impulses, but preserving and even improving human life in the process. The early fourteenth-century penitential manual, *Handlyng Synne*, recommends hunting to 'emperorus and to kyngys . . ./ Erlës, barons, . . ./ and knygtës . . ./ þat þey ne be tempted of ouþer synne', such as robbing one's neighbors,[20] and the early fifteenth-century *Master of Game*, by Edward, Second Duke of York, asserts that 'hunting causeth a man to eschew the seven deadly sins'.[21] Next, the poem places the hunt during the 'fermesones' (8), the close season between 14 September and 24 June, when male deer were off limits; the season opens in July and lasts through August. Open season for female deer lasts from 11 November until 2 February.[22] The *Awntyrs* refers to these rules in its statement of the hunters' intent 'to fall of the femailes' (7), restricting themselves to the fair game of 'thes baraynes' (41). The enforcement of these hunting seasons moderates the environmental impact of the hunt by protecting the animals' reproductive chances. Limiting the hunt through the 'fermesones' ensures that female deer will only be killed after the young have been weaned, so that the death of a doe does not also doom the fawn to starvation, but allows it to survive to sexual maturity and ensure the abundance of future hunts. The rules of hunting ensure the future of the pastime by means of these limitations on the scope of its inherent violence.

[19] See C. Reeves, *Pleasures and Pastimes in Medieval England* (Stroud, 1995), pp. 103–104.

[20] Robert Mannyng of Brunne, *Robert of Brunne's Handlyng Synne, 1303*, ed. F. J. Furnivall, EETS 119 and 123 (London, 1901, 1903), lines 3083–3094, 2195–2200.

[21] *The Master of Game, By Edward, 2nd Duke of York, ca.1413*, ed. W. A. and F. Baillie-Grohman (London 1909), p. 4.

[22] See Shepherd, 'The Awntyrs', p. 220, n. 4. See also T. Hahn, 'The Awntyrs off Arthur', in *Sir Gawain: Eleven Romances and Tales* (Kalamazoo, 1995), n. 8.

Likewise, the duel between Gawain and Galeron provides another means of simultaneously expressing and containing a violence that might otherwise threaten the court. The exercise of the tournament allows for the violent expression of dissent or complaint, but also allows the king to determine the size, scope and location of the armed conflict. Arthur's power here reflects that of a medieval English sovereign. Richard I's regulations governing tournaments established the king's sole prerogative to license them in 1194; Edward I set up strict limits on the number of participants and the type of weapons allowed and authorized a committee to enforce the rules in his *Statuata Armorum* of 1292; and Edward III's establishment of the Order of the Garter in the 1340s made tournaments part of royal policy.[23] Thus, the *Awntyrs* acknowledges Arthur's kingship as an organizing authority for the duel. Gawain must ask for the king's permission, 'Lorde, by your leve' (468), and adhere to the conditions, the time, and the participants that 'the King gared commaunde' (481) in order to fight. Furthermore, the concatenation of 'The King commaunde(d)' between lines 481 and 482, linking commands issued in the evening with commands issued the next day, emphasizes the personal efficacy of the king in his governance of the court. Finally, this phrase resonates at the battle's conclusion when 'the King . . ./ commaunded pes' (649–650).

As the duel commences, the absolute formality of procedure follows the recommendations 'as was the manere' (498) of the *Statuata Armorum* to establish a committee to oversee the tournament. The committee of peers comprised of 'the lordes [who] bylyve hom to list ledes' (497) provides a juridical apparatus, while the 'many serjant of mace' (498) form a police force to ensure order. Michael Camille and other historians of English tournaments note that, especially in contested border areas in the north of England, such as in the vicinity of Carlisle in Cumberland where the poem locates itself,[24] 'jousting often turned into the real thing in these charged situations'.[25] For example, the outcome of William Marmion's tournament experience at Lincoln led him to engage in a very real battle, with nearly fatal results, with the Scots at the besieged Norham Castle in the 1320s.[26] This historical situation underscores the danger implicit in Galeron's request to engage Gawain in

---

[23] V. G. Kiernan discusses the establishment of the Order of the Garter with its court of honor to supervise dueling (*The Duel in European History: Honour and the Reign of Aristocracy* [Oxford, 1988], pp. 40–41), and Maurice Keen notes that in addition to promoting 'activities such as tourneying', the Order of the Garter, like other secular chivalric orders of its time, 'took pains to tap every resource of the literary mythology of chivalry to decorate and romanticise the associations that they instituted and to give them a lofty tone' (*Chivalry* [New Haven, 1984], p. 190).

[24] The poem itself locates Arthur's seat of power, and the seat of the conspiracy that will depose him, 'at Carlele' (288). Tarn Wadling lies approximately ten miles south of Carlisle, 'in Ingulwud Forest' (709), and manor houses such as Randalholme, Randasset, and Randerside Hall in the vicinity of Inglewood Forest suggest possible sources for the text's 'Rondoles Halle' (337) where Galeron issues his challenge.

[25] M. Camille, *Mirror in Parchment: The Lutrell Psalter and the Making of Medieval England* (Chicago, 1998), p. 61.

[26] Sir Thomas Gray, *Scalacronica*, ed. H. Maxwell (Glasgow, 1907), p. 61.

single combat. Galeron's introduction of himself as 'the grettest of Galwey' (418), the Scottish district immediately adjacent to Cumberland, emphasizes the personal stake he holds in the ongoing border dispute over Arthur's annexation of Galloway along with Carrick, Cunningham, Cummock, Kyle, Lanark, Lennox and Loudun Hill, all in the southwest of Scotland (419–420). His challenge explicitly calls for an alternative to war, which Galeron claims Arthur cheated at 'with a wrange wile' (421), in order to recover these territories now governed by Gawain.

But as fragile and unlikely as the peace may seem here, it nonetheless exists at the pleasure of the utopian court. In fact, the aesthetic trappings of the tournament display a greater sense of solidarity than division among the aristocratic participants on either side of the conflict. When Galeron presents himself, he follows the courtly conventions of peacetime. Instead of a military guard, 'a soteler with a symballe/ [and] A lady, lufsom of lote' (343–344) announces his entrance and requests justice, 'reson and right' (350), rather than declaring war. Immediately upon this entrance, Arthur recognizes the visitor as a fellow nobleman and, promising to uphold courtly standards of 'reson and right' (362) pursuant to his rank, acknowledges his claim to the title 'knight' (363). While the use of the familiar or contemptuous 'thou' (405–438) implies antagonism, in their interchange, the poem clearly identifies Galeron not as an outsider, but as a fully-fledged member of the aristocracy in its description of his arrival with entourage. He enjoys the same trappings of wealth and authority as any knight of Arthur's court, including a lady who 'was the worthiest wight that eny weld wolde' (365), whose courtly 'gide was glorious and gay' (366) and comparable to Arthur's queen, Gaynour, herself 'in a gleterand gide that glemed full gay' (15). Hence, the court accepts the strange knight and lady based on her appearance and comportment as one of the trappings of his nobility:

> Bright birdes and bolde
> Had ynoghe to beholde
> Of that frely to folde –
> And the hende knight.   (374–377)

The lady's appearance provides reason 'ynoghe' for the women to accept her into their fold and hence, to surmise that Galeron is as 'hende' a 'knight' as he is 'comli' (363).

Moreover, Galeron's own apparel and accoutrements signal his fully-fledged membership in the aristocracy through their use of heraldic conventions and their ostentatious display of wealth and military preparation. The first full description of Galeron begins by telling us that 'the knight in his colours was armed ful clene' (378), the concatenation of the term 'knight' (377, 378) adding emphasis. This re-statement of Galeron's status as a 'knight' (377, 378) renders conclusive the lady's assertion of his knighthood (349) along with Arthur's and the court's acceptance of this rank (363, 377) as an unassailable fact and legitimate title. Furthermore, the poem's reference to the elaborate and exacting science of heraldry in the 'colours' and black bear-head device (385) that Galeron carries further emphasizes the shared aristocratic identity and solidarity of all parties involved. The rest of his war gear, deadly and decorative, announces both the requisite wealth and military prowess proper to his estate, while his horse, equally deadly and decorated, provides the *sine qua non* of a *chevalier*.[27]

Arthur's court therefore extends its brotherly hospitality to Galeron, despite his complaint and intent to engage in juridical combat, inviting him, 'if [he] be curteys knight,/ [to] Lighte, and lenge al nyght' (414–415). The combatants hold no personal animosity toward each other. On the contrary, earlier in the poem, Gawain expresses misgivings about the way the knights of Arthur's court 'defoulen the folke on fele kinges londes,/ And riches over rymes withouten eny right' (262–263), foreshadowing Galeron's grievance, and opening a space for sympathizing with it. Thus, 'Gawayn the good glades hour gest' (458) himself, tending not only to the comfort of Galeron, but also to his retinue and even his horse, before the tournament. A description of the luxurious guest-lodgings for both man and beast occupies two and a half stanzas. It details the quality of the en-suite accommodations including 'a chapell, a chambour, a halle,/ [and] A chymné with charcole to chaufe the knight' (445–446), like a miniature, private manor house, and featuring a color scheme reserved for high ranking nobles, in the 'purpour and palle' (443) decor. Plus, a most refined dinner service features both quantity and quality with matching wine courses and elegant tableware, 'with riche dayntes dight/ In silver so shene' (454–455) for the humans, and 'hay hertly ... in haches on hight' (448) for the horse. This scene details the way that both Galeron's entourage and Arthur's court function according to the same social conventions in peacetime activities as well as in war. Moreover, Arthur's approval for the tournament itself, as a substitute for war, depends on Galeron's acceptance of this hospitality, his willingness to place himself in his adversary's care, to 'lighte, and lenge al nyght' (415), in order to prove that he is indeed, a 'curteys knight' (414) and deserves the right to engage Gawain as an equal.

Indeed, the poem itself participates in this aristocratic solidarity, not only by means of its setting, but also through the aesthetic detail that so marks the concerns of a rich warrior class in the habit of clothing itself with such things as 'griffons of golde engreled full gay,/ Trifeled with tranes and true-loves bitwene' (509–510). The loving descriptions of the deluxe armor decorated 'with graynes of rybé, that graithed ben gay' (394), but also deadly, down to the 'schynbaudes that sharp wer to shrede' (395), display the poem's keen observation, and shared interest, regarding the accoutrements of wealth and power. Even the poetic conventions in which the poem indulges – and perhaps

---

27 Denys Hay remarks that the 'origins of chivalric ideas belong to an earlier age, when only the knight was a fully-fledged member of lay society and where knights were practically all men of war. By the fourteenth century the reality was different, but the old ideas coloured literature and to some extent affected practical affairs' (*Europe in the Fourteenth and Fifteenth Centuries*, 2nd edn [London, 1989], pp. 71–72).

for our modern taste, over-indulges – hint at the its participation in the life of leisure led by the nobility. The poem plays with the possibilities of language in its alliterations and concatenations. It has a large word hoard to explore and sufficient time to exploit it.[28] It does not progress efficiently.[29] Rather, the traditional poetic diction and the repetition of commonplace superlatives, such as 'pruddest in palle' (66, 335), the use of semantically empty declarations, such as 'the trouthe for to telle' (34) and its variations (35, 314) or 'by boke and by belle' (30), and epithets adding no information, such as 'burnes so bolde' (40), 'bonkes so bare' (41), 'holtes so hare' (43), 'cliffes so colde' (44), intensifies mood, but impedes narrative progress.[30] We should further note that the highest concentration of these conspicuous words occurs in the description of the hunt (40–52), the ultimate upper-class leisure activity. The poem indulges itself and its aristocratic audience in the pure leisure of time passing through art for its own sake.[31]

Thus, as the spectacle of the tournament commences, the poem emphasizes the equality of the combatants as members of this wealthy, elite warrior-caste, in the extravagance of their armor, and in their mutual courage and prowess. A

---

28 J. P. Oakden remarks that in order to produce alliterative poetry of this sort, 'the poets in question must have had a very large common stock of such phrases from which to draw' (*Alliterative Poetry in Middle English: A Survey of the Traditions* [Manchester, 1935], p. 263). Turville-Petre also observes that 'this sort of style . . . demands a very wide vocabulary' (*The Alliterative Revival*, p. 70).

29 As Turville-Petre dryly comments, with regard to the style of such poetry, 'the poet is in no hurry to move his story along' (*The Alliterative Revival*, p. 69).

30 J. P. Oakden identifies '1415 distinct alliterative phrases and a total number of instances of roughly 4250', indicating that the poets of the 'Alliterative Revival' 'must have had a very large common stock of such phrases from which to draw' (*Alliterative Poetry*, p. 263). He provides an extensive list of such phrases, with references to their origins in Old English and early Middle English alliterative poetry (pp. 267–312), although Roger Dalrymple notes that this catalogue does not include alliterative pious formulae (*Language and Piety in Middle English Romance* [Cambridge, 2000], p. 15, n. 42). Dalrymple's catalogue of these pious formulae can be found ibid., pp. 149–250. Most scholars agree that we should not consider this large common stock of phrases as strong evidence regarding the relationships between the poems, but Dalrymple's work cautions us to attend to the semantic and literary value of common phrases, despite their formulaic nature.
   • RE: 'trouthe for to telle' see also, 'trouthe to telle' (*Richard the Redeles*, ii.41); 'þe truth for to telle' (*The Destruction of Troy*, 51, 106, *William of Palerne*, 5022).
   • RE: 'by boke and by belle,' see also, 'by bel and by boke' (*Ywain and Gawain*, 3023); 'bell oþer book' (*Pierce the Ploughman's Crede*, 115).
   • RE: 'burnes so bolde,' see also 'burneʒ (so) bolde' (*Sir Gawain and the Green Knight*, 1574, *Mum and the Sothsegger*, 144, 165); 'beryn be so bolde' (*Wynnere and Wastoure*, 126, 131); 'no buerne was so bolde' (*The Destruction of Troy*, 12887); 'euery bearne full boldlye' (*Scottish Field*, 178); 'bolde b(e)urn(e)' (*Alexander*, 9, *Sir Gawain and the Green Knight*, 1631, 2338, 2524, *The Destruction of Jerusalem*, 271, 659, *Parlement of the Thre Ages*, 110, 527, *William of Palerne*, 3817).

31 As a great many medieval poems rely on formulaic phrases to fill in alliterative and/or rhyme patterns, one might argue that courtly poetry in general engages in the idleness of time passing by means of these cliches and conventional phrases. Turville-Petre argues that, based on the idealized setting and the persona of the narrator as a court-entertainer, both commonplace to many romances, 'whatever their actual social and physical positions, however decrepit or preoccupied with mundane affairs they may be, the listeners and readers (whether in the fourteenth century or the twentieth) are invited to imagine themselves for the occasion as a noble company sitting in some baronial hall' (*The Alliterative Revival*, pp. 37–38).

single description of their virtually identical battle dress and symmetrically choreographed maneuvers suffices for both:

> Gawayn and Galeron gurden her stedes;
> Al in gleterand golde, gay was here gere.
> The lordes bylyve hom to list ledes
> With many serjant of mace, as was the manere.
> The burnes broched the blonkes that the side bledis.
> Ayther freke opon fold has fastned his spere;
> Shaftes in shide-wode thei shindre, in shedes,
> So jolilé thes gentil justed on were.
> Shaftes thei shindr in sheldes so shene;
> > And sithen, with brondes bright,
> > Riche mayles thei right.   (495–505)

After identifing Gawain and Galeron in the first line, the poem compasses them together under the third-person plural pronoun: 'her'/'here' (495, 496) in the genitive case, 'hom' (497) in the accusative, 'thei' (501, 503, 505) in the nominative. We also see them grouped together in the plural objective correlative form, 'thes gentil' (502), identifying them according to their mutual status as gentlemen, with perhaps a touch of irony, considering the occasion. Here, the 'burnes' (499) lack individuating markers. They both appear 'al in gleterand golde, gay . . . gere' (496). Both proceed to the lists with an escort of peers and guards in parade (497–498). They have the exact same battle strategy for the duel, which results in identical damage to both of their spears, which 'in shide-wode thei shindre, in shedes' (501), and identical damage to their armor, the 'riche mayles [that] thei right' (505). The poem even remarks on their well matched gallantry, 'so jolilé thes gentil justed on were' (502), extolling their internal as well as external similarities, shining in the sun of the Arthurian noon.

IV

However refractive of the splendor of the Arthurian setting, though, this military brotherhood cannot last, and this moment of resplendent violence puts the question to its efficacy as a rhetoric of civilization. After all, even here, when the court is functioning at its best, the best they can do is agree to fight. The court does not offer litigation or a peaceful compromise, but merely clothes its violence in the gorgeous trappings of peace-time games. Arthur cannot eliminate violence, only limit it to the two main disputants.

The fight itself questions the genre's implicit assertions about the efficacy of personal agency to bring about justice or to make right or even to use might for right. Despite the regulatory procedures and safety measures ostensibly present with the 'serjant of mace' (548) in attendance, the tournament goes awry. After that first perfect pass, Gawain 'strikes on stray' (511), trespassing outside the marked bounds of the lists, which causes Galeron to respond in anger at 'siche deray' (513). From this first violation of the rules, chaos encroaches on and eventually takes over the scene, such that the next exchange of blows results in a wound 'that greved Sir Gawayn to his deth day' (515). Thus the fight lapses into earnest violence with the potential for permanent injury.

Furthermore, as the physical damage mounts, the brotherly love fades. Whereas before we see the shared spirits of these two 'gentil' as they 'jolilé . . . justed on were' (502), now we see them reacting to each other in anger. Galeron 'talkes in tene' (512) at Gawain's trespass, 'lothely . . . lowe uppon hight' (523) in a display of poor sportsmanship at his advantage, and 'strikes on stray' himself when he 'swykes' by beheading Gawain's horse. In response, Gawain 'greches terwith and gremed ful sare' (524), taking the injury and affront personally, rather than with the expected professional aplomb. In contrast, one might consider the fight between Gawain and Priamus in the *Alliterative Morte Arthure*, which ends on as brotherly a note as possible. Gawain spares Priamus and admonishes him to 'Grouch not, good sir, though me this grace happen' (2644), and Priamus, far from grouching, is delighted to have been defeated by such a worthy and noble opponent, rather than just 'any priker' (2649). The *Awntyrs* dismantles the aristocratic privilege supposedly informing the tournament, as it dismantles the ostensible signs of their aristocratic privilege, their armor and horses. This demolition exposes the irony of 'thes gentil', no longer at all 'jolilé', but angrily and bloodily, engaged 'on were' (502).

Thus, as the fight degenerates into a free-for-all, the two combatants resemble one another in a deeper sense. That is to say, the vulnerable flesh beneath their armor bleeds the same color blood. At the outset of the tournament, only their heraldic colors distinguish them from one another. By the end of the tournament, the blood, gore and other violence defaces and obliterates their heraldic markings. Indeed, they are too well matched in their fighting capacities. They do each other equal damage, and as before, they are described as one:

> Hardely then thes hathelese on helmes they hewe.
> They beten downe beriles and bourdures bright;
> Shildes on shildrew that shene were to shewe,
> Fretted were in fyne golde, thei failen in fight;
> Stones of iral they strenkel and strewe;
> Stithe stapeles of stele they strike don stright.   (586–591)

Identical in their actions, they inflict identical wounds on each other, simultaneously chipping the myriad jewels and decorations from each other's armor. They strip each other of the aesthetic veneer of chivalry and deface the heraldic markers of personal identification.

Gawain's horse also dies in the fight, decapitated (541) – quite literally defaced – and Galeron offers a replacement, that 'may stonde the in stoure in as mekle stede' (552), because a fight between *chevaliers* cannot go on without *chevaus*. Indeed, the fight almost stops when Gawain's grief for this loss nearly overcomes him:

> Als he stode by his stede
> That was so goode at nede,
> Ner Gawayn wax wede,
>   So wepputte he full sare.   (556–559)

More than the defacement of the coats of arms, the loss of the horse strips the very terms of the knight's aristocratic identity, taking the *cheval* out of the *chevalier*.

This stripping away of the exterior trappings of rank and wealth reveals the underlying, inner sameness of their mortality, thus reminding us once again of the Ghost's appearance in the rotting rags of its mortal remains along with its warning to

> Muse on my mirrour,
> For, king and emperour,
>   Thus dight shul ye be.   (166–169)

As they wound each other, their injuries render them indistinguishable in their mortality, just as all, regardless of rank, become the same in death. Just as the Ghost is 'blak to the bone' (105), here as the exhausted combatants reach their physical limits, 'her blees wex blak . . . brosed for beting of brondes' (658–659). Even their faces become indistinguishable as their individuating facial features are bruised beyond recognition. Moreover, Arthur's court reacts with undifferentiated horror at the chaos. Rather than cheering on their champion, as one might expect,

> Both Sir Lote and Sir Lake
> Miche mornyng thei make.
> Gaynor gret for her sake
>   With her grey eyen.   (595–598)

Here again the poem treats the combatants with the third person plural pronoun, 'her', while insisting on the individuality of the onlookers, Sir Lote, Sir Lake and Gaynor. Insofar as the combatants have lost their individual identity in this fight, the court cannot identify with one or the other and thus finds its own identity threatened as it appears that the fight is coming to a draw. The very possibility of a stalemate here puts to doubt both the court's function as a juridical body and the romance genre's insistent premise that personal agency can effect change, progress or improvement.

The court's uniformly horrified reaction to the ungovernable extent of this violence threatens the very stability of the monarchy. The individual nobles of the court, 'both Sir Lote and Sir Lake' (595), stand united in their 'mornyng' (596). The ensuing request to stop the fight implies that the search for justice through combat no longer matters, undermining the function of the court as a legal body. Guenevere's particular part in this request even further expresses the crisis in the identity and authority of the court. As she 'wilfully . . . to the King went;/ . . . caught of her coronall and kneled him tille' (625–626), she divests herself of the symbols of her royal authority and physically lowers herself in a gesture of humility. She paradoxically insists on the corporate identity she shares with the king by virtue of their marriage contract. In her articulation of their marital status, 'As thou art roy roial . . ./ And I thi wife' (627), she lays claim to the biblical function of marriage uniting 'duo in carne una' (Gen. 2:24).[32] The image of intercession is unsettling in context, opening a rift in the court's corporate identity. For a moment here, as the Queen uncrowns herself and abases herself before her husband – her other half – the monarchy is beside itself and at odds with itself in a very literal way. Paradoxically too, in the moment of her abasement and abdication, she represents herself as the voice of the court in her declaration that 'hit were a grete conforde/ For all that here ware' (636–637) if the King would stop the fight.[33]

Stopping the fight, however, implies that justice no longer matters and undermines the procedures of law, while suggesting that the court cannot contain the violence that threatens it. When the fight finally stutters to a draw and Galeron yields the battle along with his territorial claims with the statement that, 'byfore thiese ryalle, [I] resynge the my right' (641), the terms of his withdrawal demonstrate that the contest has been ineffective on all accounts. Even though he refers to the judiciary function of the court to oversee the legal contest, his act of surrender proves it irrelevant as a juridical body, relegating it to the status of mere witness, and his articulation of his resignation retains an affirmation of his 'right' (641) to his lands. The conclusion to the fight fails to preserve the court's judiciary function.

Thus, at the height of its powers, we see the elements of the Arthurian court's eventual fall. The intrinsic failure to mitigate violence and effect justice in this display of the court's ostensible power returns us to the Ghost's prophecy with its invocation of Fortune, 'that wonderfull whelewryghte,/ [who] Shall make lordes lowe to light' (271–272), as the driving force behind history. Here too, the poem invokes the imagery of the Wheel lifting up and casting down those caught in her grasp. The end of the fight illustrates these vicissitudes:

---

[32] *Biblia sacra vulgata* (Stuttgart, 1969).

[33] Paul Strohm discusses the changing status of queens, as their roles shifted from fully involved active participants in affairs of state in the twelfth century to passive contributors whose 'influence was *petitionary*, in the sense that it cast the queen as one seeking redress rather than one able to institute redress in her own right, and *intercessory*, in that it limited its objectives to the modification of a previously determined male resolve' in the fourteenth century (*Hochon's Arrow: The Social Imagination of Fourteenth-Century Texts* [Princeton, 1992], p. 95). His analysis of Froissart's presentation of Queen Philippa's intercessory powers in Edward III's dispute with Calais and Anne of Bohemia's role as intercessor and mediatrix between Richard II and the citizens of London, in which the queens are 'linked to the king by marriage and the city by sympathy' (109), offers historical parallels for Guenevere's efficacy as *'femina ex machina*, entering from beyond the boundaries of systematized male power' (104) in the *Awntyrs*. Strohm notes the importance of the 'spontaneous emotionality attributed to the state of powerless abjection' that allows a queen to negotiate between the king's two bodies, public and private, as husband and monarch (104–105).

Downe kneled the knight
And carped wordes on hight.
The King stode upright
    And commaunded pes.   (646–650)

As Galeron yields, his fortunes fall, and we see him lowered down, kneeling, in response. Likewise, we see Arthur's fortunes rise, and reciprocally, he stands up. Indeed, the poem ends with him at the height of his fortunes, upright and commanding, but inevitably, we understand from this image that he too must someday fall. Fundamentally, the Wheel of Fortune conflicts with the narrative trajectory of romance. In its mechanical cycle of recovery and loss, it negates the prospect that individual choice, will or action can do anything to change the individual's fate. The poem's didactic dimension thus unfolds in this 'awntyr' at the apogee of the Arthurian kingdom.

V

Since the beginnings of the genre, all Arthurian stories have been overdetermined by the audience always already having known the story. In the *Awntyrs of Arthure at the Terne Wathelyne*, the poet builds an occasion for narrative reflection into the first plot element by means of the fact that the only people who do not know how the story will end are the characters themselves. Indeed, the deep tragedy of the *Awntyrs* resides in the inability of the characters to comprehend their fates despite the prophetic vision granted by the ghost. No 'mylion of masses' (706) can avert it, and we are left with the lie of the title itself.[34] The 'aunter' that provides the generic marker enclosing the poem in the concatenation of its first and last lines, here functions as a cruel moment of irony. In a conventional context of a literary romance, the term *awntyr* or *aventure* signals a chance of danger or loss offering the opportunity for the protagonists of a romance to rebound, recover and improve, but the ghost's warning itself attempts to avert the danger threatening the court.[35] So on one hand, no chance of new danger emerges with the haunting, and on the

---

34 Helen Phillips traces the title by which we know the poem to the Thornton manuscript, and notes the role that the appearance of the plural 'Awntyrs' has had in the debate over the poem's unity (or lack thereof) and meaning ('The Awntyrs', 73). For instance, we see how it might provide evidence for a bipartite reading, and how various critics have used it to argue that the poem is really about Gawain or the role of women in courtly society (see D. N. Klausner, 'Exempla and *The Awntyrs of Arthure*', *Mediaeval Studies* 34 [1972], 317; and A. C. Spearing, '*The Awntyrs off Arthure*', pp. 199–200, also noted in R. Allen, 'Some Sceptical Observations', p. 6).
35 The *Middle English Dictionary* offers the following definitions: '1. Fate, fortune, chance; plur. one's fortunes; one's circumstances; the outcome of something. 2. Something that happens, an event, an occurrence; an experience; an accident; plur. events, vicissitudes. 3. Danger, jeopardy, risk. 4. A venture, an enterprise. 5. A marvelous thing, a wonder, a miracle' (ed. H. Kurath [University of Michigan Press, 1956], A.546–549). With regard to Galeron's challenge to the court, we should also note the relationship of the term *awntyr* or *aventure* with the medieval Latin term, *adventura*, which enters the lexicon in the thirteenth century with the following definitions: '1. jousting. 2. lost or wrecked goods. 3. occasional profits of a feudal character. 4. casual judiciary profits' (*Mediae Latinitatis Lexicon Minus*, ed. J. F. Niermeyer [Leiden, 2001], p. 24).

other hand, if the ghost's warning constitutes an opportunity to avert a pre-existing danger, the total arc of the narrative thwarts any such possibility by foregrounding its own tragic conclusion. Hence, the text itself provides no opening, no opportunity to move from loss to recovery as we would expect from a romance. Instead, the pre(in)scribed 'history' – the 'legend' – of Arthur's court becomes the ghost lingering to haunt its characters, and the *awntyr* of the text, an always already missed opportunity.[36]

This meta-generic content elevates the poem beyond the scope of a moral tale and, contrary to W. R. J. Barron's assertion that 'the Arthurian world provides a casual rather than an essential setting for' the poem,[37] the Arthurian apparatus is indeed essential. The Arthurian context forces its readers to confront the ghosts of its literary ancestors even as it weaves an elaborate burial shroud for its own generic possibilities through the temporal looping and interwoven textures of its concatenations and alliterations. Form informs content joining each line and stanza to the next, the ending to the beginning, such that epic and romance both ghost their own textual reliquary in the form of the spectral history informing the poem. The power of the Ghost's warnings and prophecies depends on the vast fund of previous Arthurian literature to provide the poet and audience with a shared discourse on the genre, such that we tremble with pity at the inevitability of those predictions. Likewise, the juxtaposition of the court at its noon described in the present of the poem and its ruinous future, as prophesied by the Ghost, generate an apprehension of loss.

Usually, Arthurian romance narratives depend on the secular stability of the court to provide a point of departure for the individual knight to distinguish himself. Geoffrey of Monmouth's description of Arthur's plenary court gives us a foundational moment for the standard Arthurian point of departure. In Geoffrey's utopian vision, the world lapses into peace when 'Britain had reached such a standard of sophistication that it excelled all other kingdoms in its general affluence, the richness of its decorations, and the courteous behaviour of its inhabitants'.[38] During this time of peace and prosperity, when the court is at its apex, the knights fight only in 'imitation battle' (ix.14) for the amusement of the 'womenfolk [who] watched from the top of the city walls and aroused them to passionate excitement by their flirtatious behaviour' (ix.14). Violence and erotic desire mutually reinforce each other, such that 'the womenfolk became chaste and more virtuous and for their love the knights were ever more daring' (ix.14), and thus as these private relationships between knights and ladies work to the public good, they accrue independent

---

36 Here I pressure the Latin etymology of the term from *lego, legere, legi, lectum* 'to read' and thus in the gerundive, second periphrastic conjugation *legenda*, 'things which must be read'. See *Allen and Greenough's New Latin Grammar*, ed. Greenough, Kittredge, Howard and D'Ooge (New York, reprint, 1983), § 158.d.1.

37 W. R. J. Barron, 'Alliterative Romance and the French Tradition', in *Middle English Alliterative Poetry and its Literary Background: Seven Essays*, ed. D. Lawton (Cambridge, 1982), p. 73.

38 Geoffrey of Monmouth, *History of the Kings of Britain*, trans. L. Thorpe (Harmondsworth, 1966), ix.14.

value. As these erotic relationships ennoble the participants, inspiring greater virtue and prowess, private desire works in the service of public duty. Most of the Arthurian romances occur in the space of this heroes' holiday, in which the stakes of the adventures remain private, focused on the individual and suspended outside the concerns and outside the temporal scope of the society's epic.

The *Awntyrs* also takes place in this peaceful interlude, signaled by the ludic pastimes of the hunt and the tournament, but it continually disrupts the normative functioning of the genre. The total epic content of the Arthurian cycle intrudes on the seemingly isolated moment of romance and adventure, and the apprehension of the tragedy, the end of the story, the ruin of the court, gives the lie to the secular stability central to the functioning of romance. The poem argues that the fiction of this isolation is the very substance of romance. But the violence of the surrounding Arthurian epic continually intrudes on the typical romance elements, as the hunt leads to a vision of the infighting that will tear apart the Round Table, and the tournament reveals the price of Arthur's previous territorial conquests and stubbornly resists the romance context in which military and erotic goals align. Far from 'arous[ing] them to passionate excitement by their flirtatious behaviour' (ix.14), Guenevere and Galeron's lady both 'gret' (597, 620) in anguish over the injuries their champions inflict on each other and plead for it to stop. Thus the poem subverts the romance expectations of the erotic impetus that informs and perpetuates the violence at a tournament, even as it simultaneously argues that the territorial claims at stake in the duel here cost too much in human life for the juridical process to continue. Neither secular love nor territorial entitlement provides sufficient reward or motive for the fight to proceed.

The Ghost's intrusion into the hunt also closes down the possibilities of these typical modes of recovery in romance. Wearing the rotting rags of its mortality, 'bare . . . and blak to the bone . . . with eighen holked ful holle' (105, 116) and adorned with traditional *memento mori*, 'serkeled with serpentes that sate to the sides/ [and] todes theron' (120–121), the mere appearance of the Ghost points to the inefficacy of erotic love to ennoble and the inevitability of death. Its current punishment results from its 'luf paramour, listes, and delites' (213), and these particular sins invoke our memory of Guenevere's future adultery and its role in the dissolution of the Arthurian world. Rank, wealth and status cannot avert death, and the Ghost's exhortation to 'muse on my mirrour/ For, king and emperour,/ Thus dight shul ye be' (167–169) short-circuits the usual movement of romance from loss to recovery, even as it completes the circuit of Fortune's Wheel and looks beyond the momentary peace that enables the play of romance by insisting on the final, leveling loss that 'dethe wil you dighte, thare you not doute' (170). The present of the story must inevitably rush to meet the loss predetermined by the cycle of the Arthurian epic.

Looking backward to its literary forebearers, the poem freely borrows from the literary past to allude to the narrative future lurking around the corner. Both the *Alliterative Morte Arthure* and Geoffrey of Monmouth's *History of the Kings of Britain* provide the historical future for the *Awntyrs* with their particular details about Arthur's birth and death. The Ghost's invocation of 'False Fortune . . . That wonderfull whelewryghte' (270–271) alludes to the *Alliterative Morte Arthure*'s description of King Arthur's own prophetic nightmare in which Lady Fortune first lifts him up upon her wheel, and then casts him down:

> About sho shirled a wheel with her white hands,
> Overwhelm all quaintly the wheel, as sho sholde;
> . . .
> Sho lift me up lightly with her lene handes
> And set me softly in the see, the septer me reched;
> . . .
> In sign that I soothly was soveraign in erthe
> . . .
> But at the mid-day full even all her mood changed,
> . . .
> About sho shirles the wheel and shirles me under,
> Til all my quarters that while were quasht all to peces.[39]

The *Awntyrs* also uses Geoffrey's *History* to form a geographical circle predicting Arthur's death 'uppone Cornewayle coost' (301), five miles from Tintagel, where Geoffrey places his conception.[40] Also, the *Alliterative Morte* provides the key to identifying Mordred's coat of arms, 'sable/ With a sauter engreled of silver' (307–308).[41] And both Geoffrey's *History* and the *Alliterative Morte* include the seduction of the Queen in the list of Modred's treasonous offenses and accuse Guenevere of active complicity in this treason. In the *Alliterative Morte*, Sir Craddok announces to Arthur that 'thy warden [Mordred] is wicked and wild of his deedes' (3523), crowning himself and consorting with foreigners, and 'worst!/ He has wedded Waynor and her his wife holdes,/ . . ./ And has wrought her with child' (3549–3552). In Geoffrey's *History*, 'this treacherous tyrant was living adulterously and out of wedlock with Queen Guinevere, who had broken the vows of her earlier marriage' (x.13). In both texts, her guilt manifests itself in her broken marriage vows and flight to the convent when all is lost,[42] but the *Alliterative Morte* emphasizes the extent of her treason with her pregnancy and delivery of Mordred's child and heir, and with her betrayal of the hiding place of Arthur's ceremonial sword to Mordred: 'Wiste no wye of wonne but Waynor herselven;/ Sho had the keeping herself of the kidd wepen' (4205–4206).

---

[39] *Alliterative Morte Arthure*, ed. L. D. Benson, rev. edn E. Foster, Middle English Texts Series (Kalamazoo, 1994), 3260–3389.
[40] *History of the Kings of Britain*, viii.20.
[41] Cf. *Alliterative Morte Arthure*, 'the sauturour engreled' (4182). William Matthews argues that the two texts' agreement on the description of Mordred's device, along with the correspondences in topographical and personal names, and the similarities in their references to the Wheel of Fortune, are 'persuasive evidence of the connection of [the alliterative] *Morte Arthure* and *Awntyrs of Arthur*' (*The Tragedy of Arthur* [University of California Press, 1960], pp. 157–158).
[42] See *Alliterative Morte Arthure*, 3911–3918, and *History of the Kings of Britain*, xi.1.

Thus, in the *Awntyrs*, the Ghost's admonition to Guenevere regarding her adultery, intensified by her prediction that 'thou shal leve but a stert;/ Hethen shal thou fare' (259–260), alludes to this active treachery and links it more ominously with her warnings about the 'barne play[ing] at the balle/ That outray shall you all,/ Delfully that day' (310). The description of the traitor, Mordred, Guenevere's future lover, as a little boy playing with his toys is unique among medieval treatments of the Arthurian cycle. Indeed, it is a commonplace observation that very few medieval texts of any sort discuss the childhood of important characters, even as medieval romances begin to feature narrative patterns that show character development as *Bildungs-roman*.[43] Thus, with this added detail, the *Awntyrs* challenges the generic capacity of romance by asking us to consider the *Bildungsroman* of the present little boy into the future insurgent who will bring about the end of the Arthurian world.

On the larger scale, the poem seems to recover from this image of loss to the triumphant feast at Rondoles Halle, and it seems to recover from the savage violence that disrupts the tournament between Gawain and Galeron. True to romance expectations, it concludes with the promise of reconciliation and restored order. Arthur commands peace, redistributes lands to each of the combatants, and creates them dukes; surgical intervention heals the grevious wounds the knights had inflicted upon each other; Galeron weds his lady; and the Queen attends to the masses for her mother. This restoration of order, however, fails to address the factors that led to its crisis, and the apparent recovery is temporary and illusory. When Arthur gives Gawain 'al the Glamergan londe with greves so grene;/ The worship of Wales, at wil and at wolde' (665–666), he creates the conditions under which Gawain can honorably yield the Scottish territories to Galeron, but recreates the situation that gave rise to Galeron's grievance over Arthur's imperial annexation of his lands in the first place. The poem implies that this might only be another turn in the cycle of violence perpetuated in these territorial feuds. Somewhere in Wales, we can imagine another displaced lord arming himself for another trial by combat.

Furthermore, this Welsh land grant allows Gawain to 'gif Sir Galeron' (677) the disputed territories in southwest Scotland, 'Al the londes and the lithes fro Laner to Layre:/ Carrake and Cummake, Conyngham and Kile' (678–679).[44] And although Gawain promises to 'refeff him in felde' (685), he elides explicit acknowledgment of Galeron's 'right' (641) to them. Finally, in the ostensibly generous and conciliatory gesture of dubbing Galeron a duke,

---

43 The Middle English poem, *Havelok*, composed between 1295 and 1310, represents an early example of a romance that functions as a proto-*Bildungsroman*. It incorporates pietistic elements of hagiography (signaled by the titular line in Bodleian MS Laud Misc. 108: 'Incipit vita Havelok, quondam Rex Anglie et Denemarchie') while tracing the life of the hero from the time when 'he was litel' (6), a 'knave that was sumdel bold' (450), through the adventures that result in his accession to the thrones of England and Denmark.

44 Cf. Galeron's initial claim to the lands of 'Galwey . . ./ Of Carrake, of Cummake, of Conyngame, of Kile,/ Of Lonwik, of Lannx, of Laudoune Hillus' (418–420).

Arthur indirectly reasserts his imperial control over those very lands in contention, and thereby absorbs Galeron and his property into his kingdom by diplomatic means, but still 'with a wrange wile' (421), in the same spirit with which he first took them 'in werre' (421).

Finally, in the last stanza, as the Queen arranges the 'mylion of masses to make the mynnynge' (706),[45] the poem reminds us of the Ghost's tattered appearance with its warning that *sic transit gloria mundi*. Furthermore, the concatenating verse form rather literally leads us to review the adventures again, as it takes us back to the beginning, forming a seamless circle of verse. Simultaneously, the poem thus has no end and, in the concatenation of the last and first lines, no beginning either. Rather, it emphasizes the cyclical, circular dilemma of Fortune intruding on romance. When events of a kind as these keep repeating, no progress can be made. Indeed, the *Awntyrs* heightens the impact of the *sic transit gloria mundi* topos, insofar as it subverts the conventional religious response by neglecting to suggest the recuperatory *gloria Dei* or *caeli* in its place. The 'mylion of masses' (706) do not avail Arthur's court in averting its disaster, and although they purport to salve the misery of the dead, they represent an afterthought, rather than a program, for salvation. The *Awntyrs* even short-circuits the satisfaction of poetry's traditional intimations of immortality by linking Guenevere's penitential errands in the last stanza back to the beginning of the poem by means of the concatenation. Paradoxically, this final formal flourish exposes the poem's function, not as a celebratory immortalization of its subjects, but as a mere commemoration of the dead by the dead. As an aesthetic participant in this closed, courtly community, the poem revisits the circumstances of its own demise and thus functions as a memorialization and performative elegy for Arthurian romance itself.

---

[45] Cf. Guenevere's pledge to her mother's ghost: 'Here, hertly my honde, thes hestes to holde,/ With a myllion of masses to make thy mynnyng' (235–236).

VI

THE BLINDING OF GWENNERE:
THOMAS CHESTRE AS SOCIAL CRITIC

Dinah Hazell

What could be more fragile than a promise? How can breath bind?[1]

In *Sir Launfal*, the breath that seals a promise not only binds, but blinds, and serves as the pivotal metaphor of Thomas Chestre's poem. Many of the work's themes are treated in other Middle English romances: *trouthe* and oathkeeping, secrecy, wealth and status, generosity and charity, pride and humility, identity and individual fulfillment in society, the administration of justice, and separation, reconciliation and forgiveness. But Chestre's articulation is stronger, his criticism more pointed, and his outlook more pessimistic. His hero does not undertake a successful personal quest and eventually achieve positive integration into society. Rather, Sir Launfal is beset by negative forces that block his path to success and which he is powerless to combat. *Sir Launfal* questions how the individual can survive in a culture ruled by self-interest, and the answer is bleak.

By selecting a basic narrative that allowed him to address issues important to him and his audience, and by enhancing those elements with motifs from other works,[2] Chestre created a poem that expresses his social concerns, which reflect observations shared with other poets of the age. For Chestre,

---

[1] D. J. Canfield, *Word as Bond in English Literature from the Middle Ages to Restoration* (Philadelphia, 1989), p. xiii.

[2] Close textual parallels confirm that Chestre's primary source for *Sir Launfal* is *Sir Landevale*, an early fourteenth-century redaction of Marie de France's lai, *Lanval*. This places *Lanval* at one remove from *Sir Launfal*, and due to the lack of evidence of Chestre's direct use of Marie's work, I consider her lai secondary source material or analogous. The first known version of the folk tale that underlies the narrative, Marie's *Lanval* bequeaths a strain of social commentary that clings to future renditions. Chestre also utilized parts of the anonymous twelfth-century lai, *Graelent*, once conjectured to have been written by Marie. Its Celtic origin, possibly used by Marie for *Lanval*, resonates in *Sir Launfal*.

 In 'The Middle English *Lanval*, the Corporal Works of Mercy, and Bibliothèque National, Nouv. Acq. Fr. 1104', *Neophilologus* 72 (1988), 97–106, D. Carlson argues for a lost Middle English redaction of *Lanval* that was based on an Old French version close to the S manuscript of Marie's work. Carlson's discussion centers on the expansion of the list of the hero's good works found in *Lanval* to include several corporal acts of mercy; this adapted list appears in all Middle English versions of the narrative.

like Langland and others, social order rests on individual moral action. Chestre is not traditionally read as social critic, but *Sir Launfal* voices a reaction to the socioeconomic, political and ideological shifts that accompanied the fading of feudalism in England, and speaks for a sector of the populace often muted by more elegant, courtly poets.[3] These aspects of *Sir Launfal* have not always been recognized. In 1960, A. J. Bliss, until then the definitive Chestre critic, observed that 'there is no hint in the poem of any feeling for morality' in the poem, and that the blinding is 'repugnant to decent feeling'.[4] The complexity and relevance of *Sir Launfal* are emerging as critical orientation honours cultural context and broadens the range of texts considered worthy of serious study. However, scholars generally avoid the blinding of Gwennere in their discussions, perhaps uncertain of its importance or relevance. Nevertheless, the episode is the axis of Chestre's moral and social observations, and the absolute condemnation of Arthurian society; rather than gratuitous violence or superfluous appendage, the punishment of Gwennere recalls all of her sins and, by implication, the weaknesses of Artour and his culture.

The blinding of Gwennere results from what appears to be a 'rash' or 'casual' oath, a convention seen frequently in medieval literature. In *Sir Launfal*, her oath is more careless than casual. Gwennere's prideful oath to allow the court to 'put out my eyen gray'[5] (810)[6] if Launfal 'bryngeth a fayrer thynge' (809) than herself to court is couched in judicial procedure and language that joins it to Launfal's legal proceeding, and it becomes irrevocable.[7] The stanza in which she makes her oath is preceded by the judges'

---

3 The classification of *Sir Launfal* in the large body of 'popular' romance, based on style and cultural indications, suggests a non-courtly audience and author, probably middle class/bourgeoisie. Critics agree that *Sir Launfal*'s author was unfamiliar with the subtleties of aristocratic life and note the poem's 'blunt criticism of the court world' and mockery of wealthy urban society. A. Laskaya and E. Salisbury, eds., *The Middle English Breton Lays* (Kalamazoo, 1995), p. 203. Bliss imagines 'inarticulate . . . simpler, less sensitive listeners in market-square or inn-yard' and sees the peasantry as Chestre's avid listeners. A. J. Bliss, ed., *Sir Launfal* (New York, 1960), p. 1. I agree with critics who doubt that peasants formed the core of the popular audience; Laskaya and Salisbury, for instance, suggest a wider and more varied audience, 'perhaps not peasant but certainly mercantile' (p. 203).

4 Bliss, *Launfal*, p. 43. He also notes an 'unpleasant streak of bloodthirstiness' in the poem (ibid.), particularly the hero's encounter with Syr Valentyne. Launfal's behaviour in that episode is better understood by considering the giant's breach of his offer for single combat, and the hero's plight at facing a formidable foe and then Valentyne's vengeful host on foreign soil alone (except for the supernatural aid provided by Tryamour). His return to Bretayn 'Wyth solas and wyth plawe' (612) may be interpreted as relief and delight at homecoming rather than 'great satisfaction' for the 'indiscriminate slaughter' of Valentyne's retinue as suggested by Bliss (ibid.).

5 This may be a satiric mirror image of Tryamour, whose eyes are also grey (935), a traditional sign of moral excellence.

6 All citations from *Sir Launfal* are from *Middle English Romances*, ed. S. H. A. Shepherd (New York, 1995).

7 In 'The Trial of *Lanval*', in *Studies in French and Mediæval Literature Presented to M. K. Pope* (Manchester, 1939), pp. 115–24, E. A. Francis cites the reconstruction of legal practice in twelfth-century France contained in Pollock and Maitland's *The History of English Law before the Time of Edward II*. In summary, the only mode of bringing a felon to justice was the *appellum* (appeal), in which two litigants presented their case; the action generally involved specifically feudal crimes, a 'breach of feudal faith'. The court heard the charge and rebuttal, which were formal statements in carefully regulated language. The rebuttal was generally a flat denial of the charges, and the judges

medial verdict on Launfal, and followed by the setting of the date on which he must make his wager. The queen interjects her oath between Launfal's pledge to produce his love or lose his head, and the finding of his guarantors; her oath is therefore bound to Launfal's *wajowr* (811), which is agreed to by the court, and her 'rash promise' is transformed into a legal agreement.

But who in the court will execute the penalty when her case fails, and for what is Gwennere being punished? She ostensibly loses her wager when Tryamour's superior beauty is seen, but her conduct throughout the poem displays serious crimes. Her marriage to Artour involves personal, social and political commitment to maintain the well-being of the court and its inhabitants, and her failures are measured in their destructive impact on society. Her infidelity and lack of *trouthe*, her improper use of wealth, beauty and royal power and resultant causation of Launfal's poverty, her false accusations, and her desire for vengeance and perversion of justice undermine the stability of Artour's court. The fairy mistress is Gwennere's antithesis: loyal, generous, and supportive of Launfal's charity. She uses her wealth and power in positive ways and values Launfal for his innate attributes rather than his status. She keeps her *trouthe*, while displaying compassion and forgiveness. The issues crystallized in Gwennere and her nemesis create a consistent ethical vision and reverberate both negatively and positively in the poem's characters, motifs and episodes, and signify maladies in both Launfal's and Chestre's societies. The poet focuses on the individual's role in society, the strain between individual desire and societal expectations, fidelity and *trouthe*, the valuation of the individual, the proper use of wealth, and the ideal of justice and its implementation. Moral action by individuals embraces monarchical responsibility to maintain social integrity, and the seriousness of the regent's failure to meet that duty is emphasized by the severity of Chestre's resolution, which can be validated generically and historically.

The Individual in Society

Chestre's appropriative handling of his sources reveals a deliberate intent to create a harsh view of Artour's court, a venue that can represent contemporary rulers and be seen to embody critiques of their reigns. The Lanval tale has appeared during several particularly volatile political periods. Marie de France was the first to adapt the folktale to her purposes, during the reign of Henry II,[8] and the Landevale-poet and Chestre reworked the tale in the early

---

pronounced the medial judgment, a task the appellant must perform; the proof had to be accomplished by battle, by oath with oath helpers, or by the oaths of witnesses. Next came the wager, in which gage (surety) and pledge were given to secure the fulfillment of the judgment and performance of the task assigned (Francis, 'Trial', pp. 116–17). This legal procedure is carefully detailed by Marie in *Lanval* and believed to have been based on a contemporary trial for felony (Bliss, *Launfal*, p. 22); her description is generally followed by the *Landevale*-poet and Chestre.

8   Based on linguistic and contextual considerations, I question the traditional placement of Marie as a long-time resident of Henry's court and her dedication of *Lanval* to him. Rather, I view her as a conti-

and late fourteenth century, during the reigns of Edward II and Richard II and its transition, respectively.[9] The focus on the importance of the queen's contributory role in either maintaining or disrupting a just and stable rule resonates with dominant females in the royal arena during those periods, Eleanor of Aquitaine, Isabella, and Alice Perrers. In centering his depiction of the court on Gwennere, Chestre drew on and enhanced a long tradition of negative portrayals of the queen to create a strongly immoral character. Like his narrative, Chestre's portrayal of Gwennere is mainly a composite of elements from his sources, in which the queen's attempt to engage the hero in an adulterous affair is the catalyst of the action that demonstrates Artour's weakness as a ruler and judicial administrator. However, the manner in which her character is introduced in *Launfal* is unique; Artour's courtship of the queen and their marriage do not appear in any of Chestre's known sources, and it is supposed that this passage comes from a now unidentifiable source. This history launches the tale, and Chestre uses the scene to introduce Gwennere's propensity for infidelity and to establish the knights' distrust of her for having 'lemmannys under her lord,/ So fele ther nas noon ende' (47–8). This theme first appears in *Landevale*, during the hero's trial, and is appropriated by Chestre and moved to the opening of the poem.[10] The early revelation of Gwennere's bad reputation, the ramifications of which surface later during Launfal's trial, adds unity to the narrative and consistency to her characterization. Whether in the forefront or background, the queen and her transgressions drive the poem's movement.

Aside from the moral implications of adultery, sexual misconduct by a queen could result in illegitimate succession to the crown and was historically a serious offense. But Gwennere's infidelity is a manifestation of the breach of an equally, if not more important value: *trouthe*, a motif that pervades contemporary literature. This focus on the importance of trust and the fulfillment of commitments reflects concern over personal loyalty in the dynamic economic atmosphere of the time; as written contracts and money rents replaced fealty oaths and service as the socioeconomic base, lord/villein relationships shifted and faith in oathkeeping was imperiled.[11]

---

nental figure, possibly from the Ile de France/Vexin with close proximity to Henry's Norman court and/or travel between England and France amidst complex political associations, and that her poem is a criticism of Henry's court and his failures, particularly as a judicial administrator. His wish to be identified with Arthur to validate his rule resonates with Marie's choice of literary setting (her only Arthurian lai), and the depiction of her nameless, adulterous queen strongly recalls the reputation of Eleanor of Aquitaine.

9   I agree with the theory that dates *Sir Landevale* to the early part of the century and places *Sir Launfal* in the late fourteenth century, during which Chaucer recreated the lai in *The Franklin's Tale* and stirred a revival of the form (Bliss, *Launfal*, pp. 12–16).

10 Both *Lanval* and *Graelent* open to the scene of war: between England and Scotland in *Lanval*, and by the king of Brittany against nameless neighbors in *Graelent*. It is interesting that both the *Landevale*-poet and Chestre eliminate this element, since England and Scotland were at war throughout the fourteenth century. Perhaps they chose to remove their poems from an obviously contemporary society and allow their audience to draw social inferences from the narrative, or perhaps they did not wish to cloud the issues they raised with a seemingly irrelevant event.

11 Standard works that include discussion of the socioeconomic history of the period are M. M. Postan,

Fidelity in feudal and love relationships is tested through Launfal's character, and his attempts to fulfill the two simultaneously fail. He maintains his
loyalty to Artour and his pledge of faithfulness to Tryamour by refusing to
submit to the queen's advances, but he incurs her wrath. In defending himself
against Gwennere's slander, he commits a double breach of fidelity by
insulting her and hence the king, and breaking his oath of silence about his
lover. Launfal could have remained faithful to lover and lord without boasting
of Tryamour's beauty, but Gwennere would still have been angered by his
rejection. Launfal takes offense at the queen's charge of homosexuality:
'Thou lovyst no woman, ne no woman the;/ Thow wer worthy forlore!'
(689–90), which has been toned down from the explicit charge in *Lanval*,
'Vallez avez bien afeitiez,/ Ensemble od eus vos deduiez' (281–2) (You have
fine-looking boys with whom you enjoy yourself).[12] Launfal's pride takes
control and he commits an act of indiscretion that also injures his fealty to
Artour, for to have a lover whose beauty surpasses the queen's is a personal
affront to the king and challenges his supreme position. Artour's first charge
against Launfal is the insulting of Gwennere's beauty: 'That thy lemmannes
lodlokest mayde/ Was fayrer than my wyf, thou seyde –/ That was a fowll
lesynge!' (763–5), and the knight's alleged seduction of the queen is
secondary.[13]

For Launfal, fidelity to both lord and lover proves incompatible. On the
surface, his transgression against Tryamour would appear to be the breaking
of his oath to keep their relationship secret.[14] However, Tryamour's
commandment and Launfal's breach involve values greater than oathkeeping
and secrecy. Most critics pass over Launfal's promise as a standard folk tale
motif and fail to consider its social implications; like Gwennere, Launfal
commits a sin at a deeper level than is immediately visible. Tryamour places
two conditions on Launfal: that he 'wylt truly to me take –/ And alle wemen
for me forsake' (316–17); and what is usually interpreted as a simple vow of
secrecy but is actually an admonition against boasting: 'But of o thynge, syr
knyght, I warne the,/ That thou make no bost of me' (361–2). Boasting is
underscored several times in the poem: in Gwennere's charge against the

---

The Medieval Economy and Society (Berkeley, 1972), and M. McKisack, *The Fourteenth Century: 1307–1399* (Oxford, 1959). See also *Transition from Feudalism to Capitalism*, intro. R. Hilton (London, 1978); M. H. Keen, *England in the Later Middle Ages* (London, 1973) and *English Society in the Later Middle Ages: 1348–1500* (London, 1990); C. Dyer, *Standards of Living in the Later Middle Ages: Social Change in England c. 1200–1520* (Cambridge, 1989) and *Everyday Life in Medieval England* (Hambledon, 2000) especially chapters 9 and 10; and L. Roney, 'Depicting the Fall from Feudalism into Individualism in the *Canterbury Tales*', in *The Rusted Hauberk: Feudal Ideals of Order and their Decline*, ed. L. O. Purdon and C. L. Vitto (Gainesville, 1994).

12 Citations from *Lanval* are from *Les Lais de Marie de France*, ed. J. Rychner (Paris, 1983). Translations are from *The Lais of Marie de France*, ed. R. Hanning and J. Ferrante (Grand Rapids, 1978).

13 While modern readers' sensibilities may be offended by the depiction of women by medieval authors, and particularly by Chestre's seemingly harsh treatment of Gwennere, they might be enraged by the *Graelent*-poet, who depicts the queen as displayed by the king on a high bench, to be admired and complimented by all the knights for her beauty.

14 Launfal makes no overt promise to Tryamour; rather, his acceptance of her caveats is implicit in his acceptance of her love and gifts, and their continued relationship.

knight for having made a 'yelp' (718) about his lover; when Artour accuses him of 'yelpyng' (762); and when the judges find for acquittal if his 'yelpynge' (797) can be proven by his lover's appearance.

In *Lanval*, the fairy's initial exhortation is against his telling anyone about her, 'Ne vus descovrez a nul humme' (145) (Tell your secret to no one), but the boasting motif is articulated in the king's accusation that the knight has 'Vantez vus estes de folie' (367) (You have made a foolish boast), in Cornwall's repetition of the king's accusation concerning 'd'une amur dunt il se vanta' (441) (a love of whom he has boasted), and in the fairy lover's recognition and acquittal of Lanval's 'vantance' (622) (boast). Similarly, Graelent is warned not to 'dites parole aperte/ Dont nostre amor soit descoverte' (317–18) (speak a single word openly by which our love could be discovered) or to 'vantoiz' (333) (boast).[15] The *Landevale*-poet repeats the mistress's warning against boasting, 'Ne make ye never bost of me!' (162) and includes it in the queen's accusation, 'And of a leman bost he maide' (249).[16]

Boasting of one's lover in the Middle Ages was the enactment of a specific branch of pride that appears in literature throughout the period. This sin is *avantance*, the failure of a man to protect his female lover through the exercise of secrecy, and to commit this sin is a breach of *trouthe* that could have serious consequences. To fall prey to pride and boast of his lover, thus revealing her identity, is cautioned against repeatedly. When the fairy mistress acquits the hero's *avantance* with her presence, the knight is proven innocent of a false boast. But he is still guilty of not only revealing his relationship with her, but also of forcing her to reveal herself physically to the court, which she was not wont to do.

The convention of secrecy about love affairs is expounded by Andreas Capellanus in his *Art of Courtly Love*. In Case XXI brought before the Countess of Champagne in the court of love over which she presides, she refers to the axiom that 'All lovers are bound to keep their love secret.'[17] So, they should not sign their own names or apply their seals to letters, and their identities must be kept anonymous if a case is brought before the court; 'In this way their love will always be retained unimpaired.'[18] Andreas offers as Rule No. XIII, 'When made public love rarely endures.'[19] He does not discuss reasons for the secrecy and the consequences of breaking it, but it can be imagined that knowledge of a relationship, particularly in a culture that lacked privacy, would invite intrusions that could be injurious to the relationship and the reputation of the lovers. While the seriousness of Andreas is somewhat suspect, his discussion of secrecy in love demonstrates the cultural viability of the concept, whether or not it was being satirized by the poet.

---

[15] All citations from *Graelent* are from 'The Lay of Graelent', *Graelent and Guingamor: Two Breton Lays*, ed. and trans. R. Weingartner (New York, 1985).

[16] All citations from *Sir Landevale* are from *Sir Launfal*, ed. A. J. Bliss (New York, 1960).

[17] Andreas Capellanus, *The Art of Courtly Love*, trans. J. J. Parry (New York, 1990), p. 177.

[18] Ibid.

[19] Ibid., p. 185.

Many of Marie's lais deal with the difference between private and public love and the cultural demands placed on relationships once they are revealed, including a new set of commitments and social responsibilities. When Guigemar's affair with his married lover is discovered by her husband, the exposure of their love brings challenges and barriers from outside forces that must be overcome by both lovers before they are reunited. The *Landevale*-poet echoes this belief; when the love between the knight and his mistress was 'dern' it was 'withouten stryfe' (509), implying that once a love relationship is made public, it is subjected to pressures that threaten its stability.

In Gower's *Confessio Amantis*, the Confessor offers guidance to Amans on how to conduct a love affair properly and morally, and he includes a lesson on *avantance*. Chaucer mentions *avantance* in several of his poems. The Parson includes *avauntynge* among the 'twigges' that come from Pride and defines the *avantour* as 'one that bosteth of the harm or the bountee that he hath doon' (ParsT 385–90).[20] In the *Nun's Priest's Tale* when Chauntecleer tells Pertelote about his nightmare of the fox, the hen is repelled. She reminds him that women do not admire or love cowards, and she takes the opportunity to list the virtues of the ideal husband, who is 'hardy, wise, and free,/ And secree – and no nygard, ne no fool,/ Ne hym that is agast of every tool,/ Ne noon avauntour, by that God above!' (2914–17). Another of Chaucer's fowls, the tercel eagle in the *Parliament of Fowls*, begs his case to win the formel eagle and swears that 'And if that I be founde to hyre untrewe,/ Disobeysaunt, or wilful necligent,/ Avauntour, or in proces love a newe' (428–30), he should be 'al torent' (432) for his transgression.

Chaucer's most extensive discussion of the sin of *avantance* is in *Troilus and Criseyde*, when Pandarus admonishes the hero to protect Criseyde's reputation and honour (although Pandarus is as worried about his own reputation if his role as go-between is discovered) by keeping their love 'secree' (III line 286). Pandarus reminds Troilus of the harm that has been caused 'For makying of avantes' (III line 289) and counsels him to heed the advice of 'wise clerkes' (III line 292) that the 'firste vertu is to kepe tonge' (III line 294). Vicious gossip has made many a lady cry, 'Weilaway, the day that I was born!' (III line 304) when their reputations are lost 'through fals and foles bost' (III line 298). The length to which Pandarus carries his speech on the dangers of boasting and the need for secrecy indicates its importance to author and audience.

Like most moral and social codes, it is likely that there was a practical motive behind the concept and practice of *avantance*. An obvious possibility is that unmarried women, or adulterous married women, were viewed in a way that would bring a loss of reputation if their love relationships were made public. Windeatt observes that an 'inhibiting effect'[21] resulted from the almost claustrophobic lack of privacy in medieval English culture, and that

---

[20] All Chaucer citations are from *The Riverside Chaucer*, ed. L. D. Benson (Boston, 1987).
[21] B. Windeatt, ' "Love That Oughte Ben Secree" in Chaucer's *Troilus*', *The Chaucer Review* 14 (1979), 117–31, p. 121.

secrecy was necessary to maintain the appearance of lovers appropriate to their social standing. But perhaps more than reputation was at stake for women.

Criseyde's social standing and fortunes depend to some degree on societal expectations of chaste widowhood. While her situation is rather unique,[22] Criseyde's position also raises socioeconomic, cultural and legal issues that governed marital status and women's property rights generally. Inheritance customs during the Middle Ages are shadowy and complex, especially for women, but it is possible that Criseyde's property would be threatened through forfeiture of her possessions to a new husband if she and Troilus appeared to have entered into a secret marriage as suggested by some critics.[23] Although Tryamour does not share the vulnerability of fictive or historic women of the age, she staunchly conforms to the culture's ideals and mores such as *avantance*, and expects Launfal to do the same (within human capability).

Since *avantance* is an aspect of the 'courtly love' ethic, would it have carried the same meaning to Chestre and his audience as to those of Marie or Chaucer? Ignorance cannot be assumed because of the 'popular' designation assumed for *Sir Launfal*. Chestre was possibly well-read in both courtly and non-courtly literature, and the presence of the *avantance* theme in works by contemporary authors would have kept it in the consciousness of the literary-minded. Whether his audience would have had an appreciation of *avantance* as a courtly ethical code is questionable, but they would have recognized it as one of the facets of pride, and the ramifications of committing such a sin.

The influence of social and economic factors continues in *Sir Launfal* with the issue of property ownership, which ranges from plenty to poverty and encompasses the proper use of wealth, including largesse and charity. An important part of the courtly economy in such forms as money, land, moveable possessions and access to fortunes through marriage, largesse was at the base of the courtly social system and was used to wield power, support or destroy relationships, and to maintain status, in addition to the pragmatic function of providing life's physical needs. In *Sir Launfal*, wealth serves as poetic manifestation of personal integrity and social dynamics, intimately tied to the valuation of an individual. Its proper use by Tryamour reflects her moral stature, and its misuse by Gwennere indicates her lack of character. The hypocrisy of the mayor, based on Launfal's vacillating fortunes, similarly exposes a sycophantic and crass nature.

Like fidelity, this theme is set at the start. In the sixth stanza, Gwennere distributes gifts to establish her 'curtasye' (69) at court, using the practice for

---

22 As the daughter of a traitor, she holds her property through royal benevolence and is in an unusually precarious position. Indeed, she eventually becomes a piece of property, bartered in political negotiations.

23 By its nature, secret marriage was difficult to prove and, once failed, led to disputes between dissenting partners over property ownership and other marital issues.

apparently self-interested political and emotional reasons as evidenced when she inexplicably excludes Launfal. In Marie's version it is Arthur who 'ne l'en sovint' (19) (doesn't remember him), while in *Graelent* the king shuns the hero in response to the queen's machinations. The *Landevale*-poet discards this element from his tale, but Chestre reclaims the queen's enmity from *Graelent* and adapts it so that Gwennere withholds courtly honour from the hero by omitting him from her gift-giving during the *bredale*; 'Syr Launfal sche yaf nothying:/ That grevede hym many a sythe' (71–2). The burden of offense is placed on Gwennere rather than Artour, although the king implicitly bears responsibility for allowing the queen to behave inappropriately towards one of his courtiers. Rather than being 'quite unnecessary',[24] Chestre's borrowing of the queen's early display of malice towards the hero sets the framework in place for the construction of Gwennere's negative characterization. In combination with her adulterous reputation, which is described two stanzas earlier, the queen's character is fixed.

Launfal's primary attribute, generosity, has brought him popularity and success at court:

> He gaf gyftys largelyche –
> Gold and sylver and clothes ryche –
>   To squyer and to knyght.
> For hys largesse and hys bounté
> The Kynges stuward made was he
>   Ten yer, I you plyght.   (28–33)

There has been critical discussion about whether Launfal's beneficence, particularly after his departure, is traditional largesse or reckless spending. The text invites ambiguous readings; while his wealth is spent 'savagelych' (130) and he falls into debt at Karlyoun, this seemingly irresponsible behavior is tempered by the earlier emphasis on his generosity. Largesse must be viewed as both a political and personal act, since the donor and recipient share a bond that is supported by giving and receiving gifts; indeed, Launfal's relationship with the rulers is part of that system. But political convention does not necessarily negate the spirit in which gifts are given, and largesse could be exercised with selflessness, despite a return on the investment. In addition to a desire to share his wealth, Launfal suffers from a lack of control over his largesse and spending, so a combination of generosity, political pragmatism and extravagance is a sound characterization of the knight's magnanimity.

Rosenberg notes that Chestre has been criticized for an 'undiluted concern with money' which is the hero's major flaw. He relates the 'orthodox interpretation' of this element as the revelation of the rapacity of the lower classes, as well as that of the impoverished nobility who 'coveted the wealth they felt should be theirs as befitting their birth'.[25] While these historical influences are

---

[24] Bliss, *Launfal*, p. 30.
[25] B. A. Rosenberg, 'Medieval Popular Literature: Folkloric Sources', in *The Popular Literature of Medieval England*, ed. T. J. Heffernan (Knoxville, 1985), 61–84, p. 78.

visible in *Sir Launfal*, the poem reflects a concern with wealth and poverty at a deeper level of observation about the effects of socioeconomic pressures on the individual.

Launfal's initial rejection of the wealth and security of Artour's court is caused by Gwennere's withholding of largesse, exercised in a public setting and humiliating to Launfal. A courtier who held a trusted position in Artour's court for the virtue Gwennere refuses to display towards him, he chooses to withdraw rather than be insulted. Once away from the courtly environment, he continues to exercise largesse until he is bankrupt. Fiscal conservation in view of his altered circumstances would have been advisable but, perhaps in keeping with human nature, not readily forthcoming. Launfal is like Sir Cleges, who continues to give annual Christmas feasts 'ryall in all thynge' (40)[26] for all manner of guests, 'ryche and pore' (43) until, and after, he is deeply in debt and has lost virtually all of his wealth. Launfal also continues to live according to the social and economic rules by which he has been raised and as expected by his culture, even when he realizes he is in financial trouble. He continues exercising his outstanding virtue, despite the consequences, and he increases his charitable activities after his poverty is cured.

When deserted by Tryamour, Sir Launfal appears to be stricken with the loss of his wealth more than the disappearance of his lover; he looks first for his money and his servant. But beyond their intrinsic value, these are the tangible proofs of his adventure, love relationship, and his worthiness. Like his white armor that has 'becom of blak colour' (743), his honour is tainted by his breach of *trouthe*, and the loss of his servant, horse and money signals his failure and Tryamour's departure. Launfal's loss of his 'joye' (748) with his lover, his 'blysfull berde yn bour' (750), is his worst loss, and it drives him to despair.

The Lanval narratives are modest in their treatment of detailed opulence compared to descriptions found in works like *Erec and Enide* and *The Nibelungenlied*. The description of Tryamour's pavilion follows *Lanval* and *Landevale*, and her extravagant clothing and trappings place her on a par with royalty; they validate her social standing and related duty to *trouthe* and honour, which legitimizes her testimony at the hero's trial. All are used to vindicate Launfal and present a proper model of true regal behavior. The concern of Chestre and his sources centers not on money, but on its use and influence.

Gwennere's improper use of wealth and largesse ultimately leads to Launfal's poverty, a serious offense in a society that witnessed widespread impoverishment at the rural and urban lower strata and, increasingly, in the upper classes as economic pressures reshaped social boundaries and fortunes. Many nobles experienced adverse conditions in reaction to post-Plague influences such as a large mobile work force with high wage demands, falling rents and decreasing land values, sagging agricultural and livestock prices and

---

[26] 'Sir Cleges', *The Middle English Breton Lays*, ed. A. Laskaya and E. Salisbury (Kalamazoo, 1995).

rising commodity prices, while their need for cash continued and/or increased to meet obligations such as taxation and to support their lifestyle. Members of all classes, including knights, were unable to keep pace with living expenses and fell into debt and subsequent impoverishment. Launfal's poverty is perhaps more extreme than was historically experienced by afflicted nobility and may reflect the non-courtly nature of author and audience and the type of poverty seen in their culture. But, as seen in other romances, like *Ywain and Gawain*, the stripping away of status and external possessions offers the possibility of a realignment of values and personal growth.[27]

In contrast, Tryamour's use of her inestimable wealth is exemplary. Although it could be argued that she buys Launfal's love, her gifts are freely given and enable the knight to resume his generosity. Nothing is expected from him in return but fidelity and *trouthe*, a seemingly easy exchange. Tryamour's richness of spirit is expressed in her physical appearance, and she uses both to social good. In opposition to Gwennere's use of beauty and position to fulfill her proud and self-absorbed purposes, the fairy mistress reveals her splendor to Artour's court, rendering up her invisibility to save her lover, despite his betrayal. Magnificence, power, and 'lordly generosity' are common to Celtic fées,[28] and Chestre's use of traditional folk motifs as social commentary, seen also in the blinding episode, reflects the original force and function of such motifs as social guideposts and demonstrates his ability to invest them with current meaning.

Launfal's financial vicissitudes force the question of whether an individual should be valued for status and wealth, or for actions and character. While the mayor's daughter treats the poverty-stricken knight with compassion and generosity, her father, who once served the knight, withdraws his initial geniality when he learns that Launfal is no longer a member of Artour's court and therefore without connections or status. This reception is greeted with bitter laughter by Launfal as he tells his companions, 'Now may ye se; swych ys service/ Under a lord of lytyll pryse –/ How he may therof be fayn!' (118–20). Artour's nephews stay with him until he is no longer able to support them (or himself), but they remain faithful to him and keep their promise not to reveal his poverty to anyone. Lucas notes that the knights lie to their uncle in order to protect Launfal's reputation and keep their *trouthe* to the hero, which is an 'example, in miniature, of an ironic situation arising from

---

27 Like other Arthurian knights, Launfal's social position in the literature may not be in keeping with modern views of the medieval socioeconomic structure. Depending on their family background and relationship to the king and baronage, knights might be placed among the lower aristocracy or upper middle class with wealthy gentry and merchants and burgesses. However, since most Arthurian knights occupy a place of honor at court and often replace the peerage (although not in *Sir Launfal*, in which the magnates are visible as judges), Launfal is being treated here as literary nobility, especially in his role as court steward.

28 L. A. Hibbard, *Mediæval Romance in England: A Study of the Sources and Analogues of the Non-Cyclic Metrical Romances* (New York, 1924).

conflicting loyalties'[29] that is writ large in Launfal's obligations to both lord and lover.

When Tryamour greets the destitute knight, she is fully aware of his 'stat, ord & ende' (314) and offers her love based on his innate attributes rather than outer accouterments. Her gifts exceed his previous wealth, but the conditions she places on him test his character and inner strength; to keep her love, he must prove himself worthy through action.[30] Tryamour gives Launfal all he needs to excel: unlimited resources, her own steed and servant, her banner to carry into battle, and protection in armed combat.[31] Thus his chivalric success is assured, as long as he meets her conditions of fidelity and *trouthe*.

With Tryamour's help, Launfal reenters Artour's court and surpasses his earlier popularity, but he soon learns that an individual's behavior and trust in social contracts does not guarantee fair valuation or treatment. In fact, chivalric reputation, both military and moral, often engenders envy and vulnerability in the face of self-interest and political expediency. Sir Launfal's attributes and accomplishments do not safeguard him from mistreatment by the queen and mayor, or from inequity during his trial. His prowess invites challenges from glory seekers, and his success at court attracts Gwennere's attention. Launfal is not a perfect character; he is tinged with pride, rashness and immoderation, yet his difficulties within his culture stem largely from the failings of others, as is forcefully demonstrated during his trial.

The Judicial System

The accusation, trial and acquittal of Launfal call for reexamination and reform of the justice system and its supporting values, and exposes the forces that threaten the individual's ability to exist in a society in which self-interest is dominant. Assuming Chestre's audience was composed of middling urban (and perhaps rural) members, his poem gives a view of the judicial system from a different perspective than that of courtly writers. Despite social differences, similar criticism of the administration of justice is voiced by contemporary authors at all levels.

Chestre focuses on the corruption of judges and, because of their places in the community as barons, the entire court by extension. The Lanval narrative is set against a historical backdrop of movement toward judicial inquiry rather than trial by combat or ordeal, the weight of the written document, an

---

[29] P. J. Lucas, 'An Interpretation of *Sir Launfal*', *Medium Ævum* 39 (1970), 291–300, p. 298.

[30] If largesse is Launfal's 'only recognizable courtly quality' rather than the prowess and valor he possesses in *Lanval* (C. J. Nappholz in 'Launfal's "Largesse": Word-play in Thomas Chestre's *Sir Launfal*', *English Language Notes* [March 1988], 4–9, p. 5), one wonders whether the gifts given by Tryamour are intended to make up for the knight's lack of chivalric attributes.

[31] Chestre either ignored or was unaware of the ban on the use of any type of enchantment stated in the *Fourme of Fighting within Lists*. According to Leister, a knight who employed any such supernatural power was guilty of covetousness. G. A. Leister, 'Gawain's Fault in Terms of Counting Law of Arms', *Notes and Queries* 23 (1976), 392–3, p. 393.

emphasis on witnesses and evidence and judgment by peers, and concern over the authority of the king and shifting alliances within the court. The Old French critiques of the justiciary resonated with the judicial abuses and governmental failures observed in the fourteenth century. Like its sources, *Sir Launfal* was written during a time of unsettled monarchical control and social instability, which inevitably involves the judiciary arm of rule, an area inherently vulnerable to scrutiny.

The literary representation and examination of the respective cultures' judicial systems comprise a major portion of each version of the narrative (about one-fourth of *Graelent* and *Sir Launfal*, and nearly one-half of *Landevale* and *Lanval*). The authors' commentaries reflect the propensity, especially during times of transition, to cling to the ideal model which, although it may never have existed in reality, serves as a stabilizer. Each poet implicitly or explicitly envisions a king who rules fairly and wisely and a corresponding judicial system. In *Launfal* the intervention of a supernatural being in the administration of justice condemns the failure of ruler and court and presents a model for emulation: perfect moral and humane value and action.

Launfal reflects an ingrained wariness and suspicion by the populace, formed over a long period of time and successions of reigns. The tension between monarchical and feudal interests, corruption at all levels of judicial administration, and the threat of mistreatment and exploitation undergirded an established antagonism towards the king, his royal representatives, and local enforcement officials. While Chestre is notoriously unfamiliar with life at court, he and his audience would distrust the judiciary system from personal experience at the local level and hold the king ultimately responsible.

Assuming that *Sir Launfal* was written during the late fourteenth century, a look at the historical background provides ample evidence of erosion within the judicial system. Under Edward III, officials were widely corrupt, and impartially administered justice was not the rule. Justices held superfluous sessions to gain increased revenue, jurors were bribed, and false accusations made. Although some abuses were punished, the corruption could not be curbed. Richard II's failings as king and judge were recorded during his reign, although contemporary reports were undoubtedly slanted towards the interests of the authors. The list of his transgressions at deposition includes flagrant misuse and abuse of the law:[32]

> Item, being unwilling to protect and preserve the just laws and customs of the realm . . . frequently, from time to time, when the laws were declared and set forth to him by the Justices and others of his Council, and he should have done justice to those who sought it according to those laws – he said expressly, with harsh and insolent looks, that his laws were in his own mouth, and sometimes, within his breast; and that he alone could change or establish the laws of his realm. Deceived by which opinion, he would not allow justice to be done to

---

[32] 'The Charges Against Richard II' from the *Rotuli Parliamentorum* of 1399, in *The Past Speaks to 1688: Sources and Problems in English History*, ed. L. B. Smith and J. R. Smith (Lexington, 1981).

many of his lieges, but compelled numbers of persons to desist from suing common right by threats and fear.

The author of 'Treuth, rest, and pes' in 1401 captures the importance of equitable justice in maintaining social stability:[33]

> Trouþe is messager to ry3t,
> And ry3t is counseille to Iustice;
>   Iustice in goddis stede is dy3t.
> Do euene lawe to fooll *and* wyse.
> Set mesure in euene assise,
>   The ri3te weye as lawe ges.
> And lawe be kept, folk nyl not ryse.
>   That kyngdom shal haue reste *and* pes.   (9–16)

The corrupting influence on the judicial system of *mede* against which the poet warns is manifest in the motivation of the judges in the Lanval tale. Their behaviour is tantamount to accepting bribery; by delivering the condemnation the lord desires, they will gain his favor, which inevitably includes gifts of personal and real property, as well as social status.

Launfal's actual transgression is invisible to the outside world; his lack of *trouthe* to Tryamour is known only to the lovers (and Gyfre and Blaunchard), while he is accused publicly of seducing Gwennere and making a false boast about his lover's beauty. The obvious irony is that the consequences of Launfal's true sin prevent him from proving his innocence of the queen's perjurious accusations. There is a double-stranded action in which the manifestations of *trouthe* are tested: as fidelity in the private sphere of the lovers, and as social integrity in the public world. The poet explores the interrelationship between the values and worlds, and the effect of that dynamism on the individual.

The accusation and trial become a struggle between those who put their own interests ahead of justice and those who wish to uphold the judicial system. The initial failing lies with Gwennere, and her conduct during the trial underscores her previous willful and spiteful behavior. While in *Graelent* she remains silent, and in *Lanval* shows impatience because she has 'trop lungement jeünot' (546) (fasted too long), in *Landevale* the queen panics when the supernatural guests begin arriving and she begs Artour to 'sle Landevale thou woldest not spare' so that she is 'avenged on that tratour' (420–1). Chestre follows *Landevale* almost verbatim; Gwennere tells the king she should be 'awreke of that traytour' (920) and tells him that 'Launfal thou schuldest not spare' (922). In both fourteenth-century texts, the queen urges Artour to pass sentence on the hero because the judges, who have hesitated to make judgement pending proof of his innocence, have caused the king 'bysmare' (*Landevale* 422; *Launfal* 923).

---

[33] 'Treuth, reste, and pes', in *Twenty-Six Political and Other Poems from the Digby 102 Manuscript*, ed. J. Kail (London, 1904).

But the greater culprit is Artour who, as head judge, is responsible for ensuring equitable justice for all his subjects. From the outset, Artour allows his royal pride and emotional attachment to Gwennere to override the impartiality that marks a fair judge. Upon hearing Gwennere's tearful and wrathful accusations, he 'swor hys oth' (722) to have Launfal 'honged and to-drawe' (726).[34] This harsh punishment, standard for treason during the period, implied breaches of both moral and social order[35] and was shameful, since it was executed publicly.[36] Artour follows judicial procedure by holding a trial, but only to validate the execution of Launfal, not to determine his guilt or innocence.

The perversion of the justice system involves more than Gwennere's perjury and Artour's partiality; it also results from the political motivation of the baronage. Artour fully expects his judges to condemn Launfal because the king desires it, and many are willing 'the Kyng to queme' (879), even when it becomes apparent that Launfal is not guilty. This is perhaps the most damning social criticism in the poem, an illustration of the fissure between an individual's right action and his treatment by society.

Chestre's intentional focus on this theme is borne out by comparison with his primary and secondary source materials. In *Lanval*, the hero is an alienated figure, resented by his peers; Graelent is a well-liked but retained knight who is the king's 'soudoier' (133) (in the pay of the king/mercenary), and Carlile is an 'uncuth londe' for Landevale (27). Unlike Marie or the *Landevale*-poet, Chestre provides proof of Launfal's favor with the king, whose gifts of money and his two nephews as companions upon the knight's departure from court contrast sharply with the ruler's later rash prejudgment of his steward. Although from another land, Launfal is fully absorbed into Arthurian society and admired for his gifts, and therefore a less likely target of suspicion and malignment than a foreigner. Chestre's adaptation of Launfal's status from envied, lone stranger to integrated courtier emphasizes the judges' fickleness and indicts those barons who are willing to sacrifice a valued community member in order to fulfill their own political agenda.

Launfal is thus bound by Gwennere's falsity, Artour's vengeance, and the judges' ambition. He is saved by the humaneness of the few honest barons only long enough for the arrival of his fairy lover, her evidence, and enactment of justice. Tryamour as moral agent is not a unique theme. Supernatural beings appear in similar roles, like the appearance in *The Awntyrs off Arthure at the Terne Wathelyne* of Gaynour's dead mother to the queen and Gawayn in

---

[34] As Gwennere undermines the justice system, Artour perverts oathmaking and keeping with his precipitous promise to execute Launfal. Such negative use of oaths is seen in *Ywain and Gawain*, with Harpin the giant's 'ath' made 'depely' (2264) to kill Gawain's sister's sons and take her daughter to give as whore to his lackeys. Harpin's pledge, like Artour's, stresses the inevitability of his threatened actions and his determination to carry them through. 'Ywain and Gawain', in *Middle English Romances: Authoritative Texts, Sources and Backgrounds, Criticism*, ed. S. H. A. Shepherd (New York, 1995).

[35] W. R. J. Barron, 'The Penalties for Treason in Medieval Life and Literature', *Journal of Medieval History* 7 (1981), 187–202, p. 189.

[36] Ibid., p. 199.

order to deliver a didactic warning against pride and to counsel them to culti-vate humility and charity.[37] Tryamour functions much like another other-worldly moral agent, the Green Knight. In both *Sir Launfal* and *Sir Gawain and the Green Knight*, the heroes make promises to supernatural beings. Gawain gives two oaths to the Green Knight: one during the beheading game, and the other during the exchange of winnings game. Launfal gives a dual promise to Tryamour: to love her faithfully and to refrain from boasting about her. In both tales, the knights keep one of their oaths and fail to keep the second; the *trouthe* of both men is tested, as well as their chivalric and social honour. They are tempted through sexual seduction, and although both pass that trial, they fail the underlying test of character: Gawain to save his life, and Launfal to save his face.[38]

When the knights fail their respective tests, the supernatural beings expose the heroes' failures: the shape-shifting Green Knight by revelation of his dual identity as Bertilak and hence his knowledge of Gawain's behavior at Hautdesert, and Tryamour by her disappearance. These events are private, between the hero and the supernatural being. Both moral agents keep the oaths they made as part of their 'bargains' with the heroes; the Green Knight delivers punishment by nicking Gawain's neck when 'beheading' him, and Tryamour punishes her lover by withdrawing from his world. But both knights must also face the judgment of the 'real' courts, not for their true fail-ings but for those imagined by its members.

Tryamour and the Green Knight both perceive the true flaws of the heroes and deliver judgment and punishment that would not be exacted by society, and each acts out of mercy. The Green Knight spares Gawain's head and offers him an elevated perspective of human striving; the knight's original oath is excused and salvation offered instead. Similarly Tryamour forgives Launfal for his original transgression and offers him sanctuary. Both the *Gawain*-poet and Chestre test reality against ideality, with different results; Gawain's lesson is to accept the imperfection of human existence, and Launfal's is to reject it in favor of an ideal, moral world.

Chestre's Resolution

Although Gwennere's offenses deserve punishment, the severity of the penalty remains problematic, despite the legally binding situation in which she sets her own *wajowr*. Why did Chestre choose blinding? An obvious physical manifestation of Gwennere's moral and spiritual blindness, the motif

---

[37] See S. G. Fein, 'The Ghoulish and the Ghastly: A Moral Aesthetic in Middle English Alliterative Verse', *Modern Language Quarterly* 48, No. 1 (1987), 3–19.

[38] While nudity is not common in medieval literature, it appears in the Lanval narrative and *Sir Gawain and the Green Knight*. The near-nudity of Lady Bertilak is recalled in Tryamour's first appearance to Launfal as she lies partially clothed in bed due to the heat; in *Lanval* she is scantily clad, and in *Graelent* the fairy mistress is completely naked, bathing in a pool.

has both generic and extraliterary validation. Grouped with the Breton lais within the romance mode, *Sir Launfal* shares with those forms a dependence on folkloric elements and, as long noted by critics, Chestre's successful exploitation of the folk narrative brings his poem as near to fairy tale as to romance.

Folk tale motifs are commonplace in romances; Marie's version of the narrative is a 'true fairy story, dressed as a romance',[39] and Keightly finds the 'fairy machinery more pleasingly displayed' in *Sir Launfal* than in any other romance.[40] Critics laud, denigrate or simply observe Chestre's emphasis on the folk tale elements, but few consider the deeper implications of those attributes and their contributions to the poem's meaning.[41] While it is true that Chestre 'rationalizes' the fairy tale world and brings it 'into closer contact with the day-to-day experience of the audience',[42] it cannot be agreed that the psychologizing effects achieved by the poet distance it from the world of the Breton lai or negate the fairy tale operation of the poem. Rather, it captures the discourse of the genre as defined by Barron, who places folk tales as a subdivision of the romance 'mode' and explains that folk and fairy tales represent fundamental realities, 'what life is like'; romance adds the imagined ideal of 'what life might be'.[43] Like dreams, folk and fairy tales address the 'universal nature'[44] of the emotions, and allow the audience to confront challenges, conflicts and aspirations common to human experience.[45] While folk tales are 'the same the world over',[46] they often reflect their culture and present perceptions of the world as seen by author and audience; they tend to absorb something of the place in which they are narrated, such as a moral outlook.[47] They function as guideposts to ethical behaviour and social conformation.

---

[39] K. M. Briggs, *The Fairies in Tradition and Literature* (London, 1967), p. 9.

[40] T. Keightley, *The Fairy Mythology* (London, 1931), p. 34.

[41] B. K. Martin's attempt to defend the poem against charges of 'disquieting and inartistic' traits (p. 210) is disappointing. While trying to validate the work by placing it in the folk tale tradition, Martin trivializes both poem and tradition through observations that 'the characterization of Arthur as cuckolded husband and undignified monarch are irrelevant within the conventions . . . [they are] undeveloped motifs of the usual folktale kind' (p. 208) and that the blinding, while deserved, is another 'undeveloped motif' from which no moralizing conclusions are to be drawn. Nor does Tryamour's benevolence and affection have moral relevance. Folk tales are not meant to evoke feelings, and audiences become desensitized to the impact of the tales' harshness through familiarity with the genre (207). In short, Martin implies that since *Sir Launfal* is only a folk tale, it may be excused for its flaws but need not be taken seriously. See B. K. Martin, 'Sir Launfal and the Folktale', *Medium Ævum* 35 (1966), 199–210.

[42] D. Mehl, *The Middle English Romances of the Thirteenth and Fourteenth Centuries* (New York, 1969), p. 44.

[43] W. R. J. Barron, *English Medieval Romance* (London, 1987), p. 4.

[44] Ibid., p. 3.

[45] In 'Psychology and the Middle English Romances', Veldorn traces the development of Launfal's selfhood through his adventures. Such Jungian and Freudian approaches would seem to indicate a more complex characterization than is often considered in folk and fairy tales, but Veldorn views the romance heroes who experience such development as representative rather than individual. See B. Veldhoen, 'Psychology of the Middle English Romances', in *Companion to Middle English Romance*, ed. H. Aeertsen and A. A. MacDonald (Amsterdam, 1990), 101–28.

[46] I. Calvino, *Italian Folktales*, trans. G. Martin (New York, 1956), p. xx.

[47] Ibid., p. xxi.

These elements are clearly present in *Sir Launfal*, along with standard folk and fairy tale attributes, such as an origin in oral form, a supernatural element, a tendency toward violence, harsh retribution, and the struggles of the hero to live in an unjust, cruel world filled with adversaries. Folk/fairy tale motifs found in the poem include the offended fée, the fairy prohibition, the impoverished/spendthrift knight, the quest for a lost wife, human/fairy marriage, the vanishing bride, the journey to the Otherworld, magic gifts, combat with a giant, and a beauty competition. According to scholars, the blinding motif is unparalleled in Arthurian literature and, in the absence of a known source, appears to be Chestre's invention; it is, however, a traditional folk tale motif and therefore seems well-suited to *Sir Launfal*. In folklore, mortals who gain sight of supernatural beings often do so by means of magic ointment, usually intended for another recipient and accidentally or purposely misapplied, often by a midwife. Once the forbidden sight is discovered, the offender is blinded. Hartland recounts tales that contain these episodes; in several, the supernatural beings effect the blindness with their breath.[48]

Laskaya and Salisbury note the folk tale derivation of the blinding and suggest that in a more courtly narrative, 'shame might well have been sufficient punishment'.[49] They consider Gwennere's wager a 'casual remark' and neglect to place it within the judicial setting or to connect her blinding with her many wrongdoings. The courtly narrative imagined by Laskaya and Salisbury would have to alter the queen's character so that shame would bring self-reflection, awareness of her misdeeds, and a resolve to conform to societal expectations, which are the operative values of shame; otherwise, it would not be 'sufficient' punishment. Unlike the queen in *Graelent*, who feels 'grant honte' (604) (great shame) and leaves the court when the fairy mistress' maidens appear (although one suspects that she is more shamed by the others' beauty and demeanor than by her own actions), it is doubtful whether Gwennere would be capable of experiencing the type of shame that leads to reformed behavior, whether heartfelt or not.

The exposure of transgressions by and to the public, used as a coercive tool of 'penitential discipline',[50] presupposes a fear of humiliation in the eyes of one's peers and a conscience capable of recognizing the censured action and experiencing mortification. When the Green Knight reveals his knowledge of Gawain's lack of *trouthe*, the erring hero 'schrank for schame' and 'alle þe blode of his brest blende in his face' (*SGGK* 71–2).[51] Gawain feels neither guilt nor shame for his 'untrawþe' until a fellow knight reproaches him and

---

[48] E. S. Hartland, *The Science of Fairy Tales: An Inquiry into Fairy Mythology*, 2nd edn (London, 1925), pp. 62–9.

[49] Laskaya and Salisbury, *Lays*, p. 204.

[50] J. A. Burrow, 'Honour and Shame in *Sir Gawain and the Green Knight*', in *Essays on Medieval Literature* (Oxford, 1984), 117–31, p. 126.

[51] All citations from *Sir Gawain and the Green Knight* are from *The Poems of the Pearl Manuscript*, ed. M. Andrew and R. Waldron (Berkeley, 1978).

makes his failing externally visible,[52] at which point he assesses his sin against the ideal behavior to which he aspires and begrudgingly admits his failure.

Gwennere is capable of neither shame nor honest self-assessment, and even public exposure may not have assaulted her protective shell of pride and position. Given the queen's character in *Sir Launfal*, shame or even direct punishment, unless severe, might exact justice but still would have little or no effect on her nature. Her blindness is akin to the green sash that Gawain wears for life as a mark of his dishonour and shame, or of his humanity from the Green Knight's perspective. Gwennere is guilty of transgressions against society, individuals and her soul; her blindness, unlike transitory shame, is a permanent, visible sign of her sins. So her crimes will be forever refreshed in the court's consciousness and her own.

A desire for a similarly lasting impression on his audience may have motivated Chestre's choice of the blinding motif. Harsh corporal punishment was uncommon in England in the later Middle Ages. Punishment by mutilation, including blinding, for civil crimes appears in legal treatises in the thirteenth century, but these practices 'probably ceased by the turn of the century'.[53] If there was little historical basis for blinding as a punishment in Chestre's day, what impact would it have had on his audience? A remarkable punishment, especially one so grisly, would make a strong impression, and the motif may also have carried connotations of the severity of the crimes, particularly to folk who may have witnessed or recalled the punishment.

The exception to such harsh corporal punishment was treason, which often drew mutilation and execution.[54] In his discussion of flaying as punishment for that crime, Barron observes the paucity of records that provide evidence of flaying as a contemporary practice, compared to its frequent appearance in medieval literature. He theorizes that the punishment evoked an abhorrent association with both the execution of the act and the serious moral and social crimes it came to symbolize: 'The detestation felt for the crimes which merited [flaying], the unforgettable spectacle it must have been for anyone who ever saw it carried out, account for the traces it has left in language, folklore and literature.'[55] A similar process may have occurred with blinding, which passed into literature, carrying with it an aura of criminality and frightful justice. Folk tales may have kept blinding as punishment (particularly by a supernatural agent) alive for the medieval audience, in addition to the memory of its historical use. Salisbury notes the connection of blinding

---

[52] Burrow, 'Honour', p. 126.

[53] J. Bellamy, *Crime and Public Order in England in the Later Middle Ages* (London, 1973), p. 181.

[54] An intriguing, and perhaps not unrelated, appearance of blinding is found in Marie's fable, 'De la chalve suriz' (The Bat). Reminiscent of a folkloric 'How the Bat Lost his Sight' tale, the fable relates how the bat is punished with blinding for 'felunie' (31) and 'traïsun' (32) to his lord and community by their 'Crïere' (34) (Creator), at the request of the other animals. The moral of the fable warns against feudal infidelity, which will bring eternal shame and loss of position and honor. 'De la chalve suriz', *Marie de France: Fables*, ed. and trans. H. Spiegel (Toronto, 1994).

[55] Barron, 'Penalties', p. 197.

with the crime of rape and the irony of Gwennere receiving a punishment associated with sexual offense.[56] Although hanging was the punishment for rape by the end of the thirteenth century,[57] the memory of the threat of blinding for that crime may have retained resonance in Chestre's time.[58]

Blinding was still perceived as a menace in fourteenth-century literature, if not in practice. In *Wynnere and Wastour*, the king's knight warns the assembled armies 'That no beryn be so bolde, on bothe his two eghne,/ Ones to strike one stroke' (126–7).[59] The threat of blinding as punishment for breaking the king's peace was poetically effective and may suggest that such punishments were conventional, although generally unimplemented, tools of intimidation. Gwennere's choice of an outmoded sentence therefore might be made with no expectation of execution and seem safe. If so, this would make Gwennere's 'casual' oath even more casual, but unhappily for the queen, blinding is not beyond the scope of Tryamour's justice. Considering the grave social and political consequences to the court of the queen's misdeeds, harsh corporal punishment associated with treason is appropriate.

With the hero exonerated and taken by his lover to live in a world unmarred by greed and injustice, the Lanval narrative ends happily. Of the four knights, Launfal is the only one who returns to the 'real' world. In *Graelent* his mourning horse is the last vestige of the knight's presence and departure, a rather eerie reminder of the adventure. The horse appears in *Sir Launfal* as herald to the knight's annual return to joust with 'Ho that wyll ther axsy justus –/ To kepe hys armes fro the rustus –/ In turnement other fyghtt' (1027). Launfal returns as an ideal knight against whom others may test themselves (although his mortal vulnerability is protected by his supernatural lover). But his return is also a link with the real world, which preserves Launfal's humanity and prevents total integration into Olyroun.

Is retreating into the world of Faërie a 'happy ending'? Perhaps, if living in the ideal moral world of Tryamour is preferable to the corrupt real world. The hero's choice not to reintegrate into his society is unusual in the romance mode. Launfal tries to lead a life in which he fulfills his desires: to have his fairy mistress while living in a non-magical world. But the demands of culture, driven by human nature, prevent such a blend, and the knight must choose. His rejection of Artour's court and its values is appropriate to Chestre's commentary. But while the denouement to *Sir Launfal* at first seems

---

[56] E. Salisbury, 'Chaucer's "Wife", the Law, and the Middle English Breton Lays' (work in progress), *Le Cygne*, No. 5 (Spring 1999), p. 57.

[57] J. Bellamy, *The Criminal Trial in Later Medieval England: Felony before the Courts from Edward I to the Sixteenth Century* (Phoenix Mill, 1998), p. 164.

[58] Punishment for rape vacillated during the thirteenth century and included at different times and in different locales death, dismemberment, imprisonment and/or monetary fines. Although maiming, including blinding as prescribed by Bracton, was at times the recommended punishment, Carter points out the discrepancies between theory and practice; based on eyre roll evidence, penalties were frequently less severe than allowed by statute. J. M. Carter, *Rape in Medieval England: An Historical and Sociological Study* (Lanham, MD, 1985), p. 41. Thanks to Eve Salisbury for suggesting this source of information on blinding.

[59] 'Wynnere and Wastoure', in *Middle English Debate Poetry*, ed. J. W. Conlee (East Lansing, 1991).

ideal, on closer inspection it raises deeper questions. As in *Sir Gawain and the Green Knight*, there is ambiguity about the possibility of aligning personal ideals with societal expectations, and the role of human strength and frailty in achieving a productive symbiosis. Perhaps unintentionally, the Lanval narrative poets pose the dilemma of whether rejection of an inevitably flawed world is the right choice, or whether social integration through struggle, compromise and acceptance is part of the human challenge. Maybe Faërie is not the perfect place for a mortal after all.

VII

MALORY'S *MORTE DARTHUR*:
A POLITICALLY NEUTRAL ENGLISH ADAPTATION
OF THE ARTHURIAN STORY

Edward Donald Kennedy

Arthure. Whan he was crowned kyng was but yonge of age. but he was fayr of body and doughti of manhode and wel belouyd among alle hys peple and had many batailes ageyns the Saxsons and all the londes aboute Breteyn he made ham vnder hys abeysauns. He conquered the Romayns and slue Lucius har lorde. And whan Arthure was thus in greet trauail and in batail than Modrede the traitour that had the gouernuance of the londe toke it to hymself ageyns the kyngis entente. And whan kyng Arthure herd therof he come home to avenge hym upon that traitour and myche peple was slayn and afterward Modrede was slayn in batail and kyng Arthure was wounded to deth. And he betoke the crowne to Constantyne hys cosyn that was son to Cadors erle of Cornewaile after the incarnacion of oure lord fyue hyundred fourti and sexe yere.

(Bodleian e Mus 42)

This is a concise summary of the chronicle account of King Arthur, a longer version of which is told in hundreds of surviving manuscripts of English, Anglo-Norman, and Latin chronicles written after Geoffrey of Monmouth's twelfth-century *Historia Regum Britanniae*. It would have served as a reminder of the full story, and fifteenth-century readers, like many today, would have been able to supply the missing details. Bodleian e Museo 42, from which the quotation above is taken, is a manuscript of an English genea-logical chronicle of Edward IV produced sometime between 1467 and 1469. It is one of thirty-six surviving English and Latin pedigrees and genealogical chronicles produced as Yorkist propaganda to help establish Edward's claim to the throne: these include twenty-two pedigrees produced for Edward, with fifteen of them showing his British descent;[1] the four surviving manuscripts produced during Edward's life of a work known as the *Longer English Genealogical Chronicle of the Kings of England*, whose account of Arthur appears above; five manuscripts of the shorter version of this chronicle; and at

---

[1] S. Anglo, 'The British History in Early Tudor Propaganda', *Bulletin of the John Rylands Library* 44 (1961–62), 17–48.

least five surviving Latin versions of the longer and shorter English texts.[2] These genealogical chronicles are not well known, since most have never been edited.[3] Fourteen of them appear to have been produced at one workshop in London between 1461 and 1475, with new ones being commissioned when, for example, Edward had another child.

Edward claimed to fulfill the prophecy that a British king would once again rule Britain, not because he wanted to win favor with the Welsh but, as Alison Allan points out, because he wished to take advantage of the English public's interest in what is now known as the 'legendary history of Britain'.[4] Allan writes that the legends of early Britain formed a 'significant body of propaganda in the years after 1461' when Edward came to the throne. 'For the immediate vindication of Edward's dynastic claims,' she writes, 'only the generations of the fourteenth and fifteenth centuries were of importance; but to these were harnessed tales of earlier kings and realms to give the Yorkist king an impressive pedigree which emphasised the antiquity of the royal line he represented.'[5]

According to P. J. C. Field's estimate, Malory probably began work on *Morte Darthur* by 1467 or 1468 and completed it between March 1469 and March 1470.[6] While writing the book, he was a prisoner of Edward IV, a prisoner apparently considered so dangerous that the king excluded him from general pardons that he offered during these years.[7] Between 1467–70, at approximately the same time that Malory was in prison, Edward commissioned three of his genealogical chronicles, including Bodleian e Mus 42, chronicles that suggest both Edward's interest in his British descent and in the English chronicle version of the Arthurian story.[8] Thus Edward's interest in the Arthurian story could have given Malory incentive to compose a new version of the story of Arthur that might please the king.

---

2   See my *Chronicles and Other Historical Writing*, vol. 8 of *A Manual of the Writings in Middle English*, gen. ed. A. E. Hartung (New Haven, 1989), pp. 2676–77, 2889–90.

3   Thomas Wright, who in the nineteenth century edited parts of several French, Latin, and English genealogical chronicles dating from the thirteenth to the fifteenth centuries, explained why such chronicles had remained unedited, and his explanation still reflects the attitude of many today: '[T]he history . . . seems to be of no value, and is accompanied with equally useless genealogical tables of the fabulous kings which would give great inconvenience in printing.' See Wright's *Feudal Manuals of English History: A Series of Popular Sketches of Our National History Compiled at Different Periods from the Thirteenth Century to the Fifteenth* (London, 1872), pp. xviii–xix. Few would dispute the inconvenience of attempting to reproduce in print genealogical rolls several feet long. The history in these works, however, is of more value than Wright and others realized: the genealogical chronicles of Edward and of his predecessors and successors offer significant evidence of propaganda that kings used to establish their often dubious claims to the throne.

4   A. Allan, 'Yorkist Propaganda: Pedigree, Prophecy and the 'British History' in the Reign of Edward IV', in *Patronage, Pedigree and Power in Later Medieval England*, ed. C. Ross (Gloucester, Eng., 1979), p. 178.

5   Allan, 'Yorkist Propaganda', p. 172.

6   P. J. C. Field, *The Life and Times of Sir Thomas Malory* (Cambridge, 1993), pp. 34, 132.

7   Field, *The Life and Times*, pp. 31–32, 132.

8   See A. de la Mare, *Catalogue of the Collection of Medieval Manuscripts Bequeathed to the Bodleian Library Oxford by James P. R. Lyell* (Oxford, 1971), pp. 80–85, and Allan, 'Yorkist Propaganda', pp. 174, 190 n. 15.

Malory in all likelihood would have known something about Edward's interests in the story. In the earlier years of Edward's reign, Malory had supported Edward, and for a few years he appears to have been associated with the lower levels of Edward's court and possibly tried with little success for royal favor.[9] His name on a list of knights that accompanied Edward on a northern campaign to Alnwick and Bamburgh in 1462 could indicate, Richard Barber suggests, that although apparently not a member of the royal household, he nevertheless probably had some standing among those around the king. Edward's court was one that would probably have appealed to Malory since Edward attempted to revive the courtly culture of the court of Edward III and to imitate the contemporary courts of Burgundy and Italy, and his court was a place where, according to Edward IV's household ordinances, the 'esquiers of houshold' were accustomed to spend their evenings talking of the 'cronycles of kinges'.[10]

Since Edward claimed to be remotely descended from Arthur and included the Arthurian story in his genealogical chronicles, Malory wrote his book at a time when the Arthurian story could have had important political significance. Moreover, the book, written during the Wars of the Roses, suggests a correspondence between the contemporary civil war and the story of a nation destroyed by internal dissension. It is therefore not surprising that scholars have pointed to what they believed to have been allusions to contemporary politics and events, although there has often been disagreement over what side Malory was on and to which events he was referring. Several have attempted to show that Malory as a prisoner of Edward IV included in his work a number of allusions that were anti-Yorkist, and others have argued just as fervently that, in spite of his imprisonment and possibly to gain favor with the king, he wrote a book that was pro-Yorkist. I believe, however, that there is virtually nothing in Malory's book that could be described as either specifically anti-Yorkist or pro-Yorkist, that the book is about as politically neutral as possible, and that unlike some others writing Arthurian chronicles during the reign of Edward IV, Malory was not writing political propaganda that would support either side, was not presenting Arthur as a model for Edward, and was not commenting on contemporary policies.

I shall devote the first part of this article to discussing what I believe to be the weaknesses of the arguments for contemporary political allusions in the book and thus the improbability that Malory intended *Morte Darthur* as any kind of political propaganda. In the second part, I shall argue that although Malory was not writing political propaganda, he was nevertheless writing a version of the Arthurian story that might have pleased the king because it was an English version of the story based upon French romances that were popular with the English upper classes, but that had been available for the most part

---

[9] R. Barber, 'Malory's *Le Morte Darthur* and Court Culture under Edward IV', *Arthurian Literature* 12 (1993), 134.

[10] Barber, 'Malory's *Le Morte Darthur* and Court Culture', pp. 141–45, 137.

only in French. Thus the book, although not written as political propaganda, could nevertheless have been written to win the favor of a king interested in the Arthurian story.

1. *THE CASE AGAINST POLITICAL BIAS IN* MORTE DARTHUR

The parallel between the civil war in the Arthurian tragedy and the contemporary war between the houses of York and Lancaster would, of course, account for much of the appeal of the Arthurian tragedy to Malory and fifteenth-century readers.[11] Because of this obvious parallel and because of Malory's status as a prisoner who had been denied pardons by Edward IV, scholars have attempted to find more specific correspondences between Malory's book and contemporary politics. As I mentioned above, scholars have not agreed as to whether Malory is making statements that support the Yorkists or the Lancastrians, with some suggesting his Arthur is modeled on Henry VI and others on Edward IV or even Henry V, and efforts to determine Malory's political sentiments on the basis of the text of *Morte Darthur* have produced results of dubious validity. Field has presented the most recent, thorough and balanced survey of the supposedly contemporary allusions in Malory's work, and he rightly dismisses most of them as illusory if not ambiguous.[12] Field accepts several of the political/historical allusions that scholars have proposed, but he points out that, in a book the length of Malory's, the number is relatively few.[13] Moreover, they are inconsistent since several appear to refer sympathetically to the Lancastrians and a few to the Yorkists. Most of them are, as Field points out, geographical rather than historical or political and are thus attempts to provide more geographical verisimilitude than was present in the French romances rather than allusions to particular events.[14]

---

[11] For a good account of the historical and social context in which *Morte Darthur* was written, see F. Riddy, 'Contextualizing *Le Morte Darthur*', in *A Companion to Malory*, ed. E. Archibald and A. S. G. Edwards (Cambridge, 1996), pp. 55–73.

[12] P. J. C. Field, 'Fifteenth-Century History in Malory's *Morte Darthur*', in *Malory: Texts and Sources*, Arthurian Studies 40 (Cambridge, 1998), pp. 47–71, reprinted from *The Foundation of Culture in Medieval Britain*, ed. F. H. M. Le Saux (Lewiston, NY, 1995), pp. 39–70. Views that he dismisses include N. S. Aurner, 'Sir Thomas Malory – Historian', *PMLA* 48 (1933), 362–91; Eugène Vinaver's view that the portrait of Arthur in Malory's Tale 2 was influenced by the European campaign of Henry V (*The Works of Sir Thomas Malory*, ed. E. Vinaver, rev. P. J. C. Field, 3rd edn, 3 vols. (Oxford, 1990), 1.xxxi–xxxii, 3.1367–8, 1396–8); R. R. Griffith, 'The Political Bias of Malory's "Morte Darthur" ', *Viator* 5 (1974), 365–86; and my 'Malory and the Marriage of Edward IV', *Texas Studies in Literature and Language* 12 (1970), 155–62, an article that I, too, willingly dismiss.

[13] Field, 'Fifteenth-Century History', 70.

[14] Vinaver, for example, had thought that Malory's addition of Flanders to Arthur's itinerary in the account of the Roman campaign was to make Arthur's itinerary correspond to Henry V's; Field, however, indicates that Malory in all likelihood added Flanders to make the account of the journey geographically realistic. Malory's identificaton of Lancelot's castle Joyous Garde/Dolerous Garde with either of the northern castles Bamburgh or Alnwick could be reminders of historical events since

I agree with Field on these points but would also argue that virtually all of the others, for which Field finds some validity, should also be rejected.

Field questions, for example, but does not reject a frequently cited piece of evidence for Malory's political sentiments that was first suggested by George R. Stewart in 1935. As an instance in which, in Stewart's words, 'Malory let his anti-Yorkist feelings run away with Arthurian tradition', Malory names the parts of England that were allied with Mordred: 'people aboute London, . . . they of Kente, Southsex and Surrey, Esax, Suffolke and Northefolke' (3.1233). Stewart writes, 'The association of the south-east with a traitor's cause corresponds precisely with the situation in the Wars of the Roses, for in this district . . . lay the strength of the Yorkists.'[15] Scholars such as E. K. Chambers and Vinaver found Stewart's evidence persuasive.[16] The passage need not, however, be read as one that condemned the Yorkists, for there is some question that these areas were strongly Yorkist. Stewart cites as the souce for his information about Yorkist areas William Stubbs' *The Constitutional History of England*, but Stubbs mentions only three of them, Norfolk, Suffolk, and Kent.[17] Other areas that scholars have identified as Yorkist include Malory's London, Surrey, Sussex, and Essex, but they also cite as Yorkist a number of areas that Malory does not mention: Middlesex, Hampshire, Wiltshire, Wales and the Welsh marches, Yorkshire (after 1462) and the southwestern and central Midlands.[18] Richard R. Griffith (who attempts to show that Malory favored the Yorkists) points out that it is an oversimplification to describe the areas mentioned by Malory as Yorkist since between 1455 and 1469 allegiances in the south and east frequently shifted from one side to

---

they were castles in the North seized by the Lancastrians in 1462 and soon recaptured by a group of Yorkists that included Malory; however, as Field points out, this identification could have been made simply to give Lancelot a castle in an out-of-the-way place that was familiar to Malory. Moreover, the identificaiton of Bamburgh could, Field observes, have been suggested by the non-Arthurian section of Hardyng's chronicle which said that Bamburgh was originally called Mount Dolorous. The association of the castle of Magouns in Malory's Tale V with Arundel and Malory's reference to 'the traytoures of Magouns' is ambiguous since the Earl of Arundel had fought for both Lancastrians and Yorkists, and the allusion to Arundel again appears to be 'the product of Malory's liking for plausible geography.' See Field, 'Fifteenth-Century History', pp. 57, 68–69, 60–61, and his 'Malory's Minor Sources', in *Malory: Texts and Sources*, p. 28. A few others that Field cites are, as he acknowledges, either questionable or very minor, such as a reference to Guenevere's 'Queen's Knights' having been suggested by a group of knights that supported Henry VI's Queen Margaret or the allusion in the 'Tristram' to a character Sentrayle, whom William Matthews identified as one of the leading figures in the French wars, Poton de Saintrailles (Field, 'Fifteenth-Century History', pp. 62–65, 58–59; Matthews, *The Ill-Framed-Knight: A Skeptical Inquiry into the Identity of Sir Thomas Malory* [Berkeley and Los Angeles, 1967], p. 148n). Neither of these makes a political statement. Others, such as King Lot's allusion to footmen and a reference to a green shield, seem to have been private to Malory. See Field, 'Fifteenth-Century History', pp. 54–55, 61–62.

15 Stewart, 'English Geography in Malory's "Morte D'Arthur"', *Modern Language Review* 30 (1935), 208–9; discussed in Field, 'Fifteenth-Century History', pp. 66–68.

16 Chambers, *English Literature at the Close of the Middle Ages* (1945, second corrected impression 1947; reprinted Oxford, 1961), p. 205; Vinaver, *Works*, 3.1649. Chambers, however, doubted that Malory generally had 'his eyes much on the England of his own day' (p. 196).

17 Stubbs, *The Constitutional History of England*, vol. 3 (Oxford, 1878), pp. 180–81.

18 C. L. Scofield, *The Life and Reign of Edward IV*, 2 vols. (1923; reprinted London, 1967), 1.85; I. M. W. Harvey, *Jack Cade's Rebellion of 1450* (Oxford, 1991), pp. 183–84; both cited by Field, 'Fifteenth-Century History', p. 67; Griffith, 'Political Bias', p. 372.

the other and that 'it is possible, by selecting one's dates carefully, to present almost any combination of these counties as devoted to whichever Rose one chooses'.[19] Similarly I. M. W. Harvey, describing events of 1460 that help put Edward IV on the throne, writes: 'It would be misleading to characterize the rebels of the South-East as Yorkist. They were not partisan in that manner. They would support whoever appeared to be the best guarantor of good government. The commons of Kent in particular were a remarkably independent political force.'[20]

In addition to the fact that these counties were not indisputably Yorkist, what makes the evidence for political bias in Malory's listing of the counties even more dubious is that Malory's sources could have suggested these same areas. Mordred's control of London is implicit in both the stanzaic *Morte Arthur* and in the French *Mort Artu* since that is where Mordred is able to besiege Guenevere in the Tower. Since Stewart wrote his article, John Hardyng's chronicle has been discovered as a source for Malory, and in that chronicle Mordred controls Dover and Winchester, which would suggest that southeastern counties were under Mordred's control.[21] Hardyng (and other chroniclers) and the French *Mort Artu* indicate that Mordred's allies are the Saxons,[22] and this would have suggested areas like Essex, Sussex, and Surrey. Admittedly Norfolk and Suffolk are in former Anglian areas, but they are contiguous to the other southeastern areas Malory mentions, and in the chronicles the Saxons are the only Germanic tribes mentioned at this point in the story. Moreover, the stanzaic *Morte Arthur* mentions that parliament agrees to crown Mordred 'at Canturbery in Kente' and that Mordred celebrates in Winchester and controls Dover.[23] As Griffith points out, in the stanzaic *Morte Arthur* Mordred bribes the earls and barons along the coast on each side of Dover:

> Forthe to dover þan gan he Ryde,
> . . .
> To erlys And to barons on ylk A syde
> Grete yiftis he gaffe And lettres send,
> And for-sette the see on ylke A syde
> With bold men And bowes bente.[24]

This in itself would include most of the counties listed by Malory. Field, who presents both the views of Stewart and Griffith, observes that although both the literary and political interpretations could be true, the literary interpretation makes a political one unnecessary and that the political interpretation

[19] Griffith, 'Political Bias', p. 371.
[20] Harvey, *Jack Cade's Rebellion*, p. 184.
[21] J. Hardyng, *The Chronicle*, ed. Henry Ellis (London, 1812), pp. 145–46.
[22] Hardyng, *Chronicle*, p. 150; *La Mort le Roi Artu*, ed. J. Frappier, 3rd edn (Geneva, 1964), §§ 180–81, pp. 230–31.
[23] *Le Morte Arthur*, ed. J. D. Bruce, EETS e.s. 88 (1903; reprinted London, 1959), lines 2982–85, 3042–49, pp. 90, 92.
[24] *Morte Arthur*, ed. Bruce, lines 3042–47, p. 92; Griffith, 'Political Bias', p. 373.

'implies a degree of political commitment that would be unique in the *Morte Darthur*'.[25] What is perhaps most important in considering whether the naming of these counties had political significance is that since Arthur was arriving from France, the southeast was the only logical place for Mordred to control. Although Malory's list of areas allied with Mordred could have suggested anti-Yorkist views since the southeast was where the government was located, if he had been questioned about this, he could have replied that the areas were suggested by the sources, including Hardyng's chronicle, a work that had been dedicated to Edward IV and that appears to have been circulated as pro-Yorkist propaganda.[26]

The relatively few historical allusions that Field accepts can also be dismissed. Field, for example, agrees with earlier scholars who believed that Malory, in having the ill Uther Pendragon fight a great host from the north at St Albans, was alluding to the Lancastrian Henry VI's battle at St Albans in 1455, a battle in which 'another sick king was carried forth . . . to meet a host from the North'. Field acknowledges that Malory could have taken this from Hardyng's chronicle, but he observes, 'Even if Hardyng rather than history first made Malory think of bringing the name of St Albans into his story, he is unlikely to have added the name simply to increase the amount of real geography in his book. The two battles of St Albans [1455 and 1461] were too well-known for him to have failed to notice that he was creating an analogue of recent events.'[27] The difficulty with this explanation is that although a reference to St Albans could have reminded readers of the battles, neither Malory nor Hardyng was creating an analogue to these battles: Uther's battle at St Albans ('Verolamium' or 'Veroleyne') can be traced to Geoffrey of Monmouth's *Historia*, and Uther's battle at that location was repeated in the chronicles derived from it, including the popular English prose *Brut*, which survives in at least 173 manuscripts.[28] The same can be said concerning Uther's fighting enemies from the north. Although this coincidentally corresponds to the place from which Henry VI's enemies originated, it is also the place from which Uther's enemies came in the chronicles: Uther was fighting Octa and Oyssa (Eosa) who, according to Geoffrey and his successors, had settled in the region near Scotland.[29] Thus Malory and Hardyng were in all

---

[25] Field, 'Fifteenth-Century History', p. 68.

[26] See below, n. 54.

[27] Field, 'Fifteenth-Century History', pp. 51–52.

[28] See my *Chronicles*, pp. 2818–21, and L. M. Matheson, *The Prose Brut: The Development of a Middle English Chronicle* (Tempe, AZ, 1998). Since my list appeared in 1989, one more manuscript of the prose *Brut*, Brogyntyn 8, has been discovered. Matheson also classifies as *Brut* chronicles 'peculiar texts' which I classify as other chronicles.

[29] See Geoffrey of Monmouth, *Historia Regum Britanniae*, ed. A. Griscom (London, 1929), pp. 429 (VIII.xxxiii), 407 (VIII.viii), 420 (VIII.xviii); *The History of the Kings of Britain*, trans. L. Thorpe (Harmondsworth, 1966), pp. 209, 194, 202–3; for other chronicles, see *Wace's Roman de Brut: A History of the British*, ed. and trans. J. Weiss (Exeter, 1999), pp. 224–25, 200–1, 212–13; *Laʒamon: Brut*, ed. G. L. Brook and R. F. Leslie, vol. 2, EETS o.s. 277 (London, 1978), pp. 508, 438, 474; *Castelford's Chronicle*, ed. C. D. Eckhardt, vol. 1, EETS o.s. 305 (Oxford, 1996), pp. 523–25, 507–9; Robert Mannyng of Brunne, *The Chronicle*, ed. I. Sullens (Binghamton, 1996), pp. 318, 296, 307; *The Brut or The Chronicles of England [Prose Brut]*, ed. F. W. D. Brie, Part 1, EETS o.s. 131 (1906; reprint,

likelihood trying to make their accounts correspond to what readers would have known from older Arthurian chronicles rather than from recent events.

Similarly Field sees Malory's description of conditions in the realm after the death of Uther ('Thenne stood the reame in grete jeopardy long whyle, for every lord that was myghty of men maade hym stronge, and many wende to have ben kyng' [*Works*, 1.12]) as a 'discreet Lancastrian allusion to Malory's time' and to the machinations of Richard, Duke of York.[30] It can, however, as easily be a reference to Arthur's wars against his barons after he became king, wars that are delineated in both the Post-Vulgate *Merlin*, Malory's major source for his first tale, and the Vulgate *Merlin*, another work that Malory had at some point read;[31] in these works, the barons refuse to accept Arthur as their king and fight against him as do six kings who attempt to destroy Arthur and Merlin.[32]

In the same tale, when the lords refuse to recognize Arthur as their king after he repeatedly pulls the sword from the stone, Malory writes, 'Wherfore alle the comyns cryed at ones, "We wille have Arthur unto our kyng!"' (*Works*, 1.16). Field believes that 'this introduction of the commons' is 'apparently original to Malory' and 'may have been prompted by the events leading up to the accession of the first Yorkist king. When the Yorkists proclaimed Duke Richard's son as Edward IV, they tried to offset the short-comings in his title by having him acclaimed by the people of London.'[33] Thus, in Field's view, this reference, unlike the others cited here, is pro-Yorkist. This allusion to the support of the commons, however, is not original with Malory. The commons support Arthur in both the Vulgate

London, 1960), pp. 68, 60, 65. Field acknowledges in a note that Uther is carried in a litter in Geoffrey of Monmouth, Wace, and Laȝamon, but argues 'there is no convincing evidence that Malory knew their writings' (p. 51 n. 15). The reference in Hardyng's chronicles should, however, be sufficient to indicate that he was following a chronicle source here and not making a contemporary allusion, and the fact that it appears not just in Geoffrey, Wace, and Laȝamon but in other popular vernacular chronicles should be sufficient evidence that Hardyng was attempting to follow Arthurian tradition here and not making an allusion to local geography and a recent event.

30 Field, 'Fifteenth-Century History', p. 53.

31 R. H. Wilson suggested that the Vulgate *Merlin* influenced Malory's account of the war against the Roman emperor Lucius (Tale 2) in, for example, the survival of Kay and Bedevere, Arthur's return to England to be welcomed by Guenevere, and the position of the Roman war in the second tale immediately before the beginning of the third tale, the 'Lancelot', since the war occurs at the end of the Vulgate *Merlin* just before the beginning of the Vulgate *Lancelot*. See Wilson, 'Malory's Early Knowledge of Arthurian Romance', *Texas Studies in English* 29 (1950), 46–49. For others who have accepted the Vulgate *Merlin* as a source for Malory, see W. Matthews, *The Tragedy of Arthur* (Berkeley and Los Angeles, 1960), p. 175; L. D. Benson, '*Le Morte Darthur*', in *Critical Approaches to Six Major English Works: 'Beowulf' through 'Paradise Lost'*, ed. R. M. Lumiansky and H. Baker (Philadelphia, 1968), p. 97; and Benson, *Malory's 'Morte Darthur'* (Cambridge, MA, 1976), pp. 69–70.

32 For the Post-Vulgate *Merlin*, see *Merlin: Roman en prose du XIIIe siècle*, ed. G. Paris and J. Ulrich, 2 vols., SATF (Paris, 1886), 1.140–46; *Lancelot-Grail: The Old French Arthurian Vulgate and Post-Vulgate in Translation*, gen. ed. N. Lacy, 5 vols. (New York, 1993–96), 1.214–20, 227. The account of the rebellion of the barons against Arthur is the same in both the Vulgate *Merlin* and the Post-Vulgate account. The account of the rebellion of the six kings against Arthur is not in the edited version of the Post-Vulgate *Merlin* (and thus not in the translation of this romance in *Lancelot-Grail*), but appears in the manuscript of the Post-Vulgate *Merlin* discovered in 1944; see Vinaver, *Works*, 3.1279–82.

33 Field, 'Fifteenth-Century History', p. 54.

Merlin and the post-Vulgate *Merlin*: When Arthur pulls the sword from the stone at Candlemas, both of these works describe the reactions of the people: 'Et quant li archevesques le vit et li peuples, si plourerent de joie et de pitié et demanderent: "A il mais chelui qui contre ceste election soit?" ' ('And when the archbishop and the people saw this, they cried for joy and pity and asked, "Is there anyone who could be against this election?" ').[34] Later another reference to the support of the common people appears in the Post-Vulgate *Merlin*: ('si firent li borgois de la vile une quintine lever') and similarly in the Vulgate *Merlin* ('Et lors issi li menus pueples hors de la ville a haches & a maches & a bastons'); and Malory, following the phrasing of the Vulgate version, includes this reference to them ('the comyns of Carylon aroos with clubbis and stavys') a little later in his account.[35]

Moreover, several other references to the support of the commons appear in the Vulgate *Merlin*:

Et Antor & ses lignages se tenoient deuers artu & li communs del pueple & li baron estoient encontre. . . . Li menus pueples . . . maudient tous ceaus qui en son nuisement seroient. Qvant li menus pueples vit que la clergie se tenoit deuers le roy artu si distrent quil si tenroient. . . . Qvant li arceuesques & li menus pueples voent la desloiaute des barons si se tienent ensamble a . j . acort auoec le roy artu. . . . & li rois artus sen ala en la maistre tour & fist armer les soies gens quanques il en pot auoir . Et quant li furent tout assamble si en I ot bien . vij . Mile . de la partie au roy artu que clerc que menue gent . Mais cheualiers i auoit il moult petit . . . Et . . . li menus pueples . . . ochirent & acrauentent quanquil ataignent. & dient tout quil aiment miex a morir en la piece de terre que li rois artus I ait mal la il le puissent desfendre.

(Antor and his kinsmen stood by Arthur, and the common folk did too, but the barons were against him. . . . The common people . . . cursed those who sought to harm Arthur. When the common folk saw that the clergy were taking Arthur's side, they said that they would too. . . . When the archbishop and the common people saw the barons' faithlessness, they stood together of one accord with King Arthur. . . . And King Arthur went straight to the keep and had as many of his men as he could find arm themselves. When they had all got together, there were a good seven thousand, clerics and commoners, but very few knights indeed. . . . Then the common folk . . . killed and brought down as many as they could reach. They all said that they would rather die on the spot than that King Arthur should be harmed when they could have defended him.)[36]

Even if Malory had read the Vulgate *Merlin* long before he began writing *Morte Darthur* and did not have it at hand when writing his book, he may well

---

34 Post-Vulgate *Merlin*, ed. Paris and Ulrich, 1.141; translation my own. Similarly in Vulgate *Merlin*: see *Lestoire de Merlin*, vol. 2 of *The Vulgate Version of the Arthurian Romances*, ed. H. O. Sommer (Washington, 1908), p. 85.

35 Cambridge University Library, 7071, fol. 297vb, cited by Vinaver, *Works*, 3.1289; Vulgate *Merlin*, ed. Sommer, p. 95; Vinaver, *Works*, 1.19. This does not appear in the Huth manuscript edited by Paris and Ulrich.

36 Vulgate *Merlin*, ed. Sommer, pp. 89, 91, 95; translation from *Lancelot-Grail*, ed. Lacy, 1.214, 217, 220.

have recalled these references. Thus there is little reason to believe that Malory was alluding to popular support for Edward IV.

Field's belief that Mordred's attacking Guenevere in the tower of London and shooting 'grete gunnes' (Tale 8) is a historical allusion to the Yorkists' besieging the Lancastrian garrison in the tower of London in 1460 is also questionable.[37] Mordred's besieging the tower of London is taken directly from the Vulgate *Mort Artu* and the stanzaic *Morte Arthur*.[38] The reference to 'gunnes' could be, as Dhira Mahoney has argued, a type of siege engine that was used to cast stones to batter down walls or simply an anachronism, an appropriately unchivalric weapon to give to a villain like Mordred, similar, as Field had earlier suggested in his 1977 edition of Malory's final tales, to Milton's giving the rebel angels guns during the war in Heaven.[39]

Since Field's survey was published, two additional essays – one by Field, the other by Robert L. Kelly – have suggested parallels with still other political events. Field suggests that Arthur's final battle against Mordred was modeled to some extent on the battle of Towton, apparently the bloodiest battle that had ever been fought on British soil and that resulted in Edward IV's victory over the forces of Henry VI. Although there is no evidence that Malory witnessed that battle, it is possible that he might have been thinking of it when writing this scene; but most of the correspondences that Field cites, such as the battle's lasting from morning to night and the presence of pillagers on the field after the battle, come from the sources, and of the three that do not, two (Mordred and Arthur's being exhausted and their fighting on foot) would have been common to any battle in Malory's day (and they also occur elsewhere in Malory's book in a scene that could have no similarity to the battle of Towton).[40] The third detail that Field believes can offer a significant parallel is Malory's mentioning that Lucan sees the robbers by moonlight. The battle of Towton occurred near Palm Sunday when the moon would have been full.[41] The addition of moonlight, however, is just the kind of detail that Malory

---

37 *Works*, 3.1227; Field, 'Fifteenth-Century History', p. 65.

38 'Einsi fu la reïne assise et assaillie sovent et menu en la tor de Londres' (*La Mort le Roi Artu*, ed. J. Frappier, 3rd edn [Geneva, 1964], § 142 p. 180); similarly in the stanzaic *Morte*, ed. Bruce, lines 2992–3001, pp. 90–91.

39 D. B. Mahoney, 'Malory's Great Guns', *Viator* 20 (1989), 291–310. Field in his 1977 edition wrote that the guns 'are ascribed to Mordred here in a spirit like that in which they are ascribed to the rebel angels in *Paradise Lost*; the brutal weapons . . . match the nature of the characters who use them' (*'Le Morte Darthur': The Seventh and Eighth Tales* [1977; reprinted London, 1978], p. 275). This seems a better explanation than the political one, although Field also suggested that in the edition as well.

40 In Malory's third tale, the 'Lancelot', there is another example of knights fighting on foot and, like Mordred and Arthur, becoming exhausted. Lancelot is fighting Terquyn and 'both their horsys backys braste undir them'. The two knights 'avoided their horsys and toke their shyldys before them and drew oute their swerdys and com togydir egirly; and eyther gaff other many stronge strokys, for there might nothir shyldis nother harneyse holde their strokes. And so within a whyle they had bothe many grymme woundys and bledde passing grevously. Thus they fare two owres and more, trasyng and rasyng eyther other where they might hitte ony bare place. Than at the laste they were brethles bothe, and stode lenyng on her swerdys' (*Works*, 1.265–66).

41 P. J. C. Field, 'Malory and the Battle of Towton', in *The Social and Literary Contexts of Malory's 'Morte Darthur'*, ed. D. T. Hanks, Jr and J. G. Brogdon (Cambridge, 2000), 68–74. Field briefly suggests this correspondence in his earlier *Life and Times*, p. 126 and n. 2.

would have added. Derek Brewer has discussed Malory's tendency to add those realistic details to his narrative that are essential to the story, such as Lancelot's having his sword with him when Mordred, Agravaine and other knights find him and Guenevere together.[42] In this respect he is similar to traditional writers of biblical narrative who mention only those details that are essential to the story (Esau's having hairy hands, for example, or Zacchaeus's being short). The moonlight is precisely this type of detail: anyone who has been away from civilization in the woods on a night without moonlight knows how dark it is. Those in the Middle Ages would have been familiar with this. If Lucan were to see those who robbed the dead and dying, moonlight would have been an essential detail; robbers would not have been likely to attract attention to themselves by carrying torches. It is therefore difficult to present a convincing case for this correspondence other than to say it might be possible.

Kelly believes that Malory's *Morte Darthur* was written as a comment upon England's contemporary wars against France: '[T]he pro-French [i.e. pro-Lancelot], anti-war view the narrative advances could have been readily identifiable as a Lancastrian critique of King Edward IV's plans to reopen the Hundred Years' War.'[43] The problem with such an interpretation is that the pro-French (pro-Lancelot) view was present in the thirteenth-century French romances, and it is difficult to see how anyone could have adapted these without presenting Lancelot (and the French) favorably. Malory, in fact, turns away from the French source in the final pages to the English stanzaic *Morte Arthur* to present Arthur more positively than he appears in the French account;[44] but the pro-Lancelot and thus pro-French stance could also be found in that work, written in the late fourteenth century long before Edward was trying to reopen the Hundred Years' War.

In short, those who have attempted to find historical and political allusions in Malory's work, other than the very general parallel of the tragedy of Arthur's divided kingdom corresponding to the tragedy of an England split between Yorkists and Lancastrians, have been skating on rather thin ice. Admittedly some contemporaries who read *Morte Darthur* might have found in the book some of the allusions that modern scholars have found, whether these be to Henry V (Vinaver), Henry VI (Aurner), Edward IV (Griffith), the marriage of Edward IV (Kennedy), the regions held by Yorkists (Stewart), Edward's wars against France (Kelly), the battles of St Albans and Towton (Field) or any number of other allusions; but there is little reason to believe that Malory attempted to add such political references to his work. Field, who is rightly skeptical about many of these allusions, does not find Malory a strong partisan of either side. Although he believes that Malory's 'sympathy

---

[42] D. S. Brewer, ed., *Malory: The Morte Darthur, Parts Seven and Eight*, York Medieval Texts (London, 1968), pp. 18–19.

[43] R. L. Kelly, 'Malory's Argument against War with France: The Political Geography of France and the Anglo-French Alliance in the *Morte Darthur*', in *The Social and Literary Contexts of Malory's 'Morte Darthur'*, p. 133.

[44] See Part 2 below.

apparently extended more often to the Lancastrians than to the Yorkists, it is most naturally taken not as support for either party but as a chivalrous generosity of spirit that could encompass both'.[45] Field's belief in Malory's general neutrality presents a perceptive observation about Malory's work, and it becomes even more convincing when one realizes that the political allusions that scholars have argued for are, in all likelihood, non-existent. They can be traced to Malory's sources or they originate from his attempts to make his account consistent with earlier chronicles or from his attempts to add geographical, not contemporary political or recent historical allusions, to the material he found in his sources.

One overtly political statement, however, occurs in Malory's account of Mordred's rebellion against Arthur: Malory laments that the 'new-fangill' English people were not content with Arthur:

> Lo ye all Englysshemen, see ye nat what a myschyff here was? For he that was the moste kynge and nobelyst knyght of the worlde, and moste loved the felyshyp of noble knyghtes, and by hym they all were upholdyn, and yet myght nat thes Englyshemen holde them contente with hym. Lo thus was the olde custom and usayges of thys londe, and men say that we of thys londe have nat yet loste that custom. Alas! thys ys a greate defaughte of us Englysshemen, for there may no thynge us please no terme. (*Works*, 3.1229)

I, like others, once thought that this was the complaint of a Lancastrian longing for the return of Henry VI and at least one other scholar has interpreted the remark as that of a Yorkist opposing the contemporary rebellions against Edward IV.[46] However, as Field points out, it is ambiguous and could refer to either king.[47] Malory had once supported Edward, and Edward had been king for nine years when Malory completed his book. Edward had been trying to show for much of that time that he, and not Henry VI, had the right to the throne. Edward, in fact, faced rebellions from Richard Neville, the Early of Warwick, in 1469 and the early months of 1470, about the time Malory was completing his book.[48] In 1471 the Flemish chronicler Jehan de Waurin would, in dedicating his chronicle to Edward IV, condemn those who tried to overthrow him as usurpers.[49] Charles Ross describes the years between 1469 and 1471 as 'a period of political instability without parallel in English history since 1066'.[50] At such a time, the ambiguity of Malory's statement should not be surprising. What would have been surprising would have been the partisan pro-Lancastrian or pro-Yorkist sentiments that scholars have tried to find in

---

[45] Field, 'Fifteenth-Century History', p. 71.

[46] For those who support the Lancastrian view, see W. H. Schofield, *Chivalry in English Literature* (Cambridge, MA, 1912), pp. 92–93; Stewart, 'English Geography', p. 207; my 'Marriage of Edward IV', p. 159; for the Yorkist, see Griffith, 'Political Bias', pp. 381–82.

[47] Field, *Life and Times*, pp. 145–47, and 'Fifteenth-Century History', pp. 65–66 .

[48] C. Ross, *Edward IV*, foreword R. A. Griffiths (1974; new edn, New Haven, 1997), pp. 126–45.

[49] Jehan de Waurin, *Recueil des croniques et anchiennes istories de la Grant Bretaigne*, ed. W. Hardy and E. L. C. P. Hardy, Rolls Series 39, 5 vols. (London, 1864–91), 1.610.

[50] Ross, *Edward IV*, p. 126.

Malory's work. Malory was hoping to be released from prison, and he would have had no way of knowing which side would win. Given the uncertainty of the political situation, any intelligent person would have realized that this would have been no time to make enemies, no time to be writing political propaganda that would alienate either side.

2. *The Justification for* Morte Darthur

Although Malory was not writing political propaganda, as a prisoner of the king, he may nevertheless have been trying to please Edward by writing a work that, like Milton's *Paradise Lost*, pursued 'things unattempted yet in Prose or Rhyme', in this case an English adaptation of popular French prose romances. Many fifteenth-century English writers, encouraged by the literary triumphs of Chaucer, wished to do something about the reputation of English as a second-rate language with an impoverished literary tradition. Like many of the printer William Caxton's later publications, *Morte Darthur* could have been written to please readers at court by providing a story that had previously been unavailable in English but that had been widely read among the upper classes who knew French. Fifteen years after Malory wrote his book, Caxton would give as justification for printing *Morte Darthur* the fact that few stories about Arthur were available in English ('he is more spoken of beyonde the see') and that *Morte Darthur* was therefore filling a major gap in English literature.[51]

Edward, not surprisingly, would have been interested in the Arthurian story. Admittedly, much of the evidence for this interest, based upon his collection of books and the publications of Caxton, belongs to the years after Malory wrote *Morte Darthur*. The Flemish chronicler Jehan de Waurin, for example, presented a well-developed account of Arthur, which drew to some extent upon romances as well as a chronicle, in his massive chronicle of Britain and England, one manuscript of which he dedicated to Edward sometime after 1471;[52] and in the last ten years of his reign Edward collected among his books manuals of chivalry and chronicles.[53] The many pedigrees and genealogical chronicles mentioned at the beginning of this article, however, offer ample evidence of his interest in the Arthur of the chronicles in

---

[51] See Caxton's preface to *Morte Darthur*, *Works*, 1.cxlv.

[52] See A. Gransden, *Historical Writing in England, II: c. 1307 to the Early Sixteenth Century* (Ithaca, NY, 1982), p. 291 and n. 20.

[53] See J. Backhouse, 'Founders of the Royal Library: Edward IV and Henry VII as Collectors of Illuminated Manuscripts', in *England in the Fifteenth Century: Proceedings of the 1986 Harlaxton Symposium*, ed. D. Williams (Woodbridge, 1987), pp. 25, 39–41; M. Kekewich, 'Edward IV, William Caxton, and Literary Patronage in Yorkist England', *Modern Language Review* 66 (1971), 481–87; S. McKendrick, '*La Grande Histoire Cesar* and the Manuscripts of Edward IV', in *English Manuscript Studies 1100–1700*, ed. P. Beal and J. Griffiths (Oxford, 1990), pp. 109–38; K. Cherewatuk, ' "Gentyl" Audiences and "Grete Bookes": Chivalric Manuals and the *Morte Darthur*', *Arthurian Literature* 15 (1997), 205–16, especially p. 214, and her 'Thomas Malory's "Grete Booke" ', in *Social and Literary Contexts of Malory's 'Morte Darthur'*, pp. 42–67, especially 42–51.

the earlier years of his reign and his use of it for propaganda. I can not prove that Malory had read Edward's genealogical chronicles, but if he had been, as Barber suggests, associated with the court he would in all likelihood have been familiar with some of Edward's propaganda. In fact, the one chronicle that has been cited as a source for Malory and that offers one of the most enthusiastic portraits of Arthur in English, the final 1464 version of Hardyng's chronicle, appears to have been put into circulation as a part of Edward's propaganda campaign.[54] If Malory knew one English work circulated as propaganda for Edward, he may also have known others; and he therefore could have been aware that Edward was interested in the Arthurian stories.

As noted above, by at least 1467 or 1468 Malory had lost Edward's favor and was a prisoner excluded from general pardons that the king issued between 14 July 1468 and 22 February 1470.[55] Six of the eight explicits that conclude the major tales of *Morte Darthur* suggest not only that Malory was in prison when writing his book but also that he was feeling quite desperate: 'This was drawyn by a knyght presoner, sir Thomas Malleorré, that God sende hym good recover'; 'I pray you all that redyth this tale to pray for hym that this wrote, that God sende hym good delyveraunce sone and hastely'; 'Here endyth the secunde boke off syr Trystram de Lyones, whyche drawyn was oute of Freynshe by Sir Thomas Malleorré, knyght, as Jesu be hys helpe. . . . Therefore on all synfull, blyssed Lorde, have on thy knyght mercy'; 'Thus endith the Tale of the Sankgreal . . . by sir Thomas Maleorré, knyght. O Blessed Jesu helpe hym thorow Hys myght!'; 'And here . . . folowyth The Moste Pyteuous Tale of the Morte Arthure . . . par le Shyvalere Sir Thomas Malleorré, Knyght. Jesu, ayede ly pur vout<re> bone mercy!'; 'I praye you all jentylmen and jentylwymmen that redeth this book . . . praye for me whyle I am on lyve that God sende me good delyveraunce. . . . For this book was ended the ninth yere of the reygne of Kyng Edward the Fourth, by Syr Thomas Maleoré, Knyght, as Jesu helpe hym for Hys grete myght, as he is the servaunt of Jesu bothe day and nyght' (*Works*, 1.180, 363; 2.845–46, 1037, 3.1154, 1260).

Ingrid Tieken-Boon van Ostade revived a suggestion made but dismissed by William Matthews that Malory wrote *Morte Darthur* as an act of contrition, that Malory, imprisoned by Edward IV, attempted to show 'through the writing of a book which extolled the virtues of England's most "noble kyng and conquerour," that he knew all about the highest codes of behaviour, both moral and chivalrous'. Tieken-Boon van Ostade adds that his references to his being a prisoner and his requests in the explicits for deliverance suggest that

---

[54] A. S. G. Edwards, 'The Manuscripts and Texts of the Second Version of John Hardyng's *Chronicle*,' in *England in the Fifteenth Century: Proceedings of the 1986 Harlaxton Symposium*, ed. D. Williams (Woodbridge, 1987), pp. 75–84; F. Riddy, 'John Hardyng's Chronicle and the Wars of the Roses', *Arthurian Literature* 12 (1993), 91–108, especially pp. 102–6. Riddy suggests that Hardyng's work served much the same purpose as Edward's genealogical chronicles and may even have been read as one.

[55] Field, *Life and Times*, pp. 30–31.

he was indeed contrite.[56] To this should be added the observation that Malory, by presenting in English the French chivalric romances, was stressing not just the highest codes of behavior but was also writing a version of a story that had previously been unavailable in English but that was based to some extent upon popular British history. Another version of that story had been part of Edward's genealogical propaganda, and this new version would therefore have interested the king. Malory could not have been trying, as some have argued, to present Arthur as a model for Edward to follow or as a glorified picture of Edward; for Malory's Arthur, unlike the Arthur of the chronicles, is not ideal and has negative traits that would have made such a correspondence risky. He would instead have been trying to present a new version of the Arthurian story in English that would have appealed to Edward or anyone else interested in reading in English new stories of Arthur and his knights.

The English chronicles that told the story of Arthur were far different from the French romances to which Malory turned for most of his book. The French Vulgate cycle, upon which Malory primarily based his third, sixth, seventh, and eighth tales, began in the early thirteenth century as the story of Lancelot, not Arthur. It originally consisted of three romances, the *Lancelot* which began with the birth of Lancelot and told of development of the love of Lancelot and Guenevere, the *Queste del Saint Graal*, which narrated Lancelot's failure on the Grail Quest and the success of his son Galahad, and the *Mort Artu*, which presented the love of Lancelot and Guenevere as a primary cause for the destruction of Arthur's kingdom. Although later writers added the *Estoire del Saint Graal*, which tells of how Joseph of Arimathea brought the Grail to Britain, and the Vulgate *Merlin*, which begins with the birth of Merlin and tells of the early history of Arthur's kingdom, the original cycle was dominated by the story of Lancelot.

Judging from the manuscripts that were in England in the Middle Ages and by allusions to these romances by various English writers, the Vulgate cycle was well known there by those who could read French,[57] but even those familiar with the French romances would have found Malory's account an essentially new version of the Arthurian story. To those who could not read French, his book would have been quite different from the Arthurian stories to which they were accustomed. Although the Vulgate *Merlin* and the *Estoire*, both of which were more closely related to English chronicle tradition than the *Lancelot* or the *Queste*, had been translated into English a few times, no one prior to Malory had translated the *Lancelot* or the *Queste*;[58] and it is likely

---

[56] Tieken-Boon van Ostade, *The Two Versions of Malory's 'Morte Darthur'*, Arthurian Studies 35 (Cambridge, 1995), p. 115; Matthews, *The Ill-Framed Knight*, p. 48.

[57] See C. Meale, 'Manuscripts, Readers and Patrons in Fifteenth-Century England: Sir Thomas Malory and Arthurian Romance', *Arthurian Literature* 4 (1984), 93–126; Meale, 'Patrons, Buyers and Owners: Book Production and Social Status', in *Book Production and Publishing in Britain 1375–1475*, ed. J. Griffiths and D. Pearsall (Cambridge, 1989), pp. 201–37; M. Kekewich, 'Edward IV, William Caxton, and Literary Patronage', 481–87.

[58] The adaptations of the Vulgate *Merlin* are the metrical English romance *Of Arthour and of Merlin* (1250–1300) and the two close fifteenth-century translations, the prose *Merlin* and Harry Lovelich's

that the portrait of Arthur in these works, sometimes as a good king but often as a *roi fainéant* or *rex inutilus*, as Edward Peters describes him,[59] probably had little appeal to English readers accustomed to the heroic Arthur of the chronicles. There are negative portraits of Arthur in some of the metrical romances, but most of these are associated with northern England or Scotland and reflect the nationalist anti-British and anti-English sentiments that appear in some of the Scottish chronicles.[60]

So far as we know, prior to Malory the only attempt to adapt one of the original three parts of the Vulgate cycle for an English audience was the English adaptation of the Vulgate *Mort Artu* known as the stanzaic *Morte Arthur*, a work that was one of Malory's sources for his last two tales. The Vulgate *Mort Artu*, like the Vulgate *Merlin* and *Estoire*, had drawn on the English chronicle stories of Arthur. The stanzaic *Morte* was still further influenced by chronicles, in, for example, details such as Mordred's insisting that Arthur cede to him Kent and Arthur's fighting three battles against Mordred instead of one and by its generally more positive portrait of Arthur. The English stanzaic *Morte* took considerable liberties with its French source in its presentation of the conclusion. In the French romance Arthur blindly ignores prophetic warnings that he should wait until Lancelot returns before attacking Mordred; although Arthur in the French *Mort Artu* attributes his defeat to the workings of Fortune, it is also implicit in this work that although Arthur never seems to realize it, his pride is as much to blame as Fortune for the final disaster. The author of the stanzaic *Morte*, however, presents Arthur more positively by making his final battle more a matter of chance than of failure to heed warnings, for there Arthur tries to postpone the battle to give Lancelot

---

verse *Merlin*. The adaptations of the *Estoire* are the late fourteenth-century *Joseph of Arimathie* and Harry Lovelich's fifteenth-century *History of the Holy Grail*. For descriptions of these, see H. Newstead, 'Arthurian Legends', in *A Manual of the Writings in Middle English 1050–1500*, vol. 1, gen. ed. J. Burke Severs (New Haven, 1967), pp. 46–49, 72–75. For the prose *Merlin*, also see C. M. Meale, 'The Manuscripts and Early Audience of the Middle English *Prose Merlin*', and K. Stern, 'The Middle English *Prose Merlin*', both in *The Changing Face of Arthurian Romance*, ed. A. Adams, A. H. Diverres, K. Stern and K. Varty (Woodbridge, 1986), pp. 92–111, 112–22 respectively.

59 E. Peters, *The Shadow King: Rex Inutilis in Medieval Law and Literature 751–1327* (New Haven, 1970), pp. 194–209; E. Kennedy, 'King Arthur in the Prose *Lancelot*', trans. E. D. Kennedy in *King Arthur: A Casebook*, ed. E. D. Kennedy (New York, 1996), pp. 71–89, originally published as the second part of 'Études sur le *Lancelot en prose*', *Romania* 105 (1984), 46–62.

60 See K. H. Göller, 'King Arthur in the Scottish Chronicles', trans. E. D. Kennedy in *King Arthur: A Casebook*, pp. 173–84, originally published as 'König Arthur in den Schottischen Chroniken', *Anglia* 80 (1962), 390–404; F. Alexander, 'Late Medieval Scottish Attitudes to the Figure of King Arthur: A Reassessment', *Anglia* 93 (1975), 17–34; B. Schmolke-Hasselmann, *The Evolution of Arthurian Romance: The Verse Tradition from Chrétien to Froissart* (Cambridge, 1998), pp. 285–90; W. R. J. Barron, 'Arthurian Romance: Traces of an English Tradition', *English Studies* 61 (1980), pp. 14–17 (on *Golagrus and Gawain*). The Scottish *Lancelot of the Laik*, written after Malory's death and derived from the Vulgate *Lancelot*, presents Arthur negatively as a king who has neglected his subjects. The Scots' criticism of Arthur reflected both their anti-British and anti-English sentiments: anti-British, since the Scots were trying to prove their superiority to the British by having a Graeco-Egyptian ancestry rather than Trojan, and anti-English, since by this time the English had adopted Arthur as one of their own. Malory refers to him as an English king, not a British one. The fact that Arthur had become ruler of the Scots and that the English were attempting to do the same fueled anti-Arthurian sentiments among the Scottish chroniclers.

time to arrive with help; the final battle results from mere chance, the appearance of an adder that causes one of Mordred's knights to draw a sword to kill it, an act that the other knights interpret as a signal to begin the battle.[61]

Malory in writing for English readers a new story of King Arthur based his first tale not upon the Vulgate cycle but upon the romance of *Merlin* in another less widely circulated cycle derived from the Vulgate and known today as the Post Vulgate *Roman du Graal*.[62] The Post-Vulgate cycle follows the Vulgate Cycle very closely in its early sections; but one way that it differs from the earlier Vulgate Cycle is that it, like Malory, eliminated most of the Vulgate romance of *Lancelot*.[63] The Post-Vulgate cycle is, like Malory's book, more the story of Arthur than of Lancelot, and although the tragedy results to a considerable extent as God's punishment for Arthur's begetting Mordred by unknowingly committing incest with his sister, it is a cycle that, as Fanni Bogdanow has shown, is, on the whole, sympathetic to Arthur. The author, she writes, wanted to 'present Arthur as a tragic hero whose destiny will arouse in us "pity and fear" '.[64]

Although Malory's first tale is the only part of his book that is based upon the Post-Vulgate *Roman du Graal*, Malory appears to have known much more of this cycle. He ended his first tale with the following explicit: 'Here endyth this tale, as the Freynshe booke seyth, fro the maryage of Kynge Uther unto kynge Arthure that regned aftir hym and ded many batayles. And this booke endyth whereas sir Launcelot and Sir Trystrams com to courte' (*Works*, 1.180). Since Malory's tale ends with Pelleas and Morhalt coming to court rather than Lancelot and Tristram, Malory's statement, as several scholars have pointed out, must refer to the manuscript of Malory's source.[65] In that case, Malory would have been alluding to Launcelot and Tristan's coming to court at the beginning of the Post-Vulgate account of the Grail Quest, and this

61 See my 'The Stanzaic *Morte Arthur*: The Adaptation of a French Romance for an English Audience', in *Culture and the King: The Social Implications of the Arthurian Legend*, ed. M. B. Shichtman and J. P. Carley (Albany, NY, 1994), pp. 91–112; *Morte Arthur*, ed. Bruce, lines 3340–51, pp. 101–2.

62 The major discussion of this cycle is by F. Bogdanow, *The Romance of the Grail: A Study of the Structure and Genesis of a Thirteenth-Century Arthurian Prose Romance* (Manchester, 1966), especially pp. 197–221 ('The New Arthuriad').

63 The author of the Post-Vulgate *Merlin* explains his omission of most of the story of Lancelot: '. . . cele meisme ystoire qui doit estre departie de mon livre, ne mie pour chou qu'il n'i apartiegne et que elle n'en soit traite, mais pour chou qu'il couvient que les trois parties de mon livre soient ingaus, l'une aussi grant coume l'autre, et se je ajoustaisse cele grant ystore la moiene partie de mon livre fust au tresble plus grant que les autres deus. Pour chou me couvient il laissier celle grant ystoire qui devise les oevres de Lanscelot et la naissance.' ('That very history has to be left out of my book not because it does not belong there or is not drawn from it, but because it is fitting that the three parts of my book be equal, one as long as another, and if I added that great history, the middle part of my book would be three times as long as the other two. Therefore I must leave out this great history that tells of Lancelot's birth and his deeds.') Post-Vulgate *Merlin*, ed. Paris and Ulrich, 2.57; 'The Post-Vulgate, Part I: The Merlin Continuation', trans. M. Asher, in *Lancelot-Grail*, gen. ed. Lacy, vol. 4 (New York, 1995), p. 221.

64 F. Bogdanow, 'The Evolution of the Theme of the Fall of Arthur's Kingdom', trans. E. D. Kennedy in *King Arthur*, ed. Kennedy, p. 97. The article was originally published as 'La chute du royaume d'Arthur: Évolution du thème', *Romania* 107 (1986), 504–19.

65 T. C. Rumble, 'The First *Explicit* in Malory's *Morte Darthur*', *Modern Language Notes* 71 (1956), 564–66; Vinaver, *Works*, 3.1364; Bogdanow, *Grail*, p. 87 n. 1.

indicates that Malory would have read at least the first half of the Post-Vulgate *Roman du Graal*.[66] Since he also knew the version of the quest for the Holy Grail in the prose *Tristan*, which is basically the Post-Vulgate version of the *Queste*, he would have read most of this cycle.[67] The Post-Vulgate *Roman du Graal* could have suggested to him the structure of his book: it, like Malory's account, focuses on Arthur and has only a brief account of the adventures of Lancelot; and it alludes to some of the adventures of Tristram before its account of the Grail Quest and could have suggested Malory's placing his tale of 'Tristram' (Tale 5) immediately before his version of the Grail Quest (Tale 6).[68] It could also have suggested a new way to present the Arthurian tragedy to English readers.

Malory obviously wished to present adventures that for the most part had not yet appeared in English. But he also presumably wanted to present a portrait of Arthur that would have been acceptable to readers familiar with the heroic Arthur of the chronicles. In his adaptation of the French material, he was not able to present a consistently strong Arthur, and some critics have interpreted Malory's Arthur as a weak and degenerate king.[69] Such interpretations, however, generally overlook Malory's repeated emphasis on Arthur's basic nobility. Throughout the book, and particularly in the final tale in which critics have found most examples of Arthur's weaknesses, it is easy to find examples of Malory's describing Arthur as 'the most kynge and nobelyst knight of the worlde', a 'currageous' king, the 'noble Kynge Arthur', as one who 'ded nobely, as a noble kynge shulde do' (*Works*, 3.1229, 1236), all of which give the impression that Malory admired Arthur as a great king. But that does not mean that Malory's Arthur, any more than Lancelot or Guenevere, was flawless. The post-Vulgate *Roman du Graal*, with its portrait of Arthur as a great hero who unwittingly sinned, would have given Malory an example of Arthur as a heroic king that was presented more positively than the often weak and foolish Arthur of the Vulgate Cycle, but who had more complexity than the Arthur of the chronicles where, as Beate Schmolke-Hasselmann has observed, one finds 'a uniformly glorified picture of the monarch and a very pronounced patriotism'.[70]

Malory based his final tale primarily upon two romances, the French

---

[66] See E. D. Kennedy, 'Malory's "Noble Tale of Sir Launcelot du Lake," the Vulgate *Lancelot*, and the Post-Vulgate *Roman du Graal*', in *Arthurian and Other Studies Presented to Shunichi Noguchi*, ed. T. Suzuki and T. Mukai (Cambridge, 1993), p. 113.

[67] Malory ends his 'Tristram' with 'Here endyth the secunde boke off sir Trystram de Lyones . . . But here ys no rehersall of the thirde booke. But here folowyth the noble tale off the Sankgreall' (*Works*, 2.845). The 'thirde booke' of the French prose *Tristan* is the account of the Grail, which is the same as the one in the Post-Vulgate *Roman*; but Malory turns from it to the Vulgate version of the *Queste* for his 'Sankgreal'.

[68] See Kennedy, 'Malory's "Noble Tale" ', pp. 111–19.

[69] See E. T. Pochoda, *Arthurian Propaganda: 'Le Morte Darthur' as an Historical Ideal of Life* (Chapel Hill, 1971); G. Thornton, 'The Weakening of the King: Arthur's Disintegration in "The Book of Sir Tristram" ', *The Arthurian Yearbook* 1 (1991), 135–48; Riddy also believes that Malory's Arthur in the final pages of the book 'dwindles into enfeeblement' ('Contextualizing *Le Morte Darthur*', p. 66).

[70] Schmolke-Hasselmann, *The Evolution of Arthurian Romance*, 285.

Vulgate *Mort Artu* and the English stanzaic *Morte* Arthur. Although we do not know if Malory knew the account of the death of Arthur in the final part of the Post-Vulgate *Roman du Graal*, his additions to the information found in his other two sources indicate that he kept in mind the Post-Vulgate's suggestion that Arthur would be punished for the incest with his half-sister. The author of the Vulgate *Mort Artu* had included only two references to Mordred's being Arthur's son and none specifically to incest.[71] The stanzaic *Morte* alludes specifically to the incest once and to the fact that Arthur is Mordred's father three times.[72] Malory refers six times in the final pages of his last tale to the fact that Mordred was Arthur's son, two of which refer specifically to incest: 'bycause sir Mordred was kynge Arthurs son, he gaff hym the rule off hys londe and off hys wyff' (3.1211); Mordred wishes to marry Guenevere 'which was hys unclys wyff and hys fadirs wyff' (3.1227); the Archbishop of Canterbury rebukes Mordred: 'For ys nat kynge Arthur youre uncle, and no farther but youre modirs brothir, and uppon her he hymselffe begate you, uppon hys owne syster? Therfore how may ye wed youre owne fadirs wyff?' (3.1228); when Arthur prepares to come ashore at Dover, Mordred attempts 'to beate hys owne fadir fro hys owne londys' and tries to keep 'his owne fadir' from 'the londe that he was kynge over' (3.1229); Mordred, who does not believe Arthur sincerely wants a truce, says, 'I know well my fadir woll be avenged uppon me' (3.1235); in the account of the final battle, Mordred 'smote hys fadir, kynge Arthure' (3.1237).

Malory, however, presents the incest differently from the way it is presented in the Post-Vulgate romance. The French romance emphasizes that Arthur has been punished for his sin: At the end of the romance, the

---

71 In the Vulgate *Mort Artu*, Arthur indicates that Mordred is his son (ed. Frappier, § 164, p. 211; *The Death of King Arthur*, trans. J. Cable, Penguin Classics (Harmondsworth, 1971), p. 192), and the author near the end of the romance says that 'Einsi ocist li peres le fill, et li filz navra le pere a mort' ('the father killed the son and the son gave his father a mortal wound') (§ 191, p. 245 [Frappier], p. 220 [Cable]). The reader of *Mort Artu* would have known that Mordred was Arthur's son through an incestuous union with his half sister only if he had remembered allusions to the incest in the Vulgate *Lancelot* or *Merlin* or the Post-Vulgate *Merlin*. (Boccaccio, who used the *Mort Artu* as a source for his account of Arthur in his *De casibus virorum illustrium*, may not have realized there was incest involved since he describes Mordred as the son of Arthur's concubine. [See Boccaccio, 'De Arturo Britonum rege', *De casibus virorum illustrium*, ed. P. G. Ricci and V. Zaccaria, in *Tutte le opere di Giovanni Boccaccio*, gen. ed. V. Branca (Milan, 1983), 9.730]). In the Vulgate *Lancelot* a holy man tells Mordred that he is not, as he had supposed, the son of King Lot and prophesies that Mordred will kill his father and destroy the Round Table. After Mordred kills the holy man, Lancelot finds in the man's hand a letter that explains that Mordred's father is King Arthur and his mother the wife of King Lot of Orkney, Arthur's sister. Here, as Fanni Bogdanow has pointed out, the holy man does not reproach Arthur for incest; he instead reproaches Mordred for the evil he will do. (See Bogdanow, 'Evolution', 95; *Lancelot*, ed. A. Micha, 5 [Paris and Geneva, 1980], 219–23; *Lancelot-Grail*, ed. Lacy, 3.260–61). The Vulgate *Merlin*, written after the *Lancelot*, tells of how Arthur lay with his sister, and, like the Vulgate *Lancelot*, does not rebuke Arthur for incest (see *Merlin*, ed. Sommer, pp. 128–30; *Lancelot-Grail*, ed. Lacy, 1.237–38). In the Post-Vulgate *Merlin*, by contrast, Merlin condemns Arthur for his great disloyalty, calling him the most disloyal knight in the country, a devil, and an enemy of Christ (*Merlin*, ed. Paris and Ulrich, 1.154; *Lancelot-Grail*, ed. Lacy, 4.169).

72 'That fals traytour, sir Mordreid –/ The kynges soster sone he was,/ And eke hys owne sonne, As I rede'; the Archbishop of Canterbury rebukes him for attempting to wed his 'faders wyff'; when Arthur returns to the kingdom, Mordred fears 'Hys fader', and he attempts to defend England from 'hys owne fader' (*Morte Arthur*, ed. Bruce, lines 2954–56, 3006, 3038, 3049, pp. 89, 91, 92).

post-Vulgate Arthur says that 'God . . . has . . . cast me down because of my sin.'[73] This could have been the conception that Malory originally had for his tragedy, for in his first tale, Merlin tells Arthur, 'Ye have done a thynge late that God ys displesed with you, for ye have lyene by youre syster and on hir ye have gotyn a childe that shall destroy you and all the knyghts of youre realme. . . . hit ys Goddis wylle that youre body sholde be punyss[h]ed for your fowle dedis' (*Works*, 1.44). Moreover, Malory's Arthur attempts to destroy Mordred by having all of the children of the kingdom who 'were borne in May-day, begotyn of lordis and borne of ladyes' drowned by being put on a ship and sent out to sea; all of the children die except Mordred, who is 'cast up, and a good man founde hym, and fostird hym tylle he was fourtene yere of age' (*Works*, 1.55). In the Post-Vulgate *Merlin*, Arthur has no chance to attempt to kill Mordred since his parents put him on a ship that wrecks. Mordred is washed ashore, and Arthur, after being warned in a dream, decides against attempting to kill the other boys.[74] Malory, by contrast, makes Arthur guilty of a sin comparable to Herod's slaughter of the innocents. Thus, as he was beginning to write his book, he may have conceived of a tragedy like that of the Post-Vulgate *Roman du Graal* in which Arthur's fall is punishment for a sin committed long ago.[75] However, Malory's *Morte Darthur*, unlike the Post-Vulgate *Roman*, does not mention Arthur's being punished again, and the episode in which he has the children killed is, as Field observes, 'plainly incompatible with Arthur's character as presented elsewhere in Malory's book'.[76] Malory's first tale may have been written sometime before the rest of the book.[77] By the time he was writing the final parts of his book, he must have decided against presenting the tragedy as Arthur's punishment for sin. All of the references to Mordred's being Arthur's son in the final tale remind the reader of the relationship between Arthur and Mordred; but when there is condemnation, as in the Archbishop of Canterbury's statement, it is condem-

---

[73] F. Bogdanow, 'Evolution', 97; passages quoted in Portuguese and in translation in Bogdanow, *Grail*, 149; *Lancelot-Grail*, ed. Lacy, 5.304.

[74] *Merlin*, ed. Paris and Ulrich, 1.203–12; *Lancelot-Grail*, ed. Lacy, 4.183–85.

[75] See P.J. C. Field, 'Malory's Mordred and the *Morte Arthure*', *Malory: Texts and Sources*, pp. 89–102 (reprint of article published in *Romance Reading on the Book: Essays on Medieval Narrative Presented to Maldwyn Mills*, ed. J. Fellows, R. Field, G. Rogers and J. Weiss (Cardiff, 1996), pp. 77–93). Field believes that the suggestion for punishment for sin could have come from the Alliterative *Morte Arthure* as well as from the Post-Vulgate *Merlin*. Also see H. Cooper, 'Counter-Romance: Civil Strife and Father-Killing in the Prose Romances', in *The Long Fifteenth Century: Essays for Douglas Gray*, ed. H. Cooper and S. Mapstone (Oxford, 1997), pp. 141–62, especially pp. 150–55; E. Archibald, 'Arthur and Mordred: Variations on an Incest Theme', *Arthurian Literature* 8 (1989), 1–27.

[76] Field, 'Malory's Mordred', p. 101.

[77] The explicit ending Malory's first tale suggests that the work on his book may have been interrupted and that he may not have known if he could continue with it: 'This booke endyth whereas sir Launcelot and sir Trystrams com to courte. Who that woll make ony more lette hym seke other bookis of kynge Arthure or of sir Launcelot or Sir Trystrams; for this was drawyn by a knyght presoner' (*Works*, 1.180). Field suggests that when Malory was writing his first tale, he may not have known the sources for the later parts of his book very well ('Malory's Mordred', p. 99). Instances in Tale 1 that suggest this include Malory's erroneous statement that when Mordred was fourteen, the man who found him brought him to court 'as hit rehersith aftirward and towarde the ende of the Morte Arthure' (1.55) and his description of Pelleas as 'one of the four that encheved the Sankgreal' (1.180).

nation of Mordred, not Arthur. In another respect, however, his adaptation of the tragedy is similar. The story of the incest in the Post-Vulgate *Roman du Graal* is, Fanni Bogdanow points out, an example of the '*mescheance* which haunts Logres'.[78] The word *mescheance* can suggest punishment for sin.[79] The sin of incest is one that Arthur commits but is unaware of, and, in Bogdanow's words, the act shows that 'pure accidents unleash catastrophes'.[80] The notion that accidents can unleash catastrophes also occurs in Malory's version of the Arthurian tragedy, but there the emphasis, while not upon God punishing for sin or even upon Fortune, is upon mistakes, such as the begetting of Mordred, that are disastrous.

Judging from Malory's remarks in a few places, blame for the tragedy can be placed on two evil characters: Malory ends his seventh tale with the statement 'here I go unto the morte Arthur, and that caused sir Aggravayne' (3.1154); Malory's Arthur says 'A, Aggravayne, Aggravayne . . . Jesu forgyff hit thy soule, for thyne evyll wyll that thou haddist and sir Mordred, thy brothir, unto sir Launcelot hath caused all this sorow' (3.1184); and he later describes Mordred as 'that traytour . . . that hath caused all thys myschyff . . . the traytoure that all thys woo hath wrought' (3.1236). Judging from the text, however, Malory's tragedy is far more complex than that, and, like earlier versions of the tragedy, its causes include Fortune, fate, chance, the deliberate acts of the evil as well as the mistakes of the good.[81] What makes Malory's version different from earlier accounts of the tragedy is his emphasis upon the latter as causes for the tragedy, upon good but flawed individuals who realize too late their mistakes. The tragedy would not have occurred had it not been for the errors of basically good people.

Arthur and the other major characters make mistakes that cause catastrophes, and they realize too late that they have done so. As mentioned above, the reader is reminded of Arthur's error in begetting Mordred through the repeated references in the final pages to the father/son relationship. Arthur also makes the mistake of appointing Mordred regent because he was his son (3.1211), an appointment that in Malory's source, the stanzaic *Morte*, is made by others.[82] After the final battle, Arthur, who had earlier shown restraint by heeding Gawain's warning, makes another error in judgment, this one fatal. Only Mordred remains alive on one side; only Arthur, Lucan, and Bedevere on the other. Arthur, seeing Mordred, tells Lucan to give him his spear. Lucan warns him:

---

[78] Bogdanow, 'Evolution', p. 96.

[79] The word *mescheance* was frequently associated with punishment for sin in the earlier Vulgate cycle. See E. Kennedy, ' "Lancelot li mescheans": Mischance and Individual Responsibility in the *Lancelot-Grail*', in *De ongevalliche Lanceloet: Studies over de Lancelotcompilatie*, ed. B. Besamusca and F. Brandsma (Hilversum, Netherlands, 1992), pp. 117–35.

[80] Bogdanow, 'Evolution', p. 96.

[81] For a good discussion of the multiplicity of causes of the tragedy, see M. Lambert, *Malory: Style and Vision in 'Le Morte Darthur'*, Yale Studies in English 186 (New Haven, 1975), pp. 124–221.

[82] 'The kynges soster sone he was/ . . ./ There-fore men hym fo[r] steward chase' (*Morte Arthur*, ed. Bruce, lines 2955, 2957, p. 89).

Sir, latte hym be . . . yf ye passe this unhappy day y[e] shall be ryght well revenged. And, [good lord, remembre ye of your nyghtes dreme and] what the spyryte of sir Gawayne tolde you tonyght, and yet God of Hys grete goodnes hath preserved you hyddirto. . . . leve of thys for . . . ye have won the fylde: for yet we ben here three on lyve, and with sir Mordred ys nat one on lyve. And therefore if ye leve of now, thys wycked day of Desteny ys paste.

Arthur, however, ignores the warning: 'Now tyde me dethe, tyde me lyff . . . now I se hym yondir alone, and he shall never ascape myne hondes!' (3.1236–37). As a result, Mordred and Arthur mortally wound one another. In the Post-Vulgate *Roman* Arthur realizes as he is dying that God has punished him for his sin; Malory's Arthur, by contrast, refers implicitly to the errors he made both in opposing Lancelot and in not heeding the advice Gawain had given him to avoid fighting Mordred: 'A, sir Launcelot! . . . thys day have I sore myssed the! And alas, that ever I was ayenste the! For now have I my dethe, whereof sir Gawayne me warned in my dreme' (3.1238).

Each of the other major characters similarly acknowledges mistakes: the dying Gawain says to Arthur: 'A myn uncle, . . . thorow my wylfulnes I was causer of myne owne deth . . . And thorow me and my pryde ye have all thys shame and disease' (3.1230); Guenevere, referring to Lancelot, says, 'Thorow thys same man and me hath all thys warre be wrought, and the deth of the moste nobelest knyghtes of the worlde; for thorow oure love that we have loved togydir ys my moste noble lorde slayne' (3.1252); and Lancelot, in referring to the deaths of Arthur and Guenevere, says: 'Whan I remembre me how by my defaute and myn orgule and my pryde that they were bothe layed ful lowe . . . this remembred, of their kyndenes and myn unkyndenes, sanke so to myn herte that I myght not susteyne myself' (3.1256). Mark Lambert, referring to the speeches of Gawain, Lancelot and Guenevere writes that each takes 'absolute responsibility for the disaster because each could have prevented it, not because each entirely caused it'.[83] The same could be said for Arthur. Although the characters sometimes use the terminology of sin to refer to their actions – the pride mentioned by Gawain and Lancelot, for example – the reader does not get the impression that God has punished them. Instead they have made mistakes that, in Fanni Bogdanow's words with reference to events of the Post-Vulgate *Roman*, 'unleash catastrophes'.

Arthur's final battle also results from human error. Malory turned to the stanziac *Morte Arthur* for his conclusion in which the battle is caused not by Arthur's blindly ignoring warnings, as he does in the Vulgate *Mort Artu*, but by his heeding a warning in a dream from the spirit of the dead Gawain that he should attempt to arrange a truce with Mordred:

for and ye fyght as to-morne with sir Mordred, . . . doute ye nat ye shall be slayne, and the moste party of youre people on bothe partyes. . . . God hath sente me to you of Hys speciall grace to gyff you warnyng that in no wyse ye do batayle as to-morne, but that ye take a tretyse for a moneth-day. And proffir you

---

[83] Lambert, *Malory: Style and Vision*, p. 160.

largely, so that to-morne ye put in a delay. For within a moneth shall com sir Launcelot with all hys noble knyghtes, and rescow you worshypfully, and sle sir Mordred and all that ever wyll holde wyth hym. (3. 1234)

Arthur, following Gawain's advice, attempts to make a peace treaty with Mordred, and the final battle is caused by a knight on one side drawing a sword when he sees an adder. Malory writes that after the two sides met,

> they . . . were agreed and accorded thorowly. And wyne was fette, and [they] dranke togydir. Ryght so cam oute an addir of a lytyll hethe-buysshe, and hit stange a knyght in the foote. And so whan the knyght felte hym so stonge, he loked downe and saw the adder; and anone he drew hys swerde to sle the addir, and thought none othir harme. And when the oste on bothe partyes saw that swerde drawyn, than they blewe beamys, trumpettis, and hornys, and shoutted grymly, and so bothe ostis dressed hem togydirs. (3.1235)

As mentioned above, in the stanzaic *Morte Arthur* the knight who draws the sword is one of Mordred's men; but Malory does not indicate on which side the knight was fighting. That is irrelevant. What is relevant is Malory's explanation: 'he drew hys swerde to sle the addir, and thought none othir harme'. In Malory's account the destruction of Arthur's kingdom results from a mistake made by one who 'thought none othir harme'.

3. *Conclusion*

Most who read the brief account in Edward IV's genealogical chronicle would have been reminded of the Arthur of the chronicles, the ideal heroic king who fell, as the chronicler Hardyng observes, through the fickleness of Fortune and the treachery of Mordred. Such an interpretation is fine if an author is writing propaganda and wishes to give the king ideal ancestors.

But that is not the only interpretation one could derive from the genealogical chronicle, particularly if an author's aim is not propaganda but, like Malory's, a new uniquely English account derived from stories that had previously been known only in French and that might appeal to a king and others interested in reading more of the Arthurian legends in a language whose literature had long been thought to be impoverished. In Edward's genealogical chronicle, Arthur is certainly heroic: he is described as 'doughti' and 'wel belouyd', and he conquered the Saxons and Romans, but he is not necessarily ideal and his fall could be due to more than Fortune and treachery: the chonicle simply says: 'Modrede the traitour that had the gouernuance of the londe toke it to hymself ageyns the kyngis entente. And whan kyng Arthure herd therof he come home to avenge hym upon that traitour . . . and afterward Modrede was slayn in batail and kyng Arthure was wounded to deth.' Such a summary leaves a great deal of room for reinterpretation. Malory presented a tragedy of Arthur different from that of the Vulgate Cycle and of the Post-Vulgate *Roman* and of the chronicles. Although, as in the Vulgate Cycle and in the chronicles, Fortune and treachery are present in Malory's story, the tragedy in Malory is not primarily a medieval tragedy of fortune, and it is therefore a tragedy quite different from most of the works that Henry Ansgar Kelly discusses in his studies of medieval tragedy.[84] It is instead a tragedy that results more from human error, from good people making mistakes.

Aside from the general parallel to the tragedy of a kingdom divided by civil war, the allusions to specific historical events that scholars have noted in *Morte Darthur* have little or no claim to validity: they can be explained either as Malory's attempts to make the material in his French sources consistent with some of the events in the chronicles (Uther's battle at St Albans, for example) or as his attempts to make his stories more geographicaly precise (Joyous Garde's identification with Bamburgh or Alnwick) or as his use of material in the sources that scholars have overlooked (the support of the commons for Arthur). Scholars who have found pro-Lancastrian sentiments in Malory have seen him as a bitter anti-Yorkist who was in prison under Edward IV and whom the king refused to pardon. This view takes insufficient account of the fact that Malory, as evidenced by the comments in his explicits, was hoping to be released from prison, and this would have given him reason enough to write a new interpretation of the Arthurian tragedy that, given the uncertainties of the years 1469 and 1470, would be politically neutral and offend neither side but that would also please a king who had frequently provided genealogical advertisements of his British descent.

Malory's conception of tragedy could have come initially from the source for his first tale, the Post-Vulgate *Merlin*, which offers a tragedy resulting from human error but that was nevertheless compatible with the positive conception of Arthur held by the English. This concern with human error could have been strengthened by Malory's own experiences in the Wars of the Roses. Field, in his discussion of Malory's reference to the 'new-fangill' English people who could not be content with their true king, perceptively calls attention to Malory's use of the first person pronouns in that passage: 'men say that *we* of thys londe have nat yet loste that custom. Alas! thys ys a greate defaughte of *us* Englysshemen, for there may no thynge *us* please no terme' (3.1229; italics mine). Field writes that the passage 'does not merely condemn the English vice of volatility, but by its use of first-person pronouns three times confesses that its author too is guilty of that vice'.[85] Thus this passage could well have been intended as Malory's own *mea culpa*.

T. H. White describes Malory's tragedy as Aristotelian, as a tragedy of 'sin coming home to roost'.[86] Although White's interpretation of the Arthurian

[84] Kelly, *Ideas and Forms of Tragedy from Aristotle to the Middle Ages* (Cambridge, 1993) and *Chaucerian Tragedy* (Cambridge, 1997). Kelly says nothing about Malory in the first book and in the second draws only a brief analogy to Cresseid's realization of her sin in Robert Henryson's *Testament of Cresseid* and Malory's presentation of the final meeting of Lancelot and Guenevere (*Chaucerian Tragedy*, 246).

[85] Field, 'Fifteenth-Century History', p. 66.

[86] White, 'The Queen of Air and Darkness', *The Once and Future King* (1958; reprint New York, 1971), p. 312.

story would be applicable to the tragedy as found in the Post-Vulgate *Roman du Graal*, a tragedy that results from punishment for sin, it is not applicable to Malory's work. As indicated by Merlin's rebuke of Arthur in the first tale of *Morte Darthur* and by Arthur's killing the children born on May Day, Malory may have begun with this concept. However, as he developed the story in his final tale, human error and its recognition became more important, the errors of people who are basically good, who, like the knight who drew the sword, 'thought none othir harme', and who finally accept responsibility for what they have done. This has similarities to Aristotelian tragedy, but Malory puts emphasis upon error rather than upon sin;[87] and, of course, Malory would not have had to have been familiar with the *Poetics* to have known that good people often make mistakes that have disastrous consequences. Malory would surely have realized this as he sat writing in his cell, hoping that God, or Edward IV, would send 'hym good delyveraunce sone and hastely'.

---

[87] Like most medieval writers, Malory would in all likelihood not have been familiar with Aristotle's *Poetics*. At times, however, there are coincidental similarities between Aristotelian and medieval tragedy such as reversal and recognition. See M. V. Guerin, *The Fall of Kings and Princes: Structure and Destruction in Arthurian Tragedy* (Stanford, 1995), p. 6; Bogdanow, 'Fall', pp. 95–96.

VIII

KING, CRUSADER, KNIGHT: THE COMPOSITE ARTHUR OF THE MIDDLE ENGLISH PROSE *BRUT*

Tamar Drukker

The chronicles of late medieval England that are based on Geoffrey of Monmouth's *Historia regum Britanniae* follow its example in composing a history of the *kings* of the land, making their governance the central theme, structuring the retelling of past events around succession, and making the rulers into emblems of their times. The most important king in Geoffrey's book is, of course, Arthur, whose reign occupies almost a quarter of the work.[1] While there is mention of Arthur already in some of the earlier histories that serve Geoffrey as sources, only in the *Historia* does Arthur acquire a complete biography, decisively influencing the unfolding of the nation's past, and serving as a model of the righteous and heroic ruler.[2] Geoffrey presents in Arthur the pre-eminent British king and his reign serves as the climax of British history, even though it is a tale of failure, the story of the end of British sovereignty. Historians writing after Geoffrey, at least those who did not share his British patriotism, did not always adopt his attitude towards Arthur, but they could no longer ignore the king nor the legendary aura surrounding him and his court. The prose *Brut*, the most widely diffused and read vernacular history of Britain in late medieval England, resembles other chronicles in accepting Arthur's historicity.[3] Written in Anglo-Norman sometime soon

---

[1] Most critics agree that Arthur is the protagonist of Geoffrey's *Historia*. See, for example, H. A. MacDougall, *Racial Myth in English History: Trojans, Teutons, and Anglo-Saxons* (Hanover, London and Montreal, 1982), p. 10.

[2] For a brief survey of the Latin sources see J. J. Wilhelm, 'Arthur in the Latin Chronicles', in *The Romance of Arthur*, ed. J. J. Wilhelm and L. Z. Gross (New York and London, 1984), pp. 5–11; S. Echard, *Arthurian Narrative in the Latin Tradition* (Cambridge, 1998); and J. S. P. Tatlock, *The Legendary History of Britain: Geoffrey of Monmouth's* Historia Regum Britanniae *and its Earliest Vernacular Versions* (Berkeley and Los Angeles, 1960), pp. 180–3. On Arthur's name in Nennius's *Mirabilia* see C. Dean, *Arthur of England: English Attitudes to King Arthur and the Knights of the Round Table in the Middle Ages and the Renaissance* (Toronto, Buffalo and London, 1987), p. 51. For early Welsh Arthurian texts see O. J. Padel, *Arthur in Medieval Welsh Literature* (Cardiff, 2000).

[3] *The Brut or The Chronicles of England*, ed. F. W. D. Brie, 2 vols., EETS o.s. 131, 136 (London, 1906, 1908). Quotations from the chronicle will be followed with chapter and page references to this edition. For a general description of the chronicle see R. Albano, *Middle English Historiography* (New York, 1993), pp. 37–40; A. Gransden, *Historical Writing in England*, 2 vols. (London, 1982), II, 73–6, 220–6;

after 1333 and translated into Middle English some fifty years later, it includes a version of the life and deeds of Arthur (chapters 71–89), which shows indebtedness beyond Geoffrey, embracing varied models of kingship and sovereignty and ultimately advancing a distinctive, but composite, portrait of the legendary king.[4]

Broadly speaking, the central corpus of medieval Arthurian literature developed in two principal streams: chronicle and romance. Unlike the Arthur of romance, whose court often forms the background setting for an adventure tale of one or more of his knights, the Arthur of Geoffrey, and of the various *Brut*s that follow, is the hero of his tale. In sharp contrast to many romance treatments (to retain our trenchant classification for the moment), the king is never passive. Further, while the romances often remain vague about the geographical and temporal setting of Arthur's court, in the chronicles the legend of Arthur is integrated into – or rather imposed upon – a historical chronology of reigns. Yet there remains something ambiguous and romance-like even about the Arthur of the chronicles. He is born with the help of magic, defeats a giant, and when he dies he seems to be spirited away. Near the description of his death, in chapter 88, an early-modern reader of a prose *Brut* manuscript, Cambridge University Library Ee.4.32, has noted in the margin 'Arthur wounded', and another, in a different hand, has added 'But not known where he dyed' (fol. 47v).[5] These comments reflect the ambivalent presentation of Arthur in the *Brut*: on the one hand, Arthur is real enough to be physically wounded, and on the other, his body is never found and he has neither tomb nor shrine. Arthur evades the kind of narrative that the *Brut* tradition favours, being based on the recorded lives of kings. He forms a major presence in the *Brut*, and yet he leaves no trace.

However, the Arthurian section in the *Brut* can be considered a microcosm of the work. It includes reflection on the way supernatural forces influence history, the relationship between the distant past and the present, and between written models and lived history. In these chapters the compilers touch upon such themes as the nature of kingship, imperialism and nationalism which run as a thread throughout the prose *Brut*. Although drastically different from the other kings in the *Brut*, Arthur in many ways becomes a model and a symbol on which the kings of England depend, and to whose fame they aspire. The

---

L. Matheson, 'Historical Prose', in *Middle English Prose: A Critical Guide to Major Authors and Genres*, ed. A. S. G. Edwards (New Brunswick, 1984), pp. 209–14; and J. Taylor, *English Historical Literature in the Fourteenth Century* (Oxford, 1987), pp. 110–32.

4   This is, according to Julia Marvin, the longest episode in the work devoted to a single reign. See 'The Prose Brut Chronicle and the Lessons of Vernacular History' (unpublished dissertation, Princeton, 1997), 2 vols., I, 137. It is true that the *Brut* dedicates a long section to King Arthur, but since the chronicle continues to trace historical developments up to its time of composition, the reign of Arthur loses its weight in the work as a whole as more and more information finds its way into the work and longer chapters are devoted to more recent history. See R. Morris, *The Character of King Arthur in Medieval Literature* (Cambridge, 1982), p. 105.

5   Other readers did not sense or stress the mystery of Arthur's death, such as the reader of Cambridge University Library, MS Ll.2.14 who adds near the description of Arthur's last battle 'K. Arthur slaine. Anno 580 of Christ' (fol. 33v), thus anchoring the king's death in Christian chronology, as a datable event.

Brut was surely never considered by its readers, and never intended to be viewed, as a contribution to scholastic reasoning about dominion. Nonetheless, like the historical books of the Bible, it offers examples and precedents, demonstrating the practical problems and results of applying a monarchical form of governance.[6] The Arthurian section of the chronicle marks the *Brut*'s movement beyond the mere recording of history to engage with concerns central to late medieval literature on kingship.

The Portrayal of Arthur: Scriptural Parallels

> When thou art come into the land, which the Lord thy God will give thee, and possessest it, and dwellest in it, and shalt say: I will set a king over me, as all nations have that are about: Thou shalt set him whom the Lord thy God shall choose out of the number of thy brethren. (Deuteronomy 17:14–20)[7]

The *Brut*'s distinctive portrayal of Arthur as king would appear to have derived in part from scriptural models. The extensive commentary on kingship in Old Testament tradition centres upon God's counsel to the wandering Israelites instructing them on the nature of kingship and the ideal king. The people may have a king only when they have reached their homeland and established themselves in a territory they can call their own; this king must be one of them. Stemming from these two conditions, the king emerges as a *national* construct in the sense that his authority is based on a clear identification of a people with a land, and on some idea of common identity, ethnic or otherwise, that allows a distinction between those that belong to the group of brethren and those that do not.[8] The king must be chosen and approved by God, though he is elected by the people and on their demand. The king must ensure the well-being of his people by observing and establishing religious law in his realm; laws are essential to preserve the king's rule and to ensure the continuation of the community in his care. These instructions from God in

---

6   Medieval readers consulted the historical books of the Bible for practical and theoretical knowledge. In the prologue to the Wycliffite Bible there is repeated emphasis on the usefulness of biblical narratives, especially for rulers:
> This prosces of the iij. book of Kingis [i.e. 1 Kings] schulde stire kingis and lordis, to be mersyful and pytouse on her sugetis that trespasen aȝens hem, and in alle thingis eschewe ydilnesse, leccherie, tresoun, ydolatrie, and false counceilouris and vnwyse, and euere distroie synne, and take counceil at hooly scripture and trewe prophetis, and triste not to false prophetis, be thei neuer so manye, and crie faste aȝens oon either fewe trewe men.

The Holy Bible containing the Old and the New Testaments with the Apocryphal Books, in the Earliest English Versions made from the Latin Vulgate by John Wycliffe and his Followers, ed. J. Forshall and F. Madden, 4 vols. (Oxford, 1850), I, ch. 5, p. 15.
7   Biblical quotations are from *The Holy Bible Translated from the Latin Vulgate*, first printed by the English College at Doway, 1609, 4 vols. (1750).
8   Territorial sovereignty underlies the common medieval formula *rex in regno suo est imperator regni sui* (the king in the territory of his dominion is emperor in his own kingdom) which emphasises the relationship between ruler, people and land. On the development of this theme towards the end of the Middle Ages see W. Ullman, ' "This Realm of England is an Empire" ', *The Journal of Ecclesiastical History* 30:2 (April 1979), 175–203.

Deuteronomy form the basic guidelines of political theory in the early Hebraic tradition, while the books of Samuel and Kings present myriad narrative examples of kings and attitudes towards kingship, when the theory is put into practice.[9] In a religion which promotes the majestic image of God as the King of Kings, no human agent can achieve complete or perfect sovereignty; God is the only source of absolute rulership, excluding the possibility for any human kingship which aspires to that condition.[10] Inevitably, any human form of governance is flawed, and the king must perform under those limitations that bind him to his brethren. Much medieval commentary on the prescription of sovereignty found in Deuteronomy emphasises the sins of the two greatest Israelite kings, David and Solomon, both guilty of accumulating riches and wives against God's instructions. This leads the commentators to establish a point of political theory, namely that the election of the king is permitted by God but is not commanded by him.[11] It is not surprising therefore to find the people's wish for a monarch represented in the Bible as a sign of weakness, to which God makes a reluctant concession. The Lord explains to the prophet Samuel, who finds the people's request offensive, that 'they have not rejected thee, but me, that I should not reign over them . . . hearken to their voice: but yet testify to them, and foretell them the right of the king, that shall reign over them' (1 Samuel 8:7, 9). The idea that kingship represents a compromise by God with mankind's need for strong and human leadership forms a significant strain in medieval political thought. Based on the biblical examples, the notion has to a large extent developed independent of classical political theory, and is mostly concerned with establishing a workable Christian polity.[12]

---

9 The biblical books of Kings and Chronicles can be read as a collection of serial biographies. On this theme and its reoccurrence in medieval narrative histories see D. Mauskopf Deliyannis, 'A Biblical Model for Serial Biography: The Books of Kings and the Roman *Liber Pontificalis*', *Revue Bénédictine* 107:1 (1997), 15–23.

10 On the governance of God and the limitation of the king see S. Reynolds, 'Medieval *Origines Gentium* and the Community of the Realm', *History* 68 (1983), 375–90. On theocracy and its significance to medieval political theory see the editor's introduction to *The Cambridge History of Medieval Political Thought c. 350–c. 1450*, ed. J. H. Burns (Cambridge, 1988), especially pp. 6–7. This Judeo-Christian tradition in which the king is dependent on God as the ultimate source of governance is different from the one described by J. G. Frazer where he traces the origin of the idea of kingship to an identification of the human monarch with a god and/or his priest. See *Lectures on the Early History of Kingship* (London, 1905), pp. 28–34.

11 See for example, *Biblia sacra cum glossa ordinaria* (Antwerp, 1634), I: cols. 1568–70, or in the Facsimile Reprint of the Editio Princeps Adolph Rusch of Strassburg 1480/81 edited with an introduction by K. Froehlich and M. T. Gibson, *Biblia latina cum glossa ordinaria* (Turnhout, 1992), I, 397.

12 See C. J. Nederman's discussion of the sources for John of Salisbury's *Policraticus* in the introduction to her English translation *Policraticus; Of the Frivolities of Courtiers and the Footprints of Philosophers* (Cambridge, 1990), pp. xix–xxi. For the Latin text see *Ioannis Saresberiensis Episcopi Carnotensis sive de Nugis Curialium et Vestigiis Philosophorum libri VIII*, ed. C. C. I. Webb, 2 vols. (Oxford, 1909), and a recent edition of part of the work, *Ioannisa Saresberiensis Policraticus I–IV*, ed. K. S. B. Keats-Rohan (Turnhout, 1993). Though Aristotle's *Politics* was rediscovered in Latin Europe in the thirteenth century, this political treatise did not override persisting notions of political organisations based on biblical and early Germanic examples. For the translations and reception of Aristotle's works in England see D. Luscombe, 'The *Ethics* and the *Politics* in the Middle Ages', in *Aristotle in Britain during the Middle Ages: Proceedings of the International Conference at Cambridge 8–11 April*

One of the first medieval thinkers to comment systematically on political ideas relied heavily upon scriptural example. The *Policraticus* of John of Salisbury (1120?–80) is one of the earliest systematic treatises on good governance.[13] Completed in 1159, the work circulated widely and was considered a textbook on the nature of kingship and the application of Roman secular law in a Christian world. According to John, the just ruler must remain a servant of the Church, accountable to God and to the priesthood.[14] He sees in the institution of monarchy an existing and accepted form of rule, but adds to the biblical list of obligations other requirements that touch upon the king's personal conduct and his behaviour towards his people, to ensure his just rule for the benefit of the realm (*respublica*). The king is warned against the temptation of self-indulgence, for he must remember that his honour and power (*potestas*) belong to God and his court must not rival the divine one. The king must be kind and just in his rule and follow God's laws in every way.[15] These moral restrictions are meant to guarantee the king's welfare, by ensuring the stability of his rule and of the community. Acknowledging the possibility of a harmful kingship, John looks to the Old Testament where he finds in the rule of the judges the ideal political system compared to which monarchy is viewed as a compromise.[16] Since all forms of power emerge from God and intrinsically belong to Him, the king represents the Lord and not the people, though he must be elected and accepted by both. John devotes a long chapter

---

1994, ed. J. Marenbon (Brepols, 1996), pp. 337–49. Giles of Rome's *De regimine principum* is heavily indebted to Aristotle and became a model of the application of Aristotelian political theory to late medieval society and political thinking. On the dialogue between classical and medieval political theories in the later Middle Ages and their parallel existence see J. P. Canning, 'Introduction: Politics, Institutions and Ideas', in *The Cambridge History of Medieval Political Thought*, pp. 341–66.

13 On the work and its author see Nederman's introduction and J. Dickinson, 'The Medieval Conception of Kingship and Some of its Limitations, as Developed in the *Policraticus* of John of Salisbury', *Speculum* 1:3 (1926), 308–37; J. Huizinga, 'John of Salisbury: A Pre-Gothic Mind', in *Men and Ideas: History, the Middle Ages, the Renaissance*, trans. J. S. Holmes and H. van Marle (London, 1960), pp. 169–77; E. F. Jacob, 'John of Salisbury and the *Policraticus*', in *The Social and Political Ideas of Some Great Mediaeval Thinkers: A Series of Lectures Delivered at King's College, University of London*, ed. F. J. C. Hearnshaw (London, Calcutta and Sydney, 1923), pp. 53–84; and W. Ullman, 'John of Salisbury's *Policraticus* in the Later Middle Ages', in *Geschichtesschreibung und geistiges Leben in Mittelalter*, ed. K. Hauck and H. Mordek (Cologne and Vienna, 1978), pp. 519–45.

14 On the issue of the king's subjugation to the law – natural, divine, or human – and his status as legislator see chapter 4 in Book IV of the *Policraticus*: 'Quod diuinae legis auctoritate constat principem legi institiae esse subiectum.' (In Nederman's translation: That the authority of divine law consists in the prince being subject to the justice of law.) See also J. Dunbabin, 'Government', in *The Cambridge History of Medieval Political Thought*, pp. 477–519, see pp. 504–8.

15 As in chapters 5–7 in Book IV of the *Policraticus* entitled:
 Quod principem castum esse oportet et auaritiam declinare; Quod debet legem Dei habere prae mente et oculis semper et peritus esse in litteris et literatorum agi consiliis; Quod timorem Dei doceri debet et humilis esse et sic seruarehumilitatem quod auctoritas principis non minuatur et quod praeceptorum alia mobilia alia immobilia.
 (That the prince must be chaste and shun avarice; That the ruler must have the law of God always before his mind and eyes, and be skilled in letters and follow the counsel of the learned; That he should teach the fear of God and be humble and so preserve humility that the authority of the prince be not diminished, and that some precepts are fixed and some are flexible.)

16 Book VIII, chapter 22. According to John of Salisbury, kings would not be necessary in a perfect society. See R. Morris, *The Character of King Arthur*, p. 36.

to the nature of tyranny and the means by which the people must rid themselves of the rule of a tyrant.[17] The ideal king is set therefore not only against the unattainable utopian example of the ruling judge, but also in contrast with the worst kind of monarchy, that headed by a tyrant.

Thus theoretical discussions of various forms of political systems find their way from the Bible and associated commentaries, through political treatises like the *Policraticus*, to handbooks on good governance written for the rulers themselves, in the genre of the mirror for princes popular in the later Middle Ages. There are few works devoted purely to what is now recognised as political theory, yet the universities, the court, the papal curia and other centres of learning and writing produced many works treating social institutions, political organisations and the disposition of power.[18] Additionally, as the prose *Brut* attests, chronicles are another literary genre in which issues of just rule and the nature of kingship are of major concern, and they, too, refer back to biblical models.

Significantly, the *Brut*'s narrative of Arthur does not open with his crowning and the inauguration of his reign, as with most other kings in the chronicle, but with his birth. By tracing his history to the moment of his conception, the chronicle equates the private Arthur with the public figure, blurring the distinction between the person and his office in accord with manuals on the nature of kingship where the king's person and his political function are inseparable. The circumstances surrounding Arthur's conception mark him as an exceptional individual, brought to the world with the help of Merlin's magic.

The king's exceptional nature accordingly finds early expression in an heroic combat. When pursuing his anti-Roman campaign in Spain, Arthur hears of the kidnapping of Elaine by a giant on Mount St Bernard. Unsolicited, Arthur decides to fight the giant, delaying his battle against Rome. The narrator postpones the story of the military expedition and pauses to describe

[17] Book VIII, chapters 17–21, see especially chapter 20:
> Quod auctoritate diuinae paginae licitum et gloriosum est publicos tirannos occidere, si tamen fidelitate non sit tiranno obnoxius interfector aut alias iustitiam aut honestatem non amittat.
> (That by the authority of the divine book it is lawful and glorious to kill public tyrants, so long as the murderer is not obligated to the tyrant by fealty nor otherwise lets justice or honor slip. [Nederman, pp. 206–10])

Other thinkers struggled with the problem of unjust rule and the limits of the subjects' loyalty to their rulers. In the ninth century, for example, Hincmar of Rheims described Frankish royalty as a relationship of fidelity, trust and mutual service between king and subjects, in which case infidelity would be cause to break the 'contract' between the two. See J. Nelson, 'Kingship and Empire', in *The Cambridge History of Medieval Political Thought*, pp. 226–9.

[18] Canning, 'Introduction: Politics, Institutions and Ideas', pp. 358–60, lists various source materials for the study of medieval political theory. See also J. Simpson, *Sciences and the Self in Medieval Poetry: Alan of Lille's* Anticlaudianus *and John Gower's* Confessio Amantis (Cambridge, 1995), p. 274, justifying the use of literary works for an understanding of contemporary political thinking, and A. Black, *Medieval Political Thought in Europe 1250–1450* (Cambridge, 1992). Much of the debate was impelled by the polemics concerning *regnum* and *sacerdotium* during the Investiture Contest. For a comprehensive survey see C. Morris, *The Papal Monarchy: The Western Church from 1050–1250* (Oxford, 1989), and for the many ramifications thereafter, A. Murray, *Reason and Society in the Middle Ages* (Oxford, 1985, first printed in 1978).

this episode in detail. The narrative momentarily breaks into direct speech, a mode of narration used at other times throughout the chronicle where a moment of heightened individual struggle takes over from the national epic. The giant has not only abused and killed Elaine; he continues to sexually molest her elderly nurse, as she explains:

> When þat Elyne was dede, þe Geaunt made me to abide, to done and haunt his wille, and me most nedes it soffren. and God it wote, I do hit nouȝt wiþ my gode wille, for leuer me were to bene dede þan wiþ him to dele, so miche payne I haue when he me forleiȝ. (ch. 84, p. 85)

On one level, Arthur fights as a hero of romance, a knight who takes up arms in order to free a lady and to slay an ogre. There are various touches elsewhere in the Arthurian chapters of the *Brut* that gesture towards romance in this way, and provide a context for such a reading, as when Arthur holds a feast in the company of his knights after his victories in France. In this scene Arthur can manifest his generosity and the splendour of his court, feasting for no less than fifteen days.[19] But even in these sections we sense a recession away from the simple romance plots. Elaine is dead, so for Arthur there is no question of amatory or financial reward after the giant's defeat. Nevertheless, Arthur sets out 'priuely by nyȝt, þat none of his hoste it wiste' (p. 85) to avenge Elaine's death, to free her nurse, and to rid the people from the menacing threat of the giant.

On another level, this combat proffers Arthur as a new Brutus and symbolically, a founder. Like Brutus before him, Arthur establishes order by overcoming a monstrous being.[20] Since the first inhabitants of Britain freed the island from such creatures, Arthur must leave Britain so that, like the hero of legend, he can prove worthy to face such an opponent. The giant is a tyrant, subjecting Elaine and her nurse to his rule and to his sexual whims by force, terrorising the people, and disrupting order, with the intolerable form of monarchy described by John of Salisbury.[21]

But the Old Testament resonances are also very strong in this section. After killing the giant, Arthur presents his head to the army, 'to shewe ham for a wonder, for it was so grete & so huge' (ch. 84, p. 85). Since the battle takes place on top of Mount St Bernard, the giant's head is the only evidence informing Arthur's men and the people of Spain of Arthur's courageous act. In this scene a connection seems to be drawn between King Arthur and King

---

[19] Biblical examples of lavish banquets last at the most seven days, as the feast arranged by the Persian king at the opening of the Book of Esther, for example.

[20] The dragon-killing myth develops as a poetic symbol for the Creation. To some extent, Arthur, like Brutus, is a founding father. On the symbolic weight of the slaying of the dragon see N. Frye, 'The Mythical Approach to Creation', in *Myth and Metaphor: Selected Essays, 1974–1988*, ed. R. D. Denham (Charlottesville and London, 1990), pp. 238–54, see p. 247.

[21] On the giant as a tyrant see Marvin, 'The Prose Brut Chronicle', p. 170. John of Salisbury's discussion of the nature of tyranny concludes with the assertion that a tyrant must meet his bad end from the hands of God, but prior to that the community has an obligation to rid itself from tyrannical rule. See note 17 above and Dickinson, 'The Medieval Conception of Kingship', pp. 325–9.

David. As Jeffrey Jerome Cohen has recently demonstrated, the celebrated giant-killer of 1 Samuel informs many a romance portrait of the encounter with the monstrous.[22] Here, the sustained description of Arthur exhibiting the vanquished giant's head to his army increases the identification. Arthur follows the example of the young David, before he was made king, in fighting Goliath, a giant 'whose height was six cubits and a span' (1 Samuel 17:4), saving the Israelites from the Philistines. David overcomes Goliath in single combat and presents himself before Saul 'with the head of the Philistine in his hand' (ibid. 57). David cuts off the giant's head not only to assure King Saul and the people that their enemy is dead, as King Arthur does, but also to claim the prize offered to the one who would take up Goliath's offer to fight him. The Israelites are told that 'the man that shall slay him, the king will enrich with great riches, and will give him his daughter and will make his father's house free from tribute in Israel' (ibid. 25). This single act, often represented in iconography, portrays David as a saviour, and as the ideal figure who would come to rule the people of Israel. Although he sins later in life, David remains the most successful and beloved of biblical kings.

Arthur does not receive any tangible reward for killing the giant, yet the combat consolidates his fame. There are no political, national or personal reasons for Arthur to engage in this battle, but it serves the interests of the compilers of the chronicle. It allows them to present the reader with an image of Arthur who is no longer only a king of military history but also the hero of romance. A hero whose strongest motivations derive from personal courage and bravura, rather than from the public duties that are so dominant in the *Brut*'s account of Arthur.

The Portrayal of Arthur: Emperors and Crusaders

The composite Arthur of the prose *Brut* takes on additional dimensions in the presentation of the king's imperial aspirations. Arthur's military career reaches its climax in his overtaking of Rome, defeating the emperor, and intending to take his place as the ruler of western Christendom.[23] It is as an emperor that Arthur is presented among the Nine Worthies in the Coventry pageant in honour of Margaret of Anjou in 1456. The order in which the worthies appear differs from the usual sequence of three pagan, three Jewish,

---

[22] J. J. Cohen, *Of Giants: Sex, Monsters and the Middle Ages* (Minneapolis, 1999), pp. 65–6, 85–6.

[23] Lee Patterson argues that Geoffrey of Monmouth's entire *Historia* is structured around the opposition between Britain and Rome, culminating in Arthur's campaign against the emperor. See 'The Romance of History and the Alliterative *Morte Arthure*', in *Negotiating the Past: The Historical Understanding of Medieval Literature* (Madison, 1987), pp. 197–230, see p. 215. This theme was picked up by Henry VIII when seeking precedents for his own wish to break away from Rome. In Arthur, Henry finds the ideal ancestor. See D. Starkey, 'King Henry and King Arthur', *Arthurian Literature* 16 (1998), pp. 171–96, see pp. 171–2 where he convincingly disproves Sydney Anglo's claim that 'the Tudor use of the *British History* was not as extensive nor as important as has been supposed': S. Anglo, 'The *British History* in Early Tudor Propaganda', *Bulletin of the John Reylands Library* 44 (1961), 17–48, citation on pp. 19–20.

and three Christian heroes.[24] Julius Caesar appears last, allowing Arthur to be the first to present himself as the one who overcame the ruler of Rome. The king proclaims:

> I, Arthur, kynge crownyd & conqueroure,
> That yn this lande reyned right rially;
> With dedes of armes I slowe the Emperour;
> The tribute of this ryche reme I made downe to ly.[25]

Following Arthur, Charlemagne and Julius Caesar both introduce themselves as emperors. Arthur is grouped with them, marking him in the popular mind at the close of the Middle Ages as a sovereign not only over Britain but also as the Roman emperor ruling the entire Christian west.

Significantly, the Arthur of the prose *Brut* does not profess to be the first British ruler to reach Rome; he bases his imperial claims on a British precedent, as he clearly states in his letter to the Roman emperor:

> Uv[n]derstondes amonges ʒow of Rome, þat I am Kyng Arthure of Britaigne, and frely hit holde, and shal holde; and at Rome hastely y shal be, nouʒt to ʒeue ʒow truage, but forto axen truage; ffor Constantyne, þat was Elynus sone, þat was Emperour of Rome and of al þe honour þat þereto bilongede; ffor Maxinian conquerede al Fraunce and Almaigne, & mount Ioye passede, & conquerede al Lumbardye; and þise ij were myn ancestres; and þat þai hade and helde, I shulde haue, prouʒ Godes wille. (ch. 81, p. 82)

Arthur does not mention among his ancestors just any Roman emperor, but Constantine, the emperor who has established Christianity as the official religion of the entire Roman Empire. The *Brut* indeed firmly connects the story of Constantine I with British history by making his mother, Helena, the daughter of King Coel of Colchester. We are told that Constantine, designated emperor in York, reigned in Britain, but left it to deliver Rome from the usurping pagan, 'a sarasyne, a tyraunt, þat me callede Maxence, þat put to þe deth alle þat bileuede in God, and destroiede holy cherche by alle his power, and slought Cristen men þat he myʒt fynde' (ch. 47, p. 40). Constantine overcomes Maximus, a pagan whom the narrator of the *Brut* calls a Saracen, thus equating him with the arch-enemies of Christianity in the High Middle Ages,

---

24 On Arthur among the Worthies as a common *topos* and its political use see D. B. Tyson, 'King Arthur as a Literary Device in French Vernacular History Writing of the Fourteenth Century', *Bibliographical Bulletin of the International Arthurian Society* 33 (1981), pp. 238–41. The example above is interesting because of its diversion from the accepted presentation of Arthur among the Worthies, highlighting a specific attribute associated with these historical figures. Something similar happens in the description of the Nine Worthies in the alliterative *Morte Arthure* which begins, curiously, with Alexander. For the significance of this break from the conventional presentation see W. Matthews, *The Tragedy of Arthur: A Study of the Alliterative 'Morte Arthure'* (Berkeley and Los Angeles, 1960), pp. 34–5.

25 *The Coventry Leet Book: or Mayor's Register*, transcribed and edited by M. D. Harris, EETS 134, 135, 138, 146 (London, 1907–13), pp. 290–1. On the sources of the Nine Worthies in the pageantry see R. Withington, *English Pageantry: An Historical Outline*, 2 vols. (Cambridge, Mass., and London, 1918), I, 79–80, 149–50; see also G. Kipling, *Enter the King: Theatre, Liturgy and Ritual in the Medieval Civic Triumph* (Oxford, 1998), ch. 6, especially pp. 314–18.

and succeeds him to the throne in Rome. In addition, his mother Helena achieves the goal of all later crusaders by reaching Jerusalem, building the Church of the Holy Sepulchre and uncovering 'þat croice in þe holy londe' (ibid.).[26] The myth of the British parentage of Helena developed in the early twelfth century and seems to appear first in the writings of William of Malmesbury (c. 1095–1143).[27] Once accepted it was incorporated in other historical compositions, receiving much attention from Ranulph Higden, who could follow the career of the emperor Constantine outside Britain in his work since his *Polychronicon* was designed as a world history.[28] The ancient hero of Christendom is thus given British ancestry, thence he becomes an exemplary leader to all British kings to follow.

The medieval image of Constantine shows an ideal crusader, a soldier of Christ who frees holy sites from the rule and hands of infidels. Though placed in history many generations before the launching of the First Crusade, King Arthur, like Constantine, anticipates the crusader-kings of the English chronicles. Once the image of the ideal warrior is combined with that of the pious Christian, his battles acquire a righteousness that transforms the political and nationalistic motivations that drive him to war.

When it comes to narrating the historical crusades, the chronicle does not evoke Arthur. For although the Arthurian section of the *Brut* is central to the chronicle and germane to its presentation of the unfolding of British history, it is important to note that the compilers of the *Brut* rarely refer back to Arthur in the subsequent chapters. While English kings and their subjects identified themselves with the Arthur of the chronicle, this narrative is void of such explicit comparisons – a fact made the more striking by the parallel development of these crusaders' fortunes. Thus the *Brut* recounts how Richard I turns back to England when he hears that his brother John has taken advantage of his absence to seize control of England and Normandy. Like King Arthur before him, Richard cannot achieve his ultimate goal because of strife in his kingdom and enmity with the king of France. Though defeated and mortally wounded, Richard acts in accordance with his ideal character and sustains the crusading ethos by ending his life with an act of Christian mercy. On his deathbed he forgives his assassin, addressing him thus: 'þo saide Kyng

---

[26] In the margin of fol. 14v of a *Brut* manuscript, Bodleian Library, Ashmole 793, a reader makes note of the two ingredients of the Constantine story crucial to British history, writing, 'The holy cross; rome won by the English.'

[27] In Bk 1, section I.2 of William of Malmesbury's *Gesta regum Anglorvm: The History of the English Kings*, ed. and trans. R. A. B. Mynors, completed by R. N. Thomson and M. Winterbottom, 2 vols. (Oxford, 1998), I, 16–19.

[28] *Polychronicon Ranulphi Higden Monachi Cestresis, together with the English Translation of John Trevisa and of an Unknown Writer of the Fifteenth Century*, ed. C. Babington and J. R. Lumby, Rolls Series 41, 8 vols. (London, 1865–86; Kraus reprint, 1964). On the historiographic tradition see W. J. Mulligan, 'The British Constantine: An English Historical Myth', *The Journal of Medieval and Renaissance Studies* 8:2 (1978), 257–79, and A. Linder, 'The Myth of Constantine the Great in the West: Sources and Hagiographic Commemoration', *Studi Medievali* 3rd ser. 16 (1975), 43–95. Both explain how the myth emerges from a seemingly innocent confusion of names and gaps in historical data, but go on to show how the myth was used in a deliberate way to promote English imperial claims.

Richard: "He þat deide oppon þe croice to bryng mannus soule fram þe pyne of helle, forȝeue ȝow my deþ! and y also forȝeue hit þe" ' (ch. 145, p. 154).[29] While the name of Arthur does not appear in the section describing Richard's life, a serialistic reading of the *Brut* might well prompt reflection upon the parallels between the two heroes and the failed expeditions in the name of Christianity they both undertake. The parallel implies a cross-fertilisation of romance and history. For while chronologically it is Richard who is repeating the example set by Arthur, the historical Richard's campaign might well have inspired the way Arthur's endeavours have been transformed in the *Brut* into a crusade.

The composite Arthur of the prose *Brut* is moreover imitative of Christ. From his marvellous birth onwards, here is a devout figure, demonstrably pious and exercising a forgiveness which stands in contrast with the ruthlessness characterising him in the earliest tradition.[30] Instead of conquering the Scots by the sword as he first intended, Arthur yields to the plea of 'þe bisshoppes, Abbotes, & oþere folc of þe contre, and Ladies' (ch. 76, p. 76) who base their plea on the notion that 'ful grete dishonour it shulde be to quelle ham þat leueþ in almyȝty Gode as ȝe done' (ch. 76, p. 77). Their evocation of a common belief in the Christian God moves Arthur to take pity on the Scots and peacefully embrace them as his allies. His generosity is expressed also in the 'grete ȝiftes' (ch. 82, p. 83) he bestows on the messengers sent by the Roman emperor, and the honour and respect with which they are treated in spite of the insulting letter and the threat of war they bring with them. Arthur is kind and merciful towards those bearing the letter, but does not yield before the emperor who demands for himself what Arthur believes rightfully belongs to him. It is only when he cannot achieve justice by peaceful negotiations that Arthur sets out to wage war.

In fighting the enemies of God, Arthur fulfils one of the basic duties of the ideal Christian king. In order to achieve this goal and present Arthur in this image, the compilers of the history emphasise the inclusion of pagans among his enemies, as they join the Roman forces, which are made up 'of Sarasynes and of paynemys as of Cristen men' (ch. 85, p. 85). The emperor's act of recruiting non-Christians to help him in his war against Arthur is itself a just reason for opposing him; this is an offence against God which frees Arthur

---

[29] The same episode appears in other chronicles of the reign of Richard I, though the religious overtones are not stressed. In the continuation to William of Newburgh's *Historia rerum Anglicarum* to the year 1298 compiled by a monk of Furness Abbey, the first chapter (chapter 35) is devoted to the death of King Richard. The chronicler quotes Richard's dying words, 'Remitto tibi mortem meam' (I forgive you for my death). See *Chronicles of the Reigns of Stephen, Henry II, and Richard I*, ed. R. Howlett, Rolls Series 82, 4 vols. (London, 1885–89), II, 504. The story is repeated by modern biographers and historians, as in J. Gillingham's *Richard the Lionheart*, 2nd edn (London, 1989), p. 277.

[30] N. H. G. E. Veldhoen traces the Christ imagery in Laȝamon's *Brut* where Arthur's brutality exists alongside his religious piety: 'Towards National Identity: Literary Manipulation in the Arthurian Section of Layamon's *Brut*', *Amsterdamer Beiträge zur älteren Germanistik* 48 (1997), 19–30, especially p. 28. On Christ as the medieval model king see C. A. Conway, 'Boethius, the Liberal Arts, and Early Medieval Political Theory', in *Literature and Ethics: Essays Presented to A. E. Malloch*, ed. G. Wihl and D. Williams (Kingston and Montreal, 1988), pp. 96–110, see p. 106.

from the difficult dilemma arising when a Christian king engages in war against a fellow Christian. In setting out against a religiously-mixed army, Arthur's battle is no longer against Christianity, but for it.[31] The reality of Moslem rule in the Holy Land, increasingly important in the minds of Christians after the victory of Saladin in 1187, and the religious and political importance behind the ideal of the crusade, helped to keep it as a living aspiration in England still in the fourteenth, fifteenth and even the sixteenth centuries. By making Arthur a crusading king, the chroniclers do not only add to their favourable representation of Arthur, they also attach some of the Arthurian grandeur to the historical crusaders, seeing them as the followers of Arthur and of Constantine the Great, connecting them all in a lineage of devout warring leaders.[32]

These various idealised qualities of the prose *Brut*'s Arthur are ultimately figured not simply by example but by contrast. Such contrast is supplied by the treacherous Mordred, the usurper of Arthur's queen and realm. In the Old Testament, disregard for the social and religious prohibitions regarding sexual relations is a characteristic of evil kings, and it is one such usurper monarch who brings about Arthur's downfall.[33] Having entrusted his home, his wife and his crown to the hands of Mordred, Arthur leaves Britain to conquer Rome. The moment of his greatest achievement is also the moment of reversal and the beginning of his fall. The victorious king is defeated by treachery, epitomised in the figure of Mordred, but evident in other incidents earlier on in Arthur's life, and like other major themes recurring in the Arthuriad, this is central to the *Brut* as a whole.[34] The young Arthur becomes king after his father has been deviously poisoned (chapter 72). Secret plotting and falsehood reappear in Arthur's life and eventually bring him to ruin. The first to take advantage of Arthur's benevolence is the Saxon king Cheldric, to whom Arthur grants the freedom to leave Britain unharmed on the condition that he never return. But when Cheldric and his men sail away from Britain, 'hir wille chaungede, as þe deuel it wolde, & þai retourned hire nauye, &

---

[31] This theme recurs in the *Brut*'s treatment of the wars against the Scots, who are guilty of offending Christianity when attacking England. In chapter 190, the chroniclers write:

And in þe same tyme come þe Scottes aȝeyne into Engeland, and destroiede Northumberlond, and brent þat lande, & robbet hit, and quellede men and wymmen, & childern þat laye in cradell, and brent also holy cherche, and destroiede Cristendome, and toke & bare awaye Englisshe-mennes godes, as þai hade bene Sarasins or paynemes. and of þe wickednesse þat þai deden, all þe worlde spake þerof, þrouȝ al Cristendome. (p. 210)

The Scots behave as heathen, harming Christian sites and people in England, thus giving their enemies further justification for waging war.

[32] D. A. Trotter outlines the characteristic features of French literary descriptions of the Crusades. Religious and chivalric vocabulary is charged with specific connotations relating to the crusades. Arthur as presented in the *Brut* shares much with the fictional crusaders: *Medieval French Literature and the Crusades (1100–1300)* (Geneva, 1988), pp. 52–7, 94–9, et passim. See also E. D. Kennedy's introduction to *King Arthur: A Casebook* (New York and London, 1996), p. xix. On the ethos behind the Crusades and their appeal to clerical and lay people see J. Riley-Smith, *The First Crusade and the Idea of Crusading* (London, 1986), especially chs. 2 and 4.

[33] One such example is the biblical story of Absalom, who took his father's concubines as an initial stage in his attempt to overthrow King David and crown himself king. See 2 Samuel 16:20–2.

[34] Marvin, 'The Prose Brut Chronicle', p. 152, and Veldhoen, 'Towards National Identity', pp. 20, 24.

come aȝeyne into þis land' (ch. 73, p. 70) intending to resume their battle. Arthur defeats the Saxons in their second attempt to conquer Britain, killing many and chasing the others out of the land. Cheldric returns for the third time to Britain when Mordred sends for him asking his aid in fighting Arthur.

By recalling the Saxons to Britain, Mordred not only betrays his king, but his people and his country as well. This pattern underlies the *Brut*'s descriptions of foreign conquests of Britain, where foreign invasion succeeds only when the invaders are invited from within. Thus the earl of London sends for Julius Caesar and helps him take over the land of his compatriots (chapter 36); Buerne, to assist him in his struggle against King Osbright, invites the Danes to come with their army (chapter 103); and King Harold's own false swearing encourages William of Normandy to set sail towards England (chapters 131–2). Thus foreign rulers are helped in their conquest by civil strife and inner conflict. The *Brut*'s pattern of history is instructive, urging a moral: the greatest harm inhabitants can do to their native land is to call on other armies to wage war against their own people.[35]

As enemy within, Mordred forms a stark anti-type to Arthur's idealised qualities as sovereign. The traitor might be usefully compared with Arthur's chief combatant during his European campaigns, King Frolle of France. In Arthur's climatic combat with Frolle, the opponent is figured as adversary but nevertheless as a good king, concerned with the well-being of his people, the citizens of Paris. He offers Arthur a fair fight.

> Froll saw þat no longer he myȝt holde þe toun aȝeynes her wille, and truste greteli oppon his owen strengþ, & sent to Kyng Authure þat he shulde come to feiȝt wiþ him, body for body, and so þai shulde departe Fraunce bituene ham ij. Kyng Arthure anone graunte hit, and wolde þat none of his peple vndertoke þe batail for him. (ch. 78, p. 79)

Likewise Arthur here is not the brutal, eager commander portrayed in other histories and romances, but a refined ruler who adheres to the rules of chivalry and who keeps to law and order even in the heat of battle.[36] By contrast, Mordred the usurper-king commands little loyalty. When the inhabitants of London realise that Mordred is a traitor and their enemy as well as their king's, they refuse to give him refuge when he flees from Arthur. The scene contrasts King Frolle's successful refuge in Paris where he and his men, 'entrede þe toun, & closede þe ȝates, & þere ham helde' (ch. 78, p. 79). Frolle is Arthur's enemy, but not an enemy to his own nation. He is a brave leader, a decent rival to his slayer, King Arthur, who in a fair fight kills him and enters Paris. Unlike Frolle, Mordred does not find refuge among his own people, but

---

35 According to the chronicle of Robert of Gloucester in Pepys Library MS 2833 civil war is more destructive than threats from the outside, for 'as the bokiis seyen, that is on of the moste cause of lost of a reaume, that is to seye when ther is striff among hem self' (p. 157r).

36 Unlike the Arthur of Laȝamon's *Brut*. See J. Noble, 'Patronage, Politics, and the Figure of Arthur in Geoffrey of Monmouth, Wace, and Layamon', *The Arthurian Yearbook II*, ed. Keith Busby (New York and London, 1992), 159–78, see p. 166.

flees to Cornwall, and only with the help of the Cornish can he fight King Arthur and inflict fatal wounds upon him.

Here, to recall the *Brut*'s parallel treatment of King Arthur and King Richard I might lead to a suggestive identification of Mordred with King John, another usurper who profits from the rightful king's preoccupation with crusading endeavour. The *Brut*'s treatment of John's reign is not a favourable one; presenting a figure transgressive of rules of good governance. John loses Anjou and Normandy to the king of France, and he quarrels with the pope and with religious authorities in his land; he fails to heed good counsel; he neglects the rights of his subjects. Like a tyrant, 'he wolde none lawe holde, but dede al þing þat him likede, & disheritede meny men wiþ-outen consent of lordes & pireӡ of þe land' (ch. 153, p. 166). In order to control this leader, the lords unite against him and coerce him into signing the foundational *magna carta* (1215), outlining their rights and limiting those of the king. Like Mordred, king John is guilty of usurping the throne and seizing it against the people's wish, God's law and the laws of the land. Arthur, on the other hand, unlike these tyrants, keeps the law, respects his knights, and is careful to ask their advice and take counsel before making any significant decisions.[37] In relation to such a historical parallel, Arthur emerges as a king whose readiness to undertake single combat is balanced by a quality so much admired in the long tradition of Christian kingship, namely a willingness to take the advice of his barons and bishops. He proceeds in his great undertakings supported by a loyalty from his men gained by his readiness to heed them.

Arthur's Death

The different strands interwoven in the *Brut*'s portrayal of Arthur result in some distinctive elements in the treatment of Arthur's death and 'the Breton hope'.[38] The fight with Mordred leaves Arthur seriously wounded, yet instead of reporting the final outcome of this battle in the authoritative and omniscient mode characteristic of the narrative throughout the *Brut*, the chronicle tells us of the traditional view concerning Arthur's end, reporting only that

> Arthure himself was wondede to þe deth. but he lete him bene born in a liter to Auyoun, to bene helede of his wondes; and ӡitte þe Britons supposen þat he Leueþ in a-noþere lande, and þat he shal come ӡit and conquere al Britaigne; but certes þis is þe prophecie of Merlyn: he saide þat his deþ shulde bene dotous;

---

[37] On the king's duty to appoint counsellors and follow their advice see M. E. J. Hughes, 'Counselling the King: Perceptions of Court Politics in Poetry of the Reign of Richard II', in *France and the British Isles in the Middle Ages and Renaissance: Essays by Members of Girton College Cambridge, in Memory of Ruth Morgan*, ed. G. Jondorf and D. N. Dumville (Woodbridge, 1991), pp. 199–206. On the literature of advice in England see J. Ferster, *Fictions of Advice: The Literature and Politics of Counsel in Late Medieval England* (Philadelphia, 1996). Most relevant to my discussion is her survey in chapter three of the pseudo-Aristotelian *Secretum secretorum* addressed to Alexander the Great, and the English versions addressed to kings.

[38] For 'the Breton hope' in early sources see Tatlock, *Legendary History*, p. 204.

and he saide sothe, for men þerof ȝitte hauen doute, and shal for euermore, as men saiþ, for men weten nouȝt wheþer þat he leueþ or is dede. (ch. 88, p. 90)

As with his birth, there is something very unusual about the occasion of Arthur's death: he is taken away to a different place, and is never witnessed dead and buried. The prospect of Arthur's return forms, of course, a resonant platform for political statement in chronicle tradition. Thus the Anglo-Norman poet Wace and the anonymous author of the original Anglo-Norman prose *Brut* chronicle saw in Henry II a monarch in the model of King Arthur, the fulfilment of the Breton hope.[39] More pointed still is Stephen of Rouen's poem *Draco Normannicus* from about 1167–69 which presents a correspondence between Henry II and Arthur concerning Henry's claims over Brittany. The exchange of letters between the two monarchs is based on the assumption that Arthur is alive somewhere and bound to return. To resolve the tension between the two leaders, and to settle the rivalry between them, the poet makes Arthur appoint King Henry as his vassal, putting him in charge of his lands.[40] Hence the poem encourages the interpretation that Henry is a new Arthur, and by historicising the myth of Arthur's second coming as the accession of Henry it nullifies any Celtic 'separatism' attached to it. The Middle English prose *Brut* is markedly more cautious in its treatment of this theme. It reports the existence of such a belief, but the narrator does not pronounce Arthur's return nor comment on the validity of such a claim. Even Merlin's prophecy mentioned in the *Brut* does not touch upon the question of Arthur's return, but cites the mere fact that such a belief will always exist. The prophecy alluded to, attributed to the Eagle of Shaftesbury in Geoffrey of Monmouth's *Historia* and later ascribed to Merlin, is not included in the *Brut*.[41] The fact that Arthur inspires such a belief, that people await his second coming as a national saviour in the image of Christ, serves the chroniclers in their characterisation of King Arthur and his rule, but does not function within the historical reality following his death.

Arthur might not be dead, or some may not think he is, but the Arthur of the *Brut* is aware of the gravity of the wounds he has received, and in the manner of a responsible king he appoints an heir. The king's earlier wedding to Guinevere is inserted between a description of battles and serves as one example of Arthur's success in bringing 'his lande in pees and reste, & in gode

---

39 Noble, 'Patronage, Politics', pp. 170–1.

40 A modern edition of the poem was edited by Richard Howlett and published in *Chronicles of The Reigns of Stephen, Henry II, and Richard I*, II, 589–762. The exchange of letters between King Henry and King Arthur is on pp. 695–708. On the poem's political implications see M. L. Day, 'The Letter of King Arthur to Henry II: Political Use of the Arthurian Legend in *Draco Normannicus*', in *The Spirit of the Court: Selected Proceedings of the Fourth Congress of the International Courtly Literature Society (Toronto 1983)*, ed. G. S. Burgess and R. A. Taylor (Cambridge, 1985), pp. 153–7, and Echard, *Arthurian Narrative*, pp. 85–91.

41 On the prophecy of the Eagle of Shaftesbury see P. Strohm, *England's Empty Throne: Usurpation and the Language of Legitimation, 1399–1422* (New Haven and London, 1998), p. 7, and A. F. Sutton and L. Visser-Fuchs, 'The Dark Dragon of the Normans: A Creation of Geoffrey of Monmouth, Stephen of Rouen, and Merlin Silvester', *Quondam et Futurus* 2 (1992), 1–19, see p. 3.

state' (ch. 77, p. 77). Supplying his subjects with a queen is just another means of securing peace in the realm.[42] Since the marriage produces no issue, Arthur must overcome this handicap first by handing over his land to Mordred his nephew when he leaves to conquer Rome, and then again on his deathbed, appointing 'Constantyne, þat was Cadoreȝ sone, erl of Cornwail, his cosyn' (ch. 89, p. 90) as king. By passing on his crown, Arthur manifests his concern for the good of the realm and his people, knowing that without a male heir he must choose someone to take his place when he is no longer fit to rule. In Geoffrey's *Historia*, the fact that Arthur is childless serves both a historical and a literary function. Arthur does not create a new dynasty, and therefore his death, although not the apocalyptic end of time, clearly marks the end of the heroic chapter in British history. Geoffrey's chronicle tells of the fall of Britain, epitomised in the discontinuity of Arthur's lineage. Being without an heir, Arthur also becomes unique, one who can never be rivalled and whose glory could not be challenged by his offspring.[43] The *Brut*, by contrast, does not end with the fall of Arthur, nor with the end of British sovereignty in the land, for it continues to record historical developments up to the chroniclers' own lifetime. Arthur's Britain is revived in Anglo-Norman England. Arthur is the 'father' of kingship in England, be it British, English or Norman.

Arthur in the Brut: *An Ideal King?*

Many medieval and modern readers tend to think of Arthur as the ideal king, a perfect knight as well as a devout Christian ruler.[44] Yet from the portrait in the *Brut* it seems that there is much lacking in this king who falls short of the ideal ruler of Deuteronomy or the political treatise of John of Salisbury. We do not learn much about Arthur's behaviour as a civil ruler or the effect of his reign on those living in his kingdom.[45] In the late thirteenth century Giles of Rome,

---

[42] A king must marry and have a son in order to secure the rule over his people in the future. Being a good family man is in itself one of the duties of the king. Giles of Rome devotes the entire first part of book two of his *De regimine principum* to the value of marriage followed by an entire section on raising children. On the Latin work see note 46 below.

[43] R. Morris, *The Character of King Arthur*, p. 105. On Geoffrey's *Historia* as the story of the fall of Britain see R. M. Loomis, 'Arthur in Geoffrey of Monmouth', in *The Romance of Arthur*, 1:57–89, see p. 57.

[44] The chronicle itself uses King Arthur as the emblem of perfect kingship, notably in the comparison of Roger Mortimer, 'the king of Folly' with King Arthur in chapter 220. Another early example of the idealisation of King Arthur is found in his inclusion among the Nine Worthies. Tyson comments on medieval references to Arthur within the group of the Nine Worthies but also refers to cases where he is used simply as a model king. Some examples of such a treatment of Arthur among modern scholars can be found in K. H. Göller, 'The Figure of King Arthur as a Mirror of Political and Religious Views', in *Functions of Literature: Essays Presented to Erwin Wolff on his Sixtieth Birthday*, ed. U. Broich, T. Stemmler and G. Stratmann (Tübingen, 1984), pp. 55–79, see p. 61; F. Riddy in her introduction to the modern edition of *Brogyntyn Manuscript No. 8*, translated and transcribed by R. Voaden (Moreton-in-Marsh, 1991); B. Stone, 'Models of Kingship: Arthur in Medieval Romance', *History Today* 37:11 (November 1987), 32–8; and T. Turville-Petre, *England the Nation: Language, Literature, and National Identity, 1290–1340* (Oxford, 1996), p. 81.

[45] This is even more apparent in Geoffrey's account where, as Gillingham notes, Arthur 'founds no cities,

Archbishop of Bourges, completed a treatise *De regimine principum*, giving guidelines for the correct behaviour of any ruler, combining the theory of Aristotle's rediscovered *Politics* with Christian doctrine.[46] The work does not distinguish between the private person and the political one, and most of the instructions to the king apply to him as well as to all Christian men. The good king must be a good man in all walks of life. Therefore Giles of Rome includes all moral manners in his treatise. He explains, in the Middle English translation of John Trevisa,

> in techinge of kynges and of princes we deuyden and delen þis hoole book in þre bookes. For in þe firste book we touȝte þat kynges and princes scholde be wise and redy as a kyng and a prince is a certeyne persone in hymself and as þei scholde rewle hymself. And in þe seconde book we tauȝte a kyng to be wise and redy and in þat he is housebonde and scholde spende þe good and cataille of his hous. And in þe þridde book a kyng is itauȝt oþer a prince in þat is heed of regne oþer of a principate and in þat þei scholde ȝeue lawes and rewle citeseynes. And alle þes þre wisdomes a kyng sholde haue: particuler wisdom, wisdom of housbandrie, and wisdom of regnyng.
>
> (Book III, part iii, chapter 1, pp. 395–6)[47]

What do we know about the 'persone' of King Arthur? How does he rule his people? Unlike his forebear Brutus, Arthur inherits a civilised kingdom, and need not found new cities or establish order. He must only preserve and defend it. We are led to believe that there are no social problems or unrest within the realm, which allow the king time and freedom to extend his rule beyond the country's boundaries and to pursue imperial aspirations. The chronicle does not offer any examples of Arthur ministering justice or establishing laws that would affect the ordinary citizen in his realm.[48] There is no description of Arthur's coronation, a ceremony in which the symbolic and actual duties of a king are bestowed upon him in a public manifestation that is also a religious ceremony. Instead, the narrator lists the good qualities of the young heir when he begins to rule:

---

issues no laws, shows no concern to the well-being of farmers': 'The Context and Purposes of Geoffrey of Monmouth's *History of the Kings of Britain*', *Anglo-Norman Studies* 13 (1991), 99–118, citation on p. 116.

46 The work enjoyed wide and diverse popularity in the late Middle Ages until the introduction of print. There are some 350 surviving manuscripts of the Latin original and vernacular translations circulating in Western Europe. Though the book was originally composed for Philip the Fair and is closely connected with the French court, many manuscripts have English provenance. On the work and the manuscripts see C. F. Briggs, *Giles of Rome's* De Regimine Principium: *Reading and Writing at Court and University, c. 1275–c. 1525* (Cambridge, 1999). On Giles of Rome transmitting Aristotle's *Politics* and its fate in England see Canning, 'Introduction: Politics, Institutions and Ideas', pp. 355–6, and Luscombe, 'The *Ethics*', p. 347.

47 *The Governance of Kings and Princes: John Trevisa's Middle English Translation of* De Regimine Principum *of Aegidius Romanus*, ed. D. C. Fowler, C. F. Briggs and P. G. Remley (New York and London, 1997).

48 The stability of the socio-political order is a basic requirement for a functioning polity. The ruler has always been considered the one responsible to achieve and maintain this stability. See chapter 13 'Images of Order II: Rule and Representation', in H. Kleinschmidt, *Understanding the Middle Ages: The Transformation of Ideas and Attitudes in the Medieval Worlds* (Woodbridge, 2000), pp. 311–31.

When Arthure was made kyng of þe lande, he was but ȝonge, of xv ȝere age, but he was faire, and bolde, & douȝti of body, & to meke folc he was gode & curteise, & to prout folc he was stout & sterne; & also he was gentil and curteise, and large of spendyng, & made him wel bilouede of al men þere þat it was nede. (ch. 73, p. 69)

In the chapters that follow we are given examples of Arthur's boldness and military prowess, but not of his kindness to the poor and his inclination towards social justice. With scant time for largesse, Arthur begins his martial career when he is fifteen years old, like Brutus, with the promise 'þat Saxones neuer shulde haue pees ne reste til þat he hade drif ham out of his lande' (ibid.), followed by his immediate engagement in war, which occupies most of the section in the chronicle concerned with his reign.[49] But Arthur does exhibit his generosity when he distributes titles among the knights who have taken arms with him and have helped him in his conquests. During the feast he holds in Paris after conquering France, Arthur did 'richely . . . auaunce his knyȝtes for here seruise þat him hade holpen in his conquest' (ch. 79, p. 80). The relationship between King Arthur and the people in his court may be seen to represent his attitude towards his people. His court serves as his realm. There, Arthur establishes a new institution which comes to represent his form of civil governance, the innovative idea of the Round Table, first mentioned in Wace's *Roman de Brut*.[50] This is a political institution which shows Arthur's concern with sharing power and equally distributing it. Though only mentioned in passing when describing the court, the Round Table becomes synonymous with King Arthur so that later kings, notably Edward I and Edward III, re-established the Round Table along with a chivalric order, in an attempt to recreate Arthur's glorious reign and identify themselves with him.[51] The chroniclers remark on these attempts, ridiculing Roger Mortimer's

---

[49] It is no coincidence that Clovis, the first Christian king of the Franks, is also said to have been crowned at the age of fifteen. Gregory of Tours (538–594) ends his section devoted to Clovis with a brief summary of his life:

> At long last Clovis died in Paris. He was buried in the church of the Holy Apostles, which he and his Queen Clotild had built. He expired five years after the battle of Vouillé. He had reigned for thirty years and he was forty-five years old.

The History of the Franks, translated with an introduction by L. Thorpe (Middlesex, 1974), Bk II, ch. 43, p. 158.

[50] See I. Arnold's introduction to *Le Roman de Brut de Wace*, 2 vols. (Paris, 1938–40), I, lxxi, and Göller, 'The Figure of King Arthur', p. 63. Wace writes for a courtly audience adding detailed descriptions of Arthur's court, in a manner which reflects the Norman court of his days, to his adaptation of Geoffrey's *Historia*. Arthur's knights, in Wace's version, are Anglo-Normans, as the king is made to seem. Noble, 'Patronage, Politics', p. 167.

[51] On the Arthurian aspirations of thirteenth-century English kings and the reinstitution of Round Tables see M. E. Giffin, 'Cadwalader, Arthur, and Brutus in the Wigmore Manuscript', *Speculum* 16 (1941), especially the example of the Mortimers, pp. 111–16; Dean, *Arthur of England*, pp. 43–8; R. S. Loomis, 'Edward I, Arthurian Enthusiast', *Speculum* 28 (1953), 114–27; and J. Vale, *Edward III and Chivalry: Chivalric Society and its Context 1270–1350* (Woodbridge, 1982), pp. 1–3, 18–24 and ch. 5 on the Order of the Garter. The interest behind the composition and translation of the *Brut* might stem from this obsession with Arthurian material; the chronicles create King Arthur in the image of or at the instigation of Edward I. See Marvin, 'The Prose Brut Chronicle', pp. 164–6, and F. Riddy, 'Reading for England: Arthurian Literature and National Consciousness', *Bibliographical Bulletin of the International Arthurian Society* 43 (1991), 314–332, see p. 325.

Arthurian aspirations. According to the account in the *Brut*, Mortimer's Round Table fails because Mortimer never lives up to the model of the king he impersonates. The chronicle explains that

> openly he failede, ffor þe noble Kny3t Arthure was þe moste worþi lord of renoun þat was in al þe worlde in his tyme, and 3itte come neuer non soche after him, for alle þe noble kny3tes þ[r]ou3 Cristendome of dede of Armes alosede, du[e]llede wiþ Kyng Arthure, and helde him for her lord. (ch. 220, p. 262)

Arthur's fame arises from the company of worthy knights he has assembled in his court, an achievement never outdone by any king after his time.

The Round Table develops into a significant mark of British past achievements, but those sitting around it represent the world-empire to which Arthur aspires.[52] There is no narrow ethnic allegiance here:

> Kyng Arthure hade at þat table Britons, Fraunchemen, Normannes, Flemynges, Burgoyners, Mansers, Loherin3, and of alle þe landes a þis half þe mount of Gorie, and of his lande of Britaigne, and of þe grete Cornwaile, of Walys, & of Irland, & of Scotland; and shortely to telle, of alle þe landes þat wolde worshipe and chyualry seche, comen to Kyng Arthurus court. (ch. 77, p. 78)

Arthur sits at the head of an international chivalric order. The king is honoured for uniting diverse Christian peoples under his rule.[53] This in part explains the case by which different European nations adopt the Arthurian story and develop their own legends, myths and romances about the king and his court. But Arthur is not cosmopolitan, and the ethnic diversity of his knights does not diminish his status as a national hero, who leads his people and those who choose to support him, as a British leader. The nationalism expressed in Arthur of the *Brut* is ultimately not ethnic or racial, but *cultural*.[54] The chivalric ethos and the culture emerging from it unite all those seated at the Round Table. The broader idea of chivalry resides in the British culture which Arthur disseminates in his imperialistic conquests. Instead of the figure of a perfect monarch, the Arthur of the *Brut* is foremost the ideal *knight*, ruling over a chivalric order, not a civil nation.[55]

---

[52] Though the Round Table is mentioned only in passing in the *Brut*, fifteenth- and sixteenth-century readers of the chronicle already drew the connection between it and King Arthur, by underlining the words in the text or adding a marginal note concerning the Round Table as a signpost marking the mention of King Arthur. The Round Table becomes a metonomy for both the king himself and his reign. Examples of these notations can be found in many *Brut* manuscripts, of which I shall mention a few: the words 'nota of þe Rounde Table' on fol. 29v of Cambridge University Library, MS Kk.1.12; 'the roud table' and in a different hand 'milites Rotunda mensa' on fol. 43v of Peterhouse College, Cambridge, MS 190.

[53] Arthur here is seen as charismatic, attracting to his court the best men of Western Europe. He is what B. N. Sargent-Baur terms 'centrelizer' (p. 30) in '*Dux Bellorum/Rex Militum/Roi Fainéant*: The Transformation of Arthur in the Twelfth Century', in *King Arthur: A Casebook*, pp. 29–43. Arthur does not become the ruler of the world, but rather of a composite people: MacDougall, *Racial Myth*, p. 13.

[54] I adopt the term 'cultural nationalism' coined by Gillingham in 'The Context and Purpose of Geoffrey of Monmouth's *History of the Kings of Britain*', p. 101.

[55] From the description of his reign, as we have it in the *Brut*, Arthur emerges as strong, courageous, loyal and generous – all adjectives which Sally North finds as characteristic of ideal knights in chivalric

And yet, there seems to linger some shadow across all descriptions of Arthur, even among writers who advocate Arthur and promote Arthurian lore.[56] It is not simply that the model offered by Geoffrey is ultimately a model of failure, intrinsically connected with the character of the king, a problem which historians rewriting the *Historia* have sensed, though did not always acknowledge. There are some medieval historical compositions, though, which openly criticise Arthur on other grounds. For some, it is the ground of historical truth, for however unlike modern notions of such truth some medieval conceptions may seem, there were, of course, writers affronted with Geoffrey's book. For others, it was the ground of false interpretation, hence they emphasise the negative aspects of the reign of a bastard engaged in violent and unjust conquests. The *Brut* does not go this far, but leaves open many questions as to the nature of Arthur's kingship and its value. His presence as it is reflected in the choices made by the compilers of the *Brut* is more of an emblematic *collage* of ideal models of great leaders than that of a historical monarch faced with the everyday duties of an anointed king.[57]

biographies and histories: 'The Ideal Knight as Presented in Some French Narrative Poems *c.* 1090–*c.* 1240: An Outline Sketch', in *The Ideals and Practice of Medieval Knighthood: Papers from the First and Second Strawberry Hill Conferences*, ed. C. Harper-Bill and R. Harvey (Woodbridge, 1986), pp. 111–32.

[56] A good reading of the problematic aspect of Arthur is D. P. Donahues' 'The Darkly Chronicled King: An Interpretation of the Negative Side of Arthur in Lawman's *Brut* and Geoffrey of Monmouth's *Historia regum Britanniae*', *Arthuriana* 8:4 (Winter 1998), 135–47. This almost intrinsic flaw aligns Arthur again with biblical kings, who never live up to the ideal of kingship. M. Buber remarks that in the Bible 'the history of the kings is the history of the failure of him who has been anointed to realize the promise of his anointing': 'Biblical Leadership', in *On The Bible: Eighteen Studies*, ed. N. N. Glatzer (New York, 1982), pp. 137–149, citation on p. 147.

[57] I would like to thank Christopher Page and James Simpson for their enlightening comments on earlier versions of this paper, and the editors of *Arthurian Literature* for careful and useful suggestions.

IX

PENDRAGON, MERLIN, AND LOGOS:
THE UNDOING OF BABEL IN *THAT HIDEOUS STRENGTH*

Janina P. Traxler

That Hideous Strength, part three of C. S. Lewis's space trilogy,[1] defies simple categorization and simplistic analysis. Lewis himself called the work a 'romance' and a 'modern fairy tale for grown-ups'.[2] Some critics consider it science fiction, others label it mythopoetic fantasy;[3] in its pages, Arthurian figures must save England from the despotic figures of a dystopian regime. The story depends on several specifically Arthurian elements (especially the presence of the Pendragon, also named Mr Fisher-King, and a resurrected Merlin), but the title comes from a poem by Sir David Lyndsay, a phrase referring to the tower of Babel. While the Arthurian legend, as it appears in most medieval forms, is clearly a Christianized story, it is not generally linked with biblical motifs except through the grail story and through the fact that Arthur's kingdom displays the trappings of a Christian society – the knights attend mass, and Arthur gathers his court at major Christian feast days, for example. So at the very least, Lewis has combined material from sources not normally exploited for a common purpose, and I believe he does so to portray both the greatest danger to modern culture and the form salvation will take. In Lewis's view, modern confidence in science has alienated us from our traditional sources of spiritual fulfillment: the natural world and the divine. As in the catastrophe at Babel, the alienation manifests itself through language, and for Lewis, salvation will occur because the Arthurian cohort is equipped with a most powerful weapon: Logos.

Lewis builds this romance about the menace to contemporary society on

---

1   All references to C. S. Lewis's trilogy *Out of the Silent Planet* (New York, 1938), *Perelandra* (New York, 1943), and *That Hideous Strength* (*THS* hereafter) (New York, 1946) come from the paperback edition (New York, 1986).

2   Lewis calls the story a 'fairy tale' in the preface. Elsewhere Lewis defined the fairy tale as a genre which excludes love interest and close psychology. See C. S. Lewis, 'Sometimes Fairy Stories May Say Best What's to be Said', in *Of Other Worlds: Essays and Stories*, ed. W. Hooper (New York, 1966), pp. 35–38 (p. 36). Lewis also uses the term 'romance' in discussing this story: see 'A Reply to Professor Haldane', in *Of Other Worlds*, 74–76.

3   Raymond Thompson uses this term: see *The Return from Avalon: A Study of the Arthurian Legend in Modern Fiction* (Westport, CT, 1985), pp. 93ff.

two concepts which underlie much of modern fantasy literature, especially Arthurian fantasy. First, such literature expresses a strong nostalgia for certain wholesome characteristics absent from modern society though assumed to be present long ago. In this nostalgic view, life was better in the middle ages or some vaguely defined pre-industrial past, perhaps frankly pagan but often Christianized, still under the sway of mysterious forces, both supernatural and natural. Men were braver and more courteous, women were worthier and more beautiful, right and wrong were clearer, clergy and nobility provided the social structure necessary for a decent earthly life.[4] Second, these works clearly articulate an anxiety about contemporary threats to the survival of humanity. In particular, we worry about our ability to master the potential of modern science and technology, especially when that potential falls into the hands of people driven by destructive, selfish, perhaps even non-human forces.[5] Though these two attitudes pertain especially to *THS*, those familiar with Lewis's life and work will see that this combination of nostalgia and anxiety recurs elsewhere in his thinking.

The years during which Lewis worked on this novel provided ample fodder to feed the nostalgia and anxiety just mentioned. The period between the two world wars produced a generalized Western sense of despair. The promises of positivism rang hollow as the West assessed the horrors of the Great War, and much of the Western world suspected that humanity had lost its moral strength.[6] For all of its promise, industrialization had given humans frightful ways to kill each other, the oppression of repetitive and uncreative work, the overcrowding and squalor of urban poverty, and a sense that the glories of the past were lost forever. In addition, Lewis had a firm distaste for totalitarian regimes, whether fascist or Communist, because in all cases, their success 'involves the seizure of power by a small, highly disciplined group of people', which considers that the realization of its projects is 'the supreme duty and abrogates all ordinary moral laws'.[7] Since modern society places such confidence in science, the self-interested schemes of this ruling group typically exploit the promises of science for totalitarian purposes.

Lewis himself indicates overtly in the preface to *That Hideous Strength* that in his story he aims to develop 'a serious point' which he elaborates in his

---

4   Adam Roberts discusses this aspect of Arthurian fantasy: *Silk and Potatoes: Contemporary Arthurian Fantasy* (Amsterdam and Atlanta, GA, 1998), p. 9.

5   Raymond Thompson has devoted a good deal of effort to articulating and analyzing the ways in which Arthurian fantasy responds to contemporary fears: see especially *The Return from Avalon*. Thompson has written several articles which reprise or elaborate on aspects of the basic discussion in his book. For example, see 'Arthurian Legend and Modern Fantasy', in *Survey of Modern Fantasy Literature* (Englewood Cliffs, NJ, 1983), pp. 2299–315. In this discussion, he summarizes the premise of *That Hideous Strength* thus: the war between Logres and Britain 'is being fought between those who believe in natural harmony and beauty, in love and devotion to duty, and those who would destroy all this in the name of progress toward a dehumanized and totalitarian world order, inspired by shortsighted self-interest' (p. 2310).

6   For a fuller discussion of this, especially in Victorian society, the context out of which Lewis developed, see D. N. Mancoff, *The Return of King Arthur: The Legend through Victorian Eyes* (New York, 1995).

7   'Reply to Haldane', pp. 82–84.

essay *The Abolition of Man*[8] and which clearly reflects the desire for traditional morality and concern about the preoccupations of modern society. For Lewis, modern society's faith in rational, objective thought has deluded us into thinking that we have rid ourselves of outmoded, imprecise, and subjective ideas. According to Lewis's argument, because of this faith in a scientific approach to meaning, modern man has rejected the generic ethical standards which have historically allowed people (regardless of their culture and religion) to overcome their destructive, self-interested impulses and work for the ennobling of humanity.[9] Though we believe we have conquered the weaknesses of human nature, we have increasingly turned power over to a shrinking number of people who excel at shaping our ideas. Lewis summarizes: 'For the power of Man to make himself what he pleases means, as we have seen, the power of some men to make other men what *they* please' (*Abolition*, 72). The appeal of power, specifically the basic human desire to belong to an 'in group', corrupts those who have no time-tested moral base, like Mark Studdock in *That Hideous Strength*. In order to be accepted, Mark succumbs to that temptation which will 'make men do very bad things before they are yet, individually, very bad men' (130).

Though his own references to *Abolition* in the introduction to *THS* indicate that Lewis plans to study the moral and spiritual crisis of modern society, they do not reveal why Lewis chose to combine biblical and Arthurian material to do so. An important conversation between the Arthurian characters Ransom and Merlin suggests how we can begin to understand Lewis's decision. In trying to explain to Merlin the nature of the battle before them, Ransom notes that 'Logres' suffers from a complex malaise: 'the machines, the crowded cities, the empty thrones, the false writings, the barren beds: men maddened with false promises and soured with true miseries, worshipping the iron works of their own hands, cut off from Earth their mother and from the Father in Heaven' (293). The problems threatening contemporary society are multifaceted: intellectual, environmental, and spiritual. *Biblical* material provides Lewis with a metaphor to convey the illness – the legend of Babel – as well as a response to the disaster at Babel – the miracle of Pentecost. *Arthurian* lore provides Lewis the figures he needs: a leader destined to save the land in its hour of need, a wonder-worker who can manipulate the forces of nature, a suffering figure whose physical ailment symbolizes the moral malaise of the land.[10] The phenomenon which binds this all together is language, or more properly Logos in its several senses. Logres will be saved by the weapon of

---

8   Lewis builds his discussion around the point that the fundamental, universal desire of all men is to be in the 'inner ring' ('Reply to Haldane', p. 79).

9   Lewis labels these timeless standards the 'Tao' in *The Abolition of Man* (New York, 1947), pp. 28–29. Though *Abolition* (1947) was published the year after *THS* (1946), Lewis clearly had fleshed out the ideas of both texts before either was published.

10 For a fuller discussion of the Fisher-King and the wasteland motif, see J. H. Lutton, 'Wasteland Myth in C. S. Lewis's *That Hideous Strength*', in *Forms of the Fantastic: Selected Essays from the Third International Conference on the Fantastic in Literature and Film* (Westport, CT, 1986), pp. 69–86.

meaning, by a restoration of humans' connection to the natural and metaphysical worlds.

Lewis's choice of title indicates that he pictures the problems of modern
society as a new version of the Tower of Babel legend. The biblical story of
Babel (Genesis 11:1–9) explains why the human family is so divided linguistically even though all peoples spring from a common source.[11] According to
the biblical account, everyone originally spoke the same language until some
decided to build a tower to reach the sky. This project angered God because it
suggested that humans saw no limit to their power. To frustrate this project,
God confounded speech and scattered the nations.[12] Because humans imagined a project which overstepped the boundary between human and divine,
Judeo-Christian tradition uses this story to illustrate the sin of pride and to
suggest a second fall of man.[13] Besides referring indirectly to Babel through
the choice of title, Lewis uses the reference overtly in the story: the chaos
which destroys the banquet at Belbury results from 'the curse of Babel' (350).
The title phrase recurs several times in the text, as when Ransom explains to
Merlin that 'the Hideous Strength confronts us and it is as in the days when
Nimrod built a tower to reach heaven' (288).[14]

Perhaps because Lewis intended this story to be a modern fairy tale, he
defined unambiguously the opposing sides. The wicked figures are creepy,
shadowy, destructive; fog cloaks the valley after they move in. The heroes
include the Arthurian characters as well as others who are kind, generous,
nurturing; sun often bathes their elevated site. Despite the black-white distinctions between the two sides, the struggle itself ranges from cosmic to interpersonal. At the cosmic level, good and evil *eldils* oppose each other; these are
supra-human eternal beings, something like divinities, whose struggle is
timeless. Evil eldils have long controlled Earth. The eldils work through
humans – the National Institute of Co-ordinated Experiments (ironically

---

[11] See George Steiner's discussion of this problem in *After Babel: Aspects of Language and Translation*
(New York and London, 1975). He notes that the extremely large number of languages represented in
the human family defies all logical explanation, especially if one considers the relatively small amount
of other variation among the basics of human beings – we all digest the same way, walk the same way,
etc. See especially ch. 2.

[12] Genesis 11:6, *The Interpreter's Bible*, vol. 1, 1952. The name Babel stems in part from a Hebrew term
meaning 'to confuse'. See explanatory notes to Genesis 11:9 by C. A. Simpson (p. 565).

[13] Steiner, *After Babel*, p. 59.

[14] Lewis may have been thinking of Dante in constructing the references to Nimrod in *THS*. Certainly
Lewis's characterization of the evil figures suggests Dante's image of the condemned as having 'lost
the good of intellect'. C. A. Huttar makes this suggestion in his article 'C. S. Lewis and the Demonic',
Perspectives 3.3 (1988), 6–10. Nimrod appears in the lowest ring of Dante's *Inferno* as a representation
of those who combine intellect with brute force and evil will. These figures are most dangerous to their
fellows because they can wreak havoc on society as a whole, rather than simply on individuals. Dante's
use of Nimrod's story thus matches Lewis's: in *THS* the agents of evil hope to rule humanity using
advanced science as their tool of oppression. Filostrato articulates this concept in perfectly clear terms:
'Man's power over Nature means the power of some men over other men with Nature as the instrument'
(178). If NICE succeeds, the land will be ruled by fascists, some theological and some scientific. J.
Dauphiné discusses Dante's use of Nimrod and the story of Babel, emphasizing in particular Nimrod's
role as sower of *confusion*: see 'Dante et l'énigme de Babel', in *Miscellanea Mediaevalia: Mélanges
offerts à Philippe Ménard*, ed. J.-C. Faucon (Paris, 1998), pp. 377–84.

NICE) for the evil eldils, and the Arthurian 'Company' for the good eldils. Both sides hope to enlist the aid of Jane Studdock, a visionary who can lead them to Merlin, the figure each side considers the key to its victory. In Lewis's story, the clash between good and evil manifests itself most creatively in the areas related to language, whether in the terms used for peoples' names[15] and goals or more broadly in the use and abuse of language to accomplish one's goals. In explaining the dangers of totalitarian regimes, Lewis calls attention to the importance of language: 'All men at times obey their vices: but it is when cruelty, envy, and lust of power appear as the commands of a great super-personal force that they can be exercised with self-approval. *The first symptom is in language.*'[16] George Steiner reminds us in *After Babel*[17] that language is not merely the vehicle for expressing thought; thought process and the specifics of expression are inextricably linked. Lewis uses this concept as his figures represent their ideas in patterns whose very distortion reflects the evil nature of their plans.[18]

These modern heirs to the architects of Babel devote themselves to a program whose scientific and moral horror reveals itself in the imagery they use. The bureaucrat Feverstone and the scientist Filostrato either imply or articulate specifically the facets of the plan: selective culling of the general population so that only the superior remain, scientific cleansing of the environment so that only a sterile and artificial context remains, 'perfection' of the physical so that it becomes useless, all of this with the goal of creating a human mind of unlimited power which does not need the biological world or a concept of divinity.[19] Filostrato states: 'We do not want the world any longer furred over with organic life . . . all sprouting and budding and breeding and decaying. We must get rid of it . . . Learn to make our brains live with less and less body: learn to build our bodies directly with chemicals, no longer have to stuff them full of dead brutes and weeds. Learn how to reproduce ourselves

---

15 The names of the evil-doers all carry negative connotations (Wither, Feverstone, Fairy Hardcastle) or ironic ones (Filostrato, the 'love-struck' eunuch; the institute's acronym NICE). Those in the Arthurian company have names related to nature and positive concepts: Ivy Maggs, Grace Ironwood, Edwin Ransom, etc.

16 My italics; 'Reply to Haldane', 84. Lewis specifies that this tendency to respond to the lull of power is a type of 'devil worship' (84). Lewis also discusses in *Abolition* the way language reflects a group's plans to control: 'The belief that we can invent "ideologies" at pleasure, and the consequent treatment of mankind as . . . specimens, preparations, begins to affect our very language. Once we killed bad men; now we liquidate unsocial elements' (85).

17 See esp. pp. 74, 77, 88.

18 Even before *THS* begins, Lewis suggests the coming importance of language by designating earth as 'the silent planet' – a place so tainted with evil that it has been shut off from the rest of the universe. It is literally incommunicado.

19 Feverstone states this explicitly in the text: NICE will start their conquest with 'simple and obvious things' such as 'sterilization of the unfit, liquidation of backward races (we don't want any dead weights), selective breeding'. Those steps will be followed by an ambitious 'educational' program which will produce people that the system needs. At first this will work through psychological techniques, but eventually NICE will move on to 'biochemical conditioning in the end and direct manipulation of the brain' (42).

without copulation' (173).[20] He observes 'we can make the dead live whether they wish it or not. He who shall be finally king of the universe can give this life to whom he pleases. They cannot refuse the little present' (179). At the simple level of vocabulary, the dream is already chilling. Life is something imposed on the dead; nature is an artificiality stripped of the natural cycle of birth, reproduction, death, and decay; the little present is an atrocity forced on the unwilling.

The sobering choices of vocabulary and imagery gain further power through the widespread tendency at NICE to hide evil beneath such linguistic distortion as euphemism and disinformation. Wither, the master of this strategy, uses ambiguity and feigned courtliness to manipulate emotions and control others. Wither assures people that he is thinking only of their own good when he proposes something, but his pleasant speech covers thinly a murderous need for obedience. Those who insist upon going their own way are 'liquidated' (255); others are 'provided for' (275) as soon as their usefulness is over. Even when he seems to be speaking clearly, he sends conflicting messages, as in a moment of anger when he tells Mark that there are only two errors that he should avoid: 'On the one hand, anything like a *lack of initiative or enterprise* would be disastrous. On the other, the slightest approach to *unauthorized action* – anything which suggested that you were assuming a *liberty of decision* which, in all the circumstances, is not really yours – might have consequences from which even I could not protect you' (253; my italics).

The distortion of information and creation of propaganda naturally accompany the other distortions just mentioned, a point Lewis makes through the duties assigned to Mark Studdock. Mark, a sociologist, must fabricate newspaper articles and editorials as part of the NICE strategy to control public opinion. Feverstone underscores the importance of presenting material correctly to the public: 'if it were even whispered that the NICE wanted powers to experiment on criminals, you'd have all the old women of both sexes up in arms and yapping about humanity. Call it re-education of the mal-adjusted, and you have them all slobbering with delight that the brutal era of retributive punishment has at last come to an end' (43). Mark later must write the report of a riot the evening *before* it happens (130).

NICE's perversion of language becomes even more clear when Lewis contrasts equivalent elements in NICE and the Arthurian group. In particular, each side speaks of 'family' and 'head'; each values obedience. Wither frequently uses the term family, but in his mouth, the word makes one cringe. When he explains to Mark that the institute operates 'like a family, or even, perhaps, like a single personality' (120), the suggestion of 'single personality' sounds totalitarian rather than homey. Later he mentions that they operate like

---

[20] Lewis amuses himself especially well with the irony of Filostrato's name and character. The 'love-struck' scientist wants to purge human life of anything resembling real affection, passion, and sexuality. When one of the other NICE figures refers to him as a 'eunuch' the joke reverberates even more.

so many brothers and sisters (206), that he considers NICE 'one great family' (209), that he feels a sort of 'fatherly' concern for Mark (212). As he tries to get Mark to bring Jane to NICE, he promises that Jane will 'be company for Miss Hardcastle' (212) – the same Fairy Hardcastle who had already tortured Jane. The NICE 'family' consists of unmarried figures, all aberrant in some way, whether it be Wither's deceptive politeness, Straik's religious fanaticism, Filostrato's amoral research, or Fairy Hardcastle's sadism. By contrast, the Arthurian Company truly does function as a family – the father-like Ransom inspires obedience, and life at Saint Anne's features collaboration, sharing of responsibilities, nurturing – even mothering[21] – and devotion to the common goal of saving the land from destruction. Activity centers around the kitchen, people banter and interact comfortably, pets and farm animals enliven the Manor, and the garden provides produce.

Use of the term 'head' also distinguishes the two groups. Ransom, sometimes called the Head, seems like a godhead; at Jane's first encounter with him, she is overcome with his regal aura, 'with all linked associations of battle, marriage, priesthood, mercy, and power' (143). His room is elevated, warm, colorful; his speech is relaxed but articulate.[22] By contrast, the Head at NICE is the literal severed head but more importantly the device through which evil eldils impose their will on their human toadies. Its space looks, feels, and smells like a laboratory or operating room. Laden with dials and tubes, the room resembles 'some creature with many eyes and many tentacles' (180). When the Head communicates with its visitors, the machines force air through its mouth, it starts to drool, its mouth starts to move, it licks its lips to moisten them (182). Despite the elaborate scientific apparatus that apparently assures its survival, in reality the head is a prop whose nature only Wither and Frost understand. It is a mockery of a literal head as well as a perverse version of the concept of leadership.

Finally, obedience means different things in each group. For Ransom's group, obedience comes from each person's decision to cooperate for common purposes or from a spiritual need for order and fulfillment. Ransom equates obedience with humility and deems it necessary for true love and healthy relationships (148–49). At NICE, however, obedience means silent acceptance of orders and willingness to commit crimes. When the Head of NICE speaks, it produces the horrifying command 'Adore' and then 'give me another head' (354). The differing uses of the terms family, head, and obedience reflect the radically different character of these two groups. Inside NICE, these terms and others pervert their common sense, the sense used at Saint Anne's.

---

21 Lewis's choice of name for the Arthurian Company's manor is appropriate: Saint Anne is the patron saint of motherhood.

22 Patrick Callahan elaborates on the differences between the two places (Saint Anne's and Belbury) and their characters: see 'The Two Gardens in C. S. Lewis's *That Hideous Strength*', in *SF: The Other Side of Realism: Essays on Modern Fantasy and Science Fiction*, ed. T. D. Clareson (Bowling Green, OH, 1971), p. 154.

By giving the figures at NICE imagery and thought patterns which suggest twisted thought processes, Lewis illustrates two ideas with implications beyond this story: (1) the profound connection which theorists see between language and the very process of thinking,[23] and (2) the perversion of language which accompanies totalitarian, amoral schemes. As figures at NICE describe its program, they reveal that on both the scientific and moral planes, they prepare a disaster to rival that at Babel. NICE plans to manipulate nature, to 'perfect' it, in order to perfect man. As Filostrato states, the project works for 'the conquest of death: or for the conquest of organic life . . . It is to bring out of that cocoon of organic life which sheltered the babyhood of mind the New Man, the man who will not die, the artificial man, free from Nature. Nature is the ladder we have climbed up by, now we kick her away' (177). Filostrato's antipathy for the natural world, with its messiness, fits logically with NICE's full program of ecological destruction (rerouting the local river, for example) as well as their assumption that science can elevate humans beyond the need for biology. Fanatical as that vision seems, Reverend Straik indicates that a fearsome theological vision supports the scientific program. Straik explains to Mark 'The Kingdom is going to arrive . . . The powers of science are an instrument' (79). Straik elaborates later as he offers Mark the privilege of witnessing 'the creation of God Almighty', of meeting 'the first sketch of the real God. It is a man – or a being made by man – who will finally ascend the throne of the universe. And rule forever' (179). Thus their dream rejects any concept of boundary or limit to human ambition; no moral standards shape their thinking. NICE's plans fit perfectly into the paradigm Ransom states for what is wrong with modern society. NICE wishes to destroy both the Father (the divine) and the Mother (the natural world); what they call the perfection of man presumes the destruction of all that gives life meaning.

The preceding discussion focused on how Lewis presents NICE's project as a modern reenactment of the Babel legend, especially how Lewis articulates the looming disaster through several types of linguistic distortion (imagery, euphemism, disinformation). Lewis also links the biblical legend with the cosmic battle between good and evil, represented by the eldils and their human operatives. In each of the two earlier parts of the trilogy, a brilliant physicist named Weston traveled into space. In his quest for scientific success, Weston became the tool of the evil eldils on earth. He kidnapped Ransom and took him to Malacandra in *Silent Planet*; in *Perelandra*, he arrived on Perelandra while Ransom was a guest there; in both cases his presence threatened the lives of the planet's inhabitants. Ransom explained to Merlin the cosmic importance of Weston's travels. By venturing into space, Weston and his co-workers relinquished the protection of the 'Seventh Law' –

---

[23] Steiner cites many figures who have dealt with this question. His own thoughts are part of that tradition: see *After Babel*, esp. pp. 74–77. Steiner remarks that philology is 'the quintessential historical science . . . because the study of the evolution of language is the study of the evolution of the human mind itself' (75).

the gods' self-imposed restriction against interfering in the affairs of Earth until the 'end of all things'. Ransom summarized for Merlin: 'Our enemies had taken away from themselves the protection of the Seventh Law. They had broken by natural philosophy the barrier which God of His own power would not break' (290–91). As in the legend of Babel, humans violate the frontier between divine and human at their own risk.

Lewis clearly establishes the danger of NICE's project by associating it with the biblical legend, but nothing about either NICE's project or the attempts to thwart it require any link to the Arthurian legend. Both sides seek Merlin, yet Lewis could have imagined NICE's scheme without Merlin or without Ransom's Arthurian identities. Just as Lewis's use of Babel reflects a multi-layered understanding of the myth, so too his presentation of the Arthurian motifs involves more than fascination with medieval legend. In particular, Lewis emphasizes the Arthurian figures' connection to 'real life'. The chapter which uses this phrase in its title underscores the artificiality, sterility, and deception of everything at NICE, contrasting those qualities with the fecundity, honesty, and wholesomeness of Saint Anne's. Lewis's special treatment of Pendragon and Merlin fits within his ambitious plan for a full-scale remedy for England's problems, both micro- and macrocosmic, on the eve of World War II.

Though Ransom's three identities seem too many for one character, each identity fits into the dramatic conclusion Lewis planned. Ransom comes to *That Hideous Strength* already heavily burdened from his two trips to outer space. Before he picks up any Arthurian identifiers, Ransom is a philologist, a scholar devoted to 'love of Logos', or meaning. This identity helps him acquire the other qualities he needs to battle evil. During his first trip into space (*Silent Planet*), linguistic competence and a fundamentally humane nature allow Ransom first to learn Old Solar, the language of the extraterrestrials, then to learn their ways and favorably impress the extraterrestrial divinities, the Oyéresu. Consequently, he returns to earth with a basic understanding of their theology[24] plus their good will, both of which function significantly in the Company's victory over NICE. In *Perelandra*, while a guest on Perelandra (Venus), Ransom receives a full education in theology,

---

[24] Ransom's linguistic competence also makes him the only vehicle for communication between Weston, the twisted physicist who kidnapped Ransom for the trip, and the Malacandrians. During a conversation which Ransom translates, we get an early view of the prideful and destructive scientific program which NICE will pursue. First, Weston makes himself perfectly ridiculous, treating the highly evolved and wise Malacandrians like a pack of stupid savages who can be easily frightened and even bought: in explaining why Weston and Devine (Weston's sidekick) killed one of the residents, Weston explains 'We kill him . . . Show what we can do. Everyone who no do all we say – pouff! bang! – kill him same as that one. You do all we say and we give you much pretty things.' Then he pulls out some bright beads, 'the undoubted work of Mr. Woolworth' Ransom realizes, and dangles them in the faces of his audience as if they were children to be tempted by toys (127–28). Later he explains his plan to Oyarsa: that humanity will, by all the means at its disposal, achieve a sort of immortality by conquering other worlds and continually finding new places to set up its civilization in place of whatever it finds on site (135–40).

rather specifically Christian, though couched in more generic terms. He learns the significance of his name, saves the Perelandrian rulers from a sophisticated attack on their spiritual integrity, and gains full acceptance from the Oyéresu. *That Hideous Strength* reveals another detail essential to the battle between the Company and NICE: Ransom's experience on Perelandra provides him with the link to High Heaven that Merlin must see before he will join the Company. Thus because Ransom is a philologist and accomplished speaker of Old Solar, he becomes the vehicle for Christian theology in the battle against evil and the all-important link between the good eldils and earth, the 'silent planet' in danger of succumbing to the evil eldils (290–91).

Ransom's other two identities make the battle with NICE an Arthurian struggle. Ransom is Pendragon, the seventy-eighth in a continuous line from the original. Before Merlin will cooperate with Ransom and the Company, he must know that Ransom represents the right side. This happens through a series of riddles whose answers rely on the knowledge Ransom has from his two space voyages as well as his identity as the Pendragon (273–74). By mentioning the Oyéresu, Ransom signals to Merlin that they recognize the same divinities and that Merlin must cooperate with him. The second and third riddles clearly articulate Ransom's identities as both divine and Arthurian leader. The answer to the second riddle connects Arthurian legend and Christian theology in a way that Ransom's third identity will exploit. Merlin's question: 'Where is the ring of Arthur the King? What Lord has such a treasure in his house?' Ransom's answer: 'The ring of the King . . . is on Arthur's finger where he sits in the House of Kings in the cup-shaped land of Abhalljin, beyond the seas of Lur in Perelandra. For Arthur did not die; but Our Lord took him, to be in the body till the end of time and the shattering of Sulva, with Enoch and Elias and Moses and Melchisedec the King' (274). For the third riddle, Ransom must give an answer that only Merlin knows, and the answer underscores the notion that the battle for Logres is cosmic as well as local. Merlin's question: 'Who shall be Pendragon in the time when Saturn descends from his sphere. In what world did he learn war?' Ransom's answer: 'In the sphere of Venus I learned war . . . I am the Pendragon' (274). On Venus he received the spiritual preparation he needs to fight evil as well as the military preparation to be a *dux bellorum*, the most ancient term Arthurian tradition assigns to its leader. These riddles bind together Merlin and Pendragon, mage and liege. Clearly Ransom's skills as a philologist equip him to assume the other roles Lewis assigns him, for he must wage war at Belbury, but a war for the *soul* as much as for the land of Logres.

While the title of Pendragon makes Ransom a military defender of Logres, the other Arthurian title – Mr Fisher-King – connects Ransom to the grail quest, the spiritual face of the Arthurian legend, with pre-Christian underpinnings as well as strongly Christian elements. The legend of the Fisher-King, whose wound symbolizes the physical and moral blight on his land (the wasteland), combines ancient vegetation and fertility beliefs with the Christian promise of salvation through Christ's suffering. In the grail story, the Fisher King's wound will heal and the adventures of Logres end when the grail knight accomplishes his task and goes to his heavenly reward.[25] Like the mythical Fisher-King, Ransom bears a wound that will heal only in connection with the restoration of the land. Ransom's wound serves as a physical reminder of the spiritual battle he won against the evil 'Un-Man' Weston on Perelandra. The wound will heal after the battle against NICE, when Ransom returns to Perelandra.

More importantly, Ransom's title suggests that he is a 'fisher' of men, a Christ-like figure, and reinforces the Christian theological sense of the name Ransom. In an Eden-like scene on Perelandra, Weston tempts the Lady to disobey the divinely defined limits to her freedom. To prevent the Lady's 'fall', Ransom becomes Weston's literal and metaphysical opponent. As he fights the Un-Man, Ransom understands that he may well lose his life, that he may become, like Christ, 'a ransom for many' (Matthew 20:28). He lives on a diet of red wine and bread (an unabashed allusion to the Eucharist), and at the end of the story, the gods take him back to Perelandra, where he will join other biblical figures (274). Also like Christ, Ransom gathers about him those who will accept the ways of obedience and charity. As Ransom tries to educate Jane Studdock, he emphasizes the importance of these qualities. While they are not uniquely Christian, Lewis uses them in a clearly Christian way. For example, when he tells Jane the importance of obedience, the term suggests the opposite of pride and functions much as it would within a monastic community or a sound marriage, where humility and adherence to higher authority provide the structure for healthy spiritual and communal life.[26] When the gods descend to empower Merlin, Lewis connects charity to both Venus and Christ: 'Charity, not as mortals imagine it, not even as it has been humanized for them since the Incarnation of the Word, but the translunary virtue, fallen upon them direct from the Third Heaven, unmitigated . . . So Perelandra, triumphant among planets, whom men call Venus, came and was with them in the room' (323).

Lewis's mention of the 'Incarnation of the Word' points to a theological concept which ties together many thematic threads in *THS* and also prepares the dramatic conclusion to the story.[27] Pre-Christian thinking, especially Greek and Hellenized Hebrew, saw a direct connection between the divine and the physical world. The Stoics spoke of *Logos*, the divine principle ruling the universe; Philo of Alexandria considered Logos the divine word which creates and governs all. Most importantly for this discussion, John the Evangelist's opening statement in his Gospel offers the concept that Logos is the Word of God and that Christ is the Incarnation of that Word.[28] Thus in

---

[25] For an interesting explanation of the connections between the wasteland motif and *THS*, see Lutton's 'Wasteland Myth'. In *THS*, the Fisher-King must accomplish his task before he can be healed; in the medieval story, the king and the land will return to health when grail knight has accomplished his quest.

[26] Lewis fleshes out several of these ideas elsewhere in his writings: see for example *Mere Christianity*.

[27] For a discussion of the concept of Logos and the development of the Christian doctrine of Incarnation, see J. D. G. Dunn, *Christology in the Making: A New Testament Inquiry into the Origins of the Doctrine of the Incarnation* (Philadelphia, 1980).

[28] 'In the beginning was the Word: the Word was with God and the Word was God. He was with God in

Christian theology, God provides redemption from the fall through a concrete manifestation of divine love – Christ. The Incarnation offers humanity a means for returning to something like the pre-lapsarian relationship with God. The concluding moment in the process of reconnecting man and God occurs at Pentecost, when the Holy Spirit descends on the faithful: 'And they were all filled with the Holy Ghost, and began to speak other tongues, as the Spirit gave them utterance' (Acts 2:4). The moment also repairs the rupture which occurred at Babel because people of various languages begin to understand each other: 'And at this sound the multitude came together, and they were bewildered, because each one heard them speaking in his own language' (Acts 2:6).

By giving Ransom these three identities – philologist, Arthurian leader, and salvation figure, Lewis equips him to save the land from the Babel-like horrors that NICE prepares. Logres needs its legendary leader, its Pendragon. Yet the upcoming battle is more spiritual or moral than military, so Lewis provides a 'ransom', a remedy for the blight on the wasteland. The response to Babel combines Arthurian and biblical motifs, pre-Christian and Christian, Logos and Incarnation. Through Ransom, Logos triumphs in its Christian sense – as the Incarnation, God's thought made flesh and used to redeem humanity. Yet as Ransom notes, the crisis of meaning includes something beyond the spiritual, beyond the relationship between human and 'the Father'. We are also alienated from the 'Mother', the natural world, and Ransom cannot mend this rift alone. He needs an agent, one with Merlin's special mix of traditions and abilities.

Though the gods will transform Merlin as they empower him to defeat NICE, Logos operates first in Merlin in its pre-Christian sense, as a primal link between the divine and creation. To underscore Merlin's more primitive side Lewis details the importance of the Great Tongue, the language the Company assumes it will speak with Merlin. The traits of this language suggest the nature of Merlin and by extension what the Company is trying to save. Thus, it has a nostalgic connection to what modern society has lost. As Dimble, the Arthurian scholar in the Company, practices what he will say to Merlin in the Great Tongue, the Company hears words that 'sounded like castles' and made Jane's heart 'leap and quiver' (228). They 'spoke themselves through [Dimble] from some strong place at a distance – or as if they were not words at all but present operations of God, the planets, and the Pendragon. For this was the language spoken before the Fall and beyond the Moon and the meanings were not given to the syllables by chance, or skill, or long tradition, but truly inherent in them as the shape of the great Sun is inherent in the little waterdrop' (229). Because the words communicate at a profoundly organic level, their meaning inherent or inborn rather than assigned by humans, the Great Tongue connects Merlin to humanity's orig-

the beginning. Through him all things came to be, not one thing had its being but through him . . . And the Word was made flesh, and dwelt among us' (John 1:1–3, 14).

inal unsullied state. For Lewis, this language is better than pre-Babelian; it is pre-lapsarian. As Ransom notes, Merlin 'represents what we've got to get back to, in some different way' (286).[29] Through the nature and role of the Great Tongue, Lewis reflects a traditional, especially mystical, view of pre-Babelian language. Steiner describes it thus: 'This Adamic vernacular not only enabled all men to understand one another, to communicate with perfect ease. It bodied forth, to a greater or lesser degree, the original Logos, the act of immediate calling into being whereby God had literally "spoken the world". The vulgate of Eden contained, though perhaps in a muted key, a divine syntax – powers of statement and designation analogous to God's own diction, in which the mere naming of a thing was the necessary and sufficient cause of its leap into reality' (58).

Though Merlin assumes that he can meet Logres' needs with his ancient knowledge – plant lore, medieval political and military experience, Druidic wisdom, etc. – the Oyéresu have a far more demanding task for him. As Ransom explains, the eldils' power is so great that it will destroy earth if used directly; furthermore, 'Our Fair Lord . . . will not suffer a mind that still has its virginity to be so violated. And through a black magician's mind their purity neither can nor will operate' (291). Because Merlin once dabbled in now-forbidden things, the eldils consider him an appropriate tool for their work, preferable to Ransom and his 'virginal' moral state. The gods will descend upon Saint Anne's, empower Merlin, and send him to undo the work of the evil eldils. When Merlin understands this, he also realizes that the upcoming work will likely destroy him (291), making him another ransom for Logres. Earlier paragraphs in this discussion explored how Ransom's three identities equip him to lead Logres in the upcoming battle. Ransom serves as a bridge between heaven and earth, connects the eldils to Merlin, who will directly confront NICE. While Ransom can host the gods when they descend (by virtue of his intellectual and spiritual gifts), he needs Merlin, who thus also serves as a bridge, to link past and present, human and natural worlds.

The empowerment of Merlin completes the trajectory from pre-Christian to Christian theology by presenting a version of the Pentecost. Christianity associates Pentecost with the revelation of meaning and the renewal of the spirit. It thus provides one of the most powerful moments in both the New Testament and the Arthurian *Queste del Saint Graal*. The Pentecost in *THS* begins when a great wind sweeps over the Manor, just as in Acts and in the *Queste*. For the occasion Merlin wears red, the liturgical color for Pentecost, and the influence of the gods descends on the house much like God's spirit descends on the disciples at Pentecost. When the gods approach Saint Anne's

---

29 This gives Lewis a theological card to play as he contrasts NICE with the Company. Before the Fall, mankind was permitted everything except eating from the Tree of Knowledge of Good and Evil; this presumably included sexuality, since the original couple become ashamed of their nakedness only after the temptation. By contrast, Filostrato and company are working hard to move humanity to a state of artificiality and sterility in which the preoccupations of procreation will no longer impede the perfection of Man: 'Who would try to work with stallions and bulls? No, no; we want gelding and oxen. There will never be peace and order and discipline so long as there is sex' (173).

to transform Merlin, Mercury, the Lord of Meaning, transforms the Company: it became witty, silver-tongued, eloquent beyond all norms (321). The effect on Ransom is just as dramatic, though entirely internal: 'For Ransom, whose study had been for many years in the realm of words, it was heavenly pleasure. He found himself sitting within the very heart of language, in the white-hot furnace of essential speech' (322). Similar to the apostles in Acts, Ransom and the Company experience language as inseparable from spirituality, and meaning as an almost divine experience.[30] These details echo some theologians' interpretation of the miracle at Pentecost. With the arrival of the Holy Spirit, they began speaking in tongues, but more importantly they *understood* other tongues (Acts 2:1–13). Since this linguistic event restored communication across language barriers, some theologians consider Pentecost a reversal of the disaster at Babel.[31] The descent of the gods at Saint Anne's functions for this story much as Pentecost does for early Christianity: the moment energizes the faithful, marks them as chosen, and links them to the divine mind and the logic of the universe in ways unseen before. When Merlin goes to destroy NICE the next day, he bears the combined power of his own heritage (the connection to old language and the mysteries of nature) and the forces at Ransom's disposal (the sponsorship of the gods and the moral and political obligation to defend Logres).

Merlin arrives at the NICE compound perfectly equipped to overcome the evil there: he comes dressed as a cleric and armed with the weapon of language. In scenes heavy with poetic justice and even some humor, Merlin first deceives Wither and Frost, then destroys NICE by disrupting the banquet and freeing the imprisoned animals, and finally escapes the compound as nature itself rebels against the schemes of NICE. Pretending to be the translator NICE needs to communicate with the Merlin NICE has found (really a tramp so baffled at Wither's unctuous manner and attempts to address him in various languages that he simply plays dumb rather than speak English), Merlin compels the tramp to speak unrecognizable words which Merlin then translates for Wither and Frost. Merlin essentially fights language with language, fights NICE's gibberish disguised as brilliance with 'essential' speech that NICE perceives as mumbo-jumbo. For once, Wither's loquaciousness fails him. Even Frost, the specialist in objectivity, feels the effect of Merlin's power: in Merlin's presence 'Frost found it impossible to remember any words. . . . Nothing but nonsense syllables would occur to his mind' (333).

In more powerful form, Merlin's effect on language reappears at the banquet when Merlin confounds the speech of the NICE officials. Banquet guests at first pay no attention to the speaker's words because they expect to be bored, but they soon listen avidly as the mere drivel they expected turns into true nonsense. Their amusement gives way to horror, however, as the animals liberated from the vivisection laboratories and driven by Merlin's

---

[30] Dauphiné alludes to this relationship between language and divine thought: see 'Le Mythe de Babel', in *Mythes et littérature* (Paris, 1994), p. 5.

[31] Steiner, *After Babel*, pp. 59, 61.

voice and touch attack their former captors (351). The humans also turn against each other, killing and maiming in their frenzy to escape from the animals. Merlin leaves the banquet after cursing the assembly: 'They that have despised the word of God, from them shall the word of man also be taken away' (351). Wither alone sees the truth of the situation: he understands that the 'interpreter' is really Merlin and 'that powers more than human had come down to destroy Belbury; only one in the saddle of whose soul rode Mercury himself could thus have unmade language' (352).

As mayhem reigns in the banquet hall, Wither and Frost escape, hoping to salvage the remains of their project. They did not anticipate the presence of another Arthurian figure: Mr Bultitude, the pet bear at Saint Anne's but also 'the last of the seven bears of Logres' (287). When Merlin frees Mr Bultitude, he also reawakens the beast's primal instincts, which the Company had dampened. Merlin 'laid his hand on its head and whispered in its ear and its dark mind was filled with excitement as though some long forbidden and forgotten pleasure were suddenly held out to it' (351). In a fitting match of nature in its primal form against those who would abuse nature, Mr Bultitude kills Wither (355) and mangles the Head (358). Thus Mr Bultitude performs a moral service while satisfying his natural love of 'warm, salt tastes, of the pleasant resistances of bone, of things to crunch and lick and worry' (351).

While the blend of Arthurian, biblical, and other references makes an unlikely mix, it furthers Lewis's narrative plan while affording a wealth of interconnected ideas. *THS* offers a specifically Christian vision of salvation for the world, yet Lewis presents that vision within a much broader context. According to Lewis's logic, NICE's ultimate mistake was to ally themselves with those who broke the Seventh Law and ventured into the territory of the gods. For this reason, Lewis's use of the metaphor of the Tower of Babel undergirds the entire narrative, from the title to the linguistic undoing of NICE during the banquet scene. NICE's threat to Earth is pervasive – overtly based on a 'bent' (evil) scientific scheme to perfect Man, it really implies the destruction of all that gives life meaning. It allows no place for emotions, which NICE labels mere chemical reactions and which it tries to destroy through training in the Objectivity room. NICE's project presumes a totalitarian structure for political, social, even intellectual aspects of life, a reality conveyed in the Head's macabre orders 'Adore' and 'give me another head'. New Man (a head without a body) will replace God, and Nature will be 'kicked away' like a ladder used to attain a height from which there is no descent. To counter this menace, Lewis offers Logos at the command of two complementary figures who also link pagan and Christian, ancient and modern. Through Merlin, Logres can reconnect with the forces of nature – animal, plant, and mineral – and pre-Christian mysticism. Through Ransom, Logres will return to the influence of divine forces beyond earth, specifically the promise of the Incarnation, but also the influence of the Lord of Meaning (Mercury); of Venus-Charity, with its implications for healthy interpersonal relations; of Mars, with its emphasis on strength, obedience, and order. Ransom's linguistic talents gain him entry into the circle of the gods and give the forces of good a way to descend to the 'silent planet' (Earth) and combat evil. Ransom's goals are both Arthurian and Christian, while remaining generically moral: as Pendragon, he must try to preserve Logres in its time of trial; as a Christ figure, he must restore moral order to a world driven by pride to worship 'objectivity' and amoral science; as a hero of near-mythical definition, he must overcome the trials which threaten to kill him and destroy the world. Ransom's weapon is linguistic: he represents the Word – Logos – in the Christian sense; he exploits ancient languages to bridge the divide between the contemporary and Arthurian worlds; and when the Company undoes NICE, it uses linguistic prowess to combat moral and intellectual nonsense. The 'Pentecost' of *THS* combines all of these elements, so when Merlin goes to NICE, he will reconnect Logres with Earth the Mother and the Father in Heaven because the gods have equipped him with meaning in its fullest sense.

CONTENTS OF PREVIOUS VOLUMES

Details of earlier titles are available from the publishers